Good Food Great Medicine

Ruminations & Recipes
from a small medical practice

*Making better use of food and your kitchen
in the battle against type 2 diabetes, high blood pressure,
heart disease, stroke, and cancer*

Common sense reminder:
This book is intended as a guide only, not as a medical manual.
We hope that the information given here will help you make informed decisions about your health.
It is not intended as a substitute for any treatment that may have been prescribed by your doctor.
If you suspect that you have a medical problem we urge you to seek competent medical help.
Mention of specific companies, organizations, or authorities in this book does not imply endorsement by us,
nor does it imply that they endorse this book. (Although we hope they would.)

SECOND EDITION, REVISED
Good Food, Great Medicine
Copyright © 2009, 2012 by Mea Hassell and Miles Hassell, M.D.
Ninth printing July 2012

Printed by Lithtex in Hillsboro, Oregon

Cover art by Joyce Lovro Gabriel
Cover revision by Kelli Caldwell, 1ˢᵗ + 1ˢᵗ media
Photos on back cover and page vii by Dave Lawton
Photo on page viii by Sheila Hanson

First edition 2007
Second edition 2009, revised 2011, 2012

For permission to reprint selections from this book, contact the authors at:
www.goodfoodgreatmedicine.com

ISBN 978-0-9796339-1-1

To our mother, Jane Hartt Hassell,
who says that when you are her age
you get to choose your photo.
Here she is with her first car.

Contents

Preface

Revised second edition

This 2012 revision has given us a chance to update references, including some important new findings on the niacin issue (page 51), and also refresh information in areas like *Recommended Reading* on page 34. We may or may not have found a typo to clean up. (We can neither confirm nor deny.) Also, if you use our recipe for mayonnaise (page 96) you may notice that we have replaced canola oil with light olive oil. It is less refined than canola oil and (in our opinion) has a better fatty acid profile, yet is mild mannered enough to balance the more phenolic-rich and stronger-flavored extra-virgin olive oil.

We have also added directions for using quinoa as a substitute for the couscous in the *Southwest Chicken Salad* on page 202 (yep, we changed the name). We not only think the quinoa better complements the dish, but we love it when we can find ways to replace a refined grain (couscous) with an unrefined whole food like quinoa.

Some of you have wondered why we don't include nutrition information (calories, carbohydrate, cholesterol, and so forth) with our recipes. Our reason is that we think that it is the actual ingredients, and not their chemical breakdown, that provide the most important information. When we choose whole foods instead of processed foods we are getting the fiber, the fat, the protein, the carbohydrates, and the micronutrients as close as possible to the nutritional profile of the original plant or animal. "Nutrition information" can give the *quantities* of calories, carbohydrate, and cholesterol, for example but it won't tell us anything about the *quality*. It won't describe the type of fat used, or what kind of sweetening has been added – and how much of the sweetening and fat is naturally occurring rather than added. This way of looking at the food we eat is discussed more thoroughly in the first 60 pages of this book. However, this issue does become more complex for people with diseases like diabetes, and we will be exploring this comprehensively in our next edition.

As for the continuing crisis in health care and the epidemic of obesity and type 2 diabetes, we still believe that adopting the common sense, evidence-based, grandmother-approved principles found in this book (and many others – see page 34) would be more effective at reducing human misery and health care costs than any government plan.

We appreciate the support received from physician friends, in particular David Stewart, M.D. The thoughtful suggestions from readers, cooks, physicians, and our patients continue to be tremendously helpful. Thanks also to Anna Hassell and our office team, especially our crack editors, Sagen Castellanos and Michael Lue.

And, as always, we are grateful to our friend and co-worker Lisa Uchytil for her clarity, patience, hard work, inexhaustible good humor, and management skills; all of which were invaluable in the development of this second edition and revision.

Mea and Miles Hassell, M.D.
February 2012

Miles Hassell, MD

Internist, Comprehensive Risk Reduction Clinic

Medical Director, Integrative Medicine Program, Providence Cancer Center
Providence St. Vincent Medical Center
Portland, Oregon, U.S.A.

Miles Hassell is an internist in private practice at St. Vincent Hospital in Portland, Oregon. He was born in Seattle, Washington, and grew up in Perth, Western Australia. Miles received his medical degree from the University of Western Australia, and then moved back to the United States where he completed his residency in Internal Medicine in Portland, Oregon.

Miles emphasizes a combination of evidence-based conventional and complementary approaches to the treatment and prevention of disease in his medical practice. He especially encourages the vigorous application of evidence-based nutritional and exercise interventions, using a whole food Mediterranean model.

In addition to his private practice, Miles established the Integrative Medicine Program at Providence Cancer Center in Portland. He is principal investigator in a trial using nutritional interventions to reduce side effects of conventional cancer therapies. Miles is also a clinical instructor in the training of Internal Medicine residents, twice receiving *Outstanding Teacher of the Year* award, as well as being included in *Portland's Top Doctors*.

Miles lectures widely to physician groups regarding the appropriate use of nutritional medicine, as well as working with individual consultations to develop solutions to health problems. Miles lives in Portland with his wife, Anna, and son, Tor.

For contact information see last page of this book or go to www.goodfoodgreatmedicine.com.

Introduction

Mea Hassell

This book had its beginning in the office of Miles' medical practice. He poked his head out of an exam room one day and said, "Hey, Mea, we need some brown rice recipes in here." So *Good Food, Great Medicine* was conceived.

My brother Miles and I started working together in his internal medicine practice in 1996. Since that time Miles has been tirelessly and passionately arguing the case for good food. "But you can't get people to change the way they eat," people would tell him.

It was that response which helped motivate Miles to develop a series of patient education handouts, the first of which was *Fat Is Good, Bagels Are Bad*, as seen in Chapter Two. As he sees it, *he* can't change the way people eat, but he can give them the information that can help *them* decide to make changes themselves. This book deals with ways to translate that information into practical day-to-day living and eating.

My background is notable for food, both in and out of the kitchen; working with restaurants and natural food stores as well as writing about food and teaching cooking classes. For that matter, both Miles and I have been involved in the food business all our lives, beginning with a country inn as a family business in Western Australia and continuing with natural food stores in Seattle, Pennsylvania, and Perth, Western Australia.

Miles and I were raised in Western Australia and have eaten the way we talk about in this book all our lives. Our mother always understood the importance of whole food, and we didn't realize then how ahead of the curve she was. These days, most of what is known about food and health sounds a lot like instructions from our mother. *Eat your vegetables. Beans are good for you. Finish your oatmeal. If you're still hungry, eat an apple. Clean up your plate before you have dessert. Go outside and play.*

The approach to eating in this book is just as uncomplicated. *Choose good food. Food is medicine.* It only gets complicated when good sense collides with personal tastes and tolerances (not to mention schedules). The issue is our willingness to make the changes necessary for the food-as-medicine strategy to work.

Then there's the business of cooking. There is no avoiding the fact that it takes a certain amount of time to fix your own food. We don't assume that you are in the kitchen because you love to cook or have plenty of disposable time. Chapter one reminds you of *why* you are standing in your kitchen with a knife in one hand and an onion in the other. The subsequent chapters talk more about *how* to get there, and what to do with the knife and onions once you're there – a sort of kitchen starter kit.

The recipes reflect our personal tastes as much as our philosophy. Most of the recipes are very simply constructed and designed for speed, but the agenda also calls for maximum vegetable, whole grain, and bean per square inch of plate whenever possible. And Miles assures me that my affection for extra-virgin olive oil, onions, and garlic is fully supported by epidemiological evidence and prospective randomized controlled studies.

Mea and Miles

1 Great Medicine

Food and Exercise: A Brief Review

Food and Exercise: a Brief Review

Miles Hassell, M.D.

Most of us have in our own hands the most important tools for the prevention and treatment of heart disease, cancer, type 2 (adult onset) diabetes, stroke, dementia, osteoarthritis, obesity, and high blood pressure. These tools are good food and daily exercise – in partnership with adequate sleep, a powerful but under-appreciated factor.

> **The decisions we make about the food we eat and our exercise and sleep habits are more important than the decisions our physician will make.** The thoughtful use of each of these lifestyle choices is the strongest predictor of good health for most people.

Also, the impact of those decisions can reach well beyond the goal of risk reduction, and may actually help *reverse* disease. For example, someone who already has heart disease can reduce the risk of future events such as a heart attack by 70 percent or more with diet alone, and 60 percent or more with exercise. That's better than we see from our best drugs and medical procedures! And we find that the combination of conventional medicine added to food and exercise seems to give even better results.

Good food is whole food
Most whole, minimally processed food is good for you. The term "whole food" comes up often in this book to describe food as close to its original form as possible, such as fresh fruits and vegetables, grains that are whole or at least partially intact (like steel cut oats or cracked wheat), or animal products like eggs and fresh meat. Foods like butter and yogurt should be considered whole foods, and can even be made at home.

A few examples of minimally processed whole foods would be extra-virgin olive oil, whole grains, and cheese. (You will find more on these foods in the sections starting on page 13 and 16.)

Some of the foods included in my recommendations for most people are considered controversial; for example, raw nuts, caffeine, dark chocolate, aged cheese, real butter, eggs, meat, and modest amounts of alcohol. However, the evidence shows that all of these appear to be relatively healthy *when eaten as part of a varied diet* that already includes plenty of fruits, vegetables, beans, and whole grains.

I tell my patients that any food commonly eaten for more than 150 years should be innocent until proven guilty, and any food created by man in the last 150 years is guilty until proven innocent.

The Mediterranean factor
The Mediterranean-style diet is the only dietary approach that has been associated with fewer heart attacks, less cancer, less diabetes, fewer strokes, and less dementia in large populations studied over long periods of time.

When compared head to head against low-fat diets, the Mediterranean-style diet is better than low-fat diets at controlling weight, cholesterol, blood sugar, insulin levels, and diabetes risk, and is associated with a 60 percent lower risk of cancer. *There is no other dietary lifestyle that can show evidence for these benefits.*

The mechanisms for the benefit of the Mediterranean diet are poorly understood. Some of the likely favorable effects seen in studies so far include a beneficial effect on insulin resistance and blood sugar, small improvements in cholesterol profiles, reduced homocysteine and inflammation, and higher antioxidant levels.

What is the Mediterranean diet?

There is no precise definition of the Mediterranean diet. However, it is safe to say that there is a general pattern common with most Mediterranean regions, and consistent with what has been found in the published studies. It is pretty simple.

■ Food mainly from plant sources: fruits and vegetables, breads and grains, beans, nuts, and seeds. Vegetables, fresh and cooked, as part of every meal, and fresh fruit as a typical dessert.

■ Complex carbohydrates in the form of whole grains and beans daily.

■ Extra-virgin olive oil as the main fat, replacing most other oils and fats.

■ Animal protein in the form of fish, poultry, and eggs, and small amounts of red meat.

■ Dairy food primarily in the form of cultured products such as yogurt and kefir (a yogurt-like drink) and cheese.

■ Moderate consumption of wine, generally with meals.

The whole food Mediterranean diet

The Mediterranean diet guidelines that have been shown to improve health in medical trials allow for almost all minimally processed naturally occurring foods. In this book – and in my practice – we recommend a variation we call the *whole food* Mediterranean diet.

For example, we suggest that our patients do not eat white rice, white bread, or white pasta, even though the contemporary Mediterranean diet includes all three. We replace them with brown rice, 100 percent whole wheat bread, and whole grain pasta.

The diet includes plenty of vegetables, fruit, whole grains, and beans; moderate-to-high levels of 'healthy' fat (such as extra-virgin olive oil and raw nuts) and fish; variable amounts of cheese and yogurt; and small amounts of meat.

What about other traditional diets?

You can find some impressive results from all kinds of traditional diets. The Masai in Africa have thrived on milk, blood, and beef. The Eskimos have flourished on a diet of pretty much unlimited fat from the fish and animals they kill. The Japanese have done well eating their traditional low-fat diet.

From the evidence we have today, it seems clear that pockets of people within primitive populations all over the world – Japan, China, Russia, Greece, India, Africa – with dramatically different diets have enjoyed good health and long life. *And* all without the help of modern medicine and cookbooks, it should be added.

However, when it comes to identifying the factors that are associated with the best overall health outcomes, the only traditional diet for which we have convincing and broad data is the Mediterranean model.

What about other eating programs?

Consider some other diets you may wish to follow: Atkins, Ornish, Pritikin, South Beach, Zone, Eat Right For Your Blood Type, Macrobiotic, vegetarian, vegan, and so on. While each of these diet patterns has something to recommend it, nothing can compete with the Mediterranean-style diet for verifiable benefit in large populations.

The Mediterranean diet has been studied prospectively in large numbers of people, in various parts of the world, with individual studies of over 4 to 12 years duration.

■ It has been associated with reduced deaths from the common causes found in our society such as cancer, heart disease and stroke.

■ It has successfully maintained weight loss over extended periods of time.

■ It can significantly reduce the risk of developing type 2 diabetes, cancer, high blood pressure, dementia, and Parkinson's disease.

■ It can prevent deaths in patients with heart disease.

■ It can be adapted to a wide variety of tastes and cultures.

> **So, whether or not we are dealing with ongoing disease or remote family history, none of us can afford to dismiss the importance of making optimal food choices.** If you are going to trust your health to any diet, it seems to me an easy decision to follow the whole food Mediterranean model.

Heart disease, cancer, and the Mediterranean diet

Recent studies confirm the impression gained over the last thousand years that food and exercise play a large part in whether people develop heart disease and cancer prematurely. These same studies show us how we can use food and exercise to prevent or reverse many of these diseases. We'll review some of the recent key studies here.

HALE (Healthy Aging: a Longitudinal Study in Europe)[1]

The HALE project looked at the effects of a Mediterranean diet, alcohol use, nonsmoking, and physical activity on the health of seventy-to-ninety-year-old men and women throughout eleven European countries over twelve years.

In this population, the Mediterranean diet reduced deaths by 23 percent. Moderate alcohol use (such as one alcoholic drink daily) reduced deaths by 22 percent. Regular physical activity reduced deaths by 27 percent.

To summarize: if you were an elderly nonsmoker who ate well, *and* exercised for 30 minutes or more daily, *and* drank a small amount of alcohol, *your risk of dying from* **any** **cause** *was reduced by 65 percent.* The reductions were similar for cancer, heart disease, and other cardiovascular disease such as stroke.

Nurses Health Study

Other studies have shown that if you are younger than seventy years old, this approach can be expected to work even better. For example, in the Nurses Health Study [2], studying women in North America, reductions of about 90 percent for diabetes and 80 percent for heart disease were seen in association with similar food and exercise choices as described in the HALE study.

Studies such as these show us that *nothing* your doctor can do for any chronic disease you may have can equal the degree of benefit you can achieve with sensible daily diet, exercise and lifestyle choices. *And* not smoking. Under most conditions, you determine your health outcomes to a far greater degree than your doctor does. Of course, the combination of good medical care and sensible lifestyle choices is going to give even better results.

The Lyon Study

One of the most successful diet/health trials was the Lyon Diet Heart Study. The Lyon study stands out in being one of a handful of high quality randomized controlled prospective studies examining diet and disease using a method considered the gold standard for health research.

The Lyon study followed men who had already had a heart attack, and who were randomized to either an American Heart Association Diet, or a Mediterranean diet and followed for four years. After four years, those following the Mediterranean diet had 72 percent fewer major cardiac events, 56 percent fewer deaths [3] and 61 percent fewer cancers.

Those numbers may be difficult to absorb, so I'll repeat them: *72 percent fewer major cardiac events, 56 percent fewer deaths, and 61 percent fewer cancers* [4]. We know of *no* drug trials that can give such results.

(The Mediterranean diet used in this trial emphasized more root vegetables and green vegetables, fresh fruits, beans and legumes, breads and fiber, and fish. The main fats in

---

[1] Knoops, K. et al. JAMA 2004;292:1433-39

[2] Rimm, E. and Stampfer, M. JAMA 2004;292:1490-92
[3] Lorgeril et al. Circulation 1999;99:779-85
[4] Lorgeril et al. Archives of Internal Medicine 1998;158:1181-87

the diet were to be olive or canola oil, and study participants were to eat less meat, butter, and cream. Moderate alcohol consumption was allowed.)

The Greek EPIC study

Supporting the results of the Lyon study are the findings from the Greek EPIC study, which compared the health outcomes of Greeks who eat a Mediterranean-type diet compared to Greeks who do not, and found similar reductions in heart disease and cancer risk as in the Lyon study. [1]

One recent analysis reviewed prospective studies which assessed health outcomes of groups in relation to their adherence to the Mediterranean diet. It found a reduction in overall risk of dying, heart disease, cancer, Parkinson's, and Alzheimer's disease in the groups that more closely followed the diet. [2]

The Mediterranean diet and conventional medicine for heart disease

One agreeable side effect of the Mediterranean diet is that patients find it leads to improvements in many of the risk factors for heart disease and other diseases, so they can sometimes reduce the dose or eliminate some medications altogether.

The benefits most commonly seen among my patients are improvements in cholesterol, weight, blood pressure, blood sugar, esophageal reflux (heartburn), and measurements of inflammation such as C-reactive protein (CRP). This has also been seen in many prospective randomized controlled trials.

One of the most instructive of these studies is PREDIMED, which compared a prudent low-fat diet to a Mediterranean diet, and found significant benefits for the

---

[1] Trichopoulou et al. NEJM 2003;348:2599-608

[2] Sofi, F. et al. AJCN 2010;92:1189-96

Mediterranean diet in blood pressure, blood sugar, cholesterol, and C-reactive protein. [3] In other studies, the use of the Mediterranean diet combined with conventional cholesterol lowering medicine led to a further significant drop in cholesterol and oxidized LDL cholesterol.

Weight loss and the Mediterranean diet

The moderate-fat Mediterranean diet, when followed intelligently, will help with weight reduction as well as risk reduction. Many people who need to lose weight have been taught that they need to follow a low-fat diet, and certainly there are many healthy low-fat approaches to weight loss.

The key question is this: which eating plan for weight loss is most likely to be continued for the long term? It is not the weight loss program that works for six months that is important; you should choose the weight loss program that works for the *long term*. For most of us this means it should allow for a wide variety of enjoyable foods and blend with a 'normal' life.

Because a Mediterranean-style diet allows a very broad range of foods, including a far more liberal use of certain fats, it is much more pleasant for most of us than a low-fat diet, and we are more likely to stick to the program. This is a particularly significant factor when we are talking about a *lifetime* program, not a temporary diet. (For more on weight loss, see page 30.)

Low-fat versus Mediterranean diet: two studies

As an example of this, take a look at the weight loss studies in which a fairly high-fat Mediterranean diet, with up to 35 percent of the energy from fat, are compared to low-fat diets, with 20 – 30 percent of the calories from fat. In this study the Mediterranean diet

---

[3] Estruch et al. Annals of Internal Medicine 2006;145:1-11

group was instructed to eat more nuts, olive oil, and vegetables.

After eighteen months, the group eating the higher fat Mediterranean diet had significantly better participation, weight loss, and smaller waists. The low-fat diet group _gained_ weight at eighteen months, probably not because the diet was bad, but because they had a lot more trouble following the low-fat diet compared to the tastier and more satisfying Mediterranean diet.[1]

In another study comparing the Mediterranean diet with a low-fat diet for weight loss, those on the Mediterranean diet not only had better weight loss but also better cholesterol, blood sugar, insulin, and inflammation levels.[2]

As a postscript on the subject of losing weight on the Mediterranean diet, the importance of daily exercise, portion control, and common sense can't be overstated. Also, it makes sense to minimize otherwise healthy but high-starch and high-calorie vegetables like potatoes and corn, as mentioned in _If you need to lose weight_ on page 30.

Type 2 diabetes and the Mediterranean diet

Diabetes is responsible for a large proportion of the heart attacks, strokes, blindness, and kidney failure seen in our society. Not only is it a bad disease, but it is becoming much more common, tripling in frequency in our society over the last twenty years.

For instance, it used to be that children with type 2 (adult-onset) diabetes were rare. Now, children and teenagers are the fastest growing subgroup of this disease! Yet it is largely preventable, and probably reversible in many patients.

Preventing and reversing type 2 diabetes

The Mediterranean diet can substantially reduce your risk of adult onset diabetes and can reverse the metabolic syndrome. Two groups of studies demonstrate this.

■ One group of studies shows that a Mediterranean-style diet can prevent the development of diabetes or the 'metabolic syndrome', which is the name that describes a constellation of findings (high blood pressure, central obesity, high triglycerides, low HDL cholesterol, and elevated blood sugar levels) that are precursors to most cases of type 2 diabetes.[3][4][5]

■The other studies show that food and exercise can prevent the development of type 2 diabetes in those who already have the metabolic syndrome.[6] One program instructed at-risk patients to exercise for thirty minutes daily, eat _more_ monounsaturated fat (like olive oil and nuts), whole grains, fruit, and vegetables, as well as low-fat milk and meat products, and less saturated fat. Another goal was to lose 5 percent of their weight. Overall, this program resulted in 58 percent less diabetes developing compared to the control group. When the patients who were particularly careful to follow all the instructions were studied, they found that _none_ of those patients developed diabetes![7]

In my medical practice I take this one step farther, applying the same instructions vigorously to those patients who already have type 2 diabetes. Some of those patients who are able to do the hard work this approach requires are able to completely obliterate any evidence of diabetes, and get off all of their diabetes medication and insulin. (A note of caution: never stop your diabetes medication without the supervision of your physician.)

[1] McManus, K. et al. Int J Obesity 2001;25:1503-11
[2] Shai, I. et al. NEJM 2008;359:229-41

[3] Esposito et al. JAMA 2004;292:1440-46
[4] Martinez-Gonzalez, M.A. et al. BMJ 2008;336:1348-51
[5] Shai, I. et al. NEJM 2008;359:229-41
[6] Salas-Salvado et al. Diabetes Care 2011;34:14-9
[7] Tuomilehto et al. NEJM 2001;344:1343-50

Type 2 diabetes and medication

One of the particularly important aspects of type 2 diabetes is that the use of medicines to control blood sugars has only a modest, if any, effect on controlling the risk of heart disease, stroke, and death.[1] This is a worrisome fact, given that those with type 2 diabetes are 2 to 4 times more likely to have heart disease or a stroke than non-diabetics.

So, while we use the medications to treat high blood sugar, we are very realistic about the limited benefits they appear to provide. This makes it all the more important to focus on the vigorous use of diet, exercise, blood pressure and cholesterol management – including appropriate medications – in patients with type 2 diabetes, and to reverse the disease if we possibly can.

Aging

Aging is not something that we can prevent or reverse, but we can certainly do a lot to make the process as pleasant as it should be. Good food and exercise will reduce your risk of having to face events like heart attacks, strokes, cancer, dementia, surgery, and death. When I talk to patients about reducing risk of death, some get confused. After all, don't we all have to die sometime? Of course, for the most part that is true, right along with paying taxes. But we don't need to die prematurely – or live miserably, for that matter.

■ Premature disease and graceful aging

In my practice, those in their seventies, eighties, and nineties who don't give in to the aging process have taught me a lot. They stay physically active every day. They walk, climb stairs instead of ride the elevator, work out at the gym, play tennis, go fishing, or paddle a kayak. They keep their minds active, turn off their television, read widely, get enough sleep, and spend time with others who share their interests. Some stay employed, some run businesses, and some do volunteer work.

Their joints feel pretty good, their prescriptions are few, they can breathe just fine…and it is no accident! They've made sensible decisions about what they eat and how they spend their time.

However, if a 92 year old patient of mine loves doughnuts and eats them every day, he certainly won't get a lecture from me. I think he has earned the right to eat anything he wants. Sure, he might die sooner as a result – or maybe he'll make it to a hundred years old and tell everyone that maple bars kept him young.

■ Dementia

Following a Mediterranean diet pattern lowers the risk of developing dementia by up to 40 percent, with vegetable consumption being found to be one of the most important components.[2][3] Eating more fish and other sources of omega-3 fatty acids while minimizing sugar and refined grains (like white rice and cold breakfast cereals) also helps protect the brain – just one single high-sugar meal can measurably reduce memory! Even simply reducing calorie intake improves brain function.[4]

In addition, there are many factors apart from diet that help prevent dementia. For example, maintaining your waistline, keeping up a high level of mental activity, and drinking *small* amounts of alcohol can help. Believe it or not, just getting daily exercise reduces risk of dementia up to 40 percent. Evidence continues to support the good old 30-minute walk!

The power of exercise

Exercise, even without any help from diet, is a powerful force physically, mentally, and emotionally. Making a habit of exercise has an obvious benefit of helping to control weight, but that is only a bit of the story. Its most important benefits are far more subtle.

---

[1] Skyler, J.S. et al. Circulation 2009;119:351-57

[2] Scarmeas, N. et al. Annals of Neurology 2006;59:912-21

[3] Sofi, F. et al. AJCN 2010;92:1189-96

[4] Witte, A.V. et al. PNAS 2009;106(4):1255-60

Regular (daily) exercise protects against

- heart disease (lowers LDL and triglycerides, and raises HDL)
- stroke
- peripheral vascular disease
- dementia
- cancer
- type 2 diabetes (or can help reverse it)
- osteoporosis
- arthritis

Regular daily exercise also lowers blood pressure, eases symptoms of pain and stiffness, lowers inflammatory load, improves energy, and relieves depression.

Exercise is a great drug!

What kind of exercise?

If you are not already doing so, start a *daily* exercise program. The best studied exercises appear to be brisk walking and vigorous riding of an exercise bicycle. Aim for 30-60 minutes of brisk walking daily, or 20 minutes or more of vigorous bicycle riding.

It doesn't have to be all at once. If you want to take three 20 minute walks a day, or break up your exercise in whatever chunks you choose, that's great, too. Many people just walk up and down stairs daily at home or work. Others jump rope at home, and do simple exercise such as sit-ups, pull-ups, and push-ups. Many join a gym, where a fitness trainer can help design an appropriate workout for you.

According to the leading experts in the field of exercise, the best time to start is today, even if it is only for five minutes. The best exercise is the one you'll actually do. Brief sessions of high-intensity exercise, even for just minutes a day, appear to be very valuable. Do something!

The exercise dose

There are various ways to decide on the appropriate intensity of exercise. Unless your physician instructs otherwise, we suggest that you exercise as vigorously as you comfortably can while still being able to talk. There is a possibility that smaller doses of high intensity exercise are at least as good as 30-60 minutes of moderate exercise, such as walking. So, the folks who jump rope or run stairs might have equal benefit with 10-15 minutes daily. However, I am not aware of any hard data regarding this aspect. (See page 47 for more on the subject of exercise.)

Sleep

Current evidence shows that inadequate sleep is associated with more weight problems, more type 2 diabetes, higher blood pressure, and inflammation, not to mention more grumpiness. The recommended dose is 7 – 9 hours each night. For more about the importance of sleep and its role in preventing heart disease (as well as suggestions for getting a better sleep), see page 59.

Stay open minded!

Question all diet and lifestyle dogma, including ours. Ask for evidence. Consider good nutrition as non-negotiable as seatbelts and bicycle helmets – and remember that the evidence of benefit for nutrition is stronger. Historically stable ideas that are well grounded in solid research will generally be the ones to depend on. For example, highly refined foods such as white rice and white flour have been associated with poor health outcomes for a hundred years, and that is not likely to change any time soon. But stay alert for those new ideas and fresh research that come along to keep us all humble.

Above all, *better is a dinner of herbs where love is, than a fatted calf and hatred therewith.* (Proverbs 15:17 KJV)

2   Good Food

Fat Is Good, Bagels Are Bad
So, What Can We Eat?
Notes on Some Foods and Supplements

Fat is Good, Bagels are Bad

Some Rules to Eat By

Miles Hassell, M.D.

Many of us accept that food is our best medicine. It can be harder to agree upon *which* food. However, if we have health problems, are overweight, or have a family history of heart disease, diabetes, or cancer, there are six dietary dangers we should take seriously.

The extent to which we take these seriously would depend partly on our own known risk factors, but also on our own level of determination to eat and drink sensibly. In any case, these guidelines work for most of us. (Special occasions like birthday parties are exceptions: it may be appropriate, and arguably even therapeutic, to see how many of these rules we can break at one sitting.)

> **If we were to reduce this book to just one piece of advice, it would be to <u>avoid the six items in the following list</u>.**
>
> These are nutritionally bankrupt or compromised foods that are often marketed as healthy products. They mainly supply calories without providing the vitamins, minerals, oils, nucleic acids, phenolics, or countless other nutrients found in whole food which our bodies need to build healthy skin and muscle, clean arteries, and support cancer-fighting immune systems. To simplify further, just to eliminate most refined grains and sugars is one of the most important and life-changing health care decisions we can make.

FOODS TO AVOID

1. **Hydrogenated/partially hydrogenated oils** found in most margarines, vegetable shortening, and many packaged foods.
2. **Refined grains** like instant oatmeal, cold breakfast cereal, white rice, crackers, and breads/pastas containing white flour.
3. **Sugars** like evaporated cane juice, agave nectar, raw unrefined sugar, fructose, sucrose, dextrose, glucose, fruit juice concentrate, corn syrup, and so on. And artificial sweeteners are no better.
4. **Preserved (processed) meats** like bacon, ham, deli meats, sausages, and hot dogs.
5. **Commercially-fried foods,** which means any foods you don't fry yourself.
6. **Fake or highly-altered foods** like egg and butter substitutes, non-dairy creamer, and artificial sweeteners, flavors, colors.

Hydrogenated oils

Hydrogenated and partially hydrogenated oils are the main sources of the chemically altered fats known as trans fats. Even as a small proportion of the diet, trans fats are bad for us. They raise "bad" cholesterol (LDL), lower "good" cholesterol (HDL), raise total cholesterol, and seem to contribute to arterial disease, diabetes risk, asthma, and allergies.

You'll find partially hydrogenated oils in most margarine, shortening, fast food, processed snack food, crackers, fried food, and most commercially baked food. Pay no attention to claims like *Cholesterol Free!* or *Zero Trans Fat!* Go straight to the ingredient list, and if you see the words *hydrogenated* or *partially hydrogenated*, avoid that product.

Even products that claim to have no trans fat are actually allowed to have what many of us would consider a significant amount of trans fat, due to the way the labeling rules are written. So, in my opinion, any food with hydrogenated oil should be considered suspect even if it says '*no trans fats*'. (For oils, just stick with extra-virgin olive oil and occasional canola or soy oil.)

Refined grains

The most common sources of refined grains are products made with white flour, but they also include products like 'instant' oatmeal and white rice. These are the sneakiest and most destructive of modern foods because they tend to be acceptable to otherwise sensible people who, for unclear reasons, worship the god of low-fat.

Don't underestimate the damage to whole foods caused by processing. Consider the example of a 'whole grain' cold breakfast cereal, the type that you pour milk on and eat in the morning because it's fast and easy and tasty. It's whole grain, so that's okay, right? For my reasons why it's not okay, see more about cold breakfast cereals on page 14. As a general rule of thumb, the coarser the whole grain food, and the longer it takes to cook or chew, the better it is for us.

■ **White flour:** Two of the most popular foods in this country are made from mostly white flour: bagels (white bread with attitude) and pasta (white bread with sauce). Bagels and pasta have inexplicably come to be seen as part of a healthy diet. Both are low in fiber and nutrition, and should be avoided along with any other foods containing mainly white flour or sugar, like cookies and crackers.

Read ingredient lists regardless of any promises on labels. (Remember – the more plentiful ingredients are listed first.) If it is a true 100 percent whole grain product, it will say so. Countless products claim to be whole wheat or whole grain but in most cases it just means the product contains a proportion (generally small) of whole wheat flour or whole grains. Beware the term *wheat flour,* which is just another name for white flour.

■ **White rice:** White rice is brown rice with most of the vitamins, minerals, amino acids, oils, and fiber polished off, leaving behind starch and empty calories. I usually describe it as congealed glucose to my patients. It makes no more sense for you to eat white rice than white bread. Brown rice is a superb food full of valuable nutrients, and it is worth making a serious effort to integrate it into your regular diet. (There are many varieties of brown rice, but we suggest starting with the fragrant and delicately textured brown basmati rice. See *Brown Rice* on page 170.)

Sugars

While Americans have substantially reduced their fat intake, there has been a simultaneous rise in the intake of sugar – accompanied by a rise in obesity. Fat – good *and* bad fat – has been demonized while sugar and refined grains have been given little attention, which is ridiculous. Sugar has no nutritional value apart from empty calories, and it contributes to obesity as much or more than fat. Sugar may also suppress our body's immune response. Cutting sugar from your diet is a splendid first step toward better health and ideal weight.

You will avoid a lot of excess sugar simply by avoiding packaged foods: often they contain three or four types of sugar so that it won't show up so high on the list of ingredients. Some examples of sugars are unrefined raw sugar, agave nectar, sucrose, fructose, glucose, dextrose, maltose, maltodextrin, turbinado sugar, and high fructose corn syrup. *Read ingredient lists!* All packaged food is guilty until proven innocent!

Don't be fooled by romantic descriptions like "raw unrefined organic evaporated sugar cane extract", or organic agave syrup. They're still just refined sugars. We are unaware of any practical benefit of agave syrup over high fructose corn syrup: avoid them both.

The sugar you add to food with your own hand is not as much a problem as the sugar you consume in prepared foods from the store or fast foods, because the quantity you add is usually less. So, don't fret over whether or not to put a spoonful of brown sugar on your oatmeal. Our first choice for sweetening would be raw honey (a whole food rich in antioxidants – see page 67), and pure maple syrup is probably your next best choice.

Preserved (processed) meats

Preserved meats (bacon, ham, hot dogs, sausages, deli meats, bologna, spam, and so forth) seem to be much more identified with ill health than other animal products in general. It is unclear what it is in preserved meat that tends to be associated with diseases like cancer, heart disease, and diabetes.[1] Nitrates and nitrites have been on the short list of suspects, but we may never be sure. In addition to preservatives, they generally contain excessive salt and often added sugar.

What *is* sure is that we will be taking one less chance with our health by avoiding them. Many natural food stores carry fresh sausages without additives, for instance, and these would appear to be perfectly healthy. Traditionally aged meats like prosciutto (Italian ham which has been salt-cured and air-dried) may be fine alternatives.

On those special occasions when you indulge in preserved meats, a prudent step would be to eat antioxidant-rich vegetables (like spinach and broccoli) and fruits (like berries and apples) to help combat some of the adverse effects. For example, if you are going to have bacon, fry some slices of tomato to eat at the same time.

Commercially fried foods

Obvious examples of this group include deep fried potatoes (chips or French fries) and fried meat products like corn dogs. The main problem here is the type of long-life fats (what we uncharitably call "bad fat") used in any viable commercial frying operation. Another problem is the likelihood of there being

unstated preservatives in the food, along with the relative scarcity of nutrients.

Fake foods

If a product has been made using ingredients that don't appear in nature, avoid it. Fake food would include non-dairy creamer, fake fats like olestra, egg substitutes, and artificial sweeteners like aspartame (*NutraSweet* and *Equal*) and sucralose (Splenda) commonly found in diet sodas and other 'diet' foods. (See *Diet drinks can make you fat!* on page 19.)

An additional problem with artificial sweeteners is that they maintain your sweet tooth, which can only sabotage your efforts to reach your goal of optimal health. Our palate can be trained; by gradually decreasing the sweet things we eat, we'll find we miss them less. It won't happen overnight, so start now!

As well as having the problem of being nutritionally worthless, the health effects of these fake foods or additives are controversial, and they are usually indicators of food products of dubious value. Most junk foods include artificial colors and flavors in their ingredient lists. Lots of junk food would qualify as fake food. The flagrant examples (like Twinkies) don't pretend to be anything else, but most junk food is presented as positively as possible in order to make it into our grocery cart.

---

[1] Micha, R. et al. Circulation 2010;121:2271-83

So, What Can We Eat?

Miles Hassell, M.D.

That is an easy question. Simply emphasize foods that have been minimally processed. The more recently the food has been attached to the plant or animal it came from, the better.

We have chosen seven categories to discuss – the first two of which are not foods at all. However, fiber is important enough to take first place, and flavor is a large part of what makes the whole food Mediterranean diet so easy to follow. Whole fruits and vegetables, whole grains, beans and legumes, protein, and good fat provide the foundation.

Fiber!

By avoiding refined grains and hydrogenated fats we automatically increase our fiber intake. Fiber is an amazing entity. Increased fiber is associated with *reduced* cancers, *reduced* heart disease, *reduced* diabetes, *reduced* obesity, *reduced* cholesterol … and it comes as a no-added-cost bonus with most of the food we should be eating anyway.

Beans are a great source of fiber, as are whole grains, vegetables and fruits. *Minimally processed* whole grains (like the homemade granola or muesli on page 77, or cooked whole grain cereal like oatmeal) should replace refined cold breakfast cereals, which are not nearly as beneficial despite their 'high fiber' claims. (See page 14.)

Flavor!

Eating food that is good for you doesn't mean giving up enjoying food that *tastes* good. By allowing yourself the liberty of using healthy fats and seasonings, you can easily find a wide range of delicious meals from simple whole foods.

Being too strict about food can defeat the purpose if it means the food doesn't get eaten. The presence of enough fat, salt, and sometimes sweetening can make all the difference. Something as plain as an egg can be memorable when it's scrambled in extra-virgin olive oil or butter with salt and a splash of Tabasco sauce or freshly ground pepper.

> **A simple bowl of plain beans and brown rice** is transformed when you toss it with some finely diced sweet onion and a rich mix of extra-virgin olive oil, garlic, cumin, lemon juice, salt, and pepper. Remember that most of us don't need to worry when we add salt to our food as long as we get rid of the hidden salt in prepared foods and fast foods.

Whole fruits and vegetables

Include a *minimum* of five servings (with a goal of nine servings) of vegetables and fruit in meals and snacks each day. This means *whole* fruits and vegetables, not juiced. Fiber is king, and with it come more vitamins, minerals, phenolics, and so on.

Eat as wide a variety as you can – red, orange, yellow, gold, green, blue, purple, and white. Fresh and raw is good, but cooked is fine and even preferable in some cases. (A well-known example of the benefits of cooking is the tomato, which needs to be cooked for the antioxidant called lycopene to be available to your body.) Frozen can be almost as good as fresh, but read the labels of canned vegetables and fruit carefully.

A serving could be one piece of fruit, a medium carrot or tomato, maybe two six-inch stalks of celery, a half-cup of broccoli florets, a scoop of coleslaw, or a two-inch chunk of cucumber. Depending on how dense (like squash) or fluffy (like lettuce) the item, a serving could be considered as one half to one cup.

Cold 'whole grain' breakfast cereals

Cold breakfast cereals, those crunchy little flakes and extruded shapes that Harold McGee (*On Food and Cooking*, 2004 edition, page 463) calls "a sort of early-morning junk food" should be treated with suspicion. Even when made from whole grain and without added sugar, they have been processed to such a degree that the starch molecule and fiber have been changed, and are much more likely to raise blood sugars.

The extensive processing of ready-to-eat cold cereals is precisely what gives them great mouth feel, keeping qualities, and texture. However, once a grain has been roasted and crushed and made into a batter and extruded and steamed and puffed and dried and finished with spray-on vitamins and minerals and left on a shelf for months, is it still a whole grain? It's easy to imagine the damage to the carbohydrate, the fatty acids, the nucleic acids, the vitamins, the minerals… and who knows what else? We don't even know *how* to measure the damage. Breakfast cereals also create less satiety – a sense of having eaten enough – than their cooked whole grain equivalents, such as cooked oatmeal.

Whole grains

Grains that have been left as intact as possible will have nutrients as intact as possible. A whole grain is an exquisitely practical coalition of parts – the fibrous bran, rich germ, and starchy endosperm – each with a specific function and benefit. The bran fiber slows the absorption of starch, and both bran and germ supply most of the fiber, vitamins, healthy oils, and about 25 percent of the protein. When the grain is refined, not only is this nutrient-rich outer part removed, but the now-unprotected oils in the bran and germ quickly begin to oxidize and are rancid within weeks of the milling process.

So it's easy to see that the less processed (more coarsely ground) the grains you eat, the better they will work for you, and the more slowly and steadily – thanks to the intact bran – they will raise your blood sugar as they are digested. An example of a minimally processed whole grain product would be a whole grain cereal that you have to cook. The longer it takes to chew, the better it is for you. (Making your own bread is actually a practical concept if you keep it simple and make it often enough to get familiar with the process. See the whole grain bread options starting on page 215.)

Most of us eat plenty of wheat, so try to introduce as many non-wheat options as you can. Get to know alternatives like millet and quinoa (pages 180-81). Try pasta made with whole wheat, brown rice, spelt, or corn. Find one you enjoy. Experiment with polenta (page 182) as an alternative for pasta and potatoes.

Occasionally we do limit whole grains (especially cornmeal) for certain patients struggling with diabetes or obesity, but most handle whole grains well.

Beans and legumes

Beans, lentils, dried peas and other legumes tend to be neglected but they have a remarkable nutritional profile – protein, vitamins, minerals, fiber, and antioxidants. You don't even have to cook them yourself, thanks to the convenience of canned beans. Fresh frozen beans, like baby green limas and soybeans (edamame) add yet another dimension.

Beans and whole grains historically have a warm relationship, and recipes that combine the two are useful when one is trying to ease away from being too dependent on meat as a main feature of a meal. (See *Beans* chapter starting on page 153.)

Protein

Meat is a good source of protein but in our society it is served too often and too generously. You'll find it easier to cut back on meat when your meals are rich in good fats, beans, and whole grains. Meals should frequently feature fish rich in omega-3 fatty acids, like tuna and wild salmon. (However, mild-flavored white fish like halibut is a good option when anti-salmon/tuna sentiment is a factor.)

■ **Canned tuna** is easy to work with and can form the basis of some delicious dishes, especially with the help of brown rice and whole grain pasta. (See index for recipes.) We favor "light" tuna over albacore; light tuna (which is actually darker than the albacore!) may have less mercury and more of the healthy oils. (See page 188 for more on tuna.)

■ **Beans, whole grains, tofu, and raw nuts** are good protein alternatives, too. If you get into the habit of leaving meat out of your meals, you will be more likely to explore the world of beans and grains to a greater degree. However, small quantities of meat, cheese, and eggs included in dishes made primarily with beans and whole grains can improve the flavor immensely.

■ **Eggs** are rich sources of protein and "good fat". They are also valuable as the basis for some simple and satisfying meatless main dishes with vegetables, grains, and cheese, like *Green Eggs and Rice* on page 173, *Brown Rice Pudding* on page 177, and *Zucchini Frittata* on page 210. (If you are avoiding eggs because of concern for your cholesterol levels, please see *Dietary cholesterol and saturated fat* on page 20.)

Buying true free-range eggs from a farmer, or "omega 3" eggs from the store, may have some small added benefit. You could also consider getting a few hens. Chickens are great pets. They are always delighted to see you, yet independent enough to keep busy all day while you are gone. Hens do tend to raise their voices when they lay eggs but they mostly keep their voices down to a murmur.

Good fat

We *need* good fat. We need it not only for the health of body parts such as skin, hair, and brains, but also to reduce the risks of diseases like diabetes, heart disease, and cancer. The best fats are probably those found in foods like extra-virgin olive oil and foods like fish, raw nuts, seeds, and avocados. For vegetable oils, cold pressed canola and soy oils are likely a distant second best.

Saturated fats should not be demonized, but omega-3 fatty acids (found in fish, nuts, and flaxseeds) and extra-virgin olive oil (mostly monounsaturated fat) should be more abundant in the diet than saturated fats.

> **Saturated fat in moderation appears to be fine when part of a diet that emphasizes vegetables, fruit, beans, and whole grains.** (See page 20.) One piece of advice is to keep servings of animal protein to no more than twenty five percent of your plate.

Whether you follow a high-fat *or* a low-fat diet model, the emphasis should be on eating "good" fat. The words "low-fat", unless attached to a whole, traditional food that is *naturally* low-fat, should raise red flags. Where prepared foods are concerned, low-fat usually does not mean "low calorie", it may mean "high-sugar".

Usually, you should eat food that has been messed with as little as possible, and is as close as possible to the form that food has been used for the last few hundred years. By following these rules, you generally have the highest level of nutrient content. So when a traditional food is available in a high-fat or low-fat form, I'd generally choose whichever one I enjoyed the most and make sure I kept the quantities small enough so that I didn't gain weight.

Notes on Some Foods and Supplements

Miles Hassell, M.D.

For each of us there may be individual factors which make any particular food, no matter how healthy, a poor choice. The following are recommendations that apply to the majority of people. Most of these are based on clinical studies in humans with evidence for better health outcomes. Only some of the more common foods are covered here.

Bread

Bread is important to mention for at least two reasons. One is that bread is a significant part in many peoples' diets, and is often a part of every meal. Another reason is that the search for good bread can be confusing. The problem is that **true** whole grain bread is simply not popular enough to be produced by the big bread companies, so they have figured out a way to disguise white bread.

> **When you're shopping for bread you can trust**, first look for the words "100 percent whole wheat" or "100 percent whole grain". The first flour mentioned on the ingredient list should be 100 percent whole wheat flour. Remember that the term *unbleached enriched organic wheat flour* simply means… *white flour.* 'Enriched flour' means that first the flour is stripped of all nutrients, and then about 10 percent is added back. What a deal!

Good bread is important to find *if you want bread to be a daily part of your diet.* The optimal choice is heavy bread with chunks of grain visible on the cut surface. The heavier and coarser the loaf, the better: the healthiest choice may be the heavy, moist pumpernickel-type bread mostly found under European labels.

The fragrant, chewy, European-style artisan loaves may be simple, honest, and rustic, but if the first ingredient is white flour (organic and enriched notwithstanding) they still count as white bread and should be considered special-occasion food.

When you do find a good honest specimen – *Great Harvest Bread Company* here in Oregon makes a fine whole wheat loaf containing only stone ground whole wheat flour, water, honey, yeast, and salt, for example – consider buying two and freezing one of them. (For recipes and tips on making your own, see *Bread* starting on page 215.)

Crackers

Most crackers are junk, and have no redeeming nutritional characteristics. Saltines, for example, could be described as white flour and salt held together with hydrogenated oil. The only way to find a good cracker is to read the ingredient label: if it includes 'partially hydrogenated oil' (as most do), leave it alone.

Old-fashioned *Rye Krisp, Rye Vita*, and Swedish flatbreads are good choices. Another honest cracker is *Ak-mak,* a good tasting whole wheat cracker sold in many stores. Whole grain toasted brown rice cakes come in a variety of types; most people should be able to find one that suits them. Remember to read ingredient labels.

Raw nuts

Raw nuts are good food; they're full of healthy fats and associated with better cholesterol profiles and lower rates of heart disease and diabetes.[1] If you have any problem with weight, however, remove calories from somewhere else when adding nuts to your diet. Avoid roasted nuts for five reasons:

---

[1] Salas-Salvado, J. et al. Arch Intern Med 2008;168:2449-58

1) The fats are damaged by heating, 2) there are variables, like storage times or conditions which affect the quality, 3) nuts are higher in calories if they are roasted in oil, 4) the quality of oil used in the roasting process is unknown, and 5) they taste so good they are easy to overeat.

Raw nuts are definitely easier to eat in moderation. Raw walnuts, almonds, Brazil nuts, pecans, and hazelnuts (filberts), are probably your most sensible choices. One way to naturally moderate your intake of nuts is to keep a bowl of nuts in the shell handy, and crack them yourself. Make sure to buy them from a dependable source – old nuts taste awful.

Remember that delectations like trail mixes, especially the ones with bits of chocolate and whatnot in them, are strictly for trail use, and preferably for the *uphill* portions of the trail.

Peanuts and nut butters

Strictly speaking, peanuts are not true nuts: they are legumes, like soybeans. In terms of optimally nutrition, the fatty acid profile of peanuts is not as favorable as the omega-3-rich nuts such as walnuts. Also, peanuts may be on shaky ground because of the mold (aflotoxin) associated with them, although it doesn't seem to be a problem in North America.

Nut butters are usually made with roasted nuts. (If you wonder why, compare the flavor with raw nut butter.) The roasting process damages the good fats, so any form of roasted nuts should be considered special occasion food. Nut butters are very calorie-dense, too, so if you have a weight problem, they should be used sparingly. Ideally, grind your own at one of the many stores with nut butter machines, usually in the bulk food aisle. This way you can be sure it is as fresh as possible as well as free of sugar and other additives. **If you buy bottled nut butters, make sure they have no added oils or sugars.**

Extra-virgin olive oil

Extra-virgin olive oil is a food rich in a variety of nutrients, particularly monounsaturated (omega-9) fatty acids and a family of antioxidants called phenols, both which seem to be associated with overall better health and less heart disease. The other grades of olive oils (regular and "light") are second-best, but still preferable to other vegetable oils. Extra-virgin olive oil has the highest nutrient level, particularly the phenols, so it is probably the best choice.[1]

Walnut, sesame, soy, and canola oils could be considered third best alternatives, but none have the benefit associated with extra-virgin olive oil. One problem with most vegetable oils is that they are heavily processed in order to make them edible and to give them good keeping qualities. In the process, micronutrients usually contained in the oils are removed.

Another problem with most vegetable oils apart from extra-virgin olive oil is that they are high in omega-6 fatty acids, which when oversupplied in the diet appear to be pro-inflammatory and immunosuppressive. For practical purposes, extra-virgin olive oil and virgin coconut oils are the most minimally processed vegetable oils available.

Seafood

Fish is *great* food. For the purpose of treating heart disease and diabetes, oily fish appears to be the best choice. These are generally darker and more highly flavored fish like salmon, tuna, mackerel, and trout. Some ready-to-eat examples are canned tuna, sardines, salmon, and raw pickled herring. (For more on canned tuna, see page 188.) Shellfish and less oily fish like cod and halibut may not be quite as beneficial as the oily fish, but are still good food, and great sources of protein.

Dark chocolate

One of the most surprising and heartwarming nutritional discoveries of the last 20 years is

---

[1] Perona et al. Clinical Nutrition 2004;23:1113-21

that dark chocolate appears to be associated with less heart disease[1], more flexible arteries, better cholesterol, and lower blood pressure. Much of the benefit probably is associated with a group of chemicals in dark chocolate called phenols, which are also present in tea, extra-virgin olive oil, and many other foods.

Definitive studies using dark chocolate to prevent heart disease have not been done, so don't go crazy with this idea; however, it is reasonable to use up to one ounce daily. Choose dark chocolate with a cocoa content of 70 percent or higher.

However, when you add something like chocolate to your diet, remember to remove calories somewhere else. Gaining weight on chocolate would tend to defeat the purpose. (For your chocolate in a liquid form, see recipe for *Hot Chocolate* on page 244.)

Caffeine-containing foods

If someone you know insists that caffeine in any form is harmful, ask to see the data. Tea, coffee, and dark chocolate (which also contains caffeine-like compounds) appear to be part of a healthy lifestyle and are seemingly associated with lower rates of heart disease, diabetes,[2][3] and maybe even some cancers.

Of course, caffeine doesn't work for everybody. Even in small amounts, it causes some people to have abnormalities of their heart rhythm or other problems. As with most of the advice in this book, the use of caffeine needs to be modified depending on your particular health situation.

In general, tea is lower in caffeine than coffee and may be better tolerated. Tea not only is associated with less heart disease, but also less osteoporosis. Green tea generally has less caffeine than black tea, but it is unclear whether it is 'healthier' than black tea. It is also uncertain whether decaffeinated coffee and tea have the same benefits as their full-strength versions.

Definitely *not* part of a healthy lifestyle is caffeine that comes attached to sodas, or in boutique espresso drinks with steamed milk, flavored syrups and sweetened whipped cream look-alikes.

> **Avoid fruit juices!** Contrary to popular belief, juices are very poor sources of nutrients as well as being associated with increased obesity in general and a major cause of obesity in children. Juice has limited nutritional value, with most of the precious fiber, vitamins, and minerals removed but with the sugar and calories retained. If you must drink juice, tomato and vegetable juices (like V8) are your best options. Even 100 percent fruit juice should be considered borderline junk food, especially for children with poor or picky appetites. It should neither count as a serving of fruit nor an example of whole food. There is nothing natural about removing and discarding the most valuable part of the fruit.

Carbonated and sweet drinks

Unsweetened sparkling water is an alternative to juice for some who would like something cold and refreshing in the refrigerator. Most other carbonated drinks, like cola or non-cola, diet or regular, are best avoided. All sugar sweetened drinks, regardless of breathless promises, are calorie-rich and nutrition-poor. This includes the various 'vitamin waters', sports drinks, and energy drinks.

Colas provide the additional insult of weakening your bones[4], and the 'diet' sodas maintain your sweet-tooth with chemicals that are certainly not good for you, and arguably could do harm to some people. (See the following remarks on diet drinks.) We should mainly stick with drinks like water, tea, and coffee, all of which healthy people have been drinking for millennia.

---

[1] Buijsse et al. Arch Int Med 2006;166:411-17
[2] Salazar-Martinez et al. Ann Intern Med 2004;140:1-8
[3] Arnlov et al. JAMA 2004;291:1199-1201

[4] Tucker et al. American Journal of Clinical Nutrition 2006;84:936-42

Diet drinks can make you fat![1]

The fact that sugar–sweetened sodas make you plumper is well known. What is now evident is that low-calorie diet drinks are just as bad.

Soft drinks and 'fruit drinks' are wildly popular pseudo-foods consumed in dramatically increasing quantities over the last twenty or thirty years, and served in larger and larger portions. This explosion in soft drink and juice consumption seems to be related to the dramatic increase in obesity during this same time, particularly in children. In addition, soft drinks have been associated with a growing incidence of diabetes in adults.

A recent analysis that is part of the Framingham Heart Study found that the amount of soft drinks consumed corresponded with the development of 'metabolic syndrome', a constellation of metabolic factors that relate to increased risk of stroke, heart attack, diabetes, dementia, and some cancers.

In fact, even just one soft drink – **diet or regular** – daily was associated with significant increases in:

- Waist measurement and risk of obesity
- High blood pressure
- Worsened cholesterol and triglyceride levels
- Impaired fasting glucose, a critical step in the development of type 2 diabetes

Most importantly, diet soft drinks, the ones with no or low-calories, were just as risky as the sugar sweetened drinks.

There are many potential reasons why both diet and regular soft drinks would be associated with so many negative effects, including that drinking sweet drinks leads to eating more sweets overall through adverse effects on the appetite.[2]

---

[1] Dhingra, R. et al. Circulation 2007;116:480-88

[2] Swithers, S. and Davidson, T. Behavioral Neuroscience 2008;122:161-73

Alcohol

The sometimes-uncomfortable reality is that *small amounts* of alcohol seem to substantially lower the risk of dying (by up to 50 percent) from heart disease, [3] and are associated with a lower incidence of type 2 diabetes, stroke, and dementia.

This advice is not intended for those with medical, personal or philosophical reasons to avoid alcohol. For some, any alcohol is too much. For everyone, drinking more than the suggested amount of alcohol is dangerous, causing more accidents, strokes, dementia, depression, heart disease, liver failure, high blood pressure, weight gain, and divorce.

The difficulty in making appropriate use of the benefits of alcohol lies in that phrase "small amounts", so note the *maximum* doses carefully: a maximum of one drink daily for women and two for men. **A drink is generally defined as 5 ounces of wine, 12 ounces of beer, or 1½ ounces of spirits.**

Although foods such as grapes or grape juice have high antioxidant content, they do not appear to have the same benefits as alcoholic drinks. There is something uniquely beneficial about the ethanol (alcohol) molecule itself. All forms of alcohol seem to have benefit, although the evidence appears to be stronger for red wine.

Salt

Those with high blood pressure and sensitivity to salt should probably keep their sodium intake under 2,500 mg daily. This is equivalent to about 6 grams or 1½ teaspoons of table salt. About three-quarters of the salt eaten in our society comes in commercially prepared foods. Simply by avoiding pre-packaged foods and eating a diet of mainly whole natural foods, you can reduce your salt consumption. A high potassium intake supplied by a diet high in minimally processed whole foods blunts the harmful effects of excess sodium. If buying packaged foods,

---

[3] Mukamal et al. J Am Geriat Soc 2006;54:30-7

look for products which have more potassium than sodium, as well as less than about 5 percent of the daily allowance of sodium per serving. And use restraint when adding salt.

Dietary cholesterol and saturated fat

There are several reasons I don't spend a lot of time condemning the consumption of dietary saturated fat and cholesterol. The first we mention elsewhere but will repeat here: if you are filling the majority of space on your plate with vegetables, whole grains, and beans, then you probably aren't consuming too much cholesterol and saturated fat. The idea of keeping the animal protein to no more than a quarter of your plate at any given meal is a nice pattern for moderation.

Another reason is that I am not convinced that the evidence supports the idea that simply eating foods containing saturated fat or cholesterol contribute to your risk of heart disease. Although this may seem to run counter to conventional wisdom, a review of the following evidence is sobering.

High-fat vs. low-fat

When we look at recent large, well done epidemiological studies, INTERHEART or Greek EPIC,[1][2] we see many factors related to heart disease risk identified —such as fruit and vegetable intake — but dietary saturated fat or dietary cholesterol intake is not among the significant factors.

We can also examine studies in which a low-fat diet is used to try to prevent heart disease in large populations over long periods of time. One example is the Women's Health Initiative[3] which studied 48,835 women for 8 years, randomized to either a low-fat diet, or their usual diet. No effect was seen on heart disease risk or total death rates.

Next we can look at a recent prospective randomized controlled study in which low-fat

diets, the Mediterranean diet, and a low-carbohydrate-high-fat Atkins diet were compared.[4]

Those on both the Mediterranean and Atkins diets ate *more* saturated fat and cholesterol than those on the low-fat diet, yet had better blood cholesterol levels, inflammatory and diabetes markers, and more weight loss than those eating the low-fat diets. We suspect that those on the higher-fat diets enjoyed their food more, too.

People can probably eat perfectly well and be healthy on high- or low-fat diets. What our current data tells us is that a diet with a broad range of foods using the Mediterranean pattern gives the best health outcomes of the various diets studied. Your intake of saturated fat and cholesterol should ***not*** be your focus. Far more important is your intake of vegetables and fruit, whole grains and beans, good fats and fish, daily exercise, sleep, and waist control.

Common sources of cholesterol and saturated fat

■ **Dairy:**
Dairy foods in their generally unprocessed form can be part of a healthy diet. Two or three servings per day are probably a reasonable maximum, and the evidence favors cultured dairy foods such as aged cheese, yogurt and kefir (a yogurt-like cultured milk drink) rather than milk itself. This is not to condemn milk, but simply to point out that the greatest historical evidence for benefit concerns *cultured* dairy foods.

It is reasonable to use either low-fat or full-fat dairy, but there may be evidence that full fat dairy is even superior for both weight loss (see page 30) and cardiac health.[5] A strong case *can* be made, however, against sugar delivery systems disguised as dairy foods, such as caramel lattes and pre-sweetened non-fat yogurt. Each eight ounce

[1] Yusuf, S. et al. Lancet 2004;364:937-52
[2] Trichopoulou et al. NEJM 2003; 348:2599-608
[3] Howard, B. et al. JAMA 2006;295:655-66

[4] Shai, I. NEJM 2008;359:229-41
[5] Warensjo, E. et al. Am J Clin Nut 2010;921:191-202

container can include as much as *6 – 9 teaspoons of added sugar!* As usual, it pays to read ingredient lists.

But even honest dairy foods are not critical to a healthy diet, so if you happen to be intolerant of dairy, don't fret.

■ Yogurt and kefir:
The process of culturing milk into cheese, yogurt, or kefir seems to do something to milk to make it better for adult humans. Kefir is a drink which tastes like yogurt and has similar benefits, but with a different spectrum of good microorganisms.

A plain yogurt or kefir with live cultures ('probiotics') is anti-bacterial, immune boosting, and has high available calcium content. These helpful microbes even predigest the lactose in milk, which allows some people with lactose intolerance to enjoy the benefits of yogurt without any problems.

Most sweetened packaged yogurts and have little or no live cultures. Even worse are the non-fat sweetened yogurts; not only are they loaded with extra sugar for a more acceptable taste, but studies have shown that people perceive the non-fat or low-fat label as a license to eat more. As for commercial frozen yogurt, it is both junk and fake food.

To get the value from the yogurt and kefir you eat, choose plain yogurt and kefir with their active cultures clearly noted on their labels, and add your own fruit or sweetening. *(For more about yogurt, see pages 78 and 97.)*

■ Cheese:
Arguably the healthiest people in the world live in Southern Europe and eat generous amounts of cheese. The best evidence would favor using aged, drier cheese, like sharp cheddar and authentic Italian Parmesan.

Aged cheeses are harder cheeses, and they have a higher 'satiety factor' which means they fill you up more readily for a given number of calories. Maybe it is because they tend to be more flavorful, or maybe something happens to the fats and proteins with extended aging.

You are less likely to over-indulge with the stronger flavored cheeses; extra-sharp cheddar would be a wiser choice than mild cheeses like mozzarella and Monterey jack, for example, or the popular string cheese. Minimize soft, creamy cheeses, saving them for special occasions.

■ Butter:
Butter is a special example of a dairy food. Although high in saturated fat and cholesterol, it also has many valuable nutrients. This is in sharp contrast to margarine, a chemically manipulated food which I view as nutritionally worthless, or worse. I suggest you use butter rather than margarine, use as little as you can enjoy, and don't use butter when you can use extra-virgin olive oil. To reduce your total saturated fat intake you can make 'better butter', combining about three parts butter with one part extra-virgin olive oil. *(See page 73.)* This mixture tastes good and spreads easily even when kept in the refrigerator.

■ Eggs:
Eggs are another controversial food. However, recent data shows no association between eating eggs and increased risk of heart disease.[1][2] The majority of studies do not show that eating eggs is harmful, or has any association with blood cholesterol,[3] arterial dysfunction, or diabetes.[4] An older but useful analysis is also found in British Medical Journal.[5] A cautious approach would be one per day, but my best guess is that one or two eggs daily are perfectly healthy, with both the white and yolk rich with a variety of valuable nutrients including B vitamins, protein, and folic acid.

---

[1] Djousse, L. and Gaziano, M. Am J Clin Nutr 2008;87:964-69
[2] Kritchevsky, S. JACN 2004;23:596S-600S
[3] Njike, V. et al. Nutr J 2010;9:28
[4] Djousse, L. et al. Am J Clin Nutr 2010;92:422-7
[5] Hooper et al. British Medical Journal 2001;322:757-63

■ **Meat:**

It is hard to be sure that any one type of meat, red or white, is nutritionally superior to others. Red meat, as with other land-animal proteins, seems to be a healthy food in moderation.[1] I follow the guidelines of the American Institute of Cancer Research (AICR Food, Nutrition and Physical Activity Summary 2007), which suggest that a reasonable amount of red meat is less than 1½ pounds, raw weight, weekly.

> **In any case, keep portions of meat smallish** – like no more than one quarter of your total plate area. Think of meat as a condiment, not the main part of the meal. Large servings of meat will decrease your appetite for the most important items – vegetables, beans, and whole grains.

Processed meats, like preserved sausages, ham, bacon, and lunchmeats found in the deli case of your supermarket, are associated with significantly more heart disease and diabetes,[1] so I suggest avoiding them entirely. (See pages 12, 73 and 85.)

Nutritional supplements

When we examine the evidence connecting nutrition and good health in real people in the real world, we see that good food improves health, while controlled prospective studies using nutritional supplements generally show no benefit. Some nutritional supplements have even been shown to cause harm, such as higher doses of Vitamin E and beta carotene (see page 60.)

The more we study food and its components, the more evidence we see for the benefit of the *whole* food rather than supplements or extracts. We simply don't know enough about what it is in any given food that makes it work. It may be that there is something in the combination of foods that creates some of the benefit.

Choose whole food as your source of nutrients and fiber, as close to the original formula as possible. Don't trust your health to man's ingenuity or extraction processes. Supplements cannot replace good food, adequate sleep, and daily exercise.

Be cautious of using nutritional supplements based on results of obscure blood tests or other controversial testing methods. Ask for the evidence behind the recommendation, and *examine that evidence* to see if taking the supplement can be expected to lead to a clear-cut benefit.

In my medical practice I use supplements only when there is a good reason. I treat nutritional deficiencies with supplements when I can't achieve adequate levels with food. I use supplements in the absence of documented deficiency when there is reasonable evidence for benefit, and only on a case-by-case basis.

We always remind patients that most nutritional supplements are very unnatural, and should be considered as mild drugs with potential for both benefit and harm, and not as food substitutes. When thought of in that way, nutritional supplements are used with much more discretion.

Two supplements I often prescribe are fish oil and Vitamin D.

■ **Fish oil**

Fish oil can be provided by eating oily fish three or more days a week or by taking a fish oil supplement. (For more details on the use of fish and fish oil, see pages 45-46.)

■ **Vitamin D**

Vitamin D supplements are often necessary when people don't spend much time in the sun, or they live in areas where the sunlight is too weak to provide adequate vitamin D. Having adequate levels of vitamin D in the blood is associated with less heart disease, diabetes, cancers, osteoporosis, and less muscle loss with aging. In randomized-controlled studies of vitamin D, patients given vitamin D supplements have lower death

---

[1] Micha, R. et al. Circulation 2010;121:2271-83

rates. (For references and more on vitamin D see page 60.)

I am typically guided in my dosing by checking blood levels of vitamin D, and often find that doses of 1,000 to 2,000 IU of vitamin D3 (cholecalciferol) are needed. When using vitamin D2 (ergocalciferol), slightly larger doses are needed.

Antioxidant supplements and vitamin E may be harmful

Well done studies show no benefit for most antioxidant supplements in terms of making you healthier or reducing your heart disease risk, and there is strong evidence from randomized controlled studies that vitamin A, beta carotene and Vitamin E supplements have been associated with increased risk of death. (For references see page 60.)

Vitamin E and similar antioxidant nutrients are best supplied in foods, such as minimally processed grains, beans, and raw nuts. If people insist on taking a vitamin E supplement we suggest they use a 'mixed tocopherol' form of vitamin E and keep the dose to less than 100 units daily. From time to time there may be exceptional situations where we use higher dose vitamin E. In these cases, we think of the vitamin E more as a drug than a vitamin.

Food concentrates with antioxidants or enzymes

There are many products in capsules, tablets or powders being vigorously marketed for their heart-healthy properties…and new ones are coming on the market all the time. The trouble is, whenever components are removed from food to make a concentrate, there is an excellent chance that you are removing an important benefit. We simply don't know enough about food to know which parts we can afford to discard.

Unless there are well done studies – and a simple study called a case series would be better than nothing – demonstrating a clinical benefit, I'd suggest you skip these and invest in nuts, avocados, blueberries, and walking shoes, instead.

Antioxidants are very important to good health, as are numerous other families of nutrients. However, the evidence indicates that the optimal source of those nutrients, including antioxidants, is *FOOD!*

Multivitamins

Multivitamins are hard to recommend for most people, based on the currently available data showing lack of benefit in most populations. Decades of research in many countries has so far failed to show any consistent benefit. There are exceptions that can be made on a case by case basis, but I don't recommend taking a multivitamin unless there are specific good reasons to do so. It remains a truism that your best multivitamin-mineral source is….whole food.

Be particularly cautious when using supplements that are sold by the same health care provider who is recommending them. Such conflicts of interest are troublesome.

One randomized placebo-controlled study of 77,000 people using multivitamins for ten years showed no benefit overall and some risk associated with the vitamin E component.[1] Also, an excellent review of the evidence regarding multivitamin supplements can be found in the Annals of Internal Medicine[2].

Don't be gullible!

Question any nutrition advice to avoid falling for nutty ideas. Get an opinion from a qualified, objective professional. Stay open minded and ask for the evidence. It's too easy to accept something just because it sounds sensible at the time, or comes from an "expert" – but beware the expert who is selling a product or ideology. Ask for evidence from an unaffiliated source.

---

[1] Slatore et al. Am J Respir Crit Care Med 2008;177:524-30
[2] NIH Annals of Internal Medicine 2006;145:364-71

3 Taking Steps

Transition Tips
Healthy Habits
Suggestions for Feeding Children
Recommended Reading

Transition Tips

Whether you are dealing with your own dietary changes or someone else's, the transition does not need to be traumatic or dreary. You will more likely be in for some pleasant surprises. What if you find out that you actually *like* lima beans? (Fresh baby limas, anyway – see *Luscious Lima Beans* on page 161.)

You may be surprised to find your tastes changing along with your diet, so don't give up on any healthy foods too quickly. One tip mentioned later on is to choose times when you are hungry to eat foods you are trying to learn to like. Likes and dislikes are not necessarily something we are born with; they can be learned. Following are some encouragements, observations and suggestions that may help.

Don't be overwhelmed

Don't let yourself be overwhelmed by the journey ahead of you or frustrated when progress seems too slow. Just break it down to steps you can easily handle. The one-step-at-a-time method works for most of us, although some may find change easier when it's dramatic.

Clear the house of junk food

This is the only thing that works for some of us. Sadly, this may even include ice cream, which should only have access to your freezer on birthdays. (And only birthdays of people you actually know personally.) Limit fast foods and junk food to special occasions.

No improvement is too small

Even if you start by eliminating one cookie a day, one burger a week, one fast food meal a month … these are all significant steps. Cold turkey doesn't work for everyone.

Use a reminder system

Keep a list of good snacks on the front of the fridge. (See page 82 for ideas.) Then, if you're not thinking clearly due to a sudden acute onset of Refined Carbohydrate Deficiency, the list can help you through the crisis by thinking for you. Soon you'll have built up such good habits that you won't need the list anymore.

A transition trick

One strategy that worked well for at least one former diet junkie was to divide all food into 3 categories — Toxic Treats, Treats, and Food. In the toxic category she puts things like non-dairy creamer and sodas, to be avoided almost completely. Treats are things like white bread, cookies, and fast food, to be eaten on special occasions. In the Food category she includes all unrefined whole foods (like whole grains, beans, vegetables, fruit, meat, eggs, and cheese) which she eats without restriction. She said it was easier to resist or cut back on the wrong foods when she identified them clearly in her mind first.

Try to identify food triggers

For example if you crave a sweet treat when you stop for a latté, then don't stop for a latté. If you can't stop at one scoop of ice cream, skip it altogether. Brutal, but it works. Also, be alert for the more subtle triggers that make us eat the wrong thing – like letting ourselves get too hungry, or stressed, or depressed. One solution is to make sure we eat a good breakfast (see page 72), offer ourselves a healthy snack regularly (see page 82), avoid refined carbohydrates (see refined grains and sugar on page 11), and get enough sleep (see page 59). Also, don't forget that the combination of exercise and fresh air is a powerful antidepressant.

Eat when you're hungry

Food tastes a lot better when you're hungry. This is an obvious but underrated fact. If you're learning to like something, wait until you're hungry before you eat it. It will look a lot better. And if you have to learn to like just about *everything*, only eat when you're hungry.

...but don't go shopping hungry

Go with a proper list and a firm hand, and don't let anything but good food make it into your cart. Choose *whole* foods, not juiced, powdered, dried, or instant. Buy fresh fruit that you really *are* going to eat and vegetables that you really *will* find time to prepare. While you are transitioning to a better eating pattern, stick to vegetables you know and like.

Make it taste good!

Eating well doesn't mean compromising on taste. Think rich, spicy, hot, sweet, and sour, and adjust your recipe accordingly. Think *good* fat, not *low*-fat. Remember that the enemy is not salt and butter and cheese and meat. Mankind has been enjoying these since the beginning of recorded history. The problem is generally user error – we eat too much.

Maintain a routine

Daily routine works well for many of us: an orange at breakfast, half of a banana for the mid-morning hungries, an apple before bedtime ...three servings of three different fruits without trying. (Our stomach will probably remember even if we don't.)

White versus brown bread

If you run into resistance making the transition from white bread, you don't need to move directly to 100 percent whole wheat. Find some decent compromise, like a loaf with at least half whole wheat flour, and then move on to the good stuff when the fuss dies down. (See *Bread,* starting on page 215.) Sandwiches made with whole wheat bread are not always interchangeable with white bread sandwiches: the heavier bread can easily overwhelm the filling. Slice bread as thinly as possible or switch to whole wheat pita bread.

Make sensible compromises

If you want a cookie or a muffin, consider making your own homemade whole grain muffins or oatmeal cookies. In fact, just about *anything* you make yourself is better than ready-made commercially prepared stuff you can buy. (See *Quick Breads and Treats* on page 233.)

White versus brown rice

If you are preparing meals for anyone who is finding it tough to adjust to the whole food paradigm, don't feel compelled to replace white rice with brown rice on every occasion– at least in the beginning. **However, don't present white rice as anything other than a compromise – it is a refined grain** (see page 11) **and a special-occasion food.** Brown rice is a whole food with more flavor and texture, and – properly cooked – can replace white rice in every meal or recipe. Try different kinds of brown rice; there can be significant variation in texture, flavor, cooking times, water absorption, and so on. My favorite is brown basmati rice. (See the recipes beginning on page 171.) Also, don't overlook quinoa (see page 180) as a tasty protein-rich alternative that cooks as quickly as white rice.

Soda substitute

Try to eliminate soda pop and other junk drinks. Diet soda is just as bad. (See *Diet drinks can make you fat!* on page 19) A good strategy is to keep sparkling spring water chilled in your refrigerator. (Lemon lime flavor is spunky without being distractingly fruity.) It can be useful combined with frozen 100 percent fruit juice concentrates into a sort of punch, especially when trying to wean children from drinking juices or sodas. Sparkling water can also help you resist a second glass of wine. But don't replace soda with juice!

Healthy Habits

We all battle habits, preconceptions, and our own opinions as to what tastes good, but it can be surprisingly easy to slide into new habits and tastes once we decide to get serious about our health. There is nothing complicated about eating well but it *does* require attitude and discipline. You will probably constantly fine-tune your own rules, but the most important principle will keep floating to the top: food really *is* your best medicine.

Don't say you're on a diet!

The whole food approach to eating is not a temporary program to lose weight or feel better. This is a way of life: a new perspective for some and a return to good sense for others. While you work on improving your food choices, make other changes.

Don't nag

Eating well is a privilege and not a sentence to serve, but that's not always obvious at first. If faced with family resistant to change, don't nag! Not only is change difficult for most of us, giving up food we love can be pretty painful. Just make sure there is plenty of good food available. After a while of being exposed to better food, tastes can gradually adjust. However, it certainly does not make any sense to sacrifice any relationship on the altar of good food.

Exercise any way you can

Making a habit of exercise, even without a change in diet, has a huge pay-off. As we detail on page 8, exercise protects against heart disease, stroke, cancer, type 2 diabetes, osteoporosis, arthritis, dementia, depression, and more. Exercise can take many forms. Some people do very well with short bursts (a couple of minutes or so) of maximal exercise daily, such as running stairs and skipping rope.

Most of the research has concentrated on thirty – sixty minutes of daily moderate-to-brisk walking, which is fine for most people. The most important thing is to *do some exercise every day*. And if there is any doubt about your ability to perform any particular type of exercise, check with your physician. (For more on exercise, see page 47.)

Eat more vegetables

Remember, a minimum of five servings and a goal of nine servings! But increasing your vegetable consumption can be almost effortless. Salads can be as easy as opening bags of pre-washed bite-sized greens, or even a selection of vegetables custom-cut for anything from party trays to stir-fries. Broccoli florets and snap peas ready to dip or stir fry. Mushrooms are sliced and packed in neat little cartons for you. English (hothouse) cucumbers are shrink-wrapped individually and need no peeling or seeding. You can buy bags of crunchy little baby carrots, peeled and washed and ready to dip. Leave a bowl of bite-sized vegetables on the counter for all-day snacking. And so on.

Eat more fish

Raising your omega-3 fatty acid level can be pleasant and convenient if you shop around for something to suit your tastes. Tuna comes in all forms including appetizing-looking slices in easy-open serving-sized cans. Sardines are available in all kinds of sizes and flavors with handy peel-back lids like their tasty smoked counterparts, kippered snacks. Experiment.

Read ingredient labels

Stoutly resist products admitting to sugar, white flour, hydrogenated fat, and artificial flavors. This means avoiding items like packaged cookies, snack foods, sodas, and cold breakfast cereals (see page 14), but you will be delighted at the amount of good food to add to your shopping cart. It is because of sensible choices made by brave and smart people like you that most supermarkets now have healthy options in every department.

Eat out less

If your health is at all compromised, whether by excess weight or other risk factors, it would be wise to eat out as little as possible. The degree of strictness would logically depend on your particular health problems and family history. A lean, healthy person whose parents are 100 years old and still playing tennis may be less strict than, say, a plump diabetic.

When you do eat out, don't fool yourself. Even a 'good' restaurant or deli can't afford to make *your* health a higher priority than *their* survival. This means they will tend to choose methods and ingredients that have the best effect on *their* bottom line, not yours. (For more on eating out, see page 86.)

Watch TV less

Television is associated with weight gain, diabetes,[1] and depression. Shut down your computer sooner and read more. Learn all you can about eating sensibly. (Some reading suggestions start on page 34.) If you watch less television you will be sure to eat less junk, get more sleep, have more energy, and find more time to exercise. (See page 47.)

Be thankful!

Making intelligent food choices has never been easier or more enjoyable than it is these days – mainly because nutrition is so much more of a marketable commodity than it used to be. The average person is alert to the importance of food and exercise, so restaurants and supermarkets are scrambling to keep ahead of the demand.

Drink plenty of water

Increasing your water intake is important when you increase your fiber intake and decrease your calorie intake. Happily, increasing your liquids and fiber effortlessly in the form of whole fruits and vegetables is a bonus that comes with the Mediterranean approach.

---

[1] Dunstan et al. Diabetes Care 2007;30:516-22

How much water should I drink?

I'm not sure anyone can answer that question authoritatively, but you do need to drink enough water to plump up your blood vessels, provide for tears, sweat, and saliva, and keep your colon happy. (Water is still the most important stool softener.)

Finally, you need enough water to let the kidney do its thing in excreting toxins without needing to make the urine very concentrated and to prevent kidney stones.

So how do you know if you are drinking enough water and other liquids? Pale urine is probably as good a sign as any that you are drinking enough.

Some people believe that it is important to drink eight cups of plain water a day. I'm not sure of any evidence to support that. If you are in a hot climate or are sweating very much, you'll need to drink more liquid, so use the pale urine as your test. The most common cause of bright yellow urine, by the way, is the vitamin riboflavin (B2), found in most multivitamins and B vitamins.

Get a waist

The weight you carry around your middle is more hazardous for heart disease, diabetes, and some cancers than weight elsewhere on your body. So if you are overweight, losing weight is not as important as being fit and losing inches around your waist.

One risk reduction guideline is a waist measurement of less than 35 inches for women and less than 40 inches for men. (This guideline may be inaccurate for people with a slight build.) Another useful measurement of risk that can be used is the waist-hip ratio.

Calculating waist-hip ratio

Various protocols for measuring the waist-hip ratio are used, which complicates comparisons between research papers.

One accepted approach is:

1. Measure your waist at the belly button
2. Measure the broadest point around your buttock area (your hip measurement)
3. Use a calculator to divide the first measurement (waist) by the second (hip).

If the number is greater than 0.88 for women or 0.95 for men, you'll need to lose weight to minimize your risk of dying of heart disease, diabetes, or cancer. This measurement is probably much more important than your cholesterol level. (See *Big waists can lead to bad hearts and soft brains* on page 56.)

The high-fat/weight loss paradox

When we recommend high-fat whole foods such as raw nuts, extra-virgin olive oil, and full-fat dairy and aged cheese, patients who are struggling to control their waistline often wonder if we are leading them in the wrong direction. We remind them that *high*-fat minimally processed *whole* foods are less likely to put on weight and are more satisfying than *low*-fat *processed* foods, which contain more sugars and highly refined grains.

As mentioned on page 20, the available data suggest that a higher fat diet is associated with more effective weight *loss* than a low-fat diet. When high-fat diets are compared to low-fat diets for overweight people, those eating the higher fat diets tend to lose more weight, have better cholesterol, lower blood sugar and lower triglycerides.[1] [2]

If you are overweight, reduce your intake of refined carbohydrates (like sweets, ready-to-eat breakfast cereals, white rice, and products made with white flour, including fat-free "protein bars" (see page 83) and "meal replacement" drinks (see page 81).

If the weight is still not coming off after you have eliminated refined grains and sugars <u>and</u> are eating minimally processed whole foods, reduce your portion sizes. Too much food, even very *good* food, is still too much.

[1] Shai, I. et al. NEJM 2008;359:229-41
[2] Gardner, C. et al. JAMA 2007;297:969-77

If you need to lose weight

Just about any diet works for short-term weight loss, but what works best for *long term* weight control is a diet of real food that includes healthy fats needed by you *and* your immune system. For anyone trying to control or reduce weight, here are eleven steps to try:

1. **Avoid refined carbohydrates** like cold breakfast cereal, crackers, white flour, white rice, white pasta, sweets, and sugar.

2. **Avoid sweet drinks** like fruit juices and sodas, including diet sodas (pages 18-19).

3. **Minimize or eliminate potatoes, rice, corn, dried fruit, and bread** *if weight is not coming off.* Also, stop at two handfuls of raw nuts, *one ounce* of dark chocolate, and *one serving* of alcohol per day. (Serving sizes on page 19.)

4. **Read ingredient lists** on everything you buy – junk is often disguised as food. For example, eight ounces of sweetened fat-free yogurt can hide *6 – 9 teaspoons of sugar.* See page 10 for six ingredients to avoid.

5. **Eat vegetables and whole fruit** with *every* meal including breakfast.

6. **Eat breakfast and don't skip meals:** eating breakfast (see *Breakfast* on page 72.) and frequent small meals (see pages 82 – 86) are both associated with successful weight loss.

7. **Avoid eating out:** if you work away from home, pack a lunch. Don't eat and drive!

8. **Eat good fat (not low-fat) <u>and</u> protein with every meal.** (See page 15 for ideas.) This will tend to slow the rise of your blood sugar and improve the sense of satisfaction.

9. **Monitor portion sizes.** Use smaller plates. Eat slowly, savoring each bite. Try to stop eating before you are full. Eat more vegetables. Eat whole fruit for dessert.

10. **Exercise daily** any way you can and at every opportunity. Move more! Avoid taking elevators if you can take the stairs.

11. **Schedule 7 – 9 hours of sleep** at night. (See *Get adequate sleep* on page 59.)

Suggestions *for* Feeding Children *and* Other People

Children generally like food that tastes good. This means they usually love junk food instantly, of course, and that can be a problem. The later we introduce whole foods to them, the slower they may take to them, but kids are adaptable. Even if they weep and rage and threaten to throw up or stop eating completely, there is a good chance that within a few days or weeks the formerly unacceptable may be the new status quo.

The bottom line

Providing good food for our children is a responsibility, not a choice, much like insisting that your child rides in a car seat. With type 2 diabetes now a disease known among children as young as six years old, the stakes are high. On the other hand, there has never been a generation of parents better equipped with not only good information about nutrition, but easy access to it.

The world of whole foods is not the dimly lit fringe territory it once was: it has shed its Birkenstocks and is standing before us in a white coat and stethoscope. (Come to think of it, your doctor is probably wearing Birkenstocks, as well.) Good food is everywhere, and whole food cookbooks are being published at a feverish rate.

How to do it

How do we get children to eat good food? We serve it. That's not just the short answer, it's the *only* answer. It's not an accident that children start off small and helpless: it establishes parents as protectors and providers. But somehow it happens that perfectly sane and loving people, grown-ups who make important decisions about what cars to drive and which houses to buy, become small and helpless when it comes to decisions about maintaining their child's health and well-being. "My child won't eat good food. What can I do? Let him/her *starve?*"

Answer: Definitely. Let the kid starve for a few minutes, which is all the time it should take to figure this out. The issue is all about where we draw lines. If you consider white bread in the same category as white sugar, it should be simple.

Your job will be more difficult if you have a television to provide a steady flow of mouthwatering images of junk food. There are plenty of other reasons to remove the TV, though, and this may be the best time.

Sell it!

If you think a junk-free diet is a good concept but not really practical, your child will, too. The same psychology of marketing that works in the business world works at home. If we're not enjoying *our* vegetables, why should they? Good food should taste good! Do what it takes to make it taste good to you, and you may find the job of feeding your children much easier.

When a child is very young (say, 0 – 18 months) you can prepare meals without being concerned about flavor. (Ever tasted baby food?) You really only need a blender and some leftover cooked vegetables, beans, brown rice, or whatever.

However, in the case of a child whose palate is already tuned to the fast food frequency, the vegetables, beans, and brown rice have to practically *leap* off the plate with excitement. This simply means making judicious use of things like good fat and salt, which are the ingredients that make fast food so appealing. Rich, spicy, salty, sweet, and sour: it's that simple. Make good food taste seductive, too. This is war.

Strategy

You don't have to say "no". Of course, the most direct solution is to remove the junk you don't want them to eat, but if that isn't practical you can always resort to cunning. You can say "yes, *after* you've eaten your dinner", or "yes, *after* you've eaten this apple." (By the way, this strategy works for us grown-ups, too.)

If they surprise you and actually eat their part of the bargain, make it a little more difficult to meet your terms next time you strike a deal. However, it is important that good food should not be seen as the enemy. Access to junk food is not the critical issue — the most important thing is that we *eat the good food first.*

When your children wake up one morning to find no frozen waffles or giant boxes of breakfast cereal, they will discover that it is possible to find food they can enjoy that is not nutritionally bankrupt — hot buttered toast with real fruit jam, for example, or pancakes with pure maple syrup. (See *Breakfast* on page 72.)

Mealtime discipline

Avoid asking young children what they would *like* to eat. Serve them what you know they *need* to eat. However, keep the portions small, and include tiny samples of detested food. Three peas or two carrot matchsticks or one pinto bean is neither unfair nor a wasted gesture.

Exposure to a *wide selection* of real food is important – not only for a child's immediate nutritional needs, but also as preparation for a lifetime of eating choices.

Because food is so important, stand firm. "No, we no longer stock your favorite fiber-free fructose-filled fudge-flavored flim-flams. How about a banana?" If your child refuses to eat and chooses to go to bed hungry it should be seen as the child's choice, not punishment. Food is not a reward for good behavior: food is necessary fuel.

Mealtime is a good time for teaching good manners, but it also happens to be the best time to make sure children get what they need to thrive. And *please* do not announce a child's likes and dislikes within their hearing. It can only serve to legitimize poor choices and make your job harder.

Battle plan

Make rules and *stick to them*. Don't get flustered. Once boundaries and expectations are established a certain degree of order will follow, and children do much better in order than in chaos. So do you. Everyone wins.

Don't forget the battle plan! The weapons are *good* fat and *real* flavor and the strategy is *reasonable* compromise and incremental progress. Also, commitment and personal resolve are probably the most decisive factors in the victory.

Lead your family into a diabetes-free future, striding with clean hearts, strong bones, shiny hair, clear skin, good hip-to-waist ratios, and plump, healthy brains.

Snacking suggestions for children

Over my long years of feeding children and grown-ups, certain patterns have emerged. For example, something I have noticed is that almost everybody likes food which has a balance of salty and sweet flavors.

The fact is, most food tastes better with salt. The sad thing is that most parents think they shouldn't add salt to food, which means that the food isn't as tasty, which leads to the general opinion that if you want kids to eat, bring home fast food.

Now that is logical thinking only if you're standing on your head. It makes far more sense to simply flavor good food with enough salt and good fat so children like it, and skip the fast food which is also loaded with far higher levels of salt, sugar, and bad fats.

Two time tested snacks

■ *Definitive Dip*

The recipe for this bright green dip is on page 100. It's rich with cheese, tart with yogurt and lemon juice, and explosively flavored with garlic and Tabasco sauce. I wouldn't have expected a small child to like it but I — and countless parents — have been surprised almost every time.

The most successful dipping vegetables have been baby carrots and bite-sized florets of broccoli that have been dropped in boiling water for a couple of minutes so they are bright green and tender-crisp. (Watch out — sometimes they just suck the broccoli and poke it right back into the dip bowl.)

■ *Luscious Limas*

One of the more dramatic examples of the success of *Luscious Limas* (recipe on page 161) was with a 6-month-old whose family had invited me to dinner.

I arrived with a bowl of *Luscious Limas* because it was a favorite with one of the other children there. We ate our meal while the baby played with any food that came her way, cramming it into her bib pocket, smashing it into the corners of her highchair tray, and squishing it in her little fists and then leaning out of her highchair to see if she could dislodge it onto the floor.

So I placed one little green lima bean on the tray, shiny with olive oil and lively with garlic, vinegar, salt, and pepper. The baby picked it up curiously and then ate it. I put another two on the tray, and she quickly ate them. I put a spoonful in front of her and she ate them one at a time, and then carefully searched her bib pocket for any beans that may have escaped.

Similar scenes have been played out over the years with children of various ages, and sometimes with *Seductive Soybeans* (see page 158), instead. It's worth a try.

Smoothies for littlies

■ **Why a smoothie?**

The smoothie strategy is possibly the easiest way to significantly boost a small child's daily nutritional intake, especially on a hectic day when an instant infusion of good calories is called for. And when you have to pack a child in the car and go somewhere, few things are as convenient as a cup or two of smoothie to feed him on the road. There are recipes for smoothies starting on page 79, and I would definitely recommend making fortified versions where possible. *(See page 80 for fortification ideas.)*

■ **Start young**

Children generally aren't as conflicted by preconceptions about textures and flavors as adults, so they can be a lot more satisfying to feed. A child's smoothie can be more basic and sensible, while still tasty. A child who is started on fiber-packed smoothies very young has no expectations, and will cheerfully suck down a smoothie fortified with his leftover breakfast oatmeal or a half-cup of yesterday's brown rice. If you must make the smoothie more like a milkshake for any reason, simply leave out the grain … but you may be amazed at the adaptability of a child in the hands of a cunning and confident parent. A chunk of ripe avocado, some fresh spinach or leftover vegetables, a tablespoon or two of cooked beans…you'd be surprised what a child can enjoy.

■ **Feeding tips**

Colored plastic cups with spouted lids make wonderful smoothie receptacles. If the spout won't allow the free flow of a thick smoothie, carefully slice off the top ¼-inch with a sharp knife; they virtually never get clogged that way. (Make sure the cut edges are child friendly.)

(For grown up smoothies see pages 78 – 81.)

Recommended Reading

We have chosen a smattering of books to briefly review here. There will always be some disagreement between the various authors (and occasionally they even disagree with *us)*, but that shows the degree of uncertainty existing in this field. Stay flexible and keep reading. You will be constantly fine-tuning your own rules, but the most important principle will keep floating to the top: good food is great medicine.

Food Rules
An Eater's Manual
(Michael Pollan © 2009)

If you only have time to read one book on this reading list, make it *Food Rules.* Actually, it is so short that you can easily read it at one sitting, which is a good thing because it is hard to put down. In the introduction, Pollan points out two things he has learned in his search for the answer to a simple question: "What should I eat?"

The first thing he found out is that eating has gotten needlessly complicated. However: "The deeper I delved into the confused and confusing thicket of nutritional science, sorting through the long-running fats versus carbs wars, the fiber skirmishes and the raging dietary supplement debates, the simpler the picture gradually became."

The picture focused on two undisputed facts: first, populations that eat a so-called Western diet (more processed foods and meat, less whole foods and vegetables, lots of added fat and sugar) have high rates of the so-called Western diseases – obesity, type 2 diabetes, heart disease, and cancer. And fact two – populations that eat traditional diets with more minimally processed food generally don't suffer from these chronic diseases. As Pollan observes, "what an extraordinary achievement for a civilization to have developed the one diet that reliably makes its

people sick!" He then points out a very important third fact that flows from the other two – people who get off the Western diet see dramatic improvements in their health. "I realized that the answer to the supposedly incredibly complicated question of what we should eat … could be boiled down to just seven words: Eat food. Not too much. Mostly plants."

Pollan then unpacks those seven words into sixty-four simple rules: "It's not food if it arrived through the window of your car." "Treat treats as treats." "Don't get fuel from the same place your car does." (We especially liked his mention of the Dutch proverb, "A land with a lot of herring can get along with few doctors.")

In Defense of Food
An Eater's Manifesto
(Michael Pollan © 2008)

In Defense of Food is the much longer (but just as enjoyable) precursor to *Food Rules.* We don't always agree with his take on the social/political aspects of food production, but we have come to the same conclusions about what to eat and why. The blend of common sense and humor delivered by such a superb writer is particularly refreshing.

The Mediterranean Diet Cookbook
(Nancy Harmon Jenkins © 2009)

One of the best reasons to buy this book (or check it out from the library) is the 7-page examination of the Mediterranean diet on page 467 by Antonia Trichopoulou, M.D. and Dimitrios Trichopoulos, M.D., Professor of Cancer Prevention and Epidemiology at the Harvard School of Public Health. Their analysis combined with Nancy Jenkins's introduction and first two chapters make up a perfect little primer on the Mediterranean diet. Jenkins' Mediterranean credentials are solid – she lived there for a long time and can talk about the food and lifestyle (and the neighbors with the Lamborghini tractor) from the inside looking out. Her authenticity will be refreshing to any serious Mediterranophile.

Eat, Drink, and Be Healthy
The Harvard Medical School Guide to Healthy Eating
(Walter C. Willett, MD © 2001)
An enjoyable read (Willett is a good writer) and a valuable source of information on the science and common sense of eating well. The book lays out the evidence and conclusions for healthy eating and includes a large section on "the practical translation of nutritional science to food selection and preparation." His chapter on calcium is worth the price of the book.

Eat, Drink, and Weigh Less
(Mollie Katzen and Walter Willett, MD © 2006)
The author of *Eat, Drink, and Be Healthy* has collaborated with the author of *Moosewood Cookbook* (and many other cookbooks) to remind us that sensible eating and weight loss don't have to mean avoiding fat and feeling deprived. However (*sigh*), Mollie Katzen's recipes are disappointingly stingy with good fat, and the authors seem to be too forgiving of heavily processed breakfast cereals, sugary granola-type bars, and fat-free/high-sugar yogurt. Except for these puzzling endorsements in the Shopping Guide, most of the book is helpful.

Passionate Vegetarian
(Crescent Dragonwagon © 2002)
Whether or not you are vegetarian – and we are not – Crescent Dragonwagon is a woman we could all use in our kitchens. As well as having a name that is fun to say, she is practical and entertaining. There are more than 1,000 exuberant pages of recipes and food-talk to inspire even reluctant cooks.

The New American Plate Cookbook
(American Institute for Cancer Research © 2005)
This book is the work of a team of cooks, writers, and scientists working with the American Institute for Cancer Research (AICR). Their mission was to produce a cookbook that would "satisfy your conscience while it dazzles your palate", and at the same time helping to reduce our risk of serious health problems like cancer and heart disease as well as maintain a healthy weight. The photographs are glorious.

The Schwarzbein Principle: The Truth About Losing Weight, Being Healthy and Feeling Younger
(Diana Schwarzbein M.D. and Nancy Deville © 1999)
This is an excellent book to acquaint the reader with the concept of using a whole foods diet to minimize insulin resistance, a metabolic problem that is related to the majority of cases of obesity, type 2 diabetes, heart disease, stroke, and some cancers.

On Food and Cooking: The Science and Lore of the Kitchen (Harold McGee © 2004)
One of the best books on food ever written. The author is fascinating, too. Enthralled by chemistry and physics growing up, he decided to study astronomy, and then switched to English literature. He wrote the first edition of this book in 1984, but says, "A lot has changed in twenty years! It turned out that *On Food and Cooking* was riding a rising wave of general interest in food, a wave that grew and grew, and knocked down the barriers between science and cooking, especially in the last decade."

What to Eat
(Marion Nestle © 2006)
Marion Nestle is one of the greats of contemporary academic nutrition but she is also a food lover and consumer. These aspects come together well in this easily-read yet powerful book which takes you on a tour of a North American supermarket. In each section there is a discussion of the food's origin, what has gone on during its production

to affect the food, and her recommendations for the consumer.

The breadth of material she covers is vast; production methods, historical comparisons, political and environmental controversies, federal government and special interest group influences, and practical applications of nutrition research are all blended into a very useful set of realistic and humbly presented recommendations. The assumptions and thought processes she uses are laid out clearly to help the reader see whether her conclusion is something they can share. Often her conclusions are amusingly simple: "Milk is just a food. There is nothing special about it. Cow's milk is not necessary and it is not perfect (at least not for humans). But cow's milk is also not a poison."

We do not always share her concerns or solutions. A couple of areas of disagreement would be her position on saturated fats, and her "Taking Action" conclusions that seem to encourage the imposition of centralized controls over which foods the consumer can buy. However, excellent tools are given to allow the consumer to practice personal responsibility and take control of their own food environment, and the disagreements we may have are far outweighed by the rich store of practical knowledge you will gain from reading this book.

Eating Well Magazine

This is a self-described "intelligent magazine bringing together food and health." It does a decent job of presenting evidence-based information, but mixed with enough puzzling dietary recommendations to give the reader a confusing picture. We are still hoping they will wake up to the serious problem of sugar in the diet (the *Hot Fudge Pudding Cake* recipe from one of their "weight loss experts" says it all) and stop tip-toeing around the good-fat-versus-low-fat issue. Enjoy this magazine, but with a healthy serving of discernment.

www.eatingwell.com

Subscribe online or call toll-free (800) 337-0402

In the interests of open-minded and healthy intellectual hiking, we are also including books that test confrontational waters on some of the controversial nutritional issues.

The Fat Fallacy: The French Diet Secrets to Weight Loss
(William Clower, Ph.D. © 2003)

A lively, funny, well-written book contrasting the French disregard for fat and carbohydrate restrictions with the American obsession with low-fat dogma. The author points out the much higher rate of obesity and heart disease in this country, and tries to show how the prudent use of chocolate, butter, eggs, and cheese can help us lose weight and gain health.

French Women Don't Get Fat
(Mireille Guiliano © 2005)

Yet it was precisely the experience of getting fat, albeit as an exchange student in the U.S. that inspired the author – who is French – to write this book! Regardless of the accuracy of the title, the book is full of practical advice, real-life case histories, and recipes. She says the book is for women who need to lose up to thirty pounds, but anyone would benefit from her message.

Nourishing Traditions
The Cookbook that Challenges Politically Correct Nutrition and the Diet Dictocrats
(Sally Fallon, Mary G. Enig Ph.D. © 2001)

This book delivers *exactly* what the title promises, and does so with the efficiency of a machine gun and the firmness of an Italian grandmother. It is an encyclopedic blend of old-fashioned liver-and-onions and Adele Davis at her most radical. Each page is crowded with recipes as well as often-fascinating facts on diet, history, religion, sociology, and medicine. This is a book to read on a desert island even if you disagree with something on every page. It may also be the only place you'll find a recipe for *Brain Omelet* when you need one.

4 Heart Disease

Preventing Heart Disease *and* Heart Attacks

using food, exercise, and medications

Featuring the ten most important choices
you can make for your heart,
even if you already have
a diagnosis of
heart disease

Preventing Heart Disease *and* Heart Attacks

Miles Hassell, M.D.

Heart disease is the most common cause of chronic disease and death in most industrialized countries. This chapter is an overview for those who have already been diagnosed with heart disease – but it is just as relevant for anyone who wants to do everything in their power to *prevent* a diagnosis of heart disease.

This first section contains some basic information to help you navigate the subject of heart disease (coronary artery disease) as well as understand some of the processes that lead to cause heart disease.

The remainder of the chapter will outline the ten most important choices we can make to prevent and reverse heart disease.

A few foundational concepts

■ Practically speaking, the process by which arteries to the heart become clogged can usually be stabilized or reversed to a significant degree using food, exercise, and appropriate medicine.

■ If you don't have heart disease, you can minimize your risk of getting it, even when you have multiple risk factors, such as high cholesterol, high blood pressure, or a significant family history of heart disease.

■ Most of your heart disease risk factors are modifiable using lifestyle choices.

■ If you already have heart disease, you can usually prevent further events, such as heart attacks, by making good medical and lifestyle choices.

Preventing heart attacks

The subject of heart disease prevention is often classified into two broad categories.

■ **Primary prevention** is the prevention of heart disease in those patients who have not yet been diagnosed with any arterial damage.

■ **Secondary prevention** means preventing further cardiac events, such as angina and heart attacks, in those who are already known to have coronary heart disease.

Patients with diabetes are a special group.
The risk of a diabetic patient having undiagnosed 'silent' heart disease is so high that we simply treat most diabetic patients as if they already have coronary artery disease.

For practical purposes, we will not distinguish between primary and secondary prevention because the steps that we need to take to protect our arteries from future insults are similar. All of us should make the kinds of lifestyle choices that will minimize our risk of heart disease.

To further complicate the issue, many people who do not have a ***diagnosis*** of heart disease ***can*** have significant cholesterol buildup in their arteries which has not yet manifested itself (silent heart disease).

Happily, the same lifestyle choices that reduce your risk of heart disease also reduce your risk of stroke, high blood pressure, type 2 diabetes, peripheral arterial disease, cancer, dementia, and macular degeneration. What a bonus!

A few important definitions

■ **Heart disease** is a term covering many conditions which affect the heart. However, for the purposes of this discussion the term 'heart disease' will be synonymous with its most common cause, coronary artery disease, also known as ischemic heart disease.

■ **Coronary artery disease** is the process of injury and blockage of the arteries (coronary arteries) that provide blood to your heart. This may lead to a 'heart attack', or myocardial infarction (MI).

■ **Heart attacks** occur when a blocked artery does not provide sufficient blood to the heart, which damages part of the heart muscle. This damage can lead to a heart that does not pump effectively (congestive heart failure or CHF), heart rhythm problems (arrhythmias), and death.

■ **Angina** refers to the discomfort that occurs when blood flow to the heart is reduced, and manifests as pain or pressure in the chest, arm, back, neck, or jaw. Angina is common in patients with coronary artery disease and can be present whether or not the patient has had a heart attack.

Narrowed or blocked arteries

The narrowing and blockage of coronary arteries is a complicated process and can involve both gradual and sudden events. The *gradual* process includes the hardening of the wall of the arteries or **atherosclerosis**. This is an accumulation of inflammatory cells, proteins, calcium, fibrosis, and oxidized cholesterol which leads to gradual loss of space for blood flow within the artery. The atherosclerotic mass is called **plaque** and the narrowing is called **stenosis.**

In contrast, the *sudden* process often involves the rapid appearance of a blood clot (**thrombosis**) in the artery that completely blocks the flow of blood. This leads to a heart attack, or damage to the heart muscle. When this happens, the health outcomes are much better for those who have immediate medical care, and for those who are more fit and have made better dietary choices.

Typically the two processes, atherosclerosis and thrombosis, are linked: the thrombosis will be precipitated by a rupture or breakdown or of the atherosclerotic plaque. As with most biological systems, many other biochemical factors are also involved.

Narrowed arteries can involve more than just the heart

Our emphasis is on heart disease, but it is important to know that the same processes of atherosclerosis and thrombosis can occur in almost every part of the body.

When atherosclerosis involves the blood supply to the brain, it can lead to a stroke. When it occurs in the legs, it is called peripheral arterial disease and can cause leg pain and amputations. When it involves arteries in the abdomen, it can cause damage to any of the abdominal organs, such as the kidneys or intestines.

Medical procedures

If you have angina or a heart attack and end up at a hospital, you will sometimes get a coronary artery **angiogram**. An angiogram is a procedure in which the cardiologist puts a special dye into the arteries supplying the heart to see if any narrowing (stenosis) or blockage is seen in the arteries.

Sometimes a blockage will be opened with a special balloon device (**balloon angioplasty**), and a **stent**, a tiny flexible tube, may be inserted in the most narrowed part of the artery to maintain blood flow by keeping it open. When an angioplasty is not a good option, patients will sometimes have a **coronary artery bypass graft (CABG)** performed. This is a surgery in which arteries or veins from elsewhere in the patient's body will be plumbed into the heart circulation to provide an alternate route for blood to supply the heart muscle, bypassing the diseased portions.

> **Although both angioplasty and bypass grafting can be lifesaving** and reduce symptoms in certain situations, they both carry some risk to the patient, and they do not 'fix' the diseased arteries elsewhere in the heart. Think of these procedures as potentially valuable partial or temporary treatments. Look to your diet, exercise, and selected medications to actually treat the disease that is causing this problem in the first place.

Reduce your risk of progressive heart disease (even if you have already had a heart attack, angioplasty, or bypass graft)

The mere existence of atherosclerotic plaque narrowing (stenosis) within an artery is usually not much of a problem if you take steps to help your body keep the plaque from undergoing changes that can damage your heart. If an artery is becoming clogged, your body has a variety of protective responses to prevent damage from occurring, including:

■ **Allowing the arterial walls to adapt** and new arteries to develop (do-it-yourself bypass!) to allow adequate blood flow despite the blockage

■ **Keeping the plaque stable**, or even reversing the stenosis, using functions such as your built-in anti-inflammatory and anti-oxidant mechanisms so that the plaque doesn't break open and cause a clot to form

■ **Having a healthy clotting system**, with the right control over blood clot formation and clot breakdown, to prevent a sudden blockage in an important artery at the wrong time

■ **Protecting the electrical system in your heart**, so that if you do have an episode of

reduced blood flow to your heart, the electrical system will be stable enough to keep the heart pumping evenly, instead of flying off into a deadly unstable rhythm (such as ventricular fibrillation)

The most powerful tools we have to encourage these protective responses within our own bodies are the kitchens in our homes and our activity choices. There are important medications we also recommend to reduce risk, but they are not as powerful as your body's own healing mechanisms.

> ## Food and exercise are effective even if you already have heart disease
>
> As you will read elsewhere in this book, food and exercise are your most powerful tools for avoiding heart disease events. In patients with known severe atherosclerosis and who have already had a heart attack:
>
> ■ The Mediterranean diet (see next page) reduces the future risk of heart disease by about 72 percent. (See page 4 for information about the Lyon Heart Study.)
>
> ■ A daily exercise program reduces future risk by about 60 percent.[1]
>
> ■ Appropriate use of fish oil supplements reduces the risk of death by up to 30 percent.[2]
>
> ■ A program to reduce LDL ('bad') cholesterol and triglycerides while increasing the HDL ('good') cholesterol in patients with low HDL, using high doses of niacin (vitamin B3) plus other cholesterol lowering medicines (such as simvastatin), may reduce risk of future heart disease by up to 85 percent.[3] (See page 51.)

[1] Taylor et al. Am J Med 2004;116:682-92
[2] Lee, J. et al. Mayo Clin Proc 2008;83:324-32
[3] Superko, R. and King, S. Circulation 2008;117:560-8

The whole-food Mediterranean diet[1]

Although the Mediterranean diet has been discussed previously, this approach is central to my approach to heart disease prevention, so here is a quick review of the details. This whole food version combines conventional Mediterranean diet concepts with minimally processed foods that have their nutrients largely intact.

- **Eat food mainly from plant sources:** vegetables, fruits, whole grains, beans and legumes, raw nuts, and seeds. Vegetables, fresh and cooked, as part of every meal, and fresh fruit as a typical dessert.

- **Eat complex carbohydrates in the form of whole grains and beans daily.** I suggest that our patients do not eat white rice, white bread, or white pasta: although the contemporary Mediterranean diet includes all three, I replace them with brown rice or quinoa, 100 percent whole grain bread, and whole grain pasta.

- **Use extra-virgin olive oil as main fat**, replacing most other oils and fats.

- **Eat plenty of fish**, but keep portions of other animal proteins smallish – like no more than one quarter of your total plate area. Think of meat as a condiment, not the main part of the meal. Save your appetite for the most important items – vegetables, beans, and whole grains.

- **Eat dairy food primarily in the form of cultured products** such as yogurt and kefir (a yogurt-like drink) and cheese. Most authorities recommend low-fat dairy foods but I am not aware of good data showing that low-fat dairy is preferable to regular dairy. (See page 20)

- **Drink small amount of wine**, generally with meals. (See page 19.)

Lifestyle choices appear to be *more* effective than medications

At the end of the previous page I mentioned a 60 – 85 percent heart disease risk reduction by combining lifestyle and HDL-raising therapies. In contrast, using statin cholesterol-lowering drugs reduces the risk of future heart disease by 20 – 44 percent. This is good, but as you can see by the evidence just cited, we can do better. I advocate appropriate prescription medicine and aspirin, but encourage you to remember that the most important treatments for the heart are your food and exercise choices.

Smoking?

We are assuming that you do not smoke. Smoking *doubles* your risk of heart disease, as well as cancer, stroke, lung disease, weak bones, impotence, wrinkles, and bad breath. When you stop smoking, the risks decrease rapidly. So if you smoke, decide to stop today. Talk with your doctor about a plan. Connect with friends who have successfully quit. Don't wait.

Heart disease risk factors not discussed in this chapter

Your physician may order tests for other possible markers of heart disease risk, such as hsCRP (a measure of inflammation), Lipoprotein (a), uric acid, homocysteine, ferritin, advanced lipid testing, and others. These can give further information on your risk of heart disease and tend to be improved using the lifestyle recommendations described here.

Targeted therapies aimed solely at these risk factors, such as vitamin therapy to lower homocysteine, have not been shown to reduce risk. We'll see what the future holds for these and other novel risk factors.

---

[1] http://www.oldwayspt.org/

SUMMARY OF YOUR TEN MOST IMPORTANT CHOICES TO PREVENT AND REVERSE HEART DISEASE

1. Adopt a *whole-food* Mediterranean-style diet including oil-rich fish and fish oil

2. Make a habit of *daily* exercise

3. Improve your HDL (good) cholesterol while lowering your triglycerides

4. Control your LDL (bad) cholesterol

5. Control high blood pressure

6. Maintain a healthy waistline and weight

7. Prevent or reverse insulin resistance: high blood sugar, metabolic syndrome, pre-diabetes, and type 2 diabetes

8. Get adequate sleep

9. Be aware of the pros and cons of nutritional supplements – take vitamin D when necessary but be very cautious about other supplements

10. Use appropriate medications

These ten choices are expanded on in the rest of this chapter. The more enthusiastically you address these choices, the more they will work together to help prevent or reverse your heart disease. There is a lot of overlap between these choices. For example, the diet choices you make in Choice One and the exercise choices you make in Choice Two will help improve your waistline (Choice Six) and blood sugar (Choice Seven)

ADOPT A *WHOLE-FOOD* MEDITERRANEAN-STYLE DIET

The Mediterranean-style diet is the only dietary approach that has been associated with fewer heart attacks, death, cancer, type 2 diabetes, strokes, and dementia. When compared head to head against low-fat diets, the Mediterranean-style diet is better than low-fat diets at controlling weight, cholesterol, inflammation, blood sugar, and insulin levels. **To date, there is no other dietary lifestyle that shows these benefits.** The data behind the Mediterranean diet is covered in detail starting on page 2. In the pages to follow we'll outline some individual steps that may help you adapt the Mediterranean diet to your lifestyle.

Mechanisms for the benefit of the Mediterranean diet

Some of the effects of the Mediterranean diet seen in studies so far include a beneficial effect on insulin resistance and blood sugar, small improvements in cholesterol profiles, less oxidized LDL, reduced homocysteine and inflammation, a more favorable essential fatty acid mix, and higher antioxidant levels. However, the benefit seen cannot be accounted for by any of these effects individually. It is probable that other factors (or combination of factors) are at work.

The Mediterranean diet is not primarily a cholesterol-reducing diet

Although cholesterol levels often improve a bit when patients use the Mediterranean diet model, the effect is modest and does not account for the large reduction in heart attacks and deaths that we see. However, as you will see in the following pages, we can enhance the Mediterranean diet by including foods that significantly improve blood cholesterol levels.

Other diets

Other diets, whether low-fat like the Ornish or high-fat like the Atkins, have their successes. However, only the Mediterranean-style diets have been shown to reduce heart disease, cancer, diabetes, and death. (For more information about head-to-head trials comparing the Mediterranean diet with other eating programs, see page 3.)

Using a *whole-food* Mediterranean diet against heart disease

Here are eight foods to keep in focus when applying the Mediterranean diet to your heart disease prevention program. The first seven are dealt with only briefly here because they are already discussed elsewhere in the book.

1. Whole fruits and vegetables
2. Whole grains
3. Legumes/beans
4. Raw nuts
5. Extra-virgin olive oil
6. Alcohol
7. Dark chocolate*
8. Fish and fish oil

* Although dark chocolate is not generally part of the Mediterranean diet guidelines, we stoutly defend its inclusion, and eleven out of ten patients agree.

Whole fruits and vegetables

Goal: Eat a minimum of five servings with a goal of nine servings per day

Whole fruits and vegetables are rich in fiber, minerals, vitamins, and antioxidants. As with most other high-fiber low-calorie-density foods, they assist in lowering cholesterol, improving blood sugars, and encouraging weight loss. They are valuable whether cooked or uncooked, but juices are best minimized. The benefit is probably more robust for vegetables, particularly in keeping blood sugars and insulin levels low. Including at least one whole fruit or vegetable with every meal, including breakfast, is a wise choice. (See page 13 for more about fruits and vegetables, as well as information on serving sizes.)

Whole grains

Goal: Eat *minimally* processed *whole grains* daily and avoid *refined grains*

Eating more whole grains is associated with significantly less risk of cardiac death, stroke, and type 2 diabetes. Much of the benefit appears to be associated with the fiber content, but whole grains also contribute a high level of antioxidants, assist in lowering cholesterol, and provide a broad range of fatty acids, vitamins and minerals. Compared to refined grain products, they also help with weight loss. The more intact the grain, the better it will work for you. For more information on whole grains, see page 14.

Legumes/beans

Goal: Eat at least one serving most days

The benefits of beans and legumes are comparable to that of whole grains, with a similar broad range of soluble and insoluble fiber, essential fatty acids, antioxidants, vitamins and minerals. Their protein content tends to make them an excellent – and inexpensive – complement to whole grains. (See page 14 for more information.)

Raw nuts

Goal: Eat up to two handfuls (e.g. about 30 almonds) of raw nuts daily

Raw nuts are an integral part of the Mediterranean diet, and in epidemiologic studies are associated with a substantially lower risk of heart disease and sudden death. Their benefit is probably due to their high antioxidant and healthy fat content. Walnuts and almonds have been shown to have significant cholesterol-lowering effects and help reverse the risk of type 2 diabetes[1] and heart disease. Pecans and hazelnuts (filberts) are also on my list of favored nuts for health benefits but it is likely that all raw nuts are good for you. There is probably a much greater health benefit if you choose raw nuts over roasted and salted varieties. (For more information on raw nuts, see page 16.) All nuts are calorie dense and should replace a less valuable food in your daily diet.

Extra-virgin olive oil

Goal: **Use extra-virgin olive oil daily as your primary dietary oil**

Extra-virgin olive oil, the oil from the first pressing of the olives, has over 200 nutritional components, including a monounsaturated fat (oleic acid) and a variety of antioxidants including phenols. These components have been associated with remarkable benefits:

- Significantly reducing blood pressure (see page 55)
- Favorably modifying the clotting mechanisms in the blood, thus avoiding dangerous thrombosis
- Reducing inflammation
- Reducing cholesterol oxidation
- To a very modest degree, increasing HDL while lowering LDL and triglycerides

Other grades of olive oil have monounsaturated fats, but only extra-virgin olive oil has the other valuable micronutrients. ("Light" olive oil has no less fat than regular olive oil, by the way – just less flavor. See box on page 66 for one use for light olive oil.) If you really must use another vegetable oil, walnut, sesame, soy, and canola oils all could be considered second-best alternatives, but none have the benefit associated with extra-virgin olive oil. (See pages 17 and 66.)

Alcohol

Goal: **One drink daily** (A drink is generally defined as 4 – 5 ounces of wine, 12 ounces of beer, or 1½ ounces of spirits.) **Important note: This advice is not intended for those who have medical, personal or philosophical reasons to avoid alcohol.**

Small amounts of alcohol seem to substantially lower the risk of dying (by up to 50 percent) from heart disease or heart failure. All forms of alcohol seem to have benefit, although the evidence appears to be stronger for red wine. We don't really know how alcohol works, but some of the mechanisms identified[2] include:

- A beneficial effect on HDL
- Reduced stickiness of platelets in blood
- Improved regulation of clotting mechanisms in the artery
- Relaxation of arterial muscle
- Anti-inflammatory effects

For some, any alcohol at all is too much. For anyone, drinking more than the recommended amount of alcohol is dangerous. (See page 19.)

Dark chocolate

Goal: **Up to an ounce of dark chocolate daily (70 percent or greater cocoa content)**

Definitive studies using dark chocolate to prevent heart disease have not been done, but eating dark chocolate appears to be associated with less heart disease. (See more about dark chocolate on page 17.) It is worth noting that a *small* amount of dark chocolate daily is associated with:
- Less heart disease and less total deaths[3]
- Reduced stickiness of platelets in blood
- Improvements in HDL cholesterol and blood pressure
- Reduced harmful chemical changes (oxidation) in LDL cholesterol

[1] Salas-Salvado, J. et al. Arch Intern Med 2008;168:2449-58

[2] Hvidtfeldt et al. Circulation 2010;121:1589-97
[3] Buijsse Arch Int Med 2006;166:411-7

Fish and fish oil[1]

Goal: See primary and secondary prevention specifics on page 46

Fish and fish oil have long been associated with reduced heart disease. The benefit is thought to be mostly due to the long chain omega-3 fatty acids (EPA and DHA) found in the fish oil. The evidence for the use of fish oil for heart disease is powerful enough to make fish oil the only nutritional supplement recommended by the American Heart Association.[2]

Current evidence does not allow us to conclude with certainty that vegetarian sources of shorter chain omega-3 fatty acids are as good as fish and fish oil, although this may change as further research is done. I think the weight of the data suggest that fish oil and oily fish have a special place in any heart disease prevention program.

How fish oil works

Fish oil has many potentially beneficial mechanisms, including a small effect on blood pressure and HDL (good cholesterol), regulation of blood clotting, stabilizing the plaque that clogs arteries, and stabilizing the electrical activity in the heart. Look for the total EPA and DHA content. In our recommendations, we specify the *goal* for EPA and DHA, not the total quantity of fish oil, which contains many other compounds apart from EPA and DHA.

Reasons to use fish or fish oil daily

■ People who eat fish frequently are at a lower risk of developing heart disease or dying of heart disease

■ In people who have heart disease, using a fish oil supplement containing about 1,000 mg EPA + DHA appears to be associated with a 20-30 percent lower risk of dying[3]

■ In people with heart failure, about 1,000 mg of EPA + DHA in fish oil is associated with a 9 percent lower risk of dying[4]

■ When used with cholesterol lowering medications like 'statins' (simvastatin, atorvastatin, and others), fish oil improves the overall effect of the statin for reducing heart attacks[5] and helps to further lower triglycerides and VLDL (one of the forms of 'bad' cholesterol)[6]

[3] Studer et al. Archives of Internal Medicine 2005;165:725-30
[4] GISSI-HF Investigators Lancet 2008;372:1223-30
[5] Yokoyama et al. Lancet 2007;369:1090-98
[6] Lee, J. et al. Mayo Clin Proc 2008;83:324-32

[1] Lee, J. et al. Mayo Clin Proc 2008;83:324-32
[2] Kris-Etherton et al. Circulation 2002;106:2747-57

Using fish and fish oil for primary prevention

Goal: In people *without* known heart disease, about 500 mg daily of omega-3 fatty acids (EPA and DHA) in fish or fish oil are recommended

This dose can be achieved by eating oily fish 3 or 4 days of the week. Examples of oily fish include sardines, salmon, herring, tuna, trout, halibut and shellfish. The USDA website (www.ars.usda.gov/nutrientdata) gives the actual quantities of the oil found in these fish.

If you don't eat fish, you can use a fish oil supplement containing about 500 mg of EPA + DHA. Read labels carefully – some products have much higher concentrations.

Some of us prefer to use liquid fish oil, which can be found in the nutrition section of many stores. Read the label to find out how much oil will provide about 500 mg of EPA + DHA. You probably wouldn't need to take the liquid fish oil supplement daily, but could instead take a larger dose three or four days per week.

---

[1] Lee, J. et al. Mayo Clin Proc 2008;83:324-32

Using fish and fish oil for secondary prevention

Goal: In people who *have* a diagnosis of heart disease, about 1,000 mg of omega-3 fatty acids (EPA + DHA) in fish or fish oil are recommended

This dose is associated with a 20 percent decrease in death rate in the GISSI trial.[2] This amount of EPA + DHA is difficult to obtain from oily fish alone; a more reliable way is to use a fish oil supplement. To find out how much oil it takes to equal 1,000 mg of EPA + DHA, read the label. Either capsules or liquid fish oil will work equally well. For fish oil supplements you will need to use enough to equal a dose of 1,000 mg of EPA + DHA or one Lovaza capsule. (Lovaza is prescription fish oil.)

Using fish and fish oil for high triglycerides

Goal: About 3,000 - 4,000 mg of omega-3 fatty acids (EPA + DHA) in fish or fish oil are recommended for those who have triglycerides over 150 mg/dl despite good diet and exercise choices

Fish oil is an outstanding agent to effectively lower triglycerides by up to 45 percent. More detailed information on the use of fish oil is found in the HDL/triglyceride portion.

Dealing with the taste and the after effects of fish oil (burping)

To get around taste objections, we use fish oil with lemon, orange or other flavors, and most people find them very acceptable. To minimize the burping, store the oil in the refrigerator and take it immediately before your largest meal. The same holds for fish oil capsules, and some people report a greater burp-free effect if they are stored in the freezer.

---

[2] GISSI-Prevenzione Investigators Lancet 1999 354:447-55

MAKE A HABIT OF DAILY EXERCISE

Goal: 30-60 minutes brisk walking daily, or at least 20 minutes of vigorous bicycle riding or equivalent – ask your physician

Note: If the above goal is too ambitious for your situation, any exercise is better than none, so 5 minutes is a fine start

Exercise for preventing heart disease is such a powerful tool that many people can't quite believe it. (See more on exercise starting on page 7.) The specific benefits of exercise which work together to reduce your risk of heart disease include raising HDL, lowering LDL, lowering triglycerides, and lowering blood pressure. For example, just brisk walking for 30 to 45 minutes a day for five or six days a week may lower your blood pressure up to ten points – similar to a prescription drug!

■ Regular exercise is associated with up to four years of increased disease-free lifespan.[1]

■ People who exercise 30 minutes or more on most days of the week have about 50 percent lower risk of dying than similarly healthy people who don't exercise.[2] This benefit persists even when the people are between 70 and 80 years old![3]

■ People with heart disease who do regular exercise have a 20 percent lower death rate than similar patients who don't exercise regularly.[4]

■ People with a single blocked artery to the heart who exercise daily and don't have the artery opened up are 60 percent less likely to have another heart attack or other 'event' than those who don't exercise and have the artery opened with angioplasty and a stent.[5]

---

[1] Franco et al. Arch Intern Med 2005;165:2355-60

[2] Leitzmann et al. Arch Intern Med 2007;167:2453-60

[3] Chakravarty, E. et al. Arch Intern Med 2008;168:1638-46

[4] Taylor et al. Am J Med 2004;116:682-92

[5] Hambrecht et al. Circulation 2004;109:1371-78

How exercise helps your heart

The benefits of exercise which work together to reduce your risk of heart disease include:

■ Lowering blood pressure

■ Improving triglycerides and cholesterol levels

■ Lowering inflammatory load

■ Reducing cholesterol oxidation

■ Improving flexibility in the arterial walls

■ Favorably modifying blood clotting function

■ Slowing aging within the genetic material of your cells

■ Improving neurohormonal function and immunity

Exercise intensity

Unless your physician instructs otherwise, I suggest that you exercise as vigorously as you can while still being able to talk. If you can still talk easily, you probably aren't overdoing exercise. A useful rule of thumb is that you should get a bit short of breath and sweaty on a daily basis. Check with your physician for advice concerning your particular situation. Many people get additional benefit with using a physical trainer or exercise physiologist.

Exercise daily

Something as simple as a brisk 30 minute walk is a great idea – besides, fresh air and natural light are helpful, too. But any exercise is better than none, so 5 minutes is a fine start. If your job requires a lot of sitting, make a point of moving around frequently. One reasonable approach is to exercise on every day that you do not want to have a heart attack or stroke. Some authorities suggest exercising on every day ending in ' y '.

IMPROVE YOUR HDL AND LOWER YOUR TRIGLYCERIDES

Goal: Raise HDL to more than 45 mg/dl for men and 55 mg/dl for women, and lower triglycerides to less than 150 mg/dl (less than 100 mg/dl may be optimal)

Both low HDL and high triglycerides are important risk factors for heart disease, and the management of both disorders is similar. This section will combine the management of these two separate issues.

HDL cholesterol explained briefly

High density lipoprotein (HDL) is known as the 'good' cholesterol, and is one of the important predictors of future heart attacks – *the higher your HDL, the lower your risk.* For example, a person with an HDL of less than 35 mg/dl has a risk of future heart attack up to 3 or 4 times greater than a person with a high HDL, even if their LDL cholesterol is the same.

HDL is called 'good' for many reasons: it acts to transport cholesterol back to the liver (away from the arteries) and favorably alters the blood clotting process. HDL also helps protect LDL cholesterol from oxidation, which discourages the development of atherosclerosis.

Another way to make use of HDL in assessing risk is to use the ratio of total cholesterol (TC) divided by HDL: this is called the TC/HDL ratio. For TC/HDL, lower is better: aim for less than 4.

My recommendations for the HDL goals at the beginning of this section are based on the levels of HDL cholesterol associated with 'average' heart disease risk in the Framingham Offspring study,[2] and are somewhat higher than recommendations made by national organizations.

---

[1] Hambrecht et al. Circulation 2004;109:1371-78

[2] Castelli, W. Am Heart J 1983;106:1191-200

Key HDL points to know

■ **Treating low HDL usually requires many steps.** Most steps may raise HDL about 5 - 15 percent. When done together, these steps can increase total HDL by as much as 50 - 100 percent – or even higher.

■ **Raising HDL by 7.5 percent** while controlling LDL is associated with regression of coronary artery atherosclerosis in several of the best heart disease prevention trials. This suggests that disease reversal is occurring.[1]

■ **The benefit of raising HDL probably extends far beyond a reduction in heart disease risk.** Most of the changes that improve HDL are associated with lower risk of other diseases as well; stroke, high blood pressure, cancers, obesity, and diabetes.

■ **Even *tiny* improvements in HDL are associated with reduced heart disease.** It is estimated that every 1 mg/dl improvement in HDL lowers heart disease risk by up to 4 percent. Thus, even an apparently modest 5 mg/dl increase in HDL may translate into up to 20 percent less heart disease risk.

■ **In addition to total HDL testing,** part of a routine cholesterol panel, HDL subtype testing is available. We do not usually do this because the value is still being debated.

Lowering triglycerides

Triglycerides are another form of blood fat that relate to heart disease and stroke risk. In addition, high triglycerides often indicate an increased risk of developing diabetes or insulin resistance, which in turn also raises your risk of heart disease, stroke, dementia and some cancers. The risk associated with high triglycerides is even higher for women and people with diabetes. High triglycerides are also linked to a peculiar form of LDL cholesterol (small dense LDL) that particularly increases your risk of blocked arteries.

[1] Nicholls, S. et al. JAMA 2007;297:499-508

Eight important steps to raising HDL and lowering triglycerides

1. Make a habit of **daily exercise**.
2. **Eat healthy fats.** Low-fat diets usually increase triglycerides and lower HDL.
3. **Use fish oil.**
4. **Avoid trans fats** which can *lower* HDL (avoid hydrogenated oils).
5. Eat **more minimally processed** whole grains, beans, vegetables, and fruit. Eat **less refined** grains and sugar. (See list on page 10.)
6. Maintain a **healthy waistline and weight**
7. Drink a **small amount of alcohol.** *Limit to one drink per day.*
8. Use certain medications, particularly niacin. **(See our note regarding the 2011 niacin study on page 51.)**

---

1. **Daily exercise** raises HDL up to 10 - 20 percent and lowers your risk of future heart 'events' by 30 – 60 percent. About 30 - 60 minutes on most days is advisable, and any kind of exercise will do. For raising HDL, however, the longer the duration or greater the intensity of exercise, the better. As a good alternative to formal exercise, use a pedometer and make sure you accumulate 10,000 steps daily. The same benefit may apply to triglyceride levels.

2. **Eating more 'healthy fats'** is a good step towards raising HDL and lowering triglycerides. **A person with low HDL should be on a *good* fat diet, not a *low-fat* diet!** Some of the best fats are extra-virgin olive oil, avocado, raw nuts, and oily fish such as salmon, sardines, and tuna. Moderate amounts of eggs, cheese, butter, and meats also help raise HDL. Omega-3 fats help raise HDL a little bit, and are found in nuts, canola and soy oils, oily fish, shellfish, flaxseeds, and some green leafy vegetables.

3. **Using fish oil** may have a small effect in raising HDL, and a large effect in reducing triglycerides. The subject of fish oil is discussed more on page 45 and 52.

4. **Trans fats can *lower* HDL and raise triglycerides.** Trans fats are found in variable amounts in hydrogenated and partially hydrogenated oils, most margarines, many packaged foods, and in commercially prepared foods in general, often even those that say 'NO TRANS FATS'. Legally a food can be said to have 'no trans fats' even when there is what I consider a significant amount of trans fats per serving. So, I suggest you read labels carefully and avoid hydrogenated oils completely. They are generally nutritionally worthless anyway.

5. **Eating more minimally processed whole grains and beans and less refined grains and sugars** will help raise HDL and lower triglycerides. (Examples of refined grains and sugars are cold breakfast cereals, white rice, sweets and sweet drinks, and all white flour products.)

6. **Maintain a healthy waistline and weight.** Losing weight around the middle helps raise HDL 5 – 10 percent, and lowers triglycerides. Measure your waistline risk by calculating your waist-hip ratio. (See page 56 for why *Big waists can lead to bad hearts* and to find out your ideal ratio. Tips on weight loss are on page 30.)

7. **A *small* amount of alcohol** may help raise HDL up to 5 – 10 percent. If you do not have medical or philosophical reasons to avoid alcohol, consider drinking up to 1 drink per day. (See page 44.) Larger amounts of alcohol *raise* triglycerides.

8. **Medications for raising HDL and lowering triglycerides.** While lifestyle changes are very effective for lowering triglycerides in most people, medications can help a great deal. I advocate the use of niacin and fish oil because there is

evidence that these improve health outcomes. Unfortunately, some of the medications used to treat HDL and triglycerides have been associated with higher total death rates. When you discuss medications with your physician, I suggest that you request *only* medications that have been associated with less heart attacks and deaths. You would be surprised to discover how many prescription drugs used to treat cholesterol or triglycerides have *not* been shown to improve overall health.

Niacin, fish oil, statins, and fibrates

The two main non-food items I use for treating low HDL cholesterol and high triglycerides are niacin and high-dose fish oil. When I use niacin and fish oil it is often in combination with a class of prescription drugs called statins, such as simvastatin, pravastatin, rosuvastatin, and atorvastatin. Another class of medications used to improve HDL and triglyceride levels are fibrates, including gemfibrozil and fenofibrate. I prescribe these very rarely, as their health outcomes data are not as favorable.

Niacin to raise HDL and lower triglycerides

Niacin is a B vitamin (B_3) and the most effective agent for raising HDL. Numerous studies have shown niacin therapy to significantly lower the risk of heart attack or death, particularly when used with a statin drug. When used in therapeutic doses niacin can raise your HDL by 30 percent or more, lowers LDL by up to 20 percent, and lowers triglycerides by up to 40 percent. When combined with other cholesterol lowering medications, usually a statin drug such as simvastatin, niacin is associated with up to an **85 percent reduction in heart event risk.**[1][2] This combination provides a greater degree of benefit than is seen with any statin drug alone.

---

[1] Superko, R. and King, S. Circulation 2008;117:560-8
[2] Bruckert, E. et al. Atherosclerosis 2010;210:353-61

How to use niacin

Common side effects from niacin are flushing, itching, and other skin symptoms which gradually go away. These reactions can be minimized by following these directions:

For immediate release crystalline (non-prescription) niacin: start with 250 mg with your evening meal. After one week, add another 250 mg at lunch. After another week, add another 250 mg at breakfast. Now you are taking 250 mg three times daily. Some people can now increase the dose to 500 mg three times daily for a month, and then increase the dose until they are taking 1,000 mg three times daily. Some get excellent results with just two doses daily. Immediate release niacin is inexpensive, and works very well for those who can tolerate it.

For extended release or slow release niacin (like Niaspan, Endur-Acin, and Slo-Niacin): start with 500 mg at bedtime and increase by 500 mg every 2 - 4 weeks, for a maximum of 2,000 mg daily:

■ **Niaspan** is *prescription* niacin and is used once a day at bedtime. Niaspan is also available combined with simvastatin, called 'Simcor', which combines the benefits of both a statin medication and niacin.

■ **Endur-Acin** *and* **Slo-Niacin** (both non-prescription) are used one or two times daily with physician supervision. If using twice

daily, close blood monitoring is required. Use only those which have been examined for efficacy and safety in peer-reviewed studies, such as Slo-Niacin and Endur-Acin.[3]

Niacinamide and No-Flush Niacin (inositol hexanicotinate) are forms of niacin that do not effectively lower cholesterol.[4]

Whichever form of niacin you use, your doctor needs to be involved. *Blood tests should be done after you reach a total daily dose of 1,000 mg, and then after every 500 mg increase.*

Give niacin time!

If you haven't used niacin before, it may seem like a nuisance. However, for most people with low HDL cholesterol, a treatment program including niacin appears to be the most beneficial in terms of reducing their risk of death or future heart attack, especially if niacin is combined with a statin medication. After a few weeks many people experience little or no side effects from niacin. Everyone is different. Some tolerate only small doses of niacin, like 500 – 1,000 mg daily, but even at lower doses there are very useful benefits.

---

[1] AIM-HIGH, NEJM 2011;365:2255-67

[2] Bruckert, E. et al. Atherosclerosis 2010;210:353-61

[3] Ito, M. et al Pharmacotherapy 2006;26:939-1010

[4] Meyers, C. et al. Ann Intern Med 2003;139:996-1002

Using fish oil to lower triglycerides

Fish oil has only a small effect on HDL or LDL cholesterol levels, but it does lower triglycerides substantially. Fish oil contains many types of fat, but what we are most interested in are the two fatty acids called EPA and DHA. When choosing fish oil, read the label to find out how much EPA + DHA it contains. (Some contain 30 percent while others contain 90 percent.) **A total of about 3,000 – 4,000 mg daily of EPA + DHA will lower triglycerides by 30 – 50 percent.** In order to get that dose you have a number of options:

■ **Prescription fish oil:** 4 Lovaza capsules daily. It is expensive but convenient, as it has a higher percentage of DHA + EPA than most others so you can take less capsules. It is also the brand used in the most important fish oil study (GISSI).

■ **Over-the-counter fish oil capsules:** these are usually lower concentration, and it takes up to 12 daily to get the required dose of EPA + DHA. These are best stored in the freezer, and taken before meals. It is fine to take them all just before your largest meal, to avoid fishy reminders.

■ **Liquid fish oil:** this is the best option for many people. Generally 1 tablespoon daily of fish oil will provide the required dose of EPA + DHA, but read the label; some are more concentrated than others and there are a variety of flavors. Store in the refrigerator – using cold fish oil before your largest meal reduces the potential for unpleasant burping. Cod liver oil is a good choice, too, and gives you a useful dose of vitamin D at the same time. When using cod liver oil, check the label for the vitamin A content, and make sure you are not getting more than about 5,000 IU daily of vitamin A.

CONTROL YOUR LDL (BAD) CHOLESTEROL

Goal: **LDL of less than 160 mg/dl in low risk patients, and less than 100 mg/dl or even 70 mg/dl in high-risk patients**
(Ask your doctor what your target should be.)

Low-density lipoprotein (LDL) is a form of cholesterol strongly related to increased risk of heart disease, particularly in those who have other risk factors for heart disease. Although controlling LDL is important, don't rely solely on a low LDL to prevent a heart attack: most people who have heart attacks in the US are already at their recommended LDL goal.[1]

There are many drugs I use to lower LDL cholesterol. However, with consistent use of food choices you may not need medications at all, or you may get by with a smaller dose of medication, reducing expense and side-effects.

Mediterranean diet and LDL

In studies using the Mediterranean diet without the goal of lowering LDL, the LDL may stay the same or fall up to 10 percent. More importantly, the Mediterranean diet is associated with a reduction in LDL oxidation, a benefit which may be more important than simply lowering the total amount of LDL.

Some foods to lower LDL

When assessing the LDL-lowering effects of food, compare the expected effect with the fact that doubling any given dose of a statin drug will typically lower your LDL by only another 6 – 9 percent. Many patients use the foods mentioned on the following page in order to keep their statin dose low. LDL-lowering foods can easily be incorporated into your diet, and each could typically lower LDL by 5 – 10 percent. Using several measures

---

[1] Sachdeva, A. et al. Am Heart J 2009;157:111-17

together can lower your LDL cholesterol up to 30 percent, an effect similar to that of a medium dose of a statin drug.

These LDL-lowering foods can also lower your triglycerides, raise HDL, improve your blood sugar control, and are associated with lower levels of inflammation. The more of these steps you take, the more of an improvement you will see in your LDL.

These foods do not work for everyone, unfortunately, but they can have some amazing results. A couple of our patients have seen their LDL cholesterol drop by 50 percent with the vigorous use of these foods. The higher your LDL, the better these foods work. Give any food program about 6 weeks to work.

■ **Psyllium (e.g. Metamucil) to lower LDL**
A daily dose of 10 grams of psyllium (about 2 heaping teaspoons) can sometimes reduce LDL by about 7 percent.[1] In some studies, psyllium has failed to lower LDL but has had a beneficial effect in raising HDL and lowering triglycerides.[2] A method that works well is to stir it into a small amount of water or juice, drink it quickly before it gels, and then follow with 12 ounces of water. Psyllium is a great anti-constipation agent, too.

■ **Oat bran to lower LDL**
Using 4 tablespoons (¼ cup) of oat bran each day may give about 10 – 26 percent reduction in LDL.[3] Oat bran can be added to cereal, stirred into yogurt or smoothies, or added to muffins. (See *Extreme Muffins* on page 236.)

■ **Raw nuts to lower LDL**
About two handfuls of raw nuts (about 30 almonds or two ounces) daily can reduce LDL by 7 – 10 percent. Raw walnuts, hazelnuts, Brazil nuts, almonds, and pecans are good choices. Adding raw nuts to your diet also has the important benefit of reducing oxidized LDL as well as another risk factor called

Lp(a).[4] [5] (See *Heart disease risk factors not discussed in this chapter* on page 41.)

■ **Eggplant and okra to lower LDL**
About 6 ounces of eggplant or about 3 – 4 ounces of okra every other day can also lower LDL. These foods have not been studied by themselves, but when used in combination with other factors, have been found to lower LDL by 28 percent. Inflammation was reduced as well.[6]

■ **Soy and other beans to lower LDL**
Soy foods modestly reduce cholesterol. These are probably best included in the diet in the form of whole traditional soy foods such as soybeans (edamame), tofu, miso, and tempeh. (See recipes for soybeans and tofu on pages 158-60.) I am less enthusiastic about the highly refined soy products like soy milk. For those who use soy milk because of dairy intolerance, read the ingredient label carefully. Some other beans also lower LDL to a similar degree, particularly pinto beans. A half-cup of cooked pinto beans or 25 grams of soy protein will lower LDL 5 percent or more.[7]

■ **Stanols to lower LDL**
There are a variety of stanol-containing margarines that can lower LDL cholesterol. I don't tend to recommend them because of concerns over the problems with hydrogenated oils in the margarine, and the debate over whether stanols at these doses have potential for harm.[8] Time will tell.

Medications to lower LDL

Most people who need significant LDL lowering are also likely to need prescription medication, usually a statin. However, some people are able to control their cholesterol with a whole food diet enhanced on a daily basis with the foods described above.

[1] Anderson et al. Am J Clin Nutr 2000;71:472-9
[2] Sola, R. et al. Am J Clin Nutr 2007;85:1157-63
[3] Romero et al. JACN 1998;17:601-8

[4] Jenkins et al. Circulation 2002;106:1327-32
[5] Sabate, J. Arch Intern Med 2010;170:821-7
[6] Jenkins et al. JAMA 2003;290:502-10
[7] Winham et al. JACN 2007;26:243-9
[8] Fransen, J. et al. Nutrition 2007;137:1301-6

CONTROL HIGH BLOOD PRESSURE

<u>**Goal blood pressure:**</u> **less than 135/85**
Your physician may recommend an even lower target

Although many drugs are available to treat high blood pressure, it is wise to also emphasize the steps you can take apart from medication to get your blood pressure under control. Not only will you probably need less medicine, you will also be healthier.

Factors that can raise blood pressure

■ Medications
Discuss all of the medications you take with your doctor to see if any of them could be making your problem worse. A medicine that can raise blood pressure in one person may have no effect on another. Dozens of different medications can be a problem, so look over **all** of them carefully. Read the package insert. If you don't have one, ask your pharmacist to provide one. Common examples of medications which may cause high blood pressure when used frequently include:
- Most decongestant medications
- Non-steroidal anti-inflammatory medications (NSAIDS) such as ibuprofen, naproxen, and many others
- Acetaminophen may also cause high blood pressure

(Aspirin appears *not* to raise blood pressure at normal doses.)

■ Alcohol
Keep alcohol to *no more than* 1 drink daily for women and 2 drinks daily for men. A drink is generally defined as 5 ounces of wine, 12 ounces of beer, or 1½ ounces of spirits. (See page 19.)

■ Excess weight
If you are overweight, aim to lose a few pounds. Ten pounds of weight loss can lower your risk of developing high blood pressure by 65 percent. If you are hypertensive, this may drop your blood pressure to the same degree as a prescription drug. (For more on weight loss, see page 30.)

Salt (Sodium)
This tends to be more of a problem for some people than others. Those who are salt sensitive should probably keep their sodium intake at less than 2,500 mg daily, equivalent to about 6 grams or 1½ teaspoons of salt.

Most of the salt (probably around 75 percent) eaten in our society comes in commercially prepared foods, so simply avoiding pre-packaged and restaurant food while emphasizing minimally-processed whole foods will reduce your salt intake. Sodium intake can be more liberal when the diet is high in potassium-rich whole foods. A diet naturally high in potassium will blunt the harmful effects of excess sodium.[1]

If buying packaged foods, check the nutrition panel and choose products which have more potassium than sodium, and 5 percent or less of the daily allowance of sodium per serving. And use restraint when adding salt – including sea salt – at the table.

■ Licorice
Licorice can raise blood pressure in a small number of people. Only **real** licorice (usually from Finland, Holland, or Australia) has this effect. However, if you enjoy licorice and do not have high blood pressure, it is fine to eat it in small amounts. Just remember it's candy.

---

[1] Cook, N. et al. Arch Int Med 2009;169:32-40

Factors that can lower blood pressure

■ Exercise

As mentioned on page 47, brisk walking for 30 - 45 minutes daily five to seven days a week may lower blood pressure up to ten points.

■ Extra-virgin olive oil

Good fats such as extra-virgin olive oil (3 - 4 tablespoons daily) have a beneficial effect on high blood pressure. In one study, this dose was enough to completely eliminate the need for medications in one third of patients with high blood pressure who were being treated with blood pressure medications.[1]

■ Dark chocolate

Dark chocolate tends to improve high blood pressure, as well as being associated with less heart disease, less diabetes, and happier people. Look for dark chocolate with at least 70 percent cocoa content. Up to about an ounce a day might be beneficial.

■ Hibiscus tea[2]

Try drinking 3 cups of hibiscus tea daily.

■ Supplements

Nutritional supplements are *usually* not helpful for lowering blood pressure. Some that have been successful in limited studies, and may be worth trying for a month or two, are:

- **Magnesium oxide** 400 mg once or twice a day (magnesium may cause loose stools)

- **Vitamin D** 1,000 IU daily or more, or 1 tablespoon cod liver oil

■ The Resperate device

This is a little FDA-approved gadget which apparently works by teaching you to alter the timing of your breathing slightly. It is used for 15 minutes three to four times per week, and seems to lower blood pressure by up to 14 mm Hg in about 8 weeks, which compares very favorably to most drugs. (For more information see www.resperate.com.)

Lifestyle changes that can help lower your blood pressure: the Mediterranean diet (surprise!) and the DASH diet

The best studied diet for lowering blood pressure is the DASH diet. The name DASH (Diet and Systolic Hypertension) arises from some elegant studies that used this dietary approach to lower blood pressure.[3]

The DASH diet can lower your blood pressure by 10 points or more. This diet is high in fiber, minerals, and antioxidants, and is associated with far less heart disease and cancer. As you might guess, it is very similar to the whole-food Mediterranean diet but is more restrictive in fat. To combine the benefits of a DASH diet with those of the Mediterranean diet, emphasize:

- Grains and cereals, particularly whole grain versions such as oatmeal, brown rice, and whole grain pasta. Adding 2 tablespoons of oat bran to your whole grain cereals during cooking will help blood pressure, blood sugar, and cholesterol levels even more

- Five or more servings of whole fruits and vegetables daily, cooked or raw

- Two to three servings of low-fat dairy foods daily

- Raw nuts, seeds, dried beans and peas

- Fish at least twice each week, and small amounts of poultry and meat

- Extra-virgin olive oil as the preferred kitchen oil

[1] Ferrara et al. Arch Intern Med 2000;160:837-42

[2] McKay, D.L. et al. Journal of Nutrition 2010;140(2):298-303

[3] Ard, J.D. and Svetkey, L.P. J Clin Hypertens 2000;2:387-91

MAINTAIN A HEALTHY WAISTLINE AND WEIGHT

Goal:
A waist measurement of less than 35 inches for women and less than 40 inches for men

Alternative goal:
A waist-hip ratio of less than 0.88 for women and less than 0.95 for men

Weight and waistline are often not as appreciated as the very significant risk factors that they are. Carrying extra weight around your middle (central, visceral or abdominal obesity) is much more harmful than extra weight elsewhere in the body, leading to:

- Insulin resistance, a precursor to type 2 diabetes
- Changes in cholesterol and other blood fats that increase risk of heart disease, even when the overall amount of cholesterol is on the low side
- Higher levels of inflammation
- Strikingly increased risk of dying from heart disease, diabetes, and some cancers

Big waists can lead to bad hearts and soft brains

It appears that carrying too much weight around your middle triples your risk of dying of heart disease (this is an increase in risk similar to that of a smoker) and doubles your risk of dementia.[1] An oversized waist strikingly elevates your risks even if you are 'normal' weight as defined by a Body Mass Index (BMI) of 18.5 to 25 kg/m.[2]

The BMI is a calculation based on height and weight and is often used to determine 'correct' weight. However, the BMI does not tell you how much weight you are carrying

[1] Whitmer et al. Neurology 2008;71:1057-64
[2] Zhang, C. et al. Circulation 2008;117:1658-67

around your middle. Therefore, we often look at overweight-associated risk in terms of waist measurement, aiming for the goal levels shown at the beginning of this page.

However, this measurement can be misleading in many people, particularly those of slight stature: another useful measurement of risk that can be used is the waist-hip ratio. This measurement is probably much more important than your cholesterol level.

Calculating waist-hip ratio

There are various protocols for measuring the waist-hip ratio. One accepted approach is:

1. Measure your waist at the (belly button)
2. Measure the broadest point around your buttock area (your hip measurement)
3. Now, use a calculator to divide the first measurement (waist) by the second (hip).

A woman's waist-hip ratio should ideally be less than 0.88, and a man's less than 0.95.

Waist reduction
One encouraging finding is that the harmful effects of excessive weight are mostly reversed when the weight goes down. When you decide to take steps to reduce your waistline, my recommendation is that you do not go on a diet. Instead, adopt a set of habits in your food choices and daily exercise that you can maintain for the rest of your life. Choose to adopt these with sufficient zeal that you are losing a little weight each week. For many people, losing one pound per week is an achievable goal.

And remember that it is better to be fit than slim. If you *are* overweight, it is all the more important to exercise daily. For weight loss ideas, see our eleven tips on page 30. In addition to these ideas, many people find a dietician or other weight loss specialists can be very helpful.

PREVENT OR REVERSE INSULIN RESISTANCE

- **HIGH BLOOD SUGAR**
- **METABOLIC SYNDROME**
- **TYPE 2 DIABETES**

Goal:

- **For patients who do not have a diagnosis of type 2 diabetes but have one of the insulin resistance syndromes: high blood sugar or metabolic syndrome; aim for a fasting blood sugar of less than 90 - 100 mg/dl, and an HbA1c (see below) of less than 5.5 - 6 percent**

- **For patients with diagnosed type 2 diabetes; follow your physician's recommendation**

Insulin resistance disorders (high blood sugar, metabolic syndrome, and most cases of type 2 diabetes) are associated with 2 – 4 times increased risk of heart disease, as well as increased stroke, cancers, and dementia. To understand the increased heart disease risks associated with even mildly elevated blood sugar, it helps to understand the range of disorders characterized by high blood sugar due to insulin resistance.

Insulin resistance

Insulin resistance means that your cells have become less responsive to the effects of insulin, and is the result of a complex interplay between food, activity, body weight, genetics, and medication.

If it is allowed to progress, insulin resistance will eventually lead to high blood sugar and type 2 diabetes. These high blood sugar syndromes are not only associated with increased risk of heart disease, but also some cancers, liver cirrhosis, stroke, and dementia. It is often not appreciated that *any* form of insulin resistance is associated with heart disease risk similar to that from type 2

diabetes. Don't wait to be told that you have diabetes before choosing to reverse your insulin resistance and therefore your risk of type 2 diabetes.

Metabolic syndrome: Get serious about your lifestyle choices if …

- Your fasting blood sugar is typically greater than 100 mg/dl (sometimes called impaired fasting glucose or pre-diabetes), or

- You develop metabolic syndrome. One of the definitions of metabolic syndrome is the presence of three or more of the following five conditions:

  - blood pressure greater than 135/85 or being treated for high blood pressure
  - triglycerides greater than 150mg/dl
  - HDL cholesterol lower than 40 mg/dl
  - fasting blood sugar greater than 100 mg/dl or being treated for high blood sugar
  - waistline greater than 35 inches for women or 40 inches for men; or less for small framed people

Of course, if you have type 2 diabetes, which in most cases is the result of insulin resistance, the advice in this section is all the more relevant.

HbA1c (glycosylated hemoglobin)

Another way to measure blood sugar levels is something called the HbA1c, or glycosylated hemoglobin. This is a measurement that reflects your average blood sugar over time.

- **For people not taking medicines to lower blood sugar** the level should be less than 6 percent, and maybe even less than 5.5 percent, to minimize your heart disease risk.

- **For people using medications to lower blood sugar**, the current recommended goal for HbA1c is 7 percent.

Medications to control blood sugar levels in patients with type 2 diabetes may not protect the heart

Many people with type 2 diabetes feel that the prescription medicines they take to lower blood sugar will also lower their risk of heart disease. However, it is far from clear that using medications to treat high blood sugar (see page 7) in type 2 diabetes has much benefit for reducing your risk of heart disease, stroke, or death. So while it may be wise to use the available prescription therapies to control blood sugar, they cannot be depended upon to protect your heart.[1] Therefore the lifestyle choices known to reduce heart disease risk and control high blood sugars are all the more important, along with blood pressure and cholesterol medications.

Lifestyle modifications for above-normal blood sugar due to insulin resistance, including type 2 diabetes

Patients with one of the insulin resistance syndromes are often treated with a variety of medications to control associated cardiac risk factors, such as blood pressure and high cholesterol. It is also particularly important to follow the basic lifestyle approaches that are associated with both less insulin resistance and a dramatically reduced risk of heart disease and stroke. By adopting the eight lifestyle modifications in the following list, many patients can actually reverse their diabetes or pre-diabetes and achieve normal blood sugars *without* medications.

1. **Exercise daily** (moderate to vigorous, 30 to 60 minutes, 7 days per week) which improves insulin resistance.

2. **Adopt a whole food Mediterranean-style diet**, shown to be more effective at reducing insulin resistance than other diet patterns.[2]

3. **Eat smaller portions** and eat slowly, savoring your food.

4. **Avoid refined carbohydrates** like sweets, sweet drinks, cold breakfast cereals, and white flour products. In contrast, minimally processed whole grains, legumes and beans are associated with less insulin resistance.

5. **Eat vegetables and whole fruits** with every meal, while avoiding the very starchy vegetables like potatoes and corn.

6. **Have some 'good fat' with every meal** (see page 15). For example, if you have a cooked wholegrain cereal, eat some raw nuts too. This will tend to lower the amount that your blood sugar rises after the meal and improve the sense of satisfaction (satiety).

7. **Work toward achieving ideal body weight** which may completely reverse insulin resistance. For weight loss goals based on your waistline, see page 56. For one approach to weight loss, see page 30.

8. **Get adequate sleep** (7-9 hours night).

The very low carbohydrate approaches to insulin resistance

The very low carbohydrate approach to treating insulin resistance, as characterized by books such as *Dr. Bernstein's Diabetes Solution* by Richard K. Bernstein, M.D., can often have spectacular effects on reducing blood sugar levels. It is unclear whether this approach improves health outcomes, but it probably does. Many patients have been helped by *The South Beach Diet* by Arthur Agatston, M.D., which offers another approach to losing weight and improving insulin resistance that emphasizes a lower carbohydrate approach.

---

[1] Skyler, J.S. et al. Circulation 2009;119:351-57
[2] Shai, I. et al. NEJM 2008;359:229-41

GET ADEQUATE SLEEP

Goal: 7 – 9 hours per night

It is useful to think of sleep as a valuable nutrient needed in adequate quantities for good health. Current evidence shows that inadequate sleep is associated with more obesity, more insulin resistance and diabetes, greater susceptibility to infection, higher blood pressure, and inflammation. It is not surprising that patients who get less than about 7 hours of sleep each night develop much more calcification in their coronary arteries, which is a measure of arterial damage.[1]

Steps to a better sleep

If you follow all the following suggestions and sleep still eludes you, there are other behavioral techniques and medications that may be helpful. Your doctor can point you in the right direction.

■ Have a sleep schedule. Go to bed about 7 or 8 hours before you plan to get up.

■ Avoid daytime naps.

■ Avoid afternoon or evening caffeine.

■ Check all prescriptions, over-the-counter medications and herbs to see if they can be blamed for your insomnia.

■ Try to resolve concerns and worries before bedtime. Lack of sleep will only intensify stress.

■ Some find that a hot mug of a caffeine-free herbal tea is helpful. (Chamomile is a traditional soother.)

■ Get daily exercise, preferably in the first half of the day. (Some find that exercise close to bedtime makes sleeping more difficult.)

■ Keep the television out of the bedroom, and have the bedroom as dark as possible (no night lights, and close the curtains).

■ Keep alcohol intake to one drink per day. Alcohol can act as a stimulant as well as a depressant, and has an unpredictable effect on sleep.

■ If you can't sleep, do quiet activities such as reading, or listening to relaxing music. Avoid watching TV, and turn your computer off.

■ Have a bedtime snack. What works the best for some people is a combination of protein, fat, and calcium. For example, an apple with cheese, or plain yogurt (sweetened with honey) with a handful of raw nuts. (See *Snacking Suggestions* on page 82.)

■ Take a deep hot bath for 20 - 30 minutes in the late evening – this helps many people sleep better.

■ Sleep apnea is associated with many health problems and is a very treatable disorder, particularly with weight loss. Talk to your doctor about whether sleep apnea could be your problem.

Light therapy

Exposure to bright light when you wake up can be effective sleep therapy. Depending on the time of year, this can be accomplished with a walk outside or other exposure to outside light first thing in the morning. Another way to use this effect is to sit in front of a 10,000 lux light for 30 - 40 minutes on awakening. This is the same kind of very bright light that is used to treat Seasonal Affective Disorder. (There are a number of sources of these special lights, including www.bio-light.com)

---

[1] King, C.R. JAMA 2008;300:2859-66

KNOW YOUR VITAMIN D LEVEL

<u>Goal:</u> **Typically 1,000 or 2,000 international units (IU) of vitamin D$_3$ (cholecalciferol) daily as a supplement is required to achieve adequate blood levels of greater than 30 ng/ml**

Vitamin D deficiency is very common, and having a low level of vitamin D is associated with a substantially higher risk of heart disease.[1] I generally measure the blood level of *25-hydroxy Vitamin D* and recommend supplementation based on the result. Although we aim for a blood level of at least 30 ng/ml, the optimal level is unknown and may be higher.

Although specific studies looking at high dose vitamin D supplements for heart disease have not been done, we do have evidence from randomized controlled studies that vitamin D supplements at doses up to 2,000 IU are associated with a reduced risk of death.[2]

Fortified dairy foods have a small amount of vitamin D. Sardines, salmon, and sunlight are also good sources of vitamin D. I would like to see sunlight used more as a source of vitamin D: having your arms and legs exposed to the sun, without sunscreen, for about 20 minutes 3 times per week in sunny months may be enough for many people. The farther from the equator that you live, the more difficult it will be to get vitamin D from the sun.

Often people believe that when they take vitamin D they need to also take a calcium supplement. However, most people who eat 2 – 3 servings of dairy each day are unlikely to need calcium supplements, and in fact excess calcium may increase risk of heart disease.[3]

Other supplements for heart disease

In specific situations, there are many other nutritional supplements I sometimes recommend for certain clinical heart disease scenarios. We have already discussed niacin and fish oil, but others include magnesium, coenzyme Q$_{10}$, l-carnitine, and hawthorn berry. Because of the difficulty in making general recommendations concerning these, I usually only discuss them in consultation with a specific patient.

Be aware of the pros and cons of nutritional supplements

The more we study food and its components, the more evidence we see for the benefit of the whole food rather than extracts or supplements. Furthermore, controlled prospective studies using nutritional supplements have generally shown no health outcomes benefit. Some have even been shown to cause harm, such as higher doses of Vitamin E and beta carotene. Supplements cannot replace good food, adequate sleep, and daily exercise.

Antioxidant supplements and vitamin E may be harmful
(From page 23)

Well done studies show no benefit for most antioxidant supplements in terms of improving health or reducing heart disease risk. There is also strong evidence from randomized controlled studies that vitamin A, beta carotene and Vitamin E supplements have been associated with increased risk of death.[4][5] Vitamin E and similar antioxidant nutrients are best supplied in foods, such as minimally processed grains, beans, and raw nuts. (See page 22 for more on supplements.)

---

[1] Kim et al. Am J Cardiol 2008;102:1540-44
[2] Autier, P. and Gandini, S. Arch Inten Med 2007;167:1730-37
[3] Bolland, M. et al. BMJ 2008;336:262-6

[4] Lee at al. JAMA 2005;294:56-65
[5] Kris-Etherton et al. Circulation 2004;110:637-41

HEART CHOICE TEN

USE APPROPRIATE MEDICATION

Goal: Work with your physician to select medications that have demonstrated efficacy at preventing heart disease and saving lives

There are many good drugs for people at risk of heart disease, and in our medical practice we use conventional medications with enthusiasm where appropriate: for example, to lower cholesterol, improve blood pressure, and make platelets in blood less sticky. I use them all. However, the available scientific evidence supports the idea that, for optimal health, the emphasis should be on lifestyle choices.

If you do not tolerate certain medications (like cholesterol-lowering statins), diet and lifestyle choices are particularly important. I have many patients who have done very well despite being unable to tolerate some important medications. Typically, they are also people who have taken their diet and exercise choices seriously.

Happily, most people can use both lifestyle *and* medications to achieve maximal reduction in their risk for heart disease. While evidence-based medications are valuable, your lifestyle choices bring the greatest total health benefit. Don't neglect them!

PUTTING HEART DISEASE CHOICES INTO PRACTICE

I have chosen the stories of two of my patients, both who were faced with major cardiovascular events at a relatively young age. One had a heart attack and a quintuple bypass graft at 45, and the other had a stroke at 53. Both adopted the vigorous risk reduction strategies we've been talking about in this chapter. Here is a recap of the four foundational heart disease concepts that I mentioned earlier.

■ The process by which arteries to the heart become clogged can usually be stabilized or reversed to a significant degree using food, exercise, and appropriate medicine.

■ If you don't have heart disease you can minimize your risk using sound preventative choices, even if you have multiple risk factors.

■ Most of your heart disease risk factors are modifiable using lifestyle choices.

■ If you already have heart disease, you can usually prevent further events by making good medical and lifestyle choices.

The two cases following are representative of the results I often see when patients put lifestyle choices – and appropriate medicines – to work.

PATIENT SUCCESS STORY ONE

Steve was a 45 year old senior executive and father of two when he had his first heart attack, followed by a quintuple bypass graft. He was prescribed a statin and blood pressure medications, and went on a variety of diets.

When we first began treating him, his total cholesterol was 229 mg/dl, with high-risk triglycerides of 463 mg/dl and a HDL of only 29. His total cholesterol to HDL ratio (TC:HDL) was a dangerous 7.9.

Although his LDL cholesterol was treated aggressively with medications to recommended levels, he continued to have further progression of disease that required another angiogram and a coronary artery stent.

He then got serious and decided on a more comprehensive approach. In addition to the cholesterol and blood pressure medicine he was already taking, he adopted a Mediterranean diet pattern emphasizing more good fats, fish oil every day, and began a daily exercise program. A prescription form of niacin (Niaspan) was added, and he built that up to 1,500 mg daily.

The combination of diet, exercise, weight loss, and medications improved his cholesterol panel remarkably. His total cholesterol dropped 40 percent, from 229 to 141 mg/dl. His HDL (good cholesterol) rose 186 percent, from 29 to 54 mg/dl, a change that is associated with a risk reduction of about 50 percent or greater, and in some studies a reversal of arterial blockage.[1] His triglycerides dropped 76 percent, from 463 to only 111 mg/dl. His TC:HDL improved strikingly, from 7.9 to 2.6, and his LDL (bad cholesterol) was now a very favorable 65 mg/dl. He gradually dropped his weight from 184 lbs to 161 lbs, and his waist from 39 inches to 34½ inches.

Compared to the results we see when we just use medications to treat heart disease, these results seem almost unbelievable. Yet his amazing success, in spite of a rocky beginning, shows us what can be achieved when we take our heart disease risk seriously and vigorously use appropriate medications, excellent dietary choices, portion control, and daily exercise.

Steve turned 70 in 2011, with a dramatically lowered risk of progressive heart disease. Although he started with a sobering prognosis, he now feels great and is living a very active life 24 years after his bypass graft.

[1] Nicholls, S. et al. JAMA 2007;297:499-508

PATIENT SUCCESS STORY TWO

Sandy was a 53 year old health professional when she had a stroke. Her initial recovery was excellent, leaving her with only minimal persistent brain damage.

However, her risk factors for a repeat stroke, including being overweight, and having elevated blood sugars and abnormal cholesterol and triglycerides, were unchanged. She continued to be at a very high risk of another stroke, perhaps much more disabling than the last one.

We looked more carefully at what she thought was a healthy diet and made changes. First, we identified several parts of her diet that had hidden calories, such as pre-sweetened yogurt, highly-refined breakfast cereals, and dried fruit. She started buying plain yogurt and sweetening it herself, using less total sweeteners in the process.

She also started cooking her own whole grain cereal, or eating eggs and other protein foods for breakfast. She dramatically reduced her use of breads and pasta, and increased her intake of vegetables and protein (including fish and other animal protein) foods. She ate out less.

Another critically important change she made was to exercise every day, including climbing the stairs at work. She gradually built up to climbing up and down a total of 20 flights of stairs daily.

In other words, she didn't go on a diet or program: she changed her habits. After 8 weeks, she had lost 15 pounds, on her way to eventually losing a total of 30 pounds. Her cholesterol panel improved, with a drop in total cholesterol of 40 points, lower triglycerides, and markedly better total cholesterol to HDL ratio. Her fasting glucose also dropped 42 points, and she was able to reduce her medications.

Sandy feels good, has more energy, and her future risk of stroke or heart disease has been substantially reduced.

5

Kitchen Strategy

Pantry Basics
Important Ingredients
Useful Cooking Tools

Pantry Basics

I f you have the basic ingredients on hand it's much easier to put together meals without any planning and with little effort. When we're tired and wanting to do anything but cook or even *think* about cooking, the right inventory can make the difference between preparing a truly delicious meal or succumbing to the temptation to eat out or order in. With this selection of mix-and-match whole foods (and the absence of junk food) it's also easier to stay on the wagon where food choices are concerned.

These are the foods I can generally count on having in my refrigerator, freezer, or cupboards at any given time. Of course, the recipes I use most often in this book lean heavily on this list. You can prepare most of the recipes from these supplies without any need to shop. I would consider this a sort of master shopping list.

Fresh Fruits and Vegetables
(Store in a cool, dry place)
- apples
- oranges
- bananas
- lemons/limes
- tomatoes
- onions (sweet if possible)
- garlic
- butternut squash
- yams (orange-fleshed sweet potatoes)
- russet, red, or Yukon gold potatoes

Refrigerated Food
- carrots
- celery
- napa cabbage
- butter
- milk (2 percent)
- plain yogurt (see page 97)
- sharp cheddar cheese
- Parmesan (see page 67)
- eggs

- mayonnaise (page 96)
- vinaigrette (page 95)
- whole grain mustard
- horseradish
- tahini (sesame seed paste)
- extra-firm tofu
- whole flaxseeds
- raw almonds
- raw walnuts
- raw sesame seeds
- raw sunflower seeds
- dry active baking yeast

Frozen Food
- baby lima beans
- green soy beans (in and out of the pod)
- chopped spinach
- petite peas
- petite yellow corn
- baby green beans
- blueberries and strawberries
- (back-up butter and sliced bread)

Grains and beans
(Store in a cool, dry place)
- millet
- bulgur
- quinoa
- whole barley
- brown basmati rice
- toasted buckwheat(kasha)
- old-fashioned rolled oats
- Scottish oatmeal and oat bran
- steel-cut oats
- whole oat groats
- stone-ground cornmeal (polenta)
- unbleached white bread flour
- stone-ground whole wheat flour
- stone-ground whole wheat pastry flour
- brown rice pasta
- brown and red lentils
- Anasazi and pinto beans
- cannellini and small white beans
- chick peas (garbanzos)

Canned Food
- 15-ounce black beans
- 15-ounce chickpeas

- ❑ 15-ounce red kidney beans
- ❑ 15- and 32-ounce chicken broth
- ❑ 5- and 12-ounce evaporated whole milk
- ❑ 14- and 28-ounce diced tomatoes
- ❑ 14- and 28-ounce crushed tomatoes
- ❑ 3.75-ounce sardines
- ❑ 6-ounce light solid tuna in olive oil
- ❑ 12-ounce solid white tuna in water
- ❑ 4- and 7-ounce whole mild green chiles
- ❑ 14-ounce coconut milk (not *lite*)

General Supplies

- ❑ extra-virgin olive oil
- ❑ light olive oil
- ❑ apple cider vinegar
- ❑ cold pressed canola oil
- ❑ non-stick canola spray
- ❑ raisins
- ❑ currants
- ❑ dried prunes
- ❑ honey
- ❑ pure maple syrup
- ❑ sugar, brown and white
- ❑ baking powder
- ❑ baking soda (see box below)
- ❑ dried unsweetened shredded coconut

> **Baking soda** is the best cleaner I've found for just about everything from coffee stained mugs to the kitchen sink – literally. It cleans stainless steel or porcelain, and improves (if not removes) the baked-on residue from non-stick spray that can collect on baking sheets and pans. You can even use it to brush your teeth – just put a half-teaspoon or soon your palm and dip your wet toothbrush in it.

Special Effects

- ❑ salsa
- ❑ capers
- ❑ anchovies
- ❑ kalamata olives
- ❑ soy sauce
- ❑ fish sauce
- ❑ toasted sesame oil
- ❑ mirin (rice wine)
- ❑ almond essence

Seasonings

- ❑ salt (kosher and table)
- ❑ peppercorns (for grinder)
- ❑ Tabasco sauce
- ❑ crushed chilies
- ❑ chili powder
- ❑ paprika
- ❑ basil
- ❑ thyme
- ❑ oregano
- ❑ cinnamon
- ❑ cloves
- ❑ garam masala
- ❑ ground cumin
- ❑ curry powder
- ❑ turmeric
- ❑ fresh ginger (see page 160)

Some favorite Portland sources:

Most of these items are available from supermarkets, but don't forget resources like local farmers' markets and bee-keepers. Eating well is simple and inexpensive if you make use of the bulk food section of your local supermarket for whole food items like spices, raw nuts, whole grains, and beans. We find the following sources useful:

Bob's Red Mill Natural Foods
www.bobsredmill.com

Fred Meyer
www.fredmeyer.com

New Seasons Market
www.newseasonsmarket.com

Trader Joe's
www.traderjoes.com

Whole Foods Market
www.wholefoodsmarket.com

WinCo Foods
www.wincofoods.com

Important Ingredients

There are some fundamental ingredients that are nonnegotiable essentials in my kitchen, like extra-virgin olive oil, apple cider vinegar, salt, peppercorns, and honey. For my tastes, these basics work even when a recipe calls for specialty oils or vinegars, black salt, pink peppercorns, or lavender honey.

Other ingredients, like Parmesan cheese, lemons or limes, cilantro, and parsley, fall somewhere between necessities and luxuries. These are necessary for their contribution to certain recipes but not always in the kitchen when I need them. (Onions and garlic are dealt with in the *Vegetable* chapter starting on page 111.)

Extra-virgin olive oil

Our kitchen has two kinds of oil: extra-light olive oil for making mayonnaise (see recipe on page 96) and a 3-liter tin of extra-virgin olive oil for everything else, including frying eggs, popping popcorn, and sautéing vegetables. Extra-virgin olive oil is remarkably versatile oil, considering its distinctive flavor. In terms of health benefits, extra-virgin olive oil (the oil from the first pressing of the olives) is the richest and least processed of the grades of olive oil.

You can use extra-virgin olive oil for almost any recipe where oil is used. I use extra-virgin olive oil in all my Asian and Mexican recipes, too. If your sensibilities are not too offended, you should try it yourself. The only recipes where I *don't* use exclusively olive oil are the few times when flavor is an issue: for example, we prefer mayonnaise made with about 30 percent extra-virgin olive oil and 70 percent extra-light olive oil.

Also, in the case of the *Tofu in Soy Ginger Marinade* on page 160, there is no substitute for toasted sesame oil.

As for choosing from the dozen or more brands you are faced with in most stores, my suggestion is to buy the best selling extra-virgin olive oil from any serious food store: it will be moderately priced and it may be their house brand. The turnover of lower-priced oil in a busy food store is far more assured than with any of the expensive imported brands, regardless of how magnificent they were when they left Italy, Greece, or Spain. (Store away from light and heat.)

> *Light Olive Oil?* If you have been using light or regular olive oil in your kitchen, consider moving it into your bathroom, too: it is a wonderful moisturizer when used on a just-washed face. (A little goes a long way.) Moist skin will absorb the oil and look radiantly healthy, but olive oil applied to a completely dry face gives an oily look and feels itchy. Olive oil is also a skin-friendly treatment to get pine pitch off your skin or hair.

Apple cider vinegar

Apple cider vinegar is probably more pungent than most types of wine vinegar, but you can use it in place of any vinegar a recipe may call for, in my opinion. A major role for vinegar in my kitchen is in vinaigrette, and my boisterous recipe (page 95) is no place for exotic or nuanced varieties.

Studies have shown 1 – 2 tablespoons a day improves insulin resistance, leading to small improvements in blood sugar in diabetic patients. Apple cider vinegar is also a hero in the field of folk medicine. Some find that drinking a glass of water mixed with a couple of tablespoons of apple cider vinegar can settle a roiling tummy, and sipping a mixture of equal proportions of apple cider vinegar and honey can ease a cough.

Honey

Honey is our sugar substitute of choice. Raw honey especially qualifies as a whole food, and contains vitamins, minerals, amino acids, and antioxidants. It has an infinite shelf life, and honey that has crystallized will flow freely again when warmed. For anyone unused to handling honey it pays to be respectful of its ability to drip almost invisibly. (For peanut butter and honey sandwiches, combine the two before spreading so the honey won't sneak out.)

To measure honey, first swirl a bit of oil in the measuring spoon or cup and you'll find the honey will slip out cleanly. For most purposes we suggest the mildest tasting, lightest colored honey you can find, which will probably be clover honey. For most of my cooking purposes – like bread dough, vinaigrette, marinades, and sauces – honey is the perfect sweetener. It dissolves more slowly than sugar, of course, but an extra twenty seconds of whisking is hardly an issue.

Salt

Salt is the difference between food and feast. It's not just another seasoning: without salt, the other big flavors – like hot, sweet, and sour – are wasted. Salt is also part of a healthy lifestyle. If you get rid of all hidden salt in your diet, which means avoiding most prepared foods, you probably don't need to be concerned about adding salt to your food. (See page 54 for more on salt.) I tend to call for more salt (and freshly ground pepper) in my recipes than most, but it is no accident.

For most baking purposes table salt works fine. (I also use it as a dry scrub to clean cast iron cookware instead of using water.) For stovetop cooking and for salting vegetables and meat before roasting, I prefer the coarser texture of kosher salt, which I keep handy in a salt box beside the stove. (It doesn't clump like table salt.) I keep table salt in a lidded jar next to the salt box – it's easier to measure salt by scooping it than to use the pouring spout on the container.

Pepper(corns)

The sweet heat and potent richness of freshly ground pepper make a tremendously important contribution to food, in my opinion. I happen to use black peppercorns rather than pink or red or green or white: the important issue is not the color but whether or not it is freshly ground.

It is also important to have a grinder that works well. (See page 69.) A cheap, poorly designed pepper mill with a fitful grinder that spits out a mixture of powdered and cracked pepper at the same time is almost – but not quite – worse than the alternatives. My grinder produces a teaspoon of pepper in approximately 60 grinds; I never have to bother using measuring spoons as long as I count as I grind.

Parmesan

Freshly grated Parmesan cheese turns up quite a bit in these pages: it generally means *Parmigiano-Reggiano*, the imported Italian original. You may find domestic Parmesan that you like as well, but I haven't yet. Should you have doubts as to what the fuss is about, just do a side-by-side taste comparison. Who knows? You may disagree with me.

Parmigiano-Reggiano is expensive so shop around for the best price (avoid high-end delicatessens) and buy chunks with the least rind. Check cut edges for freshness; if they don't give at all when you press them and don't look as creamily opaque as the rest of the cheese, keep looking. Also, random cut and hand wrapped Parmesan from serious food stores is generally superior to the commercially packaged wedges in the supermarket.

When I say 'freshly grated Parmesan', I mean Parmesan you have grated yourself. It is useful and perfectly acceptable to keep a cup or so of grated Parmesan well sealed in the refrigerator. The quantities in my recipes are for Parmesan grated on the ⅛-inch teardrop-shaped holes of my box grater; 4

ounces of Parmesan (weight includes the rind) makes about 1¼ cups. It keeps nicely for weeks, and adds instant flavor and richness to tossed salads (page 132), bowls of minestrone (page 143), or dishes like *Polenta with Vegetables* (page 185) or *Tuna and Broccoli Pasta* (page 190).

Fresh lemons and limes

Both lemon and lime juice are invaluable flavor spikes, especially when cooking with confident ingredients like beans, tuna, and whole grains. Sometimes just a tablespoon of lemon or lime juice can make all the difference to a recipe. (Commercially bottled juice (from concentrate) is not a substitute for fresh, in my opinion.)

> **Zest**, which is the colored part of citrus peel, also makes a critical contribution in recipes like *Brown Rice Pudding, Tuna Tetrazzini*, and *Tuscan Bean Salad*. If you don't have a citrus zesting tool you can use a vegetable peeler, but it's important to peel with almost no pressure to remove only the thin yellow or green layer that holds the aromatic oils. The white pith is bitter. Just mince or finely slice the strips that you remove.

I have a general preference for limes because they have no seeds to fuss with and for my purposes are interchangeable with lemons, but price and quality decide the issue. If you buy lemons or limes at a good price, don't let them die before you use them! Extract the juice and store it in the refrigerator, and try to use it within a week.

One average lemon or lime will give you somewhere between ¼ - ½ cup. (They can still give plenty of juice even after the rinds stiffen but watch that your knife doesn't slip when you're slicing a hard-skinned one.) The juiciest limes or lemons are those with thin skins and a bit of give when you press them. When shopping for any citrus avoid hard fruit with deep dimpling.

(In the case of oranges and grapefruit, soft fruit with baggy-feeling peels are to be avoided no matter how large and photogenic they may be. Like a good lemon or lime, they should be thin skinned and feel heavy for their size.)

Cilantro and parsley

These are the two most useful of the fresh herbs, in my opinion. Cilantro can be an acquired taste (or possibly never acquired, as in the case of my mother). It has an aggressive flavor I've heard described as 'funky' and 'musty', but to cilantro lovers the flavor is seductive and evocative. It also has the additional convenience of tender stems that can be chopped along with the leaves. Cilantro is a natural partner to the flavors of cumin, chilies, and lime or lemon juice, and it turns up in just about all of my Asian, Mexican, and Middle Eastern dishes.

Flat leaf (Italian) parsley usually costs more than regular curly parsley but doesn't seem to have any flavor advantage. Parsley is sturdier than cilantro, but both can lose their essential flavor edge after a few days even if they keep their looks.

Clean them in a few changes of cold water as needed – some cilantro can come attached to a lot of dirt – and dry them well. (You really need a salad spinner for this, if you don't have one already.) Pack them loosely in a sealed plastic container or bag. Try to avoid any excess water hanging on the leaves and store with a couple of clean, dry paper towels. If you don't use them within a couple of days, check them daily thereafter for any signs of yellowing or pockets of blackened leaves.

I have been amazed at how long fresh herbs like basil, parsley, thyme, and rosemary will stay fresh if I poke them into a glass with a half-inch or so of water and leave them loosely covered in plastic in the fridge or uncovered for days on a window sill. They seem to like the feel of water on their feet and wind in their hair.

Useful Cooking Tools

Cooking is like gardening in that your choice of tools can make a big difference to your fun. A person can make do (or do without) in many cases, but for me there are a handful of things I use almost every day. Naturally this list is very subjective. Every home cook would have a different list, and may even feel passionate about a different garlic press.

Knives

I really only need two knives – an 8-inch chef's knife and a 3-inch paring knife. There is no substitute for a good chef's knife. And it's true that a dull knife is more dangerous than a sharp one. Protect the blade in a knife block, which holds the knife handle out and ready to grab. Make that *three* knives – a serrated bread knife is essential for slicing bread and pretty nice for slicing tomatoes.

Cutting board

A heavy hardwood board, at least 15 x 25 inches, is my choice. Mine lives permanently on the countertop. (Wood is apparently as safe as plastic boards, as bacteria are thought to be neutralized by the wood.) Some cooks prefer the polyethylene cutting boards; they're easier to handle and store if you don't have room for a permanent block.

Oyster knife

I also like my oyster knife, with its comfortable wooden palm-friendly handle and sturdy, stiff blunt blade. I use it for serious poking or prying – generally whenever I'm tempted to use a knife but shouldn't. Scraping the garlic skin out of a garlic press, for example, or drilling a hole in a fresh coconut. (See page 205.)

Vegetable peeler

The Oxo brand with the fat black handle and tip designed for digging is comfortable and efficient, and doesn't remove any more of the vegetable than necessary.

Metal dough scraper

The one I reach for is a 4-inch square piece of stiff metal with a round wooden grip, and it is pretty much an extension of my hand. It scrapes dried dough off counters after I've made bread, separates and scoops up chopped vegetables, and is generally indispensable. I also have one that has a ruler etched on the blade, which is handy when you need to remind yourself what a quarter inch looks like.

Garlic press

For me, the cleanest and most efficient way to extract garlic is the plain old press method. (See more about crushing garlic on page 119.) I like the Zyliss brand: it is solidly built but not heavy.

Pepper grinder

Freshly ground pepper is generally underrated as an ingredient. I use and recommend a 12-inch wooden Peugeot pepper grinder – it holds a decent amount of peppercorns and the wood has a friendly feel to the hands. Also, the grinder feels comfortable even after fifty or sixty grinds, which is what it takes to give me a teaspoon of ground pepper.

Citrus reamer

This means the simple little all-wooden tool I use to squeeze juice from lemons and limes. Cheap, minimalist, and easy to store.

Kitchen scissors
Their most important purpose is to keep me from using knives in ways that may either damage the knives or me. Opening packages, cutting string, trimming stems, and so forth.

Salad spinner
This is a colander-within-a-bowl with a lid mechanism that spins the colander, and it's the best way I know to clean and dry lettuce and greens as well as parsley and cilantro. My pull-string Zyliss model has been working steadily for over ten years.

Collapsible basket steamer
These are widely available and come in at least a couple of styles and sizes. I use both large and small sizes, depending on the size of pot. They are mainly used for steaming vegetables, of course, but are also the best way I've found yet to reheat leftover rice. (See page 170.)

Silicone (heatproof) spatulas
Nonnegotiable. I use a large one with a curved head (called a *spoonula*) that holds a handy 2 tablespoons of extra-virgin olive oil. I suggest at least a couple of regular sized scraping-type spatulas as well as a skinny one for narrow spaces.

Pyrex measuring jugs
Clear, solidly built, and invaluable. You need the 1-cup, 2-cup, 4-cup, and 8-cup. The big one doubles as a mixing bowl, and it can be useful to know how much mixture you have. I mix casseroles and muffins and such in the 8-cupper and crepe batter in the 4-cupper, for example. You can even find them with lids, which saves on plastic wrap.

Measuring spoons and cups
If I had only one set of each (and I don't), my choice would be the medium weight metal. In the case of measuring spoons, the ones with slim bowls that fit into spice jars are convenient. While we're on the subject of measuring spoons, I love my two-tablespoon (⅛ cup) measuring spoon, not always easy to find in kitchen supply stores.

Timer
I strongly recommend one of those irritating timers that don't shut up until you poke them. You'll probably agree if you ever forget a loaf of bread in the oven because you didn't happen to hear the polite beep of a one-chance-is-all-you-get timer. You can also bring a timer anywhere you go to remind yourself no matter how distracted you get.

Measurpour gadget
I don't exactly know what to call this but the label says *'Measurpour'* and I've seen it in several kitchen stores. It is a plastic gadget that fits tightly into a standard (¾-inch) bottleneck and pours out extra-virgin olive oil in one-tablespoon doses. No more oily measuring spoons.

Immersion blender
Also called a stick blender, this transforms the business of making mayonnaise (page 96) and soups (starting on page 138), allowing you to create creamy ready-to-serve soups with minimum fuss. (You can purée a soup or sauce directly in the pot rather than transferring to and from a food processor or regular blender.) It can also replace a conventional blender in the making of smoothies – you just have the simple blender stick to clean rather than a blender to take apart and wash. I prefer one with variable speed, and a removable mixer which makes cleaning easier.

Food processor
My current choice for most purposes is the eleven-cup KitchenAid because it has a mini-work bowl which is just the right size for making mayonnaise and vinaigrette. However, my seven-cup Cuisinart is better for mixing bread dough, for some reason. Either size is useful for grating vegetables and to puree dips, sauces, and soups.

6 Practical Eating

Breakfast
Oatmeal Options
Smoothies
Snacking Suggestions
Lunch and Dinner
Menu for One Week

Breakfast

Mornings arrive at an uncivilized hour and leave too soon. If there are strong opinions about what is and what is not an acceptable food choice, this is not the time to argue. One effective way to avoid an argument with yourself or anyone else is to simply stop buying poor food choices. Whether it's hot oatmeal or coffee and toast, figure out something you can enjoy even if you wake up on the wrong side of the bed.

Plus, there is compelling evidence that eating breakfast is associated with less diabetes and obesity in many studies, which are two risk factors for heart disease.

Avoid fruit juice

Or have a *very* small glass. If possible, remove fruit juices from your refrigerator and your life completely. Even if freshly squeezed, juice is low in nutrition and fiber and high in sugar and calories. It is safe to say that most of us *can't afford* extra calories. Juice takes the place of the whole fruit we *should* be eating instead. So, consider juice as a treat rather than a staple. (See page 18.)

Include whole fruit

As long as our goal is to eat 5 – 9 servings of fruit and vegetables every day, why not start here? An orange or grapefruit is particularly welcome in the morning, especially if you have been used to a glass of orange juice. A banana works well for some people sliced and added to yogurt or eaten on toast with some sort of nut butter. A smoothie like the one on page 79 can easily give you at least three servings of fruit in one glass.

Avoid commercial cold cereals

Keep in mind that even seemingly honest breakfast cereals that claim whole grain status are still refined grains. Even if technically made from whole grain, conventional breakfast cereals have been processed to such a degree that the structure of the starch molecule has been changed, and acts more like sugar in your body. (See page 14.) If you are a cold-breakfast-cereal eater, try replacing it with something like crunchy toasted granola or raw muesli, both of which you can buy ready made or construct yourself. (See page 77) Be alert when buying ready-made granola – it is often over-sweetened and may contain fats and nuts that have been heated and stored for an unknown time.

Include whole grain cereals

For cold cereal you can try rolled oats, muesli, or granola served with milk, fresh fruit, or dried fruit. For hot cereal there are options like oatmeal, barley, cornmeal, brown rice, toasted buckwheat, or millet. (See page 181.) Some like hot cereal with milk and honey, some like it with butter and salt, and you may prefer brown sugar, cinnamon, and cream. Muesli makes a delicious cooked cereal, too, or soaked overnight in the juice from a couple of oranges. (Eat the pulp!)

Avoid refined grains

This includes foods like bagels, store-bought muffins, biscuits, white flour pancakes and waffles, cream-of-wheat-type cereals, and all cold breakfast cereals. Try to include as wide a spectrum of whole grains as you can, whether in the form of bread, muffins, or cereals. Custom-built, whole grain, fiber-packed nutrient-dense muffins are actually practical to make yourself. (See page 235.) Don't compromise: if you don't have the real thing in genuine whole grains, spend your breakfast calories on something else. (… but one does have to sympathize with those who question the validity of a 100 percent whole wheat bagel. When is a bagel not a bagel? Is it enough just to look like a bagel?)

Include (real) eggs

Eating an egg a day is a reasonable choice for most of us, as discussed on page 21. Don't eat fake eggs, which are neither food nor medicine. Eggs are rich in protein, folic acid, and other B vitamins and cook quickly. They can be fried, scrambled, poached, boiled (page 106), or included raw in a smoothie (page 80). Try cooking your eggs in extra-virgin olive oil, instead of butter. Butter is fine but olive oil is optimal.

Omelets or frittatas (see page 74) are also tasty ways to sneak extra vegetables into your diet – tomatoes, onions, bell peppers, mushrooms, spinach, and so on. Or just chop up a tomato and toss it into the hot pan with your morning egg as it cooks. The tomato is a perfect complement to the egg even if it is just warmed through. (The tomato, not the egg.)

Avoid preserved (processed) meat

This means bacon, ham, and cured sausages, of course. They contain added sugar, salt, and preservatives, and should be reserved for special occasions, if possible. Exactly what it is about these processed meats that seems to lead to diseases like cancer, diabetes and heart disease is not clear.

Use real butter

Real butter is a legal substance, but use it sparingly. Avoid any butter substitutes or any partially hydrogenated product like margarine. If you want to reduce your butter intake, an option is to make 'better butter', a mixture of 75 percent soft butter and 25 percent extra-virgin olive oil blended until smooth. It will be spreadable even when cold from the refrigerator. If you use mild oil like soy or canola you can make the mixture 50-50.

Use honey

If you want something sweet on your toast or in your cereal, don't overlook the perfect sweetener – antioxidant-rich honey. Clover honey has the mildest flavor. (More about honey on page 67.)

Breakfast suggestions

Eggs: fried, scrambled, coddled, poached, boiled, or in an omelet or frittata (see page 74), with whole grain buttered toast.

Hot whole grain cereal: like oatmeal, barley, cornmeal, brown rice, kasha (toasted buckwheat groats), or millet, and served with milk, dried fruit, honey, or brown sugar. (See following pages as well as whole grain chapter beginning on page 169.) Muesli is good cooked, too.

Cold whole grain cereal made from grains that have not been processed, like muesli, granola, or rolled oats served with milk, fresh fruit, or dried fruit. (See page 77.)

Whole grain muffins, which you probably need to make yourself to get a good enough nutrient profile. (See pages 235–6.)

Whole grain pancakes (see page 74) with butter and pure maple syrup.

Smoothies made with yogurt or kefir, fresh fruit, cooked grain, soft tofu, and any number of other options. (See pages 79-80.)

Plain yogurt or kefir with live cultures (see page 21) mixed with fresh fruit or canned fruit packed in its own juice. Some even like yogurt mixed with granola or muesli. Avoid sweetened and fruited yogurts! The sugar in yogurt appears to reduce the live cultures over time and load you up with extra calories.

Whole grain toast: toasted whole wheat bread, bagels, or English muffins, with nut butter, honey, or 100% fruit spread.

Whole grain French toast with honey, pure maple syrup, or a 100% fruit spread.

Fresh fruit: whole or chopped, with cereal, yogurt, kefir or cottage cheese.

Fast Frittata
with Tomato and Onion

The only difficult thing about a frittata is remembering whether to put the two *t*'s in the middle or the end of the word. Frittatas have all the advantages of an omelet but are more like a thick, tender egg pancake.

(Serves 1 – 2)

1 – 2 eggs, lightly beaten with fork
salt and freshly ground pepper
2 teaspoons extra-virgin olive oil
1 tomato, diced
¼ cup sliced green onions

1. Prepare eggs and set aside. Heat a small skillet over medium heat and add oil. When oil is hot enough it should spit when you add a drop of water. Add green onion. Sauté for 10 seconds, or until sizzling but still bright green.

2. Add the tomato. Sauté only long enough to heat the tomato through. Add the egg and distribute it evenly around the vegetables. Cook until the eggs are set, lifting sections of cooked egg to let any uncooked egg flow underneath.

3. Flip so the golden-brown underside shows, slice into wedges, and serve.

Note:

▶ You can use diced regular onion instead of green onion; sauté until tender enough for your taste. (I like it a bit crunchy.) Any ingredients you would use for an omelet would work here.

▶ This recipe expands any way you like — just adjust the size of your pan. (See *Zucchini Frittata* on page 210.)

Oatmeal Pancakes
Hearty and slightly sweet

These are deliberately substantial and oaty, and constitute a breakfast by themselves. This recipe also makes fine waffles.

(Makes about 14 x 5-inch pancakes)

1 cup cold milk
1 cup very hot water
½ cup honey
¼ cup extra-virgin olive oil
3 cups old-fashioned rolled oats
4 eggs, beaten

1 cup whole wheat pastry flour
1½ teaspoons salt
1 tablespoon baking powder

1. In a mixing bowl combine milk, water, honey, oil, and oats. Add beaten eggs.

2. Combine whole wheat flour with salt and baking powder. Add to the liquid mixture and whisk until smooth.

3. Cook pancakes on hot griddle and flip after bubbles form, but before they pop.

Oatmeal pancakes, yeast raised

1. Combine milk and water in a large mixing bowl and sprinkle **1 tablespoon of yeast** over the warm mixture. Add oats and flour (no baking powder, of course), but don't stir; set aside for 10 minutes, then stir until smooth. Cover and set aside for 30 – 60 minutes or until mixture almost doubles.

2. In a separate (smaller) bowl, whisk eggs, and then add honey, oil, and salt and whisk until mixed well. Combine yeast mixture with egg mixture and blend thoroughly. That's it – the batter is ready to use. (Follow cooking directions above.)

Oatmeal and *Rolled Oat Options*

Oats are among the best sources of soluble fiber. They reduce cholesterol, stabilize blood sugar, have antioxidant qualities, and even contain psychoactive compounds that may combat nicotine cravings and may even have antidepressant powers![1]

Rolled oats as hot cereal

Do not use quick-cooking oats! They are too refined and are digested too quickly. They also become gluey when cooked. We recommend old-fashioned rolled oats.

(Makes about 2 cups cooked oatmeal)

1 cup old-fashioned rolled oats
½ teaspoon salt
1¾ cups water

1. Bring water to a boil in a small saucepan. Add rolled oats and salt and reduce heat. Cook uncovered on the stove, stirring often, until the water is absorbed and the consistency suits you (about 5 minutes). *Oatmeal thickens as it sits, so if it seems too thin, just give it 5 minutes.*

2. Sweeten to taste with honey, raisins, or fresh fruit. **The addition of salt, by the way, is critical in oatmeal**, not only for flavor but to reduce the need for sweetening. Some people love oatmeal with just salt and a teaspoon of butter.

▶ **Microwave option:** Place rolled oats, salt, and water in 4-cup Pyrex measuring jug. (A 2-cup jug may boil over.) Microwave uncovered for 2 – 3 minutes. Stir and microwave uncovered for another 1½ – 2 minutes. Also, for a hot oatmeal breakfast that cooks while you sleep, try the overnight crock pot recipe on following page.

---

[1] Jean Carper *Food-Your Miracle Medicine* 1994

▶ **Oat bran:** Oat bran is a rich source of soluble fiber. You can add it to breakfast cereal, muffins, or pancakes but don't confuse it with Scottish oatmeal. Oat bran is flaky and can be added directly to cold cereals.

Scottish and steel-cut oatmeal

Scottish oats should not be confused with the much chunkier steel-cut (or Irish) oatmeal. Scottish oats are finely cut oat groats that provide a pleasant variation on rolled oats. They are generally cooked but are even good uncooked. (For an uncooked option try combining ⅓-cup of Scottish oatmeal with ½ cup of milk and let the mixture soak for about 30 minutes, or leave in the refrigerator overnight.)

Steel-cut oats (also called Irish oatmeal) are the coarsest form of oatmeal, made from whole groats that have been cut into two or three pieces. Steel-cut oats make the best porridge, in my opinion, but they are not for the faint-of-heart and will take at least 30 minutes to cook. You can soak the oats and water overnight to reduce the cooking time. Some folks suggest that for the best flavor, first toast the oats in a hot skillet for a few minutes or in a 350-degree oven for about 5 minutes or until fragrant.

(Makes about 3 cups cooked oatmeal)

3 cups water
1 cup of Scottish or steel-cut oats
½ - ¾ teaspoon salt

1. Bring liquid to the boil in a 2-quart pot and stir in oats and salt.

2. Simmer 10 minutes for Scottish oats *or* 30 minutes for steel cut oats.

Whole grain cereal
(overnight crock pot method)

There are at least two compelling reasons to cook grains this way. The first is that it is so easy. The second is that we are more likely to eat whole grain cereal when we can wake up to a fragrant, hot, fully-cooked breakfast.

(Makes 4 cups cooked whole grain cereal)

1 cup whole oats groats
Or whole hulled barley (not pearl barley)
½ teaspoon salt
4 cups cold water

1. Combine grain, salt, and water in your crock pot or slow cooker and stir briefly. Set crock pot on its very lowest (keep warm) setting. Cook for 8 – 10 hours or overnight.

2. In the morning, scrape anything you don't eat into a storage container while it's still warm. It will firm as it cools, and you can store it in the refrigerator to slice and heat for breakfast the next morning.

3. Serve with milk and honey, or berries, brown sugar, and cream, or sliced banana and sunflower seeds, or nuts and raisins, or – some just like hot cereal with butter.

For a larger-sized crock pot
(like 6-quart size), I recommend the water-bath method. Combine the grain, water, and salt in a bowl big enough to hold 4 cups of cooked cereal (I use a 2-quart Pyrex measuring jug), set it inside the crock pot, and add water to the crock pot until the level reaches the water level in the bowl. Then put the lid on the crock pot and set the temperature to low. Eight hours later it is ready, and with no crock pot to clean.

Note:
▸ Variations in crock pot temperature settings may mean you will need to adjust the amount of water you use.

▸ You could add raisins or chopped dried fruit with the grain to cook overnight for a different effect.

▸ Adding 1 tablespoon flaxseeds with the grain gives a subtle nutty crunch and valuable omega-3 fatty acids.

▸ ***Don't ignore the salt*** – it is a critical ingredient in oatmeal. Some prefer oatmeal flavored only with salt. Oats have a natural richness brought out by salt.

▸ Steel cut oats can be substituted for whole oats in this recipe, but other grains – like rye or wheat – absorb water differently. Play around with your proportions until you end up with the consistency you like. (See page 75 for stovetop cooking method and chapter 11 for other grain options.)

Overnight Thermos Method

This method cooks the cereal overnight but it won't be hot in the morning.

⅔ cup whole grain
¼ teaspoon salt
2 cups boiling water

1. Preheat wide mouth Thermos (3-cup size) with hot water.

2. Place grain and salt in thermos, add boiling water, and seal Thermos. Leave for 8 hours or overnight. *(Your cereal will be warm, not hot, in the morning.)*

Note:
▸ We don't recommend including dried fruit – the cereal won't cook as well.

Rolled oats as cold cereal

People who don't like hot oatmeal should try the cold version, either in the simplest form or as muesli. Just pour ½ cup of milk over ½ cup of old-fashioned rolled oats. Drizzle some honey over the top or sprinkle with raisins or a chopped banana for sweetness.

Muesli

Muesli is a rolled-oat-based cereal that doesn't need cooking, and is usually eaten with milk. (You can also cook the muesli like oatmeal.) Either buy it ready-made from a reputable local source (like *Bob's Red Mill* in Milwaukie, Oregon) or create your own. The list of ingredients that follows is more suggestion than recipe. The point is to emphasize variety, fiber, and good fat while still enjoying breakfast.

(Makes about 8 cups)

5 cups old-fashioned rolled oats
or blend of rolled oats, rye, barley, etc.
½ cup toasted buckwheat (kasha)
½ cup raw sesame seeds
1 cup raw sunflower and/or pumpkin seeds
½ cup flaxseed meal or whole flaxseeds
½ - 1 cup shredded unsweetened coconut
1 cup flaked or slivered almonds
1 cup raisins/currants/chopped dried fruit

1. Combine everything in a big mixing bowl. Store muesli in a sealed container in a cool place. Serve it as you would any cold breakfast cereal, or cook it like oatmeal.

Note:

▸ The addition of the toasted buckwheat gives a surprisingly benign crunch and flavor that we love.

▸ For extra sweetness, spread muesli in a large shallow pan and drizzle with a fine stream of honey. Tip back into mixing bowl and mix very thoroughly. It works!

Granola

Granola is a cold cereal alternative that delivers whole grains and good fat. Make it yourself, though; commercial granola is guilty until proven innocent, even if the actual ingredient list passes inspection. This granola is so good it tastes like junk food to me.

(Makes about 8 cups, but it's never enough)

5 cups old-fashioned rolled oats
or blend of rolled oats, rye, barley, etc.
1½ cups flaked almonds
1 cup raw sunflower seeds
½ cup raw sesame seeds
1 cup unsweetened shredded coconut
½ cup honey or pure maple syrup
½ cup extra-virgin olive oil
½ teaspoon salt

Preheat oven to 225 degrees.

1. In a large bowl mix together all the dry ingredients. Whisk the honey and/or syrup, oil, and salt until well blended. *(Mix carefully at first — the oil may splash.)* Pour over the dry ingredients and mix until all is pleasantly sticky.

2. Spread in your largest baking pan (or two) and bake at 225 degrees for 3 hours. Stir and return to the oven for another hour. *(If your oven runs hot, your granola will be overcooked by now. Reduce the heat next time.)*

3. Turn off oven and leave granola in oven for 4 hours or overnight. When granola is completely cool store in an airtight container in a cool place.

Note:

▸ The low slow cooking is better for the valuable oils in the nuts and grains.

▸ If you like raisins or chopped dried fruit, add in the last hour of baking (or even afterwards) so they don't overcook and get bitter or too hard.

Smoothies

There are two kinds of smoothies. There are the smoothies that vaguely pose as health food but are just fortified milkshakes. The other kind of smoothie is made with honest yogurt and fruit, and it is the only one worth drinking.

Why bother?
A smoothie is one of the easiest and tastiest ways to boost daily nutritional intake, especially when the appetite is puny, or if chewing is difficult, or you don't like eating breakfast but know you should.
For the very old or the very young (see *Smoothies for Littlies* on page 33), smoothies are a nutrient-dense liquid meal that you can tweak in any direction you want. You can adjust it up or down for calories, fiber, fat, protein, or personal preference.

Why not ready-made protein drinks?
If you ever find yourself tempted to buy canned liquid meal drinks (like *Ensure* or *Boost)* or powdered protein drinks for any reason, stop and thoughtfully read the ingredient label. Don't bother reading the nutrition panel. Your body is smart enough to know the difference between real nutrition and numbers. Even the most acceptable meal drinks can't compete with whole food. If you have ever considered using commercial meal replacement drinks, please see *Meal replacement drinks* on page 81.

Why yogurt?
Cultured milk products like yogurt and kefir (a yogurt-like drink found in the yogurt section of the supermarket) are good sources of friendly bacteria that help the immune system and have an important role in improving the health of your gastrointestinal garden. Yogurt is an important addition to the diet for anyone taking antibiotics. (See page 21.)

Often the very people who need the benefits of yogurt the most are the ones who *really hate* yogurt. A cunningly constructed smoothie, however, can get yogurt into just about anyone — unless they hate fruit, too.

Why plain yogurt?
To take full advantage of the probiotic properties of yogurt, it only makes sense to choose yogurt with as large and enthusiastic a population of working microbes as possible. Because it is suspected that sugar may deplete the bacterial activity over time, choose plain yogurt whose active bacteria strains are clearly noted on the label. You can then sweeten your smoothies as much as you need to.

It also makes sense to avoid adding any extra sugar to our food. In the effort to make yogurt popular with the largest possible audience, most commercial yogurt tastes more like pudding. Some have three different forms of sugar; artificial flavoring instead of real fruit; artificial coloring to make it attractive; and cornstarch and goodness knows what else to make it creamy.

(A sad fact is that many people still have the perception that sweet, fat-free yogurt products are a health food. Hah! We would be better off drinking an honest old-fashioned milkshake with real ice cream and real fruit.)

Fruit
Not juice! Fruit juices have most of the nutrition and fiber removed but, of course, all of the sugar and calories are intact. (See page 18 for more reasons to shun juice.) Just about any fresh or frozen fruit works, but a balance between sweet (like ripe bananas) and tart (like berries) is a good idea. Experiment.

Even dried prunes can be added – check out the *Prune Smoothie Pudding* on the next page. Bananas and berries are always available because you can keep a supply in your freezer. Smoothies are a good way to use up overripe or bruised bananas.

To freeze bananas, peel them and put them into the freezer individually wrapped in plastic, or on a plate or a cookie sheet until they're hard, then transfer them to a plastic bag. Slice frozen banana into ½-inch chunks before trying to blend them.

Those of us who may object to the texture of bananas will find that they fade nicely into the background of a smoothie. Adding a frozen banana has the effect of adding ice cream, and combined with frozen berries can give a smoothie the texture of frozen yogurt, to be eaten with a spoon.

Frozen berries are available all year, and smoothies are an ideal vehicle to deliver the extra serving or two of antioxidant-rich fruit they represent. Any frozen berries are fine, of course, but if you don't like bits of berry seeds in your smoothie, stick to strawberries and blueberries. I prefer blueberries, and I think they're sweeter.

Equipment
If you don't already own a blender or a handheld immersion blender, you will need to buy one. An immersion blender is a relatively inexpensive device that looks a bit like an electric toothbrush but it can turn a few cups of chopped fruit and yogurt into a smooth drink in less than a minute. Regular blenders work great if you are making larger quantities but the immersion blender is the easiest way to make one or two servings, and clean-up is as easy as detaching and rinsing the business end. The smoothie can be left in the same container it was mixed in. No fuss, no waste.

Basic Smoothie

This smoothie is an almost-daily routine for me. It's the way that works best for me to get the three important foods I would tend to neglect otherwise — yogurt, banana, and berries. This recipe is also a safe starting point from which to wander with your own variations. The recipe below assumes you have a blender, but my smoothie mixer of choice is definitely the immersion blender.

(Makes about 2 cups)

1 ripe banana
½ cup frozen blueberries
1 cup plain yogurt or kefir
(**If necessary**, 1 – 3 teaspoons honey)

Using a regular blender:
1. Combine ingredients in any order in the blender and blend about 20 seconds at medium speed and about 20 seconds at high speed, or until smooth. (If you're lucky, you'll have a blender with a *smoothie* button.)

Using an immersion (stick) blender:
1. Combine all ingredients (in the order listed) in a 4-cup container. Blend at medium–high speed, but cautiously at first, keeping the blender head under the surface of the yogurt while poking the fruit gently with the blender until the mixture is broken down. **Keep a firm hold on the container:** the action of the blender is powerful. Within a minute the smoothie will be ready.

Note:
▸ Only add honey if you need to in order to enjoy the smoothie. Few of us can afford extra calories, and you may be surprised at how easy it is to adjust your sweet-meter.

Smoothie nutritional enhancements

Remember, *smoothies are not milkshakes!* Think of them as liquid power bars, but with all the benefits of fresh fruit and yogurt or kefir.

■ **Protein:** Yogurt and kefir already supply a lot of protein but an egg can be added for more protein, vitamins, and healthy fats. Under home conditions, we think the risk of salmonella from a raw egg is very small. (Pasteurized eggs are available for the extra cautious.) Some people like other protein sources like soft tofu or whey powder.

■ **Brewer's yeast:** This is a great source of protein, nucleic acids, B vitamins, selenium and chromium. Start with a teaspoon and see what you think of the flavor. (It's not live yeast, and can't multiply in your body or cause yeast infections.) I generally prefer it to the milder product called 'nutritional yeast' because brewer's yeast seems to have a better nutrient profile.

■ **Good fats:** A tablespoon of extra-virgin olive oil can be added to any smoothie, and will never be detected. A tablespoon of flaxseed meal (ground flaxseed) will add more fiber, lignans, and omega-3 fatty acids.

■ **Whole grain:** To add a cooked grain like brown rice (see page 170) or cooked oatmeal (see page 75) to a smoothie, combine only the yogurt and ½ cup of cooked grain first and blend them at a high speed for 20 seconds. (The grain breaks down more finely this way, and is less obvious in the finished smoothie.) Scrape down the sides and then add remaining ingredients and blend for another 20 seconds or until smooth.

■ **Vegetables:** Either fresh or cooked vegetables can be added to increase the fiber and overall vitamin and mineral content. Start with something mild, like ¼ cup of so of spinach or a fresh tomato. (Raw vegetables like carrots need a heavy-duty blender like the VitaMix for a smooth texture, of course.)

Turbo Smoothie
(Meal replacement)

A turbo smoothie is the answer to any situation where chewing is a problem (a dental crisis, for example) or time is short. If I am *really* in a hurry I just put a lid on the container and take it in the car with me.

(Makes about 2¾ cups)

½ – 1 apple, cored and chopped
1 ripe banana
½ cup frozen blueberries
1 cup plain yogurt or kefir
1 raw egg – optional
(1 – 3 teaspoons brewer's yeast – optional)

Using a regular blender:
1. Combine ingredients in any order in the blender and blend about 20 seconds at medium speed and about 20 seconds at high speed, or until smooth.

Using an immersion (stick) blender:
1. Combine all ingredients (in the order listed) in a 4-cup container. It may look impossibly chunky and too much for the container, but don't worry. Blend at medium–high speed, but cautiously at first, keeping the blender head under the surface of the yogurt while poking the chunks of fruit gently with the blender until the mixture is broken down. **Keep a firm hold on the container:** the action of the blender is powerful. Within a minute the smoothie will be ready.

Note:

▶ The tiny bits of apple skin are pretty inoffensive and the skin is a valuable part of the fruit, so think before you peel. (By the way, oranges are difficult for an immersion blender to blend smoothly.)

Prune Smoothie Pudding

This is a pleasant alternative to eating dried prunes neat. When Miles prescribes prunes for his patients, he usually recommends about ten per day, so this recipe fills the prescription nicely. This also makes a great baby food. Best eaten with a spoon.

(Makes about 1¼ cups)

1 cup plain yogurt or kefir
10 dried prunes

1. Combine yogurt and prunes in blender and blend for 30 seconds. Scrape down sides, and then blend for another 30 seconds. The mixture will be completely smooth, but if you want a pudding with no flecks of prune, blend 20 seconds longer.

Protein powders

It is difficult to see any reason to recommend any of the heavily processed protein powders, powdered diet shakes, and powdered nutrient concentrates. We are not aware of any studies using these in large populations over long periods of time, which is necessary to determine benefit or harm.

However, the more we learn about food and its effects on health, the more we realize the critical importance of the enormous spectrum and precise balance of nutrients *present only in whole foods*. Although many of the ingredients in these powdered products were originally whole food, almost all of the nutrients that would normally be present with that food have been lost in the processing.

You are much better off with a genuine whole food smoothie fortified with a genuine powdered food extract like brewer's yeast or whey powder. (See *Smoothie nutritional enhancements* on previous page.)

Meal replacement drinks

We often find it valuable to recommend meal replacement drinks; for elderly patients, for example, who have difficulty eating for various reasons, or post-surgical patients, or patients with cancer who are struggling to get enough food.

Good nutrition in a liquid form can be difficult to find in a commercial product, and the evidence argues that a heavily processed formula high in simple sugars and excessive pro-inflammatory omega 6 fatty acids is more likely to suppress a good immune response. Here is an ingredient list from a major brand: *Water, sugar (sucrose), corn maltodextrin, milk protein concentrate, soy oil, soy protein concentrate, canola oil, corn oil, natural and artificial flavors, soy lecithin, carrageenan, FD&C red #3.*

The best nutrition is from whole food sources, with their huge spectrum of micronutrients, including phenols and other anti-oxidants, nucleic acids, vitamins, minerals, fibers, healthy fats, proteins — and perhaps, just as importantly, those unknown nutrients that are present only in whole foods, not in their semi-synthetic or highly refined counterparts.

So, instead of buying a prepared meal replacement drink, consider switching to smoothies instead. By making your own yogurt and fruit smoothies you will usually get far less sugar, a better fat profile, whole food nutrients, and healthy probiotics to promote vigorous immunity. Plus, you'll save money.

There is an added bonus with smoothies in that anything you want to emphasize in the diet can be slipped in, including high-quality calories like extra-virgin olive oil or some added protein like an egg or some soft tofu. (See previous page.) Once you find a combination you like, you can make a large batch and freeze it in single serving containers.

Snacking Suggestions

Are you a snackaholic?

Snacking is such a problem for many of us that it is hard to remember sometimes that we are the aggressors. The snack is sitting quietly on the shelf, and would probably be perfectly happy to leave us alone but we insist on buying it, ripping it open and eating it, then acting like we were attacked. The wisest way to deal with snackaholism is firmly. You know what they are. **DON'T BUY THEM.**

If we make a point of always having a supply of healthy snacks that we like, we will find it a lot easier to maintain good eating habits. Find some options that work for you and don't obsess over the details. As long as we are eating good food, it's more important to enjoy whatever it is than to meet some kind of imagined criteria. (Of course, if weight is a problem, calories are a consideration.) Here are some suggestions.

■ Fruit

Fresh fruit comes in its own skin —ready-to-eat, naturally sweetened serving-sized packages. Apples, oranges, and bananas are always easily available. A handful of frozen grapes or blueberries, or frozen bananas can be waiting in the freezer, and are enjoyed by both kids *and* grown-ups. (Peel and freeze bananas *before* wrapping in plastic. See note on page 79.)

■ Vegetables

Some of our favorite combinations are baby carrots paired with sharp cheddar **cheese**, or broccoli with homemade ranch dressing (see page 99), or cucumber spears with **hummus**, or celery sticks stuffed with roasted **almond butter** or **peanut butter**. (Nut butters are perfectly good foods if you grind the nuts

yourself, which is easy to do at most natural food stores and some supermarkets.)

■ Raw nuts (especially almonds)

Raw almonds are a great snack option. (See page 16.) They can ride around in your pocket all day without making a mess, and a bag of almonds in your desk drawer is useful if your mind wanders toward food at the wrong time. A handful of raw almonds and raisins are a great combination. Keep a bowl of nuts in shell around the house. You will eat less if you have to crack them first. (Buy them from a good source. They taste awful when they're too old.)

■ Raw seeds

A handful of raw sunflower or pumpkin seeds are a sensible and satisfying snack. Buy them from a good source; like nuts, they can taste terrible if they're not fresh. Also like nuts, they taste even better mixed with raisins. Roasted and salted seeds are not a good choice unless you roasted them yourself.

■ Yogurt or yogurt smoothies

Yogurt is a remarkably healthy snack if you choose yogurt that is free of sugar (real or substitute) and without artificial flavoring and coloring. *The ingredient list is more important than the nutrition panel.* Yogurt is a simple food made up essentially of milk cultured with live organisms, and it's not meant to taste like pudding. Buy *plain* low-fat or full-fat yogurt and stir in whatever makes it taste good – like fresh fruit and honey. Smoothies made with yogurt and fruit are the easiest way to make yogurt taste delicious. (For more on yogurt, see page 21. For recipes, see pages 78-81.)

■ **Cottage cheese**
A natural cottage cheese (read the label) is wonderfully compatible with fresh fruit, vegetable sticks, or green salads.

■ **Green soybeans** *(Edamame)*
(See pages 158-59.) In or out of the pod, we like these freshly cooked or cold from the refrigerator — in a car, at a picnic, as an appetizer, in a salad, dressed or undressed.

■ **Canned beans**
Open, drain, and rinse a can of beans – black, white, red, whatever – and toss with 1½ tablespoons each of extra-virgin olive oil and apple cider vinegar, ¼-cup of minced onion, and ¼ - ½ teaspoon each of salt and pepper. Keep refrigerated and snack on as needed.

■ **Canned tuna**
You can just eat tuna directly from the can, or make some tuna salad (page 104), or serve over salad greens for an instant salad.

■ **Eggs, boiled, scrambled, or deviled**
A boiled egg can wait until you're ready to eat it (with salt and pepper, I hope) and a scrambled egg is a quickly made hot snack (cooked with salt and Tabasco, I hope). Deviled eggs are a *great* snack. (Page 106.)

■ **Whole grain muffin**
Whole grain (*100 percent!*) muffins with dried fruit and nuts are nutrition-dense yet sweet enough to satisfy the need for a treat. (See pages 234-38.)

■ **Brown rice cakes**
You can find quite a variety of sweet and savory crispy brown rice cakes in most supermarkets. A plain rice cake with roasted nut butter is tasty, especially after a brief spell in the toaster.

■ **Scottish oatcakes** (page 241.)
These barely sweet and rich cracker-like things will never be confused with Oreos, but some of us prefer them to *any* cookies. Keep them handy if you're trying to shake a cookie habit.

■ **Popcorn popped in extra-virgin olive oil**
Popcorn is a great snack. Our favorite popper is the *Stir Crazy* popcorn popper. Pop a cup of popcorn in ¼-cup of extra-virgin olive oil (don't shake your head until you've tried it), salt, and serve. The best we've had, and even good the next day.

■ **Brown Rice Power Patties** (page 174)
Make a batch of these nutty patties and store them in your refrigerator at home or at the office in zip lock bags, two per bag. One is a snack, two are lunch!

■ **Salmon (or Tuna) Cakes** (page 192)
These are good cold, warm, or hot, and have the confidence to step up and be a meal if asked. Patties keep happily in your refrigerator for a week.

■ **Marinated tofu**
You may think tofu is the last thing you would ever be caught eating by choice, but the tofu marinated in the deliciously explosive mixture on page 160 will probably change your mind.

■ **Sardine pâté**
Have you tried the recipe on page 105 yet? On little squares of buttered toast? Mmmm.

Are 'protein bars' healthy snacks?

Meal replacement bars of various kinds are hugely popular (as you can see by the expanse of retail shelf they take up!) and the reasons are poor. Most meal replacement or 'energy' bars are high in simple carbohydrates, often have suboptimal types of fat, and are generally expensive compared to whole foods.

We suggest whole food alternatives like raw nuts, dark chocolate (at least 70 percent cocoa), raw seeds like sunflower or pumpkin, and fresh fruit. (Dried fruit is not a substitute and should only be used in small quantities — it is a concentrated calorie source and probably encourages cavities.)

Lunch *and* Dinner

The prescription for maximum health and minimum risk calls for most of our daily intake to consist of whole foods like fruits and vegetables, beans, unrefined grains, and good fats. However, reality may be a full schedule and an empty kitchen. Working away from home can make lunch and dinner a challenge. Packing a lunch and limiting fast foods to special occasions are two important steps.

Avoid fast food

Picking up something on the way home can be a compelling argument that is hard to resist when you're hungry and tired, but don't give in too soon. Fast food doesn't have to compromise your eat-smarter-feel-better goals. Consider the many ready-to-eat and heat-and-serve options you can find at serious food retailers like New Seasons Market, Whole Foods Market, and Trader Joe's. In the history of civilization there has never been less excuse to eat well. Still, the value of preparing food from scratch can't be overstated in terms of health and financial benefits. Happily, toasted cheese and tomato sandwich are treats any of us can make with the most basic skills and tools.

Start cooking

If you're new to cooking it may be helpful to refer to *Pantry Basics* (pages 64) and *Useful Cooking Tools* (page 69). A few practical recipes to start with would be *Quick Little Black Bean Chili* (page 167), *Tuna Tetrazzini* (page 191), and *Green Eggs and Rice* (page 173). These are easy and make great leftovers. From a recipe like *Basic Baked Brown Rice* you can make any of the seven recipes for rice in the *Whole Grains* chapter (starting on page 169). Have a hard time making vegetables exciting? Check out the section on *Roasted Vegetables* (pages 123–28).

Eat more leftovers

Packed lunches don't have to be made to order. For cooks like me, leftovers are part of a grand strategy. Properly orchestrated leftovers take a lot of the work out of planning and cooking meals. Soups, casseroles, and chili can be reheated, and taste as good or better the next day.

Leftover polenta (page 183) can be sliced and reheated, and served topped with chili, or fried and eaten as a snack or appetizer. Leftover bean or grain salads are ready to eat straight from the refrigerator or at room temperature for days after they are made. A dish like *Tuna and Broccoli Pasta* (page 190) is great the next day at any temperature.

Three favorite leftovers for me are plain brown rice (tremendous versatility), polenta (most everyone likes fried polenta) and beans (taste the same leftover as fresh). Whether you deliberately or accidentally end up with leftovers, they will save you planning and kitchen time.

Discover whole grain salads

Salads made with grains are a smart way to combine complex carbohydrates with vegetables, and can be made in advance, languishing happily at room temperature. (There's generally no need to refrigerate a grain or pasta salad when you make it on the same day that you eat it.) They are happy to go with you to work and hang around until lunch.

Find a recipe you like – there are several in the *Whole Grains* chapter – or invent your own. One of my favorites is leftover brown rice with a diced tomato, a chopped hard-boiled egg, and either *Faux Ranch Dressing* (page 99) or *Garlic and Mustard Vinaigrette* (page 95), or leftover *Tuna Salad* (page 104), and enough salt and pepper to make it lively.

... and whole grain pasta

All kinds of whole grain pastas are available from natural food stores and supermarkets. There are pastas made from grains like corn, quinoa, soy, spelt, and brown rice as well as wheat. There is even sprouted wheat pasta, which got high marks from our tasters, although it broke up easily. I especially like brown rice pasta. It is a bit fragile but the flavor is mild and delicious and the texture is tender. Don't give up on whole grain pasta until you have found one or two that you like. Many people say they hardly notice a difference when they transition to whole wheat pasta.

Eat more beans

Beans with vinaigrette are a natural match, and it's unlikely any of us are too busy to drain a can of beans and toss them with vinegar, extra-virgin olive oil, salt and pepper. Even better, with some added diced onion and bell peppers and cilantro. Fresh frozen beans can be almost as spontaneous; baby lima beans cook in 7 minutes straight from the freezer. (*Luscious Lima Beans*, page 161) Home cooked beans are shockingly easy; you can cook up a different color and size every couple of weeks and prepare them in a dizzying number of ways. (See *Beans* chapter starting on page 153.)

Canned beans

On the subject of canned beans, *hummus* is an easy dip made with chickpeas, and a great lunch option with raw vegetables or in pita pocket sandwiches stuffed with grated carrot, cucumber, and tomato slices. (See *Hasty Tasty Hummus* on page 102.) *A Brisk Black Bean Thing* (page 101) is also easy.

I should add that both of these do have a significant garlic presence that may affect the atmosphere in the workplace. Bring enough to go around. *Hummus* is surprisingly popular once people actually try it. Ready-made hummus and all its variations are everywhere, as are recipes for hummus – but I hope you try mine.

Both beans and grains can be cooked ahead and stored in the refrigerator, and used in all kinds of combinations as you feel like it. They generally reheat with no effect on their texture or flavor, or can be served cold or at room temperature when transformed into salads. This makes them particularly heroic in last-minute meal scenarios.

Avoid the sandwich trap

The brutal truth is that the difference between white bread and most so-called whole wheat bread is color rather than fiber. It is even safe to say that the term 'whole grain bread' is meaningless without some clarification like '100 percent'.

As a general rule, deli sandwiches should be a rare indulgence. White bread is not legitimized by any amount of lettuce or tomato, but if you really must eat your sardine and onion sandwich on white bread, a loophole clause may be found.

... and preserved (processed) meats

This means the sliced deli meats that are so popular and convenient. If you can't lay your hands on sliced home-cooked meat, consider sandwich alternatives like cheese, chicken, tuna salad, or egg salad. You will get the same amount of protein but in a far better form. There is absolutely nothing good about modern preserved meats, but there is a lot that is worrisome.

Eat more tuna

You can buy single-portion rip-top cans of tuna that are perfect for personal snacks or meals, or just open a regular sized can and eat it over a couple of days. In our office a popular meal is a bowl of fresh baby spinach or mixed greens with a can of tuna tipped over it, with a splash of extra-virgin olive oil and vinegar, and freshly ground pepper. Tuna salad (see recipe on page 104) is a nutritionally optimal combination of good protein, good fat, and diced celery and onion, and is a great meal rolled up in a whole wheat pita round or tortilla. Canned tuna also expands your healthy dinner options greatly: you can use it in chowder, frittatas, fish cakes, noodle or rice casseroles, and so on. (See a few favorite tuna recipes beginning on page 189.) Tuna has also been found to be less environmentally toxic in an office lunchroom than sardines.

Give sardines a chance

Reputation-wise, sardines are a bit like liver; some people may think they actually exist only in the world of humor. A pity, because they're such nutrient-dense brain food, as well as rich in omega-3 oils, nucleic acid, and protein.

If you are new to sardines I suggest starting out with something like King Oscar Extra-Small Sardines "taken from the icy waters of Norway's purest fjords" (according to the label) and packed in olive oil in little cans with rip-off lids. If the sight of a small tail hanging off your fork might bother you, mash the sardines before you use them. Try them mashed on a thin slice of fresh whole wheat bread spread with butter or mayonnaise and sprinkled with salt and pepper. (See *Sardine Pâté* on page 105.)

Try kippered snacks if you don't like sardines. These are usually next to sardines on the grocery shelf and are tasty little smoked herring fillets that are ready to eat with a fork right out of the can. King Oscar makes a great kippered snack. (By the way, read labels carefully to make sure you don't accidentally end up with something packed in cottonseed oil.)

Avoid eating out regularly

(See *Eat out less* on page 29.)
For those of us working out of the home all week, it is easy to find ourselves eating out on a regular basis. To get away with this without gaining weight or losing our hard-won high density lipoproteins takes will, discipline, and imagination.

Don't compromise. Choose places that can offer some whole food options. Greek restaurants usually offer sides like hummus and tzatziki, sometimes served with tomato, cucumber and olives. Thai restaurants can serve up wonderful plates of vegetables, and Mexican restaurants can be sources of some whole food alternatives, like sides of black beans, pico de gallo, and fajitas with extra sauteed onions and bell peppers.

Restaurant tips

- Think about ordering from the appetizer menu – smaller servings, simpler foods. However, avoid trans fats by steering clear of fried, breaded or battered food. The coating is bad, the deep-frying is worse.

- Check the menu for options like sides of sautéed spinach or baked potato to replace sides like French fries. The restaurant may even create a side of their vegetables-of-the-day for you. Ask for brown rice or quinoa instead of white rice.

- Beware soups, sauces, dressings – these can hide lots of bad fats and sugars.

- When you're choosing a salad, pick one with the most colorful greens. When it comes to lettuce, darker green is better. Avoid trimmings like bacon bits, croutons, and roasted sunflower seeds.

- Ask for real butter. If a restaurant only has margarine, that's a bad sign.

- Just say **no** to soft drinks and fruit juice. Restrict alcohol to one drink if you're a woman or two drinks if you're a man. Skip the pre-dinner cocktail and order a tall glass of chilled sparking water with lemon instead.

- Even after choosing sensibly from a menu, we can neutralize our healthy choices by indulging in unhealthy extras that are hard to resist.

Menu for One Week

Suggesting a week's worth of dinners is relatively easy, but coming up with suggestions for breakfast, lunch, and snacks is an intimidating project. *Whose* breakfast, lunch, and snacks were we talking about? Some of us like routine but others need variety. Some need to eat snacks but some choose not to snack at all.

Furthermore, are these consumers working in an office building or at home? Do they have time to cook anything but the simplest dinner at night? Are they single or attached? With or without children?

Finally, what is in season? It is all very well to suggest asparagus and watermelon, but those menu items are impractical most of the year. Variables notwithstanding, a seven-day menu was done.

Make time for breakfast
It's a fact that people who eat breakfast find it easier to maintain a healthy weight than those who skip breakfast. And if you are going to eat breakfast, make it count: it's a good idea to include a serving of whole grains of some kind and at least one serving of fresh fruit. Some of us can eat the same thing every morning for years at a time, but for those of you who like variety there are lots of options. (See *Breakfast* starting on page 72.) It should be added that people who eat breakfast are less susceptible to the tender trap of a mid-morning snack.

Calories? We're not counting
The goal is not a number. The goal is simply to get as much good food in the form of whole grains, vegetables, and beans on your plate as possible. A side effect of this happens to be better numbers, whether you're standing on a scale or looking at your lab results.

Trying to lose weight?
If you have a weight problem, be more concerned about your intake of refined carbohydrates (products made with white flour or sugar) than you are about the healthy fat content in the whole foods you are eating. Don't let yourself fall into the low-fat mindset. Should you find yourself weakening, re-read *Fat is Good, Bagels are Bad* on page 10.

Good fat is the goal. Hidden sugar is the enemy. Cut out the calories from desserts, breads, pasta, potatoes, corn, sweet drinks, and juices. Cut back on serving sizes. Keep alcohol to a maximum of one serving daily. And exercise daily, if only for a few minutes at a time. (See page 30 for more on losing weight. See previous page for eating out tips.)

> "Of drinks and victuals and suchlike stuff, a bit too little's about enough."
>
> Piet Hein

There are no dessert suggestions
A serving of fruit is the best dessert. If our goal is optimum health and a sensible weight, there really is no place for the conventional notion of dessert, like cookies, pie, or ice cream. (...except for special occasions and holidays, of course.) If you stop having desserts, you will eventually stop missing desserts. That is a simple fact. On the other hand, if you stop having desserts *except* when you feel stressed or depressed, you are making it harder for yourself.

If you are serious about minimizing your risk factors and maximizing your health, clear the cookies out of the cupboard and the ice cream out of the freezer. If you can't find time for a walk every day, throw out your television, too. You'll be smarter as well as leaner and healthier.

Drinks

Sweet drinks with meals should be avoided. For a substitute, try chilled sparkling water. No calories, no sweetening, and it is available in handy 2-liter bottles in different natural flavors. (See pages 18-19.)

Leftovers

It's a good idea to aim to build your next meal on the last. This means (generally speaking) that a good lunch is always possible with no extra work, and dinner on the following night is much easier.

For example, you may serve *Easy, Cheesy Polenta* (page 184) with *Quick Little Black Bean Chili* (page 167) one night, and heat some up for lunch the next day. Any leftover chili could be served over hot brown rice and topped with a handful of grated sharp cheddar on another night. You can turn leftover rice into *Nutty Brown Rice* (page 172) or *Green Eggs and Rice* (page 173) on other nights that week.

When you cook meat, like *Roasted Chicken Thighs* (page 199) or *Meatloaf* (page 208), make enough for two meals. The meatloaf is just as good the second night re-heated with another couple of vegetables. You should only have to cook from scratch every other day or two. Cold chicken is a great lunch, but you could also take the meat off the bone and turn it into *Chicken Pot Pie* (page 201).

Disclaimer:

The seven days of meals in this section are not intended to represent an actual week. (My own breakfast, for example, is the same every morning.) The purpose is purely to offer ideas on how one might put into practice the principles of eating we have been talking about. Concepts like the practical use of leftovers have been only touched upon here; ideally, however, leftovers would logically play a much greater role in a sensible week's menu.

DAY ONE

Breakfast
- ☐ Orange or grapefruit
- ☐ Egg fried with sliced tomato
- ☐ Whole wheat toast

Mid morning snack
- ☐ ¼ cup mixed raw almonds and raisins

Lunch
- ☐ Whole wheat pita pocket with tuna salad
- ☐ apple or fruit in season

Afternoon snack
- ☐ 1 cup plain yogurt with banana

Evening meal
- ☐ *Quick Little Black Bean Chili* (page 167)
- ☐ *Easy Cheesy Polenta* (page 184)
- ☐ *Pico de Gallo* (page 131) *(or quick sticks of cucumber/celery/bell peppers)*

Chili and polenta are natural partners. *Easy Cheesy Polenta* tastes good by itself, and makes a filling and balanced meal with the chili. An alternative to the polenta is hot brown rice (page 171) topped with grated cheese. This combination is a quick and easy dinner to make an hour before you eat, especially if you happen to have leftover rice waiting in your refrigerator. *Pico de Gallo* goes well with this meal, or some little side dishes of diced onion, tomato, cucumber, and chopped fresh cilantro, or something as simple as sticks of fresh cucumber, bell pepper, and celery.

Both polenta and chili make wonderful leftovers. You can store chili in the refrigerator for days and reheat it for lunch or dinner served over brown rice or baked potatoes. Leftover polenta can be reheated and served with any sauce or stew, or sliced cold and fried in extra-virgin olive oil.

DAY TWO

Breakfast
- ❑ Banana or fruit in season
- ❑ Oatmeal: hot (rolled or steel cut – see page 75-6) *or* cold (page 77)

Mid morning snack
- ❑ Celery or carrot sticks with sharp cheddar cheese

Lunch
- ❑ Whole wheat pita pocket with hummus and sliced cucumber and tomato
- ❑ orange

Afternoon snack
- ❑ ¼ cup *Seductive Soy Beans* **or** ½ cup cooked *Soybeans in the Pod* (page 158-9)

Evening meal
- ❑ *Tuna Tetrazzini* (page 191)
- ❑ *Last-minute Green Beans* (page 115)

A creamy, brightly-flavored tuna noodle casserole is a dependably popular comfort food liked by most kids and grown ups, but also a natural vehicle for omega-3 rich tuna, vegetables, and whole grain pasta. It can be made a day in advance and chilled, then brought to room temperature before baking.

Warm green beans in vinaigrette contrast nicely with the rich casserole. If you're forced to throw yourself on the mercy of your freezer, you could try baby green beans or the skinny little *haricot verts* available in the frozen vegetable section of some stores. The flavor and texture is naturally never as good as fresh, but slim crisp green beans are rarely available. My solution is to toss the beans in vinaigrette.

Alternative:
A last minute one-dish meal like *Tuna and Broccoli Pasta* is a good alternative – and you can buy the broccoli in ready-to-use florets.

DAY THREE

Breakfast
- ❑ Basic smoothie (see page 79)
- ❑ *Serious Muffin* (page 235)

Mid morning snack
- ❑ Hard boiled egg, halved and salted and peppered **or** deviled egg (page 106)
- ❑ orange

Lunch
- ❑ Cheese and tomato sandwich on whole wheat bread, grilled or plain
- ❑ apple or fruit in season

Afternoon snack
- ❑ handful of raw almonds
- ❑ banana

Evening meal
- ❑ *Roasted Chicken Thighs* (page 199)
- ❑ *Quick Brown Rice Pilaf* (page 172)
- ❑ *Butternut Squash Purée* (page 144)
- ❑ *Tossed Green Salad* (page 132)

A minimum-effort-maximum-effect type dinner that is pretty safe with any audience: hot roasted chicken thighs sitting on a bed of rice, a scoop of bright butternut purée, and a vivid green salad. Thighs are my favorite chicken body part both to eat and to prepare, and cooking it with skin and bone intact is best for the meat. You can also turn it into a very simple meal by roasting some vegetables in the same pan as the chicken. Roasting a whole chicken is an option if you want the mix of white and brown meat or just need the wishbone.

Alternative:
An easier alternative to pilaf would be just plain rice. *Marinated Carrot Matchsticks* (page 148) is a good substitute for the squash. (The marinated carrots could then double as salad.)

DAY FOUR

Breakfast
- ❑ Orange
- ❑ Hot whole grain cereal (oatmeal, cracked rye, polenta, buckwheat, millet)

Mid morning snack
- ❑ 1 cup plain yogurt with honey and chopped fruit

Lunch
- ❑ Leftover chicken or chicken salad
- ❑ Slice of buttered whole wheat bread

Afternoon snack
- ❑ Apple

Evening meal
- ❑ *Green Eggs and Rice* (page 173)
- ❑ *Marinated Carrot Matchsticks* (page 148)

Green Eggs and Rice is a meatless main dish that begs for all kinds of variations and substitutions. You can stir the ingredients together in the morning or at the last. You can make it unctuous with extra cheese and rich milk or you can add extra vegetables like chopped cooked broccoli.

I like to pair *Green Eggs and Rice* with a marinated vegetable or substantial salad to make sure people get enough to eat. An alternative to the marinated carrots would be *A Greek Salad* (page 134) or even something more substantial like *Warm Lentil Salad* (page 166). You're free to work on a salad or vegetable once you put *Green Eggs and Rice* in the oven.

Alternative
Other brown rice main dish options are *Kedgeree* on page 193 and *Mexican Brown Rice with Black Beans* on page 175.

DAY FIVE

Breakfast
- ❑ Grapefruit
- ❑ Egg scrambled with cheese and tomato
- ❑ Whole wheat toast

Mid morning snack
- ❑ Celery sticks with *hummus* (page 102) or *Definitive Dip* (page 100)

Lunch
- ❑ *Tuna Salad* (page 104) in pita pocket
- ❑ Pear or peach

Afternoon snack
- ❑ 2 brown rice cakes with almond butter

Evening meal
- ❑ *Black Bean Polenta* (page 211)
- ❑ *Napa Cabbage Salad with Cilantro* (page 132)

Black Bean Polenta is an easy vegetarian meal featuring layered polenta, cheese, and black beans with a bright salsa accent. It can be prepared an hour ahead or a day or more ahead. Once *Black Bean Polenta* is put together, it technically only requires heating. So whether you bake it as a casserole or take a serving to work to heat for lunch, it works just as well. *Pico de Gallo* (page 131) is another particularly good accompaniment: the flavors are harmonious but the crunch is a refreshing contrast to the richness of the polenta.

Alternative
Another vegetarian option would be the *Spinach and Cheese Crêpes* (page 212) with *Tomato Sauce* (page 109). I would serve the crêpes with asparagus in season, or steamed broccoli and cauliflower florets tossed in *Garlic and Mustard Vinaigrette* (page 95) as a sort of warm vegetable salad.

DAY SIX

Breakfast
- ❑ *Oatmeal Pancakes* (page 74) with butter and pure maple syrup
- ❑ Plain yogurt with fresh fruit

Mid morning snack
- ❑ Carrot sticks with sharp cheddar cheese **or** leftover *pico de gallo* with ½ cup cottage cheese

Lunch
- ❑ *Tabbouleh* (page 178) with chickpeas **or** leftover *Black Bean Polenta*
- ❑ Apple or cluster of grapes

Afternoon snack
- ❑ Popcorn (popped with extra-virgin olive oil – see page 83)

Evening meal
- ❑ *Tuna and Broccoli Pasta* (page 190)
- ❑ *Fresh Tomato Salad* (page 129)

Tuna and Broccoli Pasta is a fast feast. When a dish is this simple, though, it can be easy to ruin by being casual about the details. Every ingredient matters. The only real work is slicing the florets off the broccoli stalks, and that could easily be done in advance. For the pasta I would suggest a spiral-type shape; something with plenty of surface to catch the sauce. This is good eaten cold the next day with a bit of added vinaigrette. The *Fresh Tomato Salad* here is an easy partner but even easier would be just sliced fresh tomatoes salted and peppered and drizzled with extra-virgin olive oil.

Alternative
The *Kedgeree* on page 193 is another tuna-based one-dish option. Also, you could replace the tuna in this dish with bite-sized cooked chicken.

DAY SEVEN

Breakfast
- ❑ Orange
- ❑ *Fast Frittata with Tomato and Onion* (page 74)
- ❑ Whole wheat toast

Mid morning snack
- ❑ 1 banana

Lunch
- ❑ 2 *Brown Rice Power Patties* (page 174) **or** leftover *Tuna and Broccoli Pasta*

Afternoon snack
- ❑ ¼ cup raw sunflower seeds and raisins

Evening meal
- ❑ *Crowded Chowder* (page 194)
- ❑ *Little Whole Wheat Honey Loaf* (page 220)
- ❑ *Apple, Broccoli, and Celery Salad* (page 130)

Main dish soups like this Crowded Chowder (which can be fish or clam or vegetarian) are options that work especially well for the times when I think I can smell smoke from my brain, but I'm committed to producing dinner (or lunch). When everything goes in one pot, there is much less to go wrong, and one is less likely to run into timing issues with side dishes. Make sure the bread you serve is truly 100 percent whole grain, preferably something like *Millet Bread* (page 224) or *Brown Rice Bread* (page 226) or *Bulgur and Oat Bread* (page 227).

Alternative
A great alternative to chowder is my version of *Tom Kah Gai* (page 196), which is a shockingly loose translation of the Thai chicken soup by the same name, and also one of the fastest and easiest emergency meals I know. *Napa Cabbage Salad with Cilantro* (page 132) or *Carrot Slaw* (page 133) would be alternative salads.

Favorite
7 Bits *and* Pieces

Vinaigrette

Vinaigrette is one of the most useful items you can have on hand. It is an instant source of flavor, a best friend of vegetables, easy to tweak in any ethnic direction, and can be always waiting on the other side of the refrigerator door. You can create it at the last minute directly in your mixing bowl and just add your salad or vegetables, or you can make a couple of cups at a time and use it for weeks. It's a simple process using basic ingredients, and is particularly gratifying for a cook who values maximum effect for minimum effort.

Vinaigrette on just about anything

Just about any collaboration of vegetables, fruit, grains, beans, pasta, and meat will benefit from an encounter with good vinaigrette. With the help of some freshly grated Parmesan, this vinaigrette will turn a head of romaine lettuce into an unforgettable tossed salad that can be a first course in its own right. (See recipe on page 132.)

It will dress up leftover brown rice (some minced celery and onion doesn't hurt) and the dowdiest canned beans, should they have to make an unscheduled appearance at the table. Toss whole mushrooms in some vinaigrette and you will have a succulent and delicious antipasto dish within a half-hour. (They turn dark and pickled by the next day, but they still taste good.) Vinaigrette will also pinch hit as a marinade for meat.

Cooked vegetables with vinaigrette

One of vinaigrette's most valuable contributions is in the area of vegetable consumption. Some children (and grownups) who may have a hard time getting excited about eating cooked vegetables will veritably *gobble* steamed or roasted broccoli, cauliflower, carrot, asparagus, and green beans if they are served dressed in vinaigrette. Even Brussels sprouts, beets, rutabagas, and turnips can be appetizing (well, in small pieces) with some help from vinaigrette. Some of the sturdier vegetables are improved after a night in vinaigrette, especially the less popular root vegetables like beets, which tend to be more enjoyable marinated or pickled, anyway.

Once vegetables have been tossed with vinaigrette they can be served at any temperature, which removes a lot of pressure from mealtimes. If temperature isn't an issue, you can blanch, steam, or roast vegetables whenever time allows; apply the vinaigrette; then move on to any part of the menu that may not be so flexible. They even taste good the next day. (Note that broccoli and green beans tend to turn a brownish-yellow by that time, however.)

Make it ahead

Vinaigrette technically lasts indefinitely if kept cold, but it does taste better when it is younger. If you store the vinaigrette in a glass jar in the refrigerator, in time the oil will solidify on top, which means you have to bring the whole bottle to room temperature to recombine it. It will return to a liquid relatively quickly once it begins to respond to the warmer atmosphere, but the warming-and-chilling routine won't be necessary if you follow my suggestion in the first **Note** below the recipe for *Garlic and Mustard Vinaigrette* on the next page.

Last-minute vinaigrette

The simplest vinaigrette can be made by combining vinegar, oil, salt, and pepper in a bottle and shaking it, or directly in a mixing bowl. (Taking the time to add a freshly crushed clove of garlic is worth the trouble.) Then all you do is add a few cups of hot beans or cooked grains or vegetables. Instant gratification. (See examples of this method with *Pico de Gallo* on page 131 or *Luscious Limas* on page 161 or *Tabbouleh* on page 178.)

Garlic and Mustard Vinaigrette

There is usually a diminishing bottle of this all-purpose vinaigrette in our refrigerator. If not, I can put it together quickly with ingredients I always have on hand. There is something about this combination that works, and I think it is both the satisfying roundness and intensity of the flavor. We splash it on just about anything that will stand still long enough to be tossed and eaten.

(Makes about 1 cup)

¼ cup apple cider vinegar
1 tablespoon freshly crushed garlic
1 tablespoon whole grain mustard
1 tablespoon honey
1 teaspoon salt
1 teaspoon freshly ground pepper

¾ cup extra-virgin olive oil

1. Combine all ingredients except olive oil in a 2-cup measuring jug and whisk thoroughly. (The honey will dissolve quickly.)

2. Slowly add olive oil in a thin stream, whisking steadily. *If oil begins to collect on top, stop pouring and whisk until oil has been blended.*

3. Transfer to a glass jar and store in your refrigerator. (*See* **Note.**) You can refrigerate the vinaigrette for weeks to use as needed. It will separate after a while, so blend it well each time before you use it.

Note:

▸ Hand-whisked vinaigrette may separate fairly quickly depending upon how vigorously you whisk. You will find it more user friendly (especially for last-minute needs) to divide the recipe into ¼-cup portions immediately after blending it. Recycled glass spice jars work well, or little Rubbermaid ½-cup containers.

▸ **If you use an immersion blender**, which I do, turn the speed to a low setting so the vinaigrette won't thicken too much before all the oil is blended in, and place the container on a damp cloth to keep it from dancing around. You can add the oil faster than with the hand-whisked method. You will create a creamy and more stable emulsion that will usually remain pourable even when chilled.

▸ A mini-processor also works well for vinaigrette: process everything but the oil for 10 seconds, and then add the oil and process for another 10 – 15 seconds.

▸ With my pepper grinder, about 60 grinds gives me a teaspoon of ground pepper. I never bother to measure.

▸ Don't forget that you will probably still need to add salt and pepper to whatever it is you are dressing with the vinaigrette.

Lemon and Cumin Vinaigrette

This simple little dressing can turn a can of beans (rinsed and well drained) and ½ cup of minced sweet onion into a respectable little side dish. Some chopped fresh cilantro is a magnificent addition. Even if you don't have any lemon and use apple cider vinegar instead, the presence of cumin, chili, and Tabasco will handle the situation.

(Makes about ⅓ cup)

2 tablespoons lemon juice
½ teaspoon ground cumin
½ teaspoon chili powder
½ teaspoon salt
¼ teaspoon Tabasco sauce
1 teaspoon honey
1 teaspoon freshly crushed garlic
3 tablespoons extra-virgin olive oil

Combine all ingredients in a small mixing bowl and whisk for about 15 seconds or until honey is blended.

Mayonnaise

Mayonnaise is one of the world's most useful foods. It is actually a noble sauce in its own right, but it also adapts instantly to flavors like curry, mustard, chutney, pickles, horseradish, anchovies, herbs, and even fruit. Best of all, it adapts to fresh garlic, as in *aioli*. (See *Rich Yogurt Aioli* on page 98.)

Remember that mayonnaise falls in the category of good fat **if it's made with good oil**. (See page 17.) We have chosen a combination of one part extra-virgin olive oil to two parts extra-light olive oil. (The flavor of the olive oil dominates if you use much more of the extra-virgin.)

Mayonnaise is easy to make, once you get your confidence. You can even make it with a whisk, if you really can't think of something more important to do. It is virtually foolproof if the directions in the recipe are followed.

The recipe here uses an immersion blender, which means you can make the mayonnaise in the same container it is stored in. (That is significant. The clean-up has always been the only real work to making mayonnaise.) Also, with the intense beating action of an immersion blender, you can use whole eggs instead of just the yolks. Even so, the mayonnaise often becomes too stiff well before all the oil is blended in.

If you make the mayonnaise in a food processor, the mayonnaise will have a softer texture. If you want a stiff texture, use only the yolks. If the processor bowl is too big, the blades may not engage enough mixture to form an emulsion. It works best in a mini-workbowl like the one that comes with the KitchenAid food processor. (Store spare egg whites in the refrigerator until you can make a batch of *Coconut Macaroons* on page 243.)

Mayonnaise
(using an immersion blender)

(Makes about 2 cups)

2 eggs
2 tablespoons apple cider vinegar
2 teaspoons whole grain mustard
1 teaspoon salt

½ cup extra-virgin olive oil
1 cup extra-light olive oil *or* canola oil

1. Combine eggs, vinegar, mustard, and salt in a bottle or container with a 3-cup capacity and a neck big enough to fit the business end of the immersion blender. Set the bottle on a wet cloth to help keep it from spinning as you blend.

2. Blend at medium high speed for about 15 seconds. **Keep a firm hold on the container:** the action of the blender is powerful. Then, with the machine running, add the combined oils in a very thin, steady stream. Once mayonnaise has thickened you can add oil faster. It will probably get too thick before the oil is all in; just drop the speed to medium low and use a mixing action with the blender stick to add the remaining oil in two batches, holding the container firmly with the other hand. It works fine.

3. That's it. The finished mayonnaise should be stiff enough to mound on a spoon. Just stick a lid on the container or jar you made it in. It can be stored for several weeks if kept cold and sealed.

Note:

▸ *Best Foods* **real** mayonnaise is a fine stand-in for emergencies. (Not "reduced fat"!)

▸ If your mayonnaise separates, pour into a 2-cup measuring jug. Beat 2 egg yolks, and then beat in failed mayonnaise in driblets.

Yogurt
In dips and sauces

Yogurt is best known as a good source of friendly bacteria that fortify the immune system, but it's also nutrient-rich, calcium-rich, and protein-rich. Even people with lactose intolerance can usually eat yogurt because the bacteria that turn milk into yogurt gobble up a lot of the lactose in the process. (See page 21 and 78). Even if yogurt didn't have a virtually legendary nutritional profile, I would still use it for the dips and sauces on the following pages – nothing but yogurt has the rich-but-clean-flavored ability to fit in just about anywhere in the diet.

Which yogurt?

All yogurts were not created equal, so buy a yogurt in which the only ingredients are milk and acidophilus with other live cultures. Natural yogurts with live cultures will cost more than the common supermarket brands, but if you consider yogurt a nutritional supplement, which it is, it's worth buying the best.

Our favorite is *Nancy's*, a genuinely natural yogurt made in Springfield, Oregon. As a rule, avoid mass-market brands. Even the unsweetened and unflavored versions generally include ingredients like gelatin and cornstarch, which keep yogurt from naturally separating and create a smooth texture.

How fat?

Yogurt made with whole milk has richer flavor, better texture, and is less tart— advantages to consider if introducing someone to yogurt for the first time. You may even find unhomogenized whole milk yogurt with a layer of cream on top. Low-fat yogurt is sold everywhere, though, and it is our usual preference.

To Drain Yogurt

Naturally made yogurt begins separating as soon as you dip a spoon into it, and the draining continues until the yogurt is gone. Draining the whey from the yogurt gives it a thick, smooth texture that makes it much more versatile. You can use it as a substitute for the sour cream, or even cream cheese, if you leave it long enough. (It is sometimes called "yogurt cheese".) Some even use drained yogurt as a replacement for mayonnaise, spreading it on bread and adding it to tuna salad. I mainly use drained yogurt with the dips and sauces on the next few pages.

(Makes about 1 – 1½ cups drained yogurt)

1. Scoop 2½ cups yogurt into a 3-cup strainer lined with a disposable, basket-style coffee filter or even a paper towel. (You can also buy an official yogurt drainer in some stores.) Remember that additives like gelatin and cornstarch will inhibit draining.

2. Aim to drain the yogurt for *at least* 1½ hours on the kitchen counter or in the refrigerator, but for a very thick and creamy texture drain the yogurt in the refrigerator overnight. In 12 hours you will end up with a scant cup of yogurt cheese. Save the liquid that is drained off. Yogurt whey is tart and refreshing; I drink it, but you can also add it to soup or a smoothie.

Note:

▸ If you sweeten the thick, drained yogurt with honey and soften the edges with a couple of tablespoons of cream, it is spectacular with fresh fruit or fruit desserts.

Rich Yogurt *Aioli*
(Goop)

This has always been known as *Goop* among family and friends. The name has neither dignity nor appetizing connotations, but it is what has become my culinary signature. Goop is a distant cousin to *aioli* (*eye-OH-lee*), which is the famous garlic-infused mayonnaise of the Provence region in France.

In this version mayonnaise is a proportionately-small (although important) part of the sauce. Its main role is to provide richness. Yogurt provides the main character. The French would be appalled by the presumption, but in any case it is used as an *aioli* substitute in our house.

It is thick and creamy when made with drained yogurt (see preceding page) and usually tongue-biting if I can lay my hands on enough good, fresh garlic. Good garlic is the key to good goop. I generally use more than my recipe calls for because I like to err on the side of **yowza!** Furthermore, you just never know who might need to have their sagging immune system boosted.

It should be added that there is nothing wrong with classic all-mayonnaise *aioli*. Mayonnaise made with good oil is good food. (My recipe is on page 96.) We much prefer the taste of the yogurt version, however, and we consider yogurt an important food in its own right. (See *Yogurt* on preceding page and also page 21 and 78.)

Goop is especially good with roasted vegetables (page 123), steamed vegetables, raw vegetables, and salad vegetables — and goop can single-handedly justify the existence of the baked potato. We also serve it as a sauce for fish (or any seafood, for that matter) as well as meat loaf or roast beef or chicken, or any rich meat dishes.

Goop
(Rich Yogurt Aioli)

Even though I call for 2½ cups of yogurt, the final volume is closer to 1 cup after it is drained overnight. Some folks (including me) enjoy goop made from yogurt that has only drained for a few hours; it is more refreshingly potent when its texture is not too thick.

(Makes about 2 cups)

2½ cups *Nancy's* low-fat yogurt
½ cup mayonnaise
1 tablespoon freshly crushed garlic
½ teaspoon of salt
½ teaspoon freshly ground pepper

1. Drain yogurt for at least 3 hours in a strainer lined with a basket-style coffee filter. (See *Draining Yogurt* on page 97.) You will probably end up with a bit more than 1 cup of drained yogurt.

2. Stir remaining ingredients into drained yogurt and mix well. Store in the refrigerator. It keeps well for over a week but the garlic loses some intensity. It's best when eaten within a few days.

Note:

▸ The proportion of yogurt to mayonnaise may vary in either direction but there must be enough garlic to raise eyebrows, and enough salt and pepper to round out the flavor. The freshly ground pepper is very important; about 30 grinds should give you close enough to a half-teaspoon.

▸ The longer you have allowed the yogurt to drain the thicker the goop. If you want the texture of thick ranch dressing, allow yogurt to drain just a couple of hours. For a very sturdy goop you will need to drain the yogurt about 12 hours.

Faux Ranch Dressing
with Yogurt and Garlic

This mixture serves two purposes for me: it makes food taste better and it gets more yogurt into the diet. Variations of this sauce can be used as dressing for salads or a sauce for any cooked vegetables, especially baked potatoes. This is very basic, which suits me, but it takes well to variations. However, don't be stingy with the garlic, salt, and pepper. If it isn't punchy, it just won't work.

(Makes about 2½ cups)

2 cups of plain yogurt (low fat or whole milk
¼ - ½ cup mayonnaise
2–3 teaspoons freshly crushed garlic
½ teaspoon of salt, or to taste
½ teaspoon freshly ground pepper

1. Stir all ingredients together. (Don't use the blender or food processor – they will break down the yogurt and make it too thin.) Store in refrigerator and

Note:

▸ I suggest starting with the smaller quantity of mayonnaise (homemade or equal quality). If the dressing tastes too stringent to you, add the extra mayonnaise. A little richness helps balance the garlic, as well.

▸ You can also adjust this dressing with additions like a tablespoon or so of vinegar, finely minced green onion, a half-teaspoon of something like celery seeds, and so forth. You might even find that a teaspoon of honey or sugar rounds out the flavor in a way that makes this a more useful dressing. (Honey is better but it isn't easy to stir in.)

Tzatziki (tzort of)
Yogurt Sauce *with* Cucumber and Garlic

I like this best served with fresh or grilled pita bread and the hummus (on page 102). You can also use it as a refreshing sauce or salad with rich meat dishes (see note about *raita* below). As a dip it should have a noticeable garlic presence. I suggest draining both yogurt and cucumber for the best results, but it's certainly optional or adjustable, depending on schedule or taste.

(Makes about 2½ cups)

2 cups plain yogurt (whole milk or low fat)
1 medium to large cucumber
1 teaspoon salt
(¼ teaspoon for salting cucumber)
1 tablespoon extra-virgin olive oil
1– 2 teaspoons freshly crushed garlic

1. Drain the yogurt for at least an hour in a strainer lined with a basket-style coffee filter. You will probably end up with about 1½ cups yogurt and almost ½ cup of liquid. *(If you would like a thicker consistency, drain yogurt overnight.)*

2. Peel, seed and grate cucumber. Place in a colander and sprinkle with ¼ teaspoon salt. Set aside for about 30 minutes and then press out excess liquid.

3. Mix together olive oil, garlic, salt, and yogurt, and blend with cucumber.

Note:
▸ If you would like a sort of *raita*, the Indian salad, add ¼ teaspoon ground cumin, about 1 cup fresh diced tomatoes, and ½ cup diced mild onion or green onions.

Definitive Dip

This is a sprightly but rich-tasting dip with the freshness of parsley, the punch of garlic, and the satisfying note of cheddar. It is remarkable how many garlic-wary people have enjoyed this dip without commenting on the garlic. The reason may be that there are so many flavors jostling for attention that the garlic just falls back into the crowd. Or maybe it is countered by the intense parsley presence. Whatever the reason, it seems to work.

(Makes about 2½ cups)

1 bunch minced fresh parsley
2 cups plain yogurt, **drained**
½ cup mayonnaise
2 cups grated extra-sharp cheddar
1 tablespoon freshly crushed garlic
1 tablespoon lemon juice
1 teaspoon salt
½ teaspoon Tabasco sauce
¼ teaspoon curry powder

1. Drain yogurt at least 3 hours, and overnight if possible. You will end up with about a cup of drained yogurt. (See page 97 for more detail.)

2. Wash parsley well, spin or blot dry, and discard stems. Process in food processor for about 15 seconds or until finely minced. (Leave parsley in processor. You should have at least 1 cup.)

3. Add drained yogurt and the remaining ingredients to the minced parsley and process until smooth. *If you mix this dip by hand, make sure the cheese is grated finely enough to blend in smoothly.* This dip is best eaten the same day, before it is chilled. (It will thicken when chilled.)

Guacamole

We probably can't do much to reduce America's consumption of tortilla chips, but a good guacamole can help offset the damage, while still tasting decadent enough to fool the consumer. What actually constitutes a good guacamole is a matter of opinion, and *this* opinion favors a simple combination of ingredients with strong notes of lime juice and garlic.

(Makes about 2 – 3 cups)

2 – 3 ripe avocados
2 – 3 tablespoons lime/lemon juice
1 teaspoon Tabasco sauce, or to taste
½ – 1 teaspoon freshly crushed garlic
½ teaspoon salt

Optional:
¼ cup minced mild onion
¼ cup chopped fresh cilantro

1. Slice avocados in half lengthwise. Remove peel and seed. Dice and then mash roughly in a bowl. *(Try to avoid baby food consistency. Some texture in the finished dip is nice, so I start by dicing the avocado first; by the time the other ingredients have been mixed in, the guacamole is pretty smooth, yet with some recognizable bits of avocado.)*

2. Make a separate mixture of lime or lemon juice, Tabasco sauce, garlic, and salt. Blend gently but thoroughly with avocado. Set on table with very good tortilla or pita chips and stand back.

Note:
▸ An alternative to guacamole, just as tasty but more versatile, is the *Avocado Salsa* on page 131.

Tofu Pâté
(or Faux Egg Salad)

For this recipe use extra firm tofu, which can be found in 5- and 10-ounce packets. Prepared this way, tofu pâté makes a convincing stand-in for egg salad. You could also use extra firm tofu to extend egg salad if you don't have enough eggs. (Tofu is soy bean curd – for more about soy beans and tofu, see pages 158-9.)

(Makes about 1½ cups)

5 ounces extra firm tofu
⅓ cup mayonnaise
½ cup finely minced celery
¼ cup finely minced onion
½ teaspoon salt
½ teaspoon prepared mustard
¼ teaspoon freshly ground pepper
⅛ teaspoon curry powder

1. Pat tofu dry with a paper towel. Mince tofu finely, or grate on the medium holes of a box grater, or dice and pulse in food processor until it looks finely minced.

2. Mix with mayonnaise, celery, onion, and seasoning, and mash together thoroughly. Serve as a dip for crackers or pita crisps, or as a filling for pita bread, or as a sandwich spread.

Note:

▶ It is shocking but true that vacuum-packed extra firm tofu can be perfectly fine after several months in your refrigerator, unopened. I have found tofu to still smell and taste fresh even after 10 months beyond use-by date, so test before you toss.

A Brisk Black Bean Thing

Whether you mash the beans or leave them whole, this is a great little side dish to serve when you find yourself with a ragged smorgasbord of leftovers, even if you don't have fresh cilantro. A good companion for guacamole and salsa, whether you serve it in the form of a dip or as a simple little bean relish to eat with a fork.

(Makes about 2 cups)

1 can (15 ounce) black beans
¼ - ½ cup finely minced mild onion
2 tablespoons lemon or lime juice
2 – 3 tablespoons extra-virgin olive oil
½ teaspoon freshly crushed garlic
½ teaspoon chili powder
½ teaspoon ground cumin
½ teaspoon salt
¼ - ½ teaspoon Tabasco sauce
¼ cup chopped fresh cilantro

1. Drain and rinse beans and set aside. Mince onion (use smaller amount if onion is not mild) and place in a mixing bowl, and add lemon or lime juice, oil, garlic, and seasonings. Add beans and cilantro (if you have it) and toss thoroughly.

Note:

▶ For a dip-able or spreadable texture, mash the beans or the whole mixture with a fork until you're happy with it. I like to mash roughly enough so that the beans are still recognizable and the onions are still crunchy.

▶ If you want something more salad-y, add finely diced celery and red or green bell peppers.

Hasty, Tasty Hummus
(Chickpea Dip)

Don't say you dislike hummus until you've tried this recipe. It is best eaten right after it's made — creamy, rich, and almost warm. Hummus is delicious as a dip for raw vegetables like carrot and celery, or pita bread, or as a spread in a vegetarian sandwich.

There are countless ways to make hummus and perhaps as many ways to spell it. (You can even buy powdered hummus but I've never wanted to get close enough to read the actual ingredients or instructions.) Few recipes call for a respectable amount of garlic, but *this one does!*

(Makes about 2½ cups)

1 can (15 ounces) chickpeas
¼ cup lemon juice
¼ cup tahini (raw or roasted)
¼ cup extra-virgin olive oil
1 tablespoon freshly crushed garlic
½ teaspoon salt
⅛ teaspoon ground cumin
¼ cup boiling water

1. Drain chickpeas thoroughly. (No need to rinse.) Combine drained chickpeas and all the ingredients except the water in a food processor and blend until smooth.

2. With the processor running, pour in the boiling water. The texture should be thick but creamy and pourable. (It will thicken more in the refrigerator.) Taste and adjust the flavor to suit yourself . . . but make sure it's *spunky*. If it's too beany it's boring.

3. Eat while freshly-made, if possible. Hummus keeps well in the refrigerator for at least a week.

Note:

▸ Tahini is sesame seed paste, and you can usually find it in supermarkets as well as natural food stores. I try to find a jar with the thinnest layer of oil on top. (The longer the tahini has been sitting, the more oil will rise to the surface, and the harder the paste will be.) Store in the refrigerator.

Roasted Chickpeas

For another tasty treatment of chickpeas — with *no garlic* — try this simple idea. Nice appetizer to serve with olives. This is a small recipe – I would double it.

(Makes about 1¼ cups)

1 can (15 ounces) chickpeas
1 tablespoon extra-virgin olive oil
¼ teaspoon ground cumin or curry powder
¼ teaspoon freshly ground pepper
¼ teaspoon salt

Preheat oven to 450 degrees.

1. Rinse and thoroughly drain chickpeas.

2. In a small mixing bowl, combine olive oil with cumin or curry powder, freshly ground pepper, and salt. Add chickpeas and toss.

3. Spread in a single layer in a shallow foil-lined baking pan and roast for about 20 – 30 minutes or until toasty. Shake pan now and them.

Note:

▸ If your oven isn't available, sauté chickpeas in one layer in a sturdy skillet over medium-high heat. Cook until chickpeas begin to brown, about 20 – 30 minutes, shaking pan now and then.

Pita Crisps

Pita crisps stand in nicely for commercially made chips and crisps and are certainly worth the ridiculously small effort they demand. You can make a more exotic version with herbs or spices or sprinkles of Parmesan and so forth, but I rarely do. This recipe is simple and has few ingredients because I'm usually making them when I'm too busy to feel ambitious.

Sometime it's hard to find whole wheat pita pockets, but even if you use pitas made with white flour it will *still* be a better snack than most commercial crackers.

(Makes about 80 crisps)

1 package whole wheat pita bread (about 5 pitas – see *Note*)
½ cup extra-virgin olive oil
salt
freshly ground pepper

(¼ teaspoon dried thyme, *optional*)

Preheat oven to 300 degrees. Lay out baking sheet.

1. Split each pita into 2 disks (kitchen scissors are the easiest way to separate the rounds) and lay them out with insides facing up.

2. Brush each round lightly with oil, and sprinkle with salt and a swift swish of freshly ground pepper over each one. (See **Note**.)

3. Slice each pita round into 8 wedges and place on *ungreased* baking sheets. (You'll probably need two.)

4. Bake in the middle of the 300-degree oven for about 20- 30 minutes, or until the wedges turn golden brown.

5. Serve pita crisps as you would potato chips, as an appetizer or accompaniment to dips. They will keep beautifully for at least a week, stored in a cool spot (but not in the refrigerator) in a plastic bag or covered container.

Note:

▸ Whatever you decide to spread or sprinkle on the crisps, don't forget how thin they are. A little flavor goes a long way.

▸ If you decide to use dried thyme, start with about ¼ teaspoon of thyme in your palm, grind it between thumb and forefinger, and then take pinches of the thyme and sprinkle sparingly over the pitas.

▸ Be sparing with the olive oil or you'll find the baking sheet awash with it. You can brush a bit more olive oil on the thicker rounds.

This is an inspired use for commercial pita bread. (I generally never use homemade pita pockets for this purpose because they always get gobbled up when they're fresh.) Look for a brand that is 100 percent whole wheat, and thinner rather than thicker. **If you can't find thin pita pockets, I wouldn't try this recipe** – thicker pita can be hard on the teeth when toasted like this. Some brands of pita pockets have a thin top and thicker bottom, in which case I separate them and cook them on two different baking sheets. The thinner disks turn brown sooner.

Tuna Salad
(As a sandwich filling or pita bread stuffing or salad topping)

*(See **Canned Tuna** on page 188.)*

We make this tuna salad most Saturdays for lunch. It is crunchy and exuberantly flavored, and very different from the traditional version. Because of the deliberate emphasis on crunch this mixture is not cohesive enough to behave properly in a sandwich. We serve it with a fork and slices of my whole wheat honey bread (see pages 220-23) on the side, or stuffed in small pita pockets, or spread on large pitas (that have been separated into two rounds) and rolled up into a sort of burrito.

Often those who think they don't like tuna salad find that they like this one. Please don't cut back on the seasoning when you try this recipe for the first time. You can halve this recipe easily but keep in mind that 2½ nephews can easily eat it all in one sitting.

(Makes about 4 – 5 cups)

12 ounces solid white tuna in water (see **note**)
1½ cups finely diced sweet onion
1½ cups finely diced celery
½ cup mayonnaise
1 tablespoon whole grain mustard
¾ teaspoon Tabasco sauce
½ teaspoon salt
¼ teaspoon freshly ground pepper

1. Open tuna can and drain tuna thoroughly. (See **Note** on draining.) You will have a scant 2 cups of drained tuna. Scrape into mixing bowl and break up clumps with a fork.

2. Add onion and celery, mayonnaise (see page 96), mustard, Tabasco, salt, and pepper. Mix thoroughly. Use as soon as possible – tuna salad tastes best freshly made.

Note:

▸ For tuna salad, the solid white tuna (albacore) is the most convenient because it is so much easier to squeeze out the liquid. Chunk light tuna is possibly higher in omega-3 fatty acids, potentially lower in mercury content, and cheaper, but it tends to be mushy. My choice would be solid light tuna packed in water but it doesn't seem to be available, and solid light tuna packed in its own juice is surprisingly expensive. A good compromise is solid light tuna packed in olive oil, as long as you save the oil and juices and any omega-3 fatty acids that have leached out of the tuna and into the oil.

▸ As with any other recipes calling for raw onion, I use the sweet variety (Walla Walla, Mayan, Vidalia, etc.). If you only have regular yellow onions on hand, use less. (How much less depends on how hot the onion is and who will be eating the tuna salad.)

▸ For a more cohesive and sandwich-friendly mixture, reduce the onion and celery to about 1 cup each.

▸ Tuna salad is best eaten on the same day it's made, but it can be stored in the refrigerator for several days; just mix before using to recombine liquid that will collect, or drain off the liquid, if you prefer. Less liquid will collect if you squeezed it out thoroughly to begin with.

On draining tuna: This is an important step in the construction of a reputable tuna salad, especially if you expect to have leftovers. The simplest method is to wring out as much of the liquid as you can by pressing the lid firmly down against the tuna and holding the can upside down. Solid tuna is easier to drain than chunk, which tends to squeeze out from under the lid. But even solid tuna has a proportion of mushy bits, so for best results squeeze the liquid from the tuna literally by hand, or in a small sieve.

Sardine Pâté

I generally like sardines, especially the dainty ones — the smoky, rich, extra-small brisling sardines. However, there are many kinds of sardine lovers out there, which probably accounts for the fact that lots of sardines are not dainty. Some are the sardine version of linebackers. If you happen to peel back the lid of a sardine tin and find yourself looking down at a row of oversized sardine torsos, it may be a good time to try this little recipe for sardine pâté.

Unless you suffer from an intractable anti-sardine bias, you should find this pâté tasty. I would not hesitate to serve it to a visiting head of state, preferably a state that maintains friendly relations with sardines, like Spain or Greece. I would serve it in teaspoon-sized scoops on crispy, thin little squares of buttered whole wheat toast.

1 tin (3 – 4 ounces) sardines*
1 tablespoon extra-virgin olive oil
1 tablespoon lemon juice
1 teaspoon lemon zest (optional; see page 68)
1 tablespoon whole grain mustard
¼ - ½ cup finely minced sweet onion
¼ teaspoon salt
¼ teaspoon freshly ground pepper

*I use the Brunswick brand packed in olive oil

1. Drain sardines. If they are packed in olive oil, I would include it but leave out the tablespoon of olive oil in the recipe.

2. Combine with oil, lemon, mustard, onion, salt, and pepper in a small mixing bowl. Mash and blend everything thoroughly.

Note:
▸ If you don't have a lemon in the house, use 2 teaspoons apple cider vinegar. Also, see *Give sardines a chance* (page 86).

Chicken or Egg Salad

Here are general directions for chicken or egg salad that can be eaten alone with perhaps a stalk of celery as a spoon, or used as a sandwich filling, or in pita pockets. If you use pita pockets you can get away with a crunchier version that includes more celery and onion.

(Makes about 2 cups)

½ cup finely diced celery
½ cup finely diced onion
¼ cup mayonnaise
1 – 2 teaspoons grainy mustard
¼ teaspoon salt
¼ teaspoon curry powder
¼ teaspoon freshly ground pepper
(¼ teaspoon Tabasco sauce)

1 cup chopped cooked chicken
or 4 peeled chopped boiled eggs

1. Dice celery and onion and combine in small mixing bowl with mayonnaise, mustard, salt, and pepper.

2. Add chopped chicken or eggs and blend thoroughly.

3. Stuff these mixtures into pita bread pockets, or make into sandwiches, or serve as a side with salads.

Note:
▸ Mayonnaise matters! See page 96.

▸ A 6-ounce can of solid white tuna packed in water or solid light tuna packed in olive oil, drained and flaked, is an alternative to the chicken and boiled eggs. See *Tuna Salad* recipe on page 104 for more details.

▸ Directions for boiled eggs are on the following page. A useful tip is to always choose brown eggs for boiling – you will find it easier to spot bits of shell on the peeled egg.

Boiled Eggs

A boiled egg is as simple and healthy (see page 21) a food as I can find to eat in a hurry. I boil seven at one time — that is how many fit in my little egg boiling saucepan — and eat one each day: peeled, halved, salted and peppered with breakfast or chopped into a favorite dinner salad with napa cabbage, sliced mushrooms, a bit of sliced sweet onion, and some tuna. Boiled eggs are main players in my *salade Niçoise* (page 135) and make occasional appearances in *Kedgeree* (page 193) or as a condiment for my lamb or chicken curry (page 204). There is a lot written about the best ways to boil eggs. This works for me.

1. Put the eggs from the fridge into a small saucepan. (The size of the pan would depend on the number of eggs: 6 – 7 eggs fit nicely in a 1-quart saucepan.) Cover with at least 1½ inches of cold water.

2. Bring the water to a boil, and then ***immediately remove the pan from the heat.*** Cover pan and set aside for 10 minutes. If you want soft boiled eggs, check one after about 4 minutes.

3. Pour off the hot water and submerge the eggs in cold water for 10 minutes. It helps to add plenty of ice to the water. *(This is supposed to shock the eggs into contracting slightly, which should make them easier to peel. HAH! Older eggs are said to peel more easily than fresh eggs, by the way.)*

Note:

▸ Results vary depending on details like the size of the pan, amount of water, and the number of the eggs, so you may need to customize these directions.

▸ I have an English friend whose favorite picnic sandwich is chopped hard-boiled eggs mixed with chutney and caught in the tender embrace of buttered bread. (See chutney on page 107.)

Deviled Eggs

Stuffed (deviled) eggs are an old fashioned but remarkably popular food. They are certainly handy on a hot summer night if you have some hard-boiled eggs waiting in your refrigerator. These directions call for four boiled eggs but I usually end up with at least one unstuffable egg white half.

(Serves 2 – 4)

4 hard-boiled eggs
1 tablespoon mayonnaise (see page 96)
1 teaspoon prepared mustard
¼ teaspoon salt
¼ teaspoon freshly ground pepper
¼ teaspoon turmeric
⅛ teaspoon curry powder
(1 tablespoon sweet pickle relish)

1. Peel and rinse eggs. Be fussy — crunchy bits of shell can ruin a good deviled egg. (This is a good reason to use brown shelled eggs instead of white, as the slight contrast is useful.) Slice eggs in half lengthwise and carefully extract the yolks.

2. Mash the yolks with the mayonnaise, mustard, salt, pepper, turmeric, and curry. (I like the sweet-sour tweak of pickle relish.) Mound the filling into each egg white.

Note:

▸ If your peeled eggs emerge as misshapen little lumps with only about half the egg whites still desperately clinging to their yolks, consider a nice egg salad (page 105).

▸ For an easy packed lunch stick the egg halves back together and wrap in a bit of plastic wrap, gathering the plastic at one end of the egg and twisting snugly, like you were wrapping a rum truffle. Yum.

Hot Stuff

This is hot. It has to be hot. If it isn't hot enough to make you exclaim when you taste it, hot it up some more. Horseradish is an effective decongestant, as is mustard, and a sensible diet supplement for anyone with chronic congestion (and a handy box of Kleenex). Try this sauce with meat loaf (page 208) or an aggressive vegetable like Brussels sprouts. You may even forget you never liked Brussels sprouts.

(Makes about 1½ cups)

2 tablespoons Coleman's dry mustard
2 tablespoons apple cider vinegar
2 tablespoons extra-hot horseradish
1 teaspoon salt
1 teaspoon honey
½ cup mayonnaise (see page 96)
½ cup drained yogurt (see page 97)

1. Combine the first five ingredients in a small mixing bowl and whisk until honey is dissolved.

2. Add mayonnaise and drained yogurt and blend until smooth. This will hold nicely in the refrigerator for weeks.

Note:

▶ 1 cup of yogurt will drain down to ½-cup. I prefer whole milk yogurt that has been drained at least overnight. Full directions and tips for draining yogurt are on page 97.

▶ It is worth going to some trouble to track down an honest, vicious horseradish with fumes that make your eyes water when you take off the lid.

Pear Chutney
Spicy sweet and sour relish

Chutney is easy to make, once all the dicing is done. I have also used Granny Smith apples and a large unripe Mexican papaya. Both make wonderful chutney. I like to make a big batch because it seems to last indefinitely in the refrigerator. (I found this out by accident when I lost a jar of chutney in the back of the refrigerator. **Two years later** it looked and tasted fresh!)

(Makes about 6 cups)

6 hard pears (or other fruit – see above)
1 medium-large onion
1 cup apple cider vinegar
1 cup honey
1 can (7 ounces) green chiles, diced
½ teaspoon crushed chilies
2 teaspoons salt
2 tablespoons black mustard seed
2 teaspoon turmeric
2 tablespoons minced fresh ginger
1 tablespoon crushed fresh garlic
1 cup golden raisins
1 cup currants

1. Peel fruit and chop into ¼-inch dice. You should have about 7 – 9 cups. Peel and chop onions into ¼-inch dice, which should give you about 3 cups.

2. Combine all ingredients in a large deep skillet and bring to a simmer. Cook for about 1½ hours. You don't want mush, you just want the flavors and textures melded into a tender, golden, vivid, fragrant chutney.

3. Cool, pack in pretty jars, and refrigerate for …years. Eat with brown bread and sharp cheddar, or with any meat dishes.

Béchamel Sauce
with Parmesan and Lemon

Béchamel (*bay-sha-MEL)* is also called white sauce, and appears anonymously in countless dishes like pot pies, soufflés, lasagna, macaroni-and-cheese, casseroles, and simple creamed vegetables like onion or spinach. It is so selfless and useful that it deserves to go on its own page under its own name.

Béchamel sauce can take on all kinds of accents just with additions like herbs, cheese, and spices – or lemon and Parmesan, as in this variation. It is based on a *roux* (pronounced as in *kangaroux*), a mixture of butter and flour which is also useful for enriching and thickening soups. Roux smells delicious, too — like shortbread cookies baking.

(Makes about 2½ cups)

½ stick butter (4 tablespoons)
¼ cup all-purpose flour (4 tablespoons)

2 cups whole milk
½ teaspoon salt
½ teaspoon freshly ground pepper

½ cup (generous) freshly grated Parmesan
2 tablespoons fresh lemon juice
(zest from 1 lemon – see page 68)

Roux:

1. Heat butter over medium low heat, preferably in a sturdy 1½-quart pot. When butter is melted sprinkle the flour over the butter and blend thoroughly. Stir over a medium-low heat until the mixture bubbles. Cook for another 2 minutes, stirring. Don't let it brown — it will gain flavor but lose thickening power.

Sauce:

2. Slide pot off heat and whisk ½ cup milk into the roux. When mixture is smooth add another ½ cup and whisk vigorously until smooth before blending in the remaining milk.

3. Place pot over medium heat and whisk in the seasoning. Bring sauce to a simmer. Simmer gently about 15 minutes, whisking often. It should be nicely thickened.

4. Stir in Parmesan and lemon juice and zest. (It's easiest to remove zest from the lemon before you halve or juice it.)

Note:

▸ You can use your choice of fresh milk or evaporated milk in this recipe, or you can use a non-dairy alternative like soy milk. You can also use a mixture of half-and-half or cream and chicken stock (or vegetable stock). And if you replace all the milk with meat stock, you have – *voila!* – *velouté* sauce.

▸ If you add about 4 cups of bite-sized shreds of cooked chicken and the *mirepoix* (sauté of onion, celery, and carrot) on page 143, you will have a lovely chicken pot pie filling waiting for a crust. (For a recipe for *Chicken Pot Pie*, see page 201.)

▸ For a delicious filling for crêpes (see the recipe for crêpes on page 212) add the cooked chicken pieces to the sauce along with a 10-ounce bag of baby spinach and a few cups of steamed broccoli florets.

Roux

A *roux* is useful if you need something to thicken a soup or a stew. Mix a half cup or so of soup or stew liquid into a couple of tablespoons of roux and blend until smooth, and then stir into the soup or stew. If you need more thickening, just add more *roux* the same way. (An instant *roux* can be made with equal proportions of soft butter and all-purpose flour mixed together into a paste and added the same way as the cooked *roux*.)

Tomato Sauce

This recipe is simple – pay no attention to the number of ingredients. It is also quick – I only simmer it for 20 minutes or so. Nobody needs to be told the many uses for tomato sauce: you can serve it over pasta, polenta, crêpes, fish, pizza, meatloaf, and so forth. However, if you decide to make this and actually *can't* think of a use for it, you can always turn it into cream of tomato soup (see note following), or add it to a pot of chili or minestrone.

(Makes about 4 cups)

¼ cup extra-virgin olive oil
2 – 3 cups finely diced onion
1 tablespoon freshly crushed garlic

1 can (28 ounces) crushed tomatoes
1 tablespoon honey
1 teaspoon salt, or to taste
1 teaspoon freshly ground pepper
1 teaspoon dried oregano
½ teaspoon dried thyme

1. Heat oil in 2½-quart saucepan over medium heat. Add onions and sauté until very soft, about 10 – 15 minutes. Add garlic and cook for another 2 minutes.

2. Stir in remaining ingredients, bring to a simmer, and simmer gently for about 20 minutes, uncovered. If making in advance, cool thoroughly before covering and refrigerating.

(If you use regular diced tomatoes for any reason, purée for a smoother texture with an immersion blender, or allow to cool slightly and purée sauce in a food processor. You can use the pulse button to retain texture rather than purée the sauce to smithereens.)

Note:

▸ For more texture, I like to use S&W 'petite-cut' diced tomatoes instead of crushed, or a 14-ounce can each of crushed and diced.

▸ For a Bolognese-style sauce, just add a pound of ground meat after you add the garlic, and sauté until the meat is mostly brown before adding the tomatoes.

▸ For a Puttanesca-type sauce, add ¼-teaspoon crushed chilies with the onions, and with the tomatoes add ½ -cup pitted and chopped oil-cured olives, 3 – 6 minced anchovies, and 2 tablespoons capers.

▸ Leftover tomato sauce is a beautiful thing. Use it to top a meatloaf (page 208) or crêpes (page 212), or add to chili (page 209), or add it to the *Smoooth Butternut Bisque* (page 141) before you purée it. For that matter, make yourself a little batch of cream of tomato soup. For example, to about 2 cups of tomato sauce you can add a cup of chicken stock or water, and a cup of half-and-half or evaporated whole milk. (A 5-ounce can of evaporated milk is ¾ cup; just add milk to make a cup.) *(See page 140 for a recipe for a Thai style cream of tomato soup.)*

Tomatoes and lycopene
Cooking tomatoes with extra-virgin olive oil improves the availability of the lycopene contained in the tomatoes. Lycopene and similar nutrients are strongly associated with reduced age-related eye diseases, cancers, and heart disease. The addition of the onions and herbs strengthens the nutritional punch with micronutrients that are anti-inflammatory and reduce cancer and heart disease risk.

8

About Vegetables

Fresh Vegetables

Frozen Vegetables
Emergency Corn Sauté
Last-Minute Green Beans
Quick Green Pea Soup
Spinach Timbale (Custard)

Vegetables to Keep Handy
Roasted Vegetables

Simple Salads
Fresh Tomato Salad
Apple, Broccoli, and Celery Salad
Spinach, Napa, and Mushroom Salad
Pico de Gallo
Avocado Salsa
Tossed Green Salad with Vinaigrette and Parmesan
Napa Cabbage Salad with Cilantro
Carrot Slaw
Mediterranean Chopped Salad
Greek Salad
Warm Potato Salad

Fresh Vegetables

Vegetables are protective against just about everything you want to be protected from, so it makes sense to take care of them. Only buy vegetables that you will realistically use in their prime. Cauliflower should be clear-complexioned, bell peppers firm-cheeked, broccoli should be alert, zucchini should refuse to bend at the waist, and spinach should be exuberant. These are not merely cosmetic issues. Nutrients die of old age just like we do. Anyway, the freshest vegetables taste the best.

Clean and trim them early

Wash vegetables such as celery and greens as soon after you buy them as possible so they will be available for instant use. A salad spinner (the Zyliss brand is my favorite) is a good investment: it's important to spin greens almost dry before storing or dressing them. Seal them in clean plastic bags lined with paper towels to help absorb excess water and keep them crisp.

Keep the more perishable vegetables like bell peppers and cucumbers toward the front of your refrigerator so they won't sneak off behind the leftovers and emerge a week later looking wrinkled and dissolute. Try to use them while they are at their best, even if you just slice them up and serve them as finger salad.

Take a few minutes to slice broccoli florets from their stems: it's easy and relatively quick to do, and you'll be so glad when you suddenly need a vegetable to serve. Store the broccoli stalks separately, ready to use for salad or soup. The stalks will keep better if you store them with peel intact, and then strip off the peel with a paring knife the same day you use them.

Keep it simple

For a busy cook it makes sense to lean heavily on vegetables that are always available, and that wait patiently until you need them. It helps if they are versatile enough to be useful raw *or* cooked, and if they are equally comfortable playing a leading or supporting role.

Some vegetables that fulfill all four qualifications are onions, celery, carrot, and napa cabbage, and potatoes. (It's true that potatoes are hardly useful raw — although you should try a slice of raw salted potato, if you haven't already.) For more on these, see *Vegetables to Keep Handy* on page 117.

Butternut squash and sweet potatoes deserve at least honorable mention. Both keep well in a cool, dry place, are easy to peel, and have bright orange and creamy-textured flesh. Both work well as solo vegetables, whether baked, puréed, or roasted. (Sweet potatoes are not related to potatoes or yams, by the way.) Both are especially rich in carotenoids (like beta-carotene).

The salad vegetables

Then there are the salad vegetables, like cucumber, bell peppers, and tomatoes. Simple sliced cucumbers and peppers make instant finger salads served crispy and cold with a side of dip, like *Hasty Tasty Hummus* or *Rich Yogurt Aioli*. It's a nice change from chopped or tossed salads and so much less work for the cook.

English (hothouse) cucumbers are seedless, thin-skinned, and ready-wrapped: a wonderfully convenient alternative when regular cucumbers are not exciting. They are generally more expensive and usually worth it, but examine them carefully, avoiding any with softened ends. Tomatoes sliced into wedges or chunks and sprinkled with salt and freshly ground pepper make a delicious salad in their own right.

... and greens

Romaine lettuce, as long as it's fat and fresh, is my general purpose choice of the lettuces. It has a crunchy stem and substantial leaf and is the easiest of the greens to clean.

However, if you want something as easy to use as iceberg lettuce, try napa cabbage. (See page 121 for more about one of my favorite vegetables.) Iceberg lettuce, by the way, is a far from optimal choice; in the world of lettuce, the deeper green, the better.

For tight schedules, it's hard to beat a bag of ready-to-use mixed greens, those colorful mixtures of lettuces, bitter greens, fresh herbs, and spinach. As for those handy bags of baby spinach, what a gift to the overextended cook! A case can no doubt be made for those fresh-picked muddy little bunches of spinach, but the cleaning and preparation are not acceptable uses of time, in my opinion. When I want fresh spinach for salads I would rather pay for the triple-washed bags of baby spinach available in most supermarkets. (Always triple-check use-by dates, by the way.)

I'm puzzled by people who wouldn't dream of spending extra money on pre-washed greens, yet think nothing of throwing out bags of vegetables that die of exposure and hypothermia before anyone finds time or energy to clean and trim them.

In season?

Vegetables are at their best in season. In the case of spring vegetables like asparagus and summer vegetables like corn on the cob, I'm perfectly happy to serve them every day while they're locally picked and at their best, and then pretty much ignore them the rest of the year. Cucumbers in season can be sweet and succulent with innocuous seeds, but most of the year they are just — ordinary. Variety is not more important than quality: it makes perfectly good sense to focus on the vegetables or fruit in season.

Zucchini, for example...

Certain vegetables like zucchini are not as distinctly seasonal, but in summer you can find skinny little zucchini with tender velvety skin and crisp, creamy flesh; these are delicious sliced raw and served with dip. I wish they were easier to find.

Although acceptable supermarket zucchini are generally available year round, they are *not* on my list of staples for a few reasons. They don't store very well, have a fleeting prime, and threaten to cook down into a translucent mush if you're not careful.

But roasted (see page 124,128), or in soup (as a substitute for peas on page 115 or in the minestrone on page 143), or shredded and then cooked fast and hot in extra-virgin olive oil, garlic, salt, and pepper, even so-so zucchini can be memorable. (For more zucchini ideas see *Zucchini Frittata* on page 210.)

The organic question

The question often comes up concerning whether or not to insist on organically grown vegetables. However, so far there is not enough data to make a strong case for an organic-only position. At this point the evidence for benefit is still lacking despite decades of research, but there is nothing vague about the evidence for eating at least five servings of vegetables and fruit each day. Whether or not they are from organically grown produce is secondary.

Unfortunately, we can't always trust the accuracy of the claim or the definition of organic in each case. However, I often find reasons to buy organic produce: for example, when I need green onions and the regular ones are limp and broken, it may be that the organic versions are exuberantly fresh. I'm happy to pay more for a superior product.

Frozen Vegetables

Frozen vegetables are considered to be nutritionally superior to canned, but they are more perishable. It usually doesn't pay to stock up on more than you will use in a month or so. (You don't know how long they have languished in the supermarket freezer, either.) Taste them before you use them.

I use a narrow spectrum of frozen vegetables because the fresh versions taste so much better and are convenient enough, for the most part. (See *Vegetables to Keep Handy* on page 117.) However, I would not like to do without a few frozen vegetables like corn, beans, peas, and chopped spinach. (For frozen baby lima beans and green soybeans (edamame), see the chapter on *Beans* starting on page 153.)

Frozen corn

This is a convenient vegetable to have available when you need an extra side dish and a good source of cholesterol-lowering insoluble fiber. It doesn't need to be cooked and stands up well to vinaigrette, so is adaptable to salads (see *Succotash Salad* and *Black Bean, Corn and Jicama Salad*) as well as hot dishes (see *Scalloped Corn*).

I always buy petite yellow corn. White corn is delicious but it can be disconcertingly sweet. (Good for snacking straight from the freezer, however. I like eating frozen corn a few kernels at a time like candy. Once the kernels thaw, the thrill is gone.)

Draining the corn well before using in salads is critical; one method that works well as a final step is to toss the drained corn in a sieve with a paper towel, replacing the paper towel until it stops getting wet. Sometimes I've shaken it in a hot skillet to cook off any residual water or roasted it briefly in the oven, but it's not necessary.

Emergency Corn Sauté

As a last minute cooked vegetable, frozen corn is almost instant. (For a premeditated frozen corn dish see page 147.)

(Serves 4 – 6)

2 tablespoons extra-virgin olive oil
⅛ teaspoon red chili flakes
1 bag (16 ounces) frozen petite corn
½ teaspoon salt
½ teaspoon freshly ground pepper

1. Heat olive oil in a skillet over medium heat and add chili flakes. When oil is hot add frozen corn and sauté until the kernels are hot, about 10 minutes. Add salt and pepper, and your corn is ready to serve.

Note:

▶ If you have some green onions, slice and sauté for about 20 seconds when oil is hot before adding corn. Or if you have time but no green onions, sauté 1 cup minced regular onion and an extra ¼ teaspoon of salt before adding the corn. *(Remember that a cup of diced onion cooks down to only ½ cup: that's none too much onion.)*

▶ If you don't have time but want some interest, add diced canned green chiles with the corn. (See box on page 147.)

▶ The flavor begs to be taken to another level, too. A pinch of dried basil rubbed between the fingers and added at the beginning of the cooking adds an unpretentious little flourish. Or for something more outspoken, ⅛ teaspoon of ground cumin added with the chilies.

▶ Leftovers are a great addition to polenta. (See page 183-85.)

Frozen green beans

Frozen baby green beans are convenient when fresh are hard to find. This is actually most of the year, in my experience. Frozen green beans can be a bit tough and watery, though, and a solution is to toss the hot, just-cooked green beans in vinaigrette and fresh-grated Parmesan, salt, and pepper. The added flavors will distract nicely from any freezer taste or texture.

Another solution is to serve them instead of peas in *Kedgeree* (page 193), or as a substitute for the broccoli in *Tuna and Broccoli Pasta* (page 190).

I usually buy the skinny little petite green beans rather than the chunkier cut green beans. The best choice is whichever has spent the least time in the freezer, so buy from a busy store and use quickly.

Frozen (petite) peas

Frozen petite peas are not as sturdy as frozen corn. They tend to shrivel and lose the plump sweetness that makes fresh-picked peas so incomparably delicious. As with all frozen vegetables, try not to let them linger long in your freezer. (Petite peas are more reliably sweet and tasty than the regular peas.)

The simplest way to prepare them as a side dish is to quickly sauté them with extra-virgin olive oil or butter, salt, and pepper. Cook them just before you serve – they cool quickly. They overcook just as fast, too, so sauté only until hot.

Plump green frozen peas need only to be thawed (under hot running water works) to be recipe-ready. If added to something like the *Kedgeree* on page 193, they only need to be heated through.

Last-Minute Green Beans
(Serves about 4 – 6)

(1 cup water and 1 teaspoon salt)
16 ounces frozen slim green beans
3 tablespoons extra-virgin olive oil
1 tablespoon apple cider vinegar
½ teaspoon freshly crushed garlic
½ teaspoon salt
¼ teaspoon freshly ground pepper
(¼ cup freshly grated Parmesan – optional)

1. Bring water and salt to a boil in 3-quart saucepan.

2. Place frozen beans in saucepan. Cover and boil briskly for approximately 6 minutes, or until beans are barely tender but not soft. Drain thoroughly.

3. Meanwhile combine olive oil, vinegar, garlic, salt, pepper, and Parmesan (optional) in serving bowl. Add drained beans and toss thoroughly. Serve hot, warm, or room temperature.

Quick Green Pea Soup
(Makes about 5 cups)

3 cups water or chicken stock
1 medium-large onion, diced
(2 stalks celery, diced – optional)
½ teaspoon freshly crushed garlic
1 teaspoon salt
½ teaspoon freshly ground pepper
1 bag (16 ounces) frozen petite peas
1 cup half-and-half or evaporated milk

1. Bring water or broth to a boil in a 3-quart soup pot. Add onion, celery, garlic, salt, and pepper. Simmer 20 – 30 minutes or until vegetables are very soft.

2. Add peas and simmer 5 minutes. Add half-and-half or evaporated milk and purée.

Note:
▶ For other green options, replace peas with a 10-ounce box of frozen spinach (my favorite) or a few cups of grated zucchini.

Frozen spinach

I only use frozen spinach as an ingredient, never as a cooked vegetable in its own right — unless you count the following recipe for *Spinach Timbale* or a speedy spinach soup, which I make just like the preceding *Quick Green Pea Soup*.

I always prefer to buy the 16-ounce bags of frozen chopped spinach, but the most commonly available form is the 10-ounce box, which amounts to about ¾-cup of thawed and well-drained spinach. (If you accidentally buy frozen *UN*-chopped spinach, which in my experience is stringy with spinach stems, you can chop it yourself after it has been thawed or cooked.)

Preparing frozen spinach

The easiest way to thaw frozen spinach is to leave it in the refrigerator overnight (in a dish to catch the draining liquid). If you use the stove or microwave for last-minute thawing, be careful not to overdo the heat or the spinach will lose its vivid color.

For the stovetop method, place the frozen spinach into a skillet or pot with a lid. Cover and place over a low heat, and heat very gently for about 20 – 30 minutes – your low heat may be hotter than mine – or until the spinach is fully thawed. (By heating it slowly you don't have to add water.) Check after 15 minutes and break up the icy center, especially if you are thawing a 10-ounce box of spinach.

For microwave method, place frozen spinach in a Pyrex dish and microwave uncovered for about 6 minutes. (Microwaving may reduce antioxidant levels but the jury is still out.)

Press out excess liquid in a sieve: you should easily collect ¼ – ½ cup, depending on whether you are working with 10- or 16-ounce packages. (Cooked spinach is harder to squeeze out than barely thawed spinach.) The extent to which you drain the spinach depends on the recipe. You don't need to be fussy for the following *Spinach Timbale*.

Spinach Timbale (Custard)

This is a side dish that allows you to serve spinach where no spinach has dared to go before. Even those hostile to the very suggestion of spinach can probably enjoy this timbale (pronounced *TIM-bul*). It is simply constructed and seasoned, with nothing to distract from the spinachness, yet with the spinachy edges softened by creaminess.

(Serves about 4 – 6)

10-ounce box frozen chopped spinach
3 eggs
5-ounce can evaporated whole milk
or ¾ cup half-and-half
¾ teaspoon salt
½ teaspoon freshly ground pepper

Preheat oven to 300 degrees

1. Place frozen spinach into a skillet or pot with a lid. Place over a low heat, covered, and cook very gently for about 20 – 30 minutes or until spinach is fully thawed and hot through. Check after 15 minutes and break up icy center if needed.

2. Meanwhile, whisk together eggs, milk, and seasoning. Add un-drained spinach and mix well. *(This may be mixed the day before and chilled. Remove from the refrigerator an hour before cooking, and stir again before the next step.)*

3. Scrape into a buttered 1½ -quart casserole dish and bake in a 300-degree oven for 45 minutes, or until no longer wet in center.

Note:

▸ For a superb and simple spinach soup, see *Quick Green Pea Soup* on the previous page. A peeled and thinly-sliced potato added with the onion in step 1 makes a more satisfying soup.

Vegetables to Keep Handy

There are certain vegetables I *always* try to have on hand: these are onions, carrots, celery, potatoes, cabbage, and garlic. (Butternut squash is also on the short list, but is *often* rather than *always* on hand.) They have year-round availability, durability, and versatility.

Last minute or unexpected meals aren't so much of a problem when you know your basic ingredients are waiting for you. It works best to have a core group of recipes that use all these vegetables so you don't need to be inventive unless you feel like it. Depending on the way you cut them, cook them, and combine them, most of these vegetables can be a main feature or just as easily play in a supporting role. (See *Roasted Vegetables* on page 123 and the vegetable recipes in this chapter.)

Onions

As this cook's best friend, the onion ranks right up there with fire and ice. If you can't decide what to fix for dinner, you are never wasting time if you peel an onion. You can serve them roasted, sautéed, pickled, marinated, and raw, alone or otherwise. The hottest onion is mild and almost sweet when cooked. At *least* one onion can disappear into any soup, stew, sauce, sauté, casserole, pilaf, stir-fry, potato dish, and even salad. Onions wait patiently, are modestly priced, and available everywhere all the time.

Choose onions that are hard and fairly smooth-skinned, and store loose in a dark, cool place. Sweet onions like Walla Walla, Vidalia, or Mayans have a shorter shelf life than the regular yellow onions. I make a point of checking them regularly for any signs of breakdown in their skins. A fine strategy is to keep a peeled and ready-to-dice-or-slice sweet onion in the refrigerator — it lasts much longer than at room temperature in its skin, and is so convenient when you just want part of an onion for sandwiches or salads.

There are *lots* of onions in my recipes, both because I love them and because the onion is a phenomenally healthy vegetable whether raw or cooked. I buy sweet onions almost exclusively. Their milder flavor allows me to use more of them, especially in recipes where I use them raw. I ignore any recipe's demands for red or white onions or shallots.

The sweet varieties are the nicest to work with and are generally available year round — although they are more expensive out of season, which is most of the year. The imported Mayans are generally available and are often competitively priced if you shop around.

Using onions

Everyday yellow onions are all-purpose and can be mild, but they are generally aggressive. Sweet onions almost never make me cry when I cut them, but any onion is kinder to the eyes if you chill it in the refrigerator first.

When chopping vicious onions, one defense is to wear swimming goggles, according to *Cooks Illustrated* magazine. Another technique is to chill the onion before slicing it, which apparently slows the chemical reaction that causes the tears. You can also burn a couple of candles right next to the chopping board; it's a tip that I believe has worked for me, and candlelight is certainly more flattering than goggles.

Recipes that call for only half an onion are generally improved by a whole onion. In my world a medium onion is about 2 cups diced, and a large onion is about 4 cups diced. (I don't know much about small onions.) Generally, 'diced' means chopped into roughly ¼ inch squares and 'minced' means finely diced into pieces smaller than ¼ inch. Cooked diced onions are reduced by about half when cooked.

Sautéed onions

1. For about 2 – 3 cups of diced onions, heat a 10-inch skillet or pot over a medium-hot burner and add 2 – 4 tablespoons extra-virgin olive oil.

2. When the oil is hot (but not smoking) add diced onion. If the oil is hot enough, the onions should sizzle when they hit the pan. Toss the onions to coat with oil and then sauté until onion is tender, shaking the pan and giving the onions a toss regularly to keep them cooking evenly.

3. Depending on the amount of onion, the level of heat, and the surface area of the skillet this can take 10 – 15 minutes. The smaller the amount of onions, the faster they will cook.

Fresh garlic

Garlic gets plenty of credit for its benefits to the immune system and its role as a natural antibiotic, but it is rare for garlic to be any more than a token presence in actual recipes.

Even in recipes that traditionally headline garlic, like *hummus* and *aioli,* one might see instructions to add *only one clove*! (One medium-sized clove, presumably.) In fact, I have found a recipe for hummus in which the chef-author calls for "¼ garlic clove, finely minced". Whether or not my interpretations happen to exceed even the most relaxed cultural limits, it still should be hard to defend the use of only ¼ clove of garlic in *anything*.

I do tend to use garlic in therapeutic quantities. The effect of fresh crushed garlic in certain dishes – the two mentioned above, for example – is critical to their success. However, something as pungent and aggressive as garlic is bound to stir up some strong feelings, especially when there are no warning labels. Even so, it is surprising how the most often requested recipes are the ones with the most lethal levels of fresh garlic.

(I do agree that garlic should be consensual. The risks of secondhand garlic fumes are very real, especially in a short car on a long trip. The chances of a tragic conclusion of some kind are high.)

Finding good garlic

Good garlic can be hard to find, even in the best supermarkets. Produce departments with otherwise high standards can occasionally offer a heap of aged and rickety garlic. It may *look* fine, but always be alert.

Hold any suspect garlic in your hand and rub it with your thumb; if it feels dented or soft, or if you can see any tips of green sprouts or hint of mold, don't buy it. A head of garlic should feel heavy for its size, and the cloves should feel hard and smooth.

If you find yourself alone in your kitchen with some veteran garlic, see if you can salvage any of it. Throw out any shriveled cloves. Split the others open with a small knife and remove the bitter-tasting green sprout, then use as usual. It won't be juicy, but it will at least have garlic flavor.)

Store garlic as you do onions, in a cool, dark, well-ventilated place — never the refrigerator! And if you feel tempted to keep a bottle of store-bought minced garlic at the back of your refrigerator in case of an emergency, be assured that there will never be an emergency serious enough.

Imitation garlic

Most people I meet who *think* they hate garlic have not been exposed to fresh garlic that has been treated with respect. Bottles of peeled or pre-crushed garlic are as close as some people ever come to fresh garlic, but in the opinion of this writer, there is simply no comparison.

Dehydrated garlic is definitely *not* interchangeable with fresh garlic. Even the broad-minded *Joy of Cooking* says "Always use fresh garlic. Powdered and salt forms tend to have rancid overtones."

Using garlic

It rarely makes sense to go to the work of mincing garlic. Garlic is sticky, potent, and often comes in cloves too small to control easily. Crushing is simple work with a well-designed garlic crusher (see page 69). I've had poorly designed models actually backfire. (The freshest garlic is pretty juicy and it hurts *horribly* if it squirts in your eye.)

Most recipes in this book call for 'freshly crushed garlic.' This is important because garlic really does taste better when used fresh. Some even feel that the flavor of garlic is better when crushed with a knife (minced and then crushed with the flat of the knife) rather than with a garlic press.

Crushing garlic with a garlic press:

■ Do not peel garlic clove. Crush medium and small cloves whole. If the clove is too large to fit into the garlic crushing compartment, cut it through its equator and place in the garlic press, cut side down and skin side up.

■ Squeeze garlic press tightly, and then scrape (an oyster knife works well) off the pure garlic pulp extruded from the press.

■ Remove the little mat of garlic stuff remaining inside the press. (Another good use for the oyster knife rather than the more delicate point of your paring knife.) Sometimes it lifts out cleanly and other times you have to scrape out bits that cling in and around the holes.

■ **Note: This only works on unpeeled cloves.** It is the husk that helps drive the flesh of the garlic so efficiently through the holes of the press, as well as leave behind the often-neatly-removed garlic remains.

■ I recommend disposing of the garlic remains off the premises. Left indoors, the smell can take over a room or maybe a house. I either throw them into the bushes outside or, in the winter, toss them into the fire.

Peeling and mincing garlic:

Some of my longer-cooking recipes, like *Ratatouille* (page 150) and *Beef Stew* (page 206), call for mincing the garlic instead of crushing it. This means you need to peel the garlic first, so take a clove of garlic and whack it firmly with a paperweight or some solid object with a flat bottom. You only need to use enough force to crack the clove, not smash it, and it will be easy to peel. You can also peel a clove of garlic by placing the flat side of a chef's knife over it and then leaning on the blade until you hear the clove crack. On older cloves I usually trim the root end and remove any green sprouts, which can be bitter...

Garlic Oil

If you want the convenience of bottled garlic, make your own garlic oil. This is a good way to use small cloves that are a nuisance to crush in the press (see peeling suggestion preceding) or for those times when you want to take advantage of a good supply of fresh, juicy garlic. For most purposes you can use it as you would fresh garlic. It's a wonderful back up when you find yourself out of fresh garlic or don't have time to crush it.

½ cup peeled whole garlic cloves
½ cup extra-virgin olive oil

1. Combine garlic and oil in a mini food processor (or in a 2-cup container if you have an immersion blender) and blend until smooth. Scrape into a bottle with a tightly sealing lid and refrigerate. It will become firm as the oil chills.

Note:

▶ *Keep garlic oil chilled*, taking it out of the refrigerator just long enough to scoop out what you want. Use within a month. Use in place of fresh garlic, according to taste.

Celery

When buying celery, check the cut ends for freshness (you don't want brown withered tips) and wiggle a stalk to make sure the celery is not tired or cracked. Celery lasts well when sealed properly in a plastic bag rather than stored in the open ventilated bag it often wears in the supermarket, and in which the celery turns limp within 2 or 3 days. (If you must leave the celery in the ventilated bag, at least seal the top of the bag.)

(Should you find yourself with a clump of dispirited celery, make some wonderful cream of celery soup using the recipe for *Quick Green Pea Soup* on page 115. Just replace the peas with about four cups of sliced celery, added with the onion and celery already in the recipe.)

Juicy, crunchy celery sticks are crucial to dips, tuna salad, potato, rice or bean salads, and, well, family life as we know it today. The coarse outer leaves and strongish-tasting outer stalks can be minced and used in soup or broken up and added to stock. The tender inside leaves should be chopped and added to salads or tuna or whatever. (I use celery leaves a bit like parsley, which I rarely have on hand.)

Celery is so useful that it pays to clean and trim it all at once, as soon after you buy it as possible. It is especially useful stuffed with something like tuna salad or peanut butter and handed to a child who is certain of imminent starvation when dinner is still an hour away.

Carrots

These are dependable vegetables to have in your refrigerator and easy to prepare. Peeled and sliced on the diagonal in thin discs, they make the perfect raw dipping vegetable.

Then, if you cut those slices into matchsticks, steam them for about 7 minutes (or until barely tender), and toss them with vinaigrette, you have a great side dish that's good warm, cold — or the next day. Add some minced fresh basil or cilantro and you have a company dish. Chopped fine and sautéed in oil or butter with celery and onion

they make a base for soups or sauces or stews. (See *Mirepoix* on page 143.)

Grated carrot salad is an easy fresh addition to a last-minute dinner, tossed with vinaigrette and a handful of raisins, and a couple of grated raw carrots can be tossed through cabbage or green salads. Carrots are definitely more popular raw than cooked, texture and flavor-wise, but they can be hard to chew raw for the very young and old.

> Speaking of last minute dinners, a 16-ounce bag of peeled baby carrots can be cooked quickly whole (or chopped, if you have a bit more time) in a skillet with a cup of water, most of which boils away by the time the carrots are just barely tender. Then you finish them off with extra-virgin olive oil or butter, salt, and freshly ground pepper. Basil is wonderfully good with cooked carrots.

One way to make cooked carrots popular is to make them explode with bold flavors like curry, cumin, fresh cilantro, and lemon juice. (See *Marinated Carrot Matchsticks* on page 148.) You could also turn them into a bright purée – just follow the instructions for the *Butternut Squash Purée* on page 144. Some also like carrots mashed in equal amounts with potatoes. Carrots are too useful and nutritious to give up on easily.

Potatoes

Nobody has to be told that potatoes are marvelously versatile and popular. I always have Yukon Gold or red skinned potatoes on hand for steaming, roasting, or potato salad, and/or some russets for baking, mashing, or soups.

The potato is especially valuable to the cook in a hurry because it can be cooked and mashed within 20 minutes, if you cut it into small enough pieces. It provides a comforting side dish for meatloaf or a satisfying base for leftover chili or a quick sauce made with onions and leftover meat. Potatoes can make it easy to be a hero.

As for versatility, they're a favorite appetizer (crisp-roasted potato slices or wedges), side dish (roasted, baked, scalloped, mashed, steamed), or main course (baked and served under some delicious mixture like chili and grated cheese, with a crunchy topping of diced onion and tomato).

You can turn potatoes into a warm or cold salad (page 135), use them in just about any soup (for example, the very different soups on pages 138 and 194), or combine them comfortably with just about any other vegetables. For instance, mashed and blended with a tender sauté of onion and cabbage, which is my interpretation of the Irish classic, *colcannon*. (See page 145.)

Stored loose in a cool, dark, and ventilated place, (**never** in a plastic bag), potatoes usually last easily for several weeks. In fact, store potatoes as you would onions, but not mixed *with* onions; apparently they shorten each other's shelf life. And please don't buy already-bagged mystery potatoes! It takes very little more time to handpick them.

A potato that is beginning to soften is fine to use but peel away any green patches. (As an aside, I have to say that there are few things that smell *worse* than a rotten potato, so don't store them where they may have any opportunity to roll out of sight.)

It is important to note that potatoes are mostly easily digested starch and should be considered a carbohydrate like white bread or white rice, rather than a vegetable.[1]

Napa (or Chinese) cabbage
In some ways this could be called the iceberg lettuce of cabbage – crispy, juicy, and mild – but with more flavor, more dignity, and more food value because of its cruciferous nature.

[1] Walter C. Willett, M.D. *Eat, Drink, and Be Healthy* (2001) 19-20, 115

(It is also the basis for *kimchee*, the very hot and crunchy Korean condiment.)

Napa cabbage has enough character to stand on its own, yet is too mild to offend anyone who hates cabbage. In fact, it's so mild that it benefits from the association with bold flavors, like green onion and cilantro. Like others in the cabbage family, it waits cheerfully in the refrigerator until you need it, and seems amazingly unaffected by age.

Napa cabbage is tender and crispy, and ideal for stir-frying because it barely needs cooking. It's also marvelous as a quick, easy last-minute salad, alone or added to other greens. Just remove any bruised or broken outer leaves, and then slice off whatever you need. The top half is fluffy and the bottom half is crunchy and juicy. I usually leave it undressed until shortly before serving it; napa cabbage wilts and weeps quickly. It is better dressed with vinaigrette — a mayonnaise-based dressing should be saved for the sturdier types of cabbage.

One of my favorite beat-the-clock company salads is the top half of a large specimen chopped into bite-sized pieces and tossed with an 8-ounce package of sliced mushrooms, a small bag of ready-to-use baby spinach, and the vinaigrette on page 95. (I toss the mushrooms first with vinaigrette to give them a head start.) Another favorite is shredded napa cabbage dressed with a lemon, garlic, and cumin vinaigrette with a few sliced green onions and cilantro. (See *Simple Salads* beginning on page 129.)

For an instant home-alone meal of soul-satisfying dimensions, I love a salad of napa cabbage (about 2 cups sliced), some finely sliced sweet onion, and either a chopped hard boiled egg or half a 6-ounce can of solid light tuna in olive oil and ½-cup of leftover brown rice and 2 tablespoons of my vinaigrette. Mmm-mm.

Green cabbage
Cabbage is a member of the *brassica* family of vegetables, which means it is a fiber-rich

nutritional powerhouse. I prefer the taste and texture of the crinkly-leafed Savoy cabbage over regular cabbage. In any case, green and red (purple, really) cabbage is available year round and lasts an astounding length of time in the refrigerator. In fact, its sturdiness and good sportsmanship is why we see so much of it, red and green, represented on the fast food front, mainly in the form of coleslaw.

Cabbage is one of my favorite cooked vegetables, although one of the most bitterly joked about, usually in the context of boarding schools or grandmother's house. If you cook cabbage quickly you can avoid the smell and texture that has made cooked cabbage so famous.

("*Even today, well-brought-up English girls are taught by their mothers to boil all veggies for at least a month and a half, just in case one of the dinner guests turns up without his teeth.*" This quote is from Calvin Trillin, who may have been thinking of cabbage.)

The easiest way to serve cooked cabbage is to include it in a minestrone-style soup, like the one on page 143. My favorite way, though, is thinly sliced and sautéed in butter until tender, and either eaten as is with lemon juice, salt, and pepper or stirred through mashed potatoes. Cabbage and potatoes are very happy together. (See *Colcannon* on page 145.)

Butternut squash

This is virtually always available, all-purpose, and bursting with beta-carotene. Even its name is delicious. It is easy to prepare for purées, soups, or curries, or to roast in bite-sized chunks as a scrumptious accompaniment to roasted meat.

People who think they don't like squash have discovered they love it roasted with extra-virgin olive oil and salt. (See *Squash* in roasted vegetable section.) I've even eaten raw grated butternut squash in salads! (It was similar to raw grated carrot.)

It will hang around happily for weeks, if necessary, but it will gradually dry out and develop a whitish layer under the skin and a spongy texture. Look for a smooth, hard butternut squash that feels heavy for its size with no sign of wrinkles. Try to pick one with the longest, fattest neck for the maximum amount of solid flesh. The flavor is best in squash 2½ pounds or smaller.

Squashes are no fun to peel raw, but butternut squash is easier than most. When I'm in a hurry I don't bother with the bulb end where the seeds are. I just use the neck, peeling it as I would a carrot while using the bulb end as a grip. (The surface of peeled squash leaves a funny coating on the hands.)

I set aside the bulb end in a cool place and use it within a week, when there's time to also roast the seeds. (See following directions.) There are plenty of ways to use a small amount of such an agreeable vegetable: simply roast it or steam it and either serve it hot with whatever else you're eating or store it in the refrigerator for another time.

If you don't need to cut it while it's raw, however, simply halve and bake on a foil-lined roasting pan until the flesh is soft when you poke it with a knife or a skewer. Then you just scoop the flesh out of the skin. This bake-with-the-skin-on method works especially well with the more hard-to-peel winter squashes.

A simple but good side for any meat dish is puréed squash. (See page 144.) A creamy squash soup like the *Smoooth Butternut Bisque* (page 141) may be a bit of a cliché, but a great one.

Roasted squash seeds

Scoop out the squash seeds and roughly separate them from the fibrous stuff they're attached to. Some rinse the squashy stuff off them but I don't. Toss the seeds with about a teaspoon of extra-virgin olive oil, and then spread them on an oiled square of tin foil on a baking sheet. Salt lightly and roast in a 325 degree oven for about 15 minutes or until they're golden-brown and crunchy. (Don't let them get too brown or they'll be bitter.)

Roasted Vegetables

Even people (children as well as adults) who think they don't like vegetables generally like roasted vegetables. The explanation is pretty simple: when you apply fat, salt, and high heat, you are simulating the fast food effect without the downside.

The fast food effect calls for a bath in boiling hot partially hydrogenated fat. The *real* food method calls for a coating of extra-virgin olive oil and a very hot oven. The roasting method intensifies the flavor of the vegetable, caramelizes the sugars, softens the inside, and crisps the outside.

At times when you would normally sauté or steam vegetables, you can usually roast them instead. It's certainly easier than sautéing and allows you to do other things while the vegetables are cooking. The roasting option also delivers a flavorful and ready-to-serve vegetable straight from the oven.

When the oven is already occupied

If you have only one oven and you need it to cook the main dish at 350 degrees but you want to roast vegetables at 450 degrees, it can be tricky. My fall-back position in that case is usually good old asparagus.

You can pull out the main dish the moment it's done, crank the temperature up to 450 degrees, then put in the waiting asparagus on the top rack, arranged in one layer in the foiled pan, lightly coated with extra-virgin olive oil and sprinkled with salt and pepper. Ten minutes later (or seven minutes for skinny asparagus) the asparagus is ready to serve.

The equipment and roasting guidelines are the same for most vegetables. The largest variable is the cooking time. Root vegetables take longer to soften and tend to improve if slightly over-roasted but run the risk of drying out. For that reason they are best eaten freshly cooked. Cold leftovers of roasted asparagus, on the other hand, are arguably as good as when first served.

On the next page is a sort of master recipe with general directions, and on the pages following are notes on some specific vegetables.

Don't forget the Goop

Most roasted vegetables at our table are accompanied with a side of an all-purpose sauce we call Goop, more formally called *Rich Yogurt Aioli*. (The recipe is on page 98.) This is a mixture of drained yogurt, homemade mayonnaise, salt, pepper, and enough freshly crushed garlic to cause an involuntary gasp.

Goop goes especially well with roasted potatoes, squash, asparagus, beets, broccoli, and cauliflower. As I may have mentioned elsewhere, it is also popular with meat (especially the meatloaf on page 208) and fish (especially grilled salmon).

This sauce is important to remember even when serving roasted vegetables to people who you feel confident will eat neither vegetables, yogurt, nor garlic. You certainly may be right, but more often than not you'll be wrong. It never pays to underestimate the teamwork of roasted vegetables and Goop.

Roasted Vegetables (Master Recipe)

(Serves about 4)

6 cups of vegetable pieces *(see following pages for suggestions)*
¼ cup extra-virgin olive oil
salt and freshly ground pepper
non-stick spray

Preheat oven to 450 degrees.

1. Find the largest roasting pan that will fit into your oven. The vegetables want plenty of elbowroom. The ideal pan will be sturdy and have at least half-inch sides to contain any liquid or wandering vegetable pieces. (Flimsy pans can seize in a hot oven and startle the vegetables.)

2. Line the pan with heavy-duty foil, a step that makes cleaning up ridiculously easy. (Regular foil rips too easily when you try to remove the roasted vegetables.)

3. Mist the foil with non-stick spray if you wish — I do only when I am roasting vegetables with less moisture. Potatoes and squash, for instance, tend to stick. For vegetables like zucchini and onions, the oil on the outside and the moisture on the inside are enough to resist sticking. If in doubt, though, mist with non-stick spray.

4. Toss vegetable pieces with olive oil and spread in one layer in the pan. If you add more vegetables than will fit in one layer, they will steam where they are stacked, and you will end up with semi-stewed vegetables.

5. Sprinkle with salt and freshly ground pepper. I prefer to apply salt using a salt grinder — takes a bit more fussing but I can control the coverage and the ground salt sticks best. The subject of pepper calls for the use of full caps. USE FRESHLY GROUND PEPPER from your pepper grinder. Pre-ground pepper is a poor and distant relative. Anyway, this is the best time to season the vegetables because you can make sure each piece gets a fair share, but no more than it needs.

6. Place uncovered in the top third of a preheated 450-degree oven for 10 – 45 minutes, depending on the vegetable and the size of the pieces. At this temperature the liquid will tend to evaporate from the vegetable instead of collecting in the pan, and you will probably notice the steam steadily escaping from the closed oven door toward the end of the roasting process. ***Be careful opening the oven!*** Make sure and turn your eyes away from the initial burst of steam.

7. There's generally no reason to interrupt a vegetable while it's roasting. Once you are comfortable with the process, and know how long to leave the vegetables in the oven, just set the timer and get busy doing something else.

8. When you test for doneness, poke the bigger pieces. It's better for the smaller pieces to be overcooked than to serve any undercooked vegetables. In fact, people who wouldn't care — or maybe even notice — if they never saw another vegetable in their life may fight over the blackened and caramelized crispy bits.

Roasted asparagus

This is the *only* way we have cooked asparagus ever since we first discovered the roasting method. To prepare asparagus, break off tough ends by holding both the top of the spear (below the head) and the stem end and bending it until it snaps. This takes longer than cutting the ends but it is the best way to remove **only** the tough ends. There is no need to use a peeler.

Clean thoroughly in a bath of cold water. If you are not going to use them the same day, store them in the refrigerator with their stem ends in about ¼ inch of water and the spears upright, like a bouquet of flowers, loosely covered with plastic or a damp paper towel. (A Pyrex measuring jug works well.)

Drain and pat dry, and coat with extra-virgin olive oil: my method is to heap them up, pour a couple of tablespoons of oil on top, then use my hands to make sure they are coated with oil. Spread in a roasting pan (crowding is fine, but one layer only), sprinkle with salt and freshly ground pepper, and roast at the top of the oven for about 10 minutes for slim asparagus and 12-15 minutes for fatter spears. The timing obviously depends on whether you prefer your asparagus tender-crisp or soft. A slight browning of the spears and crisping of the tips adds a flavorsome touch.

A plate of hot roasted asparagus can be served as an appetizer, or as a salad course tossed in vinaigrette. It is also fine on the dinner table even though the spears cool quickly.

Roasted beets

The beet is not a fiercely popular vegetable, but please read long enough for me to put in a word for a side dish of slim, gleaming deep-red beet wedges tossed in vinaigrette. You'll feel gratified when a guest notices them and cries "Beets? Are those *beets*? I *love* beets, but I haven't had any since my grandmother moved to Florida!"

To prepare for this moment, place the rinsed beets exactly as you bought them – tails intact but greens chopped to an inch in length – on a large enough piece of foil to allow you to enclose beets completely. Seal beets inside the foil and place in any old baking pan that fits. (If you use heavy-duty foil you don't necessarily even need a pan.) Roast in the middle of the oven for about 1½ – 2 hours.

(Beets can take an amazing amount of time to cook, and you don't want to have to bother unwrapping them until you're sure they're done. If you must interrupt earlier because you're in a hurry or the beets are small, test for doneness by poking with a skewer.)

When beets are cool enough to handle, poke a fork in the greens end and peel with a paring knife. Skins should slip off easily. Slice peeled beets into slim wedges (or cubes or straws) and toss while still warm in vinaigrette. Make sure to check your fingernails for beet stains.

Roasted Brussels sprouts

You thought beets were bad! Well, Brussels sprouts also have a relatively small but passionate following, and you never know when someone is going to ask you to cook some up as a special birthday treat. So, pull off loose outer leaves and trim the stem so it is almost flush with the sprout. Cut a tiny but deep **x** in the stem with the tip of your paring knife. Don't fret over this step.

(Optional step: toss sprouts into a pot of boiling salted water for about 5 minutes – you are not trying to cook them, just blanch them. Drain very well.)

Leave whole or cut in half, depending mainly on their size. Toss with a generous dose of extra-virgin olive oil and spread the Brussels sprouts in a foil-lined roasting pan. Sprinkle with salt and roast, shaking pan once or twice, for about 30 minutes or until browned and luscious. If the oven isn't available for roasting, you could just continue boiling the Brussels sprouts for another 5 minutes, or until just tender; drain well, then cut in half and roll around in garlicky vinaigrette, like the one on page 95. Good whether hot, warm, or at room temperature, and irresistible with a side of *Rich Yogurt Aioli* (page 98).

Roasted cauliflower

Roasted cauliflower is a delicacy to be shared between two or three who can be trusted to eat no more than their share. Cauliflower can vary quite a bit in size but two people can easily dispose of an average sized head if it's roasted as described below. (You should also try serving it as an appetizer straight from the oven to surprised friends.)

Separate cauliflower into clumps, and then carve or split clumps into smaller florets with a paring knife. Toss gently in extra-virgin olive oil and roast for about 15 – 25 minutes or until cauliflower is browning. We like an almost toasted effect, blackened bits and all. Eat right away, if possible.

Roasted eggplant

No-one needs roasted eggplant badly enough to buy anything but the best. Only settle for an eggplant that is firm, glossy, and smooth-skinned, with a perky-looking green cap. Try to use it the same day. (Store eggplants as you do tomatoes, at room temperature.) You're safest with a small to medium size, no more than eight ounces. The most dependable for mild flavor and tender skins are the Japanese eggplants. There is generally no need to peel an eggplant unless you suspect the skin is tough or waxed.

So, trim off the stem end, and cube the eggplant in ¾ inch chunks. A good fresh eggplant requires no salting and draining to remove bitterness. Toss with extra-virgin olive oil (which is absorbed as fast as you add it, so pay attention) and salt and roast according to the master recipe. It's ready when soft and beginning to brown, which will be about 25 minutes.

For eggplant lovers, the simplest preparation is to slice into ½ inch rounds. Line a baking sheet with foil, then brush both sides of the eggplant rounds with extra-virgin olive oil and crowd them on the sheet like cookies (except they don't spread). Sprinkle with salt, and roast for about 25-30 minutes or until eggplant is buttery soft to the touch.

Roasted garlic

You'll have to read about roasting garlic somewhere else. I don't roast garlic. Fresh garlic, however, is about the best friend a roasted vegetable can have. See recipe for Goop (*Rich Yogurt Aioli*) on page 98.

Roasted green beans

Roast these as you would asparagus. A plate of roasted and salted green beans makes a great appetizer. However, I've had mixed success; they can be tough and dryish, possibly because they weren't as fresh as they seemed. Still tasty, though.

Roasted onions

The sweeter varieties with their thicker layers are the best choice for roasted onions. Trim and peel onions, then cut the onions into wedges or big chunks (which will tend to break down when you toss them in oil) or into ¾-inch slices which you can brush with oil. Sprinkle with salt and pepper, and roast until the onion flesh is almost melting and the edges are blackened, about 30 minutes. Or you may prefer them less radically roasted. (You can even use this method on diced onions as an alternative to sautéing them.)

Some people like to roast them whole, in or out of the skin, with a chunk of butter stuck into a plug cut out of the center. Anything is fine as long as there is at least an onion for each person planning to eat. (Onions reduce by about half when they're cooked, as well as becoming mild and sweet.)

Roasted parsnips

How can you bring up the subject of parsnips with a straight face? But how can you possibly *ignore* them with a name like that? Now that we have mentioned them, though, it should be added that parsnips justify their existence, in my opinion, when roasted as described here. Choose slim and smallish ones, peel and cut them in half-inch chunks, roast them to within an inch of their lives, and don't be stingy with the oil and salt. (If your parsnips have very thick ends, cut off the thickest part, quarter it lengthwise, and remove the core, which tends to be tough.)

Roasted peppers

If there is one roasted vegetable that evokes the Mediterranean best for me, it is the sweet red (or yellow or orange) bell pepper. Especially when the peppers are broiled, skinned, and marinated, a surprisingly easy operation. (…except for the fact that it always sets off our smoke alarm with smoke I can never see.)

So, remove the stem, core, seeds, and white pithy bits, and quarter lengthwise. Lay skin-side up on a shallow foil-lined baking pan. (There's no need to oil anything, but use enough foil to allow you to enclose the peppers later.)

Place under the broiler and keep an eye on them. The skin should blacken within 20 minutes. You may choose to move them around to broil more evenly or use an egg turner to flatten any that are curving up too high. Basically the peppers are ready when most of the skin area is charred.

Pull pan out of the oven and bring the edges of the foil over and snugly wrap the peppers up for about 10 minutes. The skin will scrape off easily. (*Please* don't skin the poor peppers under running water like some instructions say. It's appalling to think of mixing water with the fragrant pepper juice just for the sake of a few bits of blackened skin or whatever.)

Roll the delicious and still warm pepper sections in a few tablespoons of vinaigrette or a quick mixture of a couple of tablespoons of extra-virgin olive oil, a tablespoon of vinegar, a half-teaspoon of crushed garlic, and some salt and pepper.

Roasted potatoes

This is a roasted vegetable that virtually everyone loves. There are lots of options here, both in method and variety (white, red, Yukon gold, russet, and so on). My favorite is baby red potatoes boiled in a big pot of water for 15 minutes and then rolled in extra-virgin olive oil, salted and peppered, and roasted for about 30 minutes or until soft inside. (You can roast them without parboiling them first, but the texture inside and the crunch outside may not be as good.) Depending on their size, you can quarter them, halve them, or leave them whole to roast them.

For roasting potato wedges I prefer Yukon gold. Aim for slimmer rather than fat specimens, scrubbed but not peeled, sliced lengthwise in at least eighths, tossed in extra-virgin olive oil, and crowded in the foil lined pan curved skin side down. (I actually take the time to set each wedge on its back, because it is least likely to stick to the foil that way. I don't disturb them while they're cooking, naturally.)

Sprinkle with salt and pepper, and roast until they are golden-brown, blistered, and crunchy on the outside and molten soft on the inside. Allow about 45 – 60 minutes, depending on the size of the pieces, and serve straight from the oven with a side of *Rich Yogurt Aioli*. (See page 98.)

To substitute for baked potatoes, cut potatoes in half lengthwise, rub with extra-virgin olive oil, sprinkle with salt and pepper, and roast about 45 minutes, or until tender inside and crisp outside.

For the quickest-cooking version and a great appetizer, make potato crisps: slice potatoes lengthwise into thin slices, crowd on an oiled foil-lined baking sheet, brush with extra-virgin olive oil, sprinkle lightly with salt, and roast until browned – about 10-15 minutes.

Roasted (butternut) squash

To me, squash automatically means butternut squash. As well as having the most appetizing name, this variety is easy to prepare with its smooth shape, thin skin, and sensible seed arrangement. When you buy, look for one with a long neck and an abbreviated bulb end – the neck is easiest to chop into regular pieces. (Use a sharp chef's knife and be careful when cutting this vegetable; it is hard and dense, and its shape makes it tricky to handle.)

Trim the stem end, and peel with a vegetable peeler. (Handling the peeled squash leaves a funny coating on the palms of the hands – I try to hold onto the unpeeled section as long as I can.) Slice the neck into about 1-inch wheels, and then cut slices into sixths or eighths, depending on the size of the squash.

Toss with extra-virgin olive oil, and lay curved side down where possible. Sprinkle with salt and pepper and roast 30 – 45 minutes, or until blackened on the points of the wedges and very soft. (If you are roasting the squash for purée or soup, see recipe for *Smoooth Butternut Bisque* on page 141. There are also directions for roasting the seeds on page 122.)

Roasted yams (sweet potatoes)

I mean the orange-fleshed sweet potatoes, which are called yams in this country, and which are among the richest sources of beta-carotene in the vegetable world. They are actually unrelated to yams *or* potatoes, oddly enough. The jewel or garnet sweet potatoes (yams) have generally smooth reddish-brown skins that peel easily, and are even delicious sliced and eaten raw – crisp and slightly sweet.

They can also be baked like potatoes in their skins (but on a piece of foil because the sugar escapes and burns late in the cooking) at 400 degrees for about an hour or until very soft when squeezed. Split and mash with a bit of butter, salt, and pepper. It tastes almost illicit.

To roast sweet potatoes or yams for a vegetable side dish, peel and slice into ¾ -inch chunks and roast them just as you would butternut squash, allowing the edges to blacken slightly. For roasted sweet potato cookies, slice peeled raw sweet potatoes into ¼ -inch slices, brush with extra-virgin olive oil, season, and roast for about 30 minutes or until starting to brown.

Roasted turnips

Buy them small and unblemished, and they are too good to cook – just peel and slice thinly and eat lightly salted and raw, or with dip. Their peppery sweetness is delicious roasted, too, and especially good with rich meat dishes like meatloaf.

Roasted zucchini

If you can't find small-to-moderate, slim, hard zucchinis, I don't recommend buying them at all. The bigger they are, the tougher the skin and the more spongy and seedy the centers.

So, clean and trim them, but don't peel them, of course. (Only the large zucchinis have tough skin.) Slice them down the middle lengthwise, and then cut them into 2-inch chunks. Toss in extra-virgin olive oil and lay them skin side down in the foil-lined roasting pan. Sprinkle with salt and freshly ground pepper, and roast high in a hot, hot oven for about 20 minutes, or until the zucchini is tender and beginning to brown. (Some like zucchini very soft, but I prefer it with some texture intact.)

A good side dish is roasted zucchini and onion: quarter zucchini lengthwise and slice in 1-inch chunks. Chop 2 onions in 1-inch dice. Add to chopped zucchini and toss vegetables in extra-virgin olive oil. Season and roast according to the master recipe for about 20 minutes, or until onions begin to blacken on the edges and the zucchini begins to brown. Beware! It shrinks quite a bit, so make sure there's enough to go around.

Simple Salads

The very simplest salad is sticks or slices of raw vegetables like celery, carrot, cucumber, tomato, bell peppers, broccoli or cauliflower, baby zucchini, jicama (see page 164 and 202-3), small turnips, radishes, and so forth, served with some sort of dip or dressing. My favorite three are *Definitive Dip*, *Hasty Tasty Hummus*, and *Goop*, but check out pages 94 – 102 for other ideas.

- Almost as simple is just about any combination of the same vegetables grated, thinly sliced, diced, or julienne (sliced into matchsticks) and dressed with vinaigrette, salt, and freshly ground pepper.

- The sturdy and versatile vegetables like carrots, celery, and cabbage are easy to recruit for salad duty just about any time. You can't be as spontaneous with the more delicate and perishable greens, but the variety is nice.

- Don't forget the option of steamed or roasted vegetables tossed with vinaigrette – salads don't have to be raw. In fact, there are many people who would ignore a conventional salad but enjoy a lightly cooked and marinated vegetable like asparagus, carrots, or green beans.

Fresh Tomato Salad

This is one of the most useful – and certainly one of the easiest – salads in existence. Good color accent on the table *and* the plate, easy to eat, and generally acceptable to most audiences. (As any tomato lover knows, there are times of the year when prime tomatoes are hard to find, but it's surprising what salt and pepper can do.) A plain tomato salad is simple to jazz up with green or white onions, diced avocado, olives, fresh herbs, and so on. The option I use most is sweet white onions. (You can usually find sweet onions year round, imported or otherwise.)

1. Just dice or slice fresh tomatoes – about 1 per person – into chunks, wedges, or slices and serve them sprinkled with salt and freshly ground pepper. You may prefer a bit of vinaigrette, but you will find that the salt draws out the juices of the tomatoes, which combines with the pepper to make its own dressing. It is best done within a half-hour of serving.

2. ***Onion Option***: Peel onion and halve lengthwise. Lay one half cut side down on cutting board and slice slim wedges (no more than ¼ inch at widest point) from the rounded edge. You will need about ½ - 1 cup of onion slices (depending on quantity of tomatoes and mildness of onions). Combine with 2 tablespoons vinaigrette and set aside to marinate for 15 minutes, if possible. Mix gently with chopped tomatoes.

Apple, Broccoli, and Celery Salad

This is my favorite way to use broccoli stems. It's a good reason to buy broccoli with nice long stems instead of paying more for broccoli crowns. Always check for solid, fresh looking stems, however – if you can bend the stems, don't buy the broccoli. Some chopped broccoli florets can help give a deeper green accent, too.

(Serves 4 – 6)

1 – 2 crisp apples, peeled or not, in ½ x ¼ inch dice (about 1½ - 2 cups)
1 – 2 cups sliced peeled broccoli stems
2 cups sliced celery, ¼ -inch or less

3 tablespoons mayonnaise
1 tablespoon apple cider vinegar or lemon juice
½ teaspoon salt
½ teaspoon freshly ground pepper

½ cup broken fresh or toasted walnuts or pecans
2 tablespoons dried currants or raisins

1. Strip thick skin from broccoli stems using a small knife, starting with the base of stem and peeling upwards. Halve lengthwise and slice in ⅛ – ¼ inch slices.

2. Mix together vinegar, mayonnaise, salt, and pepper and add to apples, broccoli, and celery with nuts and currants. Toss to blend thoroughly.

Spinach, Napa, and Mushroom Salad

The contrast of the deep smooth green spinach with the pale crinkly leaves of the napa cabbage is striking enough to make this salad get away with utter simplicity. And more often than not, I make it without the mushrooms.

(Serves 4 – 6)

8 ounces sliced mushrooms

¼ cup vinaigrette (see *Vinaigrette* on page 95*)*
4 cups sliced napa cabbage (about ½ head)
6 ounces pre-washed baby spinach
¼ - ½ cup freshly grated Parmesan

1. Place mushrooms in salad bowl and toss with 2 tablespoons vinaigrette. I do this about 10 minutes ahead to allow the mushrooms to "cook" a bit.

2. Add sliced cabbage and spinach with remaining 2 tablespoons vinaigrette and toss thoroughly. Add Parmesan, toss again, and serve as soon as possible.

Pico de Gallo (with Cabbage Variation)

Naturally you can fool around with the proportions and ingredients here, but this is a version I like to serve with rich dishes like chili and salmon.

(Serves 4 – 6)

> 2 tablespoons lime or lemon juice
> 2 tablespoons extra-virgin olive oil
> 1 teaspoon freshly crushed garlic
> 1 teaspoon salt
> 1 jalapeno chili, minced (at least 2 tablespoons or to taste)
> ½ cup chopped fresh cilantro, if available
> 1 cup diced (¼ -inch) mild onion, like Mayan or any sweet variety
>
> 2 – 4 tomatoes (about 2 cups) seeded and in ¼-inch dice
> 2 cups cucumber, peeled and seeded if necessary, in ¼-inch dice
> *or* 2 cups green cabbage in ¼ inch dice

1. In a small mixing bowl combine lemon juice, olive oil, garlic, salt, jalapenos, and fresh cilantro. Add diced onion and set aside.

2. Core and quarter tomatoes, and scoop out seeds. (Don't discard, for goodness sake! Eat them or save them for soup.) Dice tomatoes and cucumber or cabbage. (English cucumbers need no peeling or seeding.)

3. Add tomatoes and cucumber or diced cabbage and toss thoroughly.

Avocado Salsa

This is *so* good and *so* simple. It even looks and tastes fresh the next day. It works best if the avocados are on the firm side of ripe.

(Makes about 2 cups)

> 2 large or 3 small avocados, ripe but firm
> 1 cup diced sweet onion
> 2 – 3 tablespoons fresh lime or lemon juice
> 1 tablespoon extra-virgin olive oil
> ½ teaspoon freshly crushed garlic
> ¼ teaspoon salt
> ¼ teaspoon Tabasco sauce

1. Dice avocados in ¼ - ½ inch cubes, and the onion in ¼-inch dice. Combine in bowl and gently toss with lime juice, olive oil, garlic, salt, and Tabasco. Taste for flavor. Try to leave some for others.

Tossed Green Salad with Vinaigrette and Parmesan

The makeup of the greens can vary according to whatever you happen to have on hand; if you can plan ahead you can have bags of mixed greens and baby spinach to combine. The crispier and meatier romaine lettuce provides a nice contrast to the more delicate specialty greens. A handful of finely shredded red cabbage provides some nice color. Any salad greens work, but they should be clean, dry, and fresh. You can have the greens waiting in their serving bowl an hour or so ahead as long as you cover them with a damp paper towel and store them in the refrigerator. Dress the greens just before serving because they wilt quickly.

(Serves about 4, but easily adjusted for any number)

> 8 – 10 cups of bite sized greens
> ¼ cup *Garlic and Mustard Vinaigrette* (page 95)
> ½ cup freshly grated Parmesan (see page 67)

1. Toss the greens with the vinaigrette. Add Parmesan and toss again. Serve right away while greens are still perky.

Napa Cabbage Salad with Cilantro

If making this salad a day in advance, I would suggest leaving it undressed until shortly before you plan to serve it; napa cabbage is not as sturdy as regular cabbage, and so tends to wilt as its liquid drains from its leaves into the bottom of the bowl. But wilted or not, it makes a refreshing snack the next day.

(Serves 4 – 6)

> 6 cups thinly sliced napa cabbage
> 3 green onions, sliced thinly on the diagonal (optional)
> ¼ – ½ cup chopped cilantro
>
> **Lemon and Cumin Vinaigrette:** *(makes about ⅓ cup)*
> 2 tablespoons lemon juice
> ½ teaspoon ground cumin
> ½ teaspoon salt
> 1 teaspoon honey
> 1 teaspoon freshly crushed garlic
> 2 tablespoons extra-virgin olive oil

1. Combine cabbage, green onion, and cilantro in mixing bowl.

2. Whisk together vinaigrette ingredients. Just before serving, add to cabbage mixture and toss.

Carrot Slaw

This is bright looking and punchy tasting with a sweet twist.   (You could use a pre-shredded cabbage mixture instead of preparing them yourself, and dress the salad with ¼-cup of the *Lemon and Cumin Vinaigrette* from page 95.)

(Serves 4)

> 2 cups grated carrot (about 2 – 3 medium)
> 2 cups thinly-sliced green cabbage (like Savoy or Napa)
> ¼ cup raw sunflower seeds
> ¼ cup currants *or* finely minced or sliced candied ginger
>
> 1 tablespoon apple cider vinegar
> 1 tablespoon honey
> 2 tablespoon extra-virgin olive oil
> ½ teaspoon freshly crushed garlic
> ½ teaspoon salt
> ½ teaspoon freshly ground pepper

1. Combine carrots, cabbage, sunflower seeds, and ginger/currants. *(The dainty little currants or dark raisins give a vivid accent to this salad.)*

2. Mix together vinegar, honey, olive oil, garlic, salt, and pepper. Add to vegetable mixture and toss thoroughly.

Mediterranean Chopped Salad

Any variation on the theme here works. If you happen to have a few crisp radishes to slice, or a particularly fresh little zucchini to dice, add or substitute. Use whatever you like or happen to have available, adjusting amounts of each to your taste.

> 1 cucumber peeled and quartered lengthwise
> 2 medium tomatoes
> 1 sweet bell pepper, gold if possible for color
> 1 cup diced sweet onion
> ¼ cup *Lemon and Cumin Vinaigrette* or *Garlic and Mustard Vinaigrette* (page 95.)

1. Seed cucumber if seeds are large, and cut into ¼-inch dice. Dice tomatoes – I prefer Roma tomatoes for this salad, as they tend to have more meat and less juice – and bell pepper into ¼-inch dice. Add diced onion.

2. Combine vegetables with vinaigrette and toss. Add more salt and freshly ground pepper to taste.

Greek Salad

A mild onion is important in this salad — one of the sweet varieties like the seasonal Walla Wallas from Washington state, or Vidalias from Georgia, or Texas Sweets. Sweet onions from somewhere are available year-round. If you have only hot onion, make a different salad. My Greek salad needs plenty of onions, so they need to be mild. This is one of those recipes where every ingredient is critical.

(Serves 4 as side dish)

2 tablespoons apple cider vinegar
2 tablespoons extra-virgin olive oil
½ teaspoon salt
½ teaspoon freshly ground pepper
2 cups sliced sweet onion

1 cucumber, or about 2 cups chopped
4 – 6 Roma tomatoes, at least 2 cups chopped
½ cup kalamata olives, pitted and quartered
4 – 8 ounces mild feta cheese, thinly sliced
    and crumbled

1. Place vinegar, oil, salt, and pepper in mixing bowl.

2. Peel onion and halve lengthwise. Lay one half cut side down on cutting board and slice slim strips, no more than ¼ inch at widest point, from the rounded edge. *(Cut strips in half if onion is big.)* You will need 2 cups of onion slices, if onion is mild enough. Add onion to dressing in bowl and toss.

3. Peel and quarter cucumber lengthwise, and scoop out seeds. Cut in ¼-inch slices. (If you are using a thin-skinned English cucumber you don't need to peel or seed.)

4. Quarter tomatoes lengthwise and remove bits of core, then cut crosswise into ½-inch slices. Add tomatoes and cucumbers to onion mixture.

5. Prepare kalamata olives (20 olives make about ½ cup) and feta. I prefer to use the larger quantity of feta, and slice it thinly so it crumbles and blends into the salad as part of the dressing. You may prefer to leave the feta in chunks, which is certainly acceptable. Add olives and feta to salad and toss. Mmmm.

Note:

▸ If you're not a feta cheese user already, start with a mild domestic brand made from cow's milk. Don't be intimidated by the use-by date – feta lasts an amazingly long time in the refrigerator sealed in its original package. Its rich, salty bite mingles with the dressing and is not at all intrusive, even for those who think they don't like feta.

The **kalamata olive** is an almond-shaped marinated Greek olive with a succulent texture and a very distinctive flavor. Another olive will work here, but *not* the mild black olive found in buffet salad bars. You can buy kalamata olives already pitted, either in a jar on the supermarket shelf or from a good deli section olive bar where you can serve yourself. However, if you happen to find yourself with olives that haven't been pitted, here is my kalamata-pitting method. (It does not work with the tiny Nicoise olives, thankfully, they are available already pitted.)

▸ Score each olive into quarters, cutting down to the seed, then massage the olive gently, with a finger and thumb on the pointy ends, until the pit disengages from the neatly quartered flesh. (Well, they don't all quarter neatly, but it doesn't matter. The flavor is the important thing.)

▸ Don't pit the olives over the salad! Being a bit sensitive about broken fillings myself, I count the pits — which look dangerously like quartered olives — before I add the olives to the salad.

Warm Potato Salad
Steamed sliced potatoes
with onions in vinaigrette

This dish is my solution when I want to serve potatoes but I don't want to have to think about any last minute preparation. It is almost as good eaten cold the next day. The onions are a critical ingredient, a fresh and crunchy foil for the rich potatoes, and if I seem to make too much of a fuss over the slicing instructions, well, it's my salad. Diced onions are not as companionable with the potato slices, and long slices drape messily off the fork. Also, I prefer to slice the onion with rather than against the grain.

(Serves 4-6)

about 1½ pounds small red potatoes

1 – 2 cups sliced sweet onion
2 tablespoons apple cider vinegar
2 tablespoons whole grain mustard
¼ cup extra-virgin olive oil
2 tablespoons capers
1 teaspoon freshly crushed garlic
1 teaspoon salt
1 teaspoon freshly ground pepper
¼ cup chopped fresh parsley

1. Scrub potatoes and remove eyes and anything that looks like it might be harboring grit. Slice into ¼-inch slices. Steam in a basket steamer until very tender, about 30 minutes.

2. Peel onion and halve lengthwise. Lay one half cut side down on cutting board and halve again crosswise, along what would be the onion's equator. Slice thin strips, about ⅛-inch at widest point, from the rounded edge. *If the onion is truly mild, I definitely recommend doubling the quantity of sliced onion to 2 cups. If the onion fumes are making your eyes water, the onion is not mild.*

3. Combine vinegar, mustard, oil, capers, garlic, salt, pepper, and parsley in a small mixing bowl. Add sliced onion, toss to coat onions, and set aside.

4. Drain hot cooked potato slices and tip into something like a 9 x 5-inch baking pan. Pour onion and dressing mixture evenly over the potato slices and mix very tenderly, using a large rubber spatula to gently separate slices of potato. Shake the pan now and then as you mix to help expose more potato surface to the dressing.

5. Mix salad a few times over the next half hour, then transfer to serving dish.

Note:

▸ Warm potato salad is also a grand buffet dish because it is just as good hours later, even though no longer warm.

▸ Any waxy potato would work – Yukon Gold is a fine choice. Slim potatoes make smaller slices which hold together better. Also, I like to peel a strip of skin the lengthwise circumference of each potato to reduce the chances of trailing skin.

Salade Niçoise

For my version of *Salade Niçoise,* I like to showcase this warm potato salad along with sliced hard-boiled eggs, some very good tuna, steamed green beans, some wedges of sweet ripe tomatoes, roasted marinated beets (see page 125), and some very good pitted black olives. (*Niçoise* olives are tiny and impossible to pit, in my opinion, and their size makes it easy for them to ride the fork unnoticed into your mouth, right between your unsuspecting teeth. Buy them already pitted.)

136

9 Vegetable Soups *and* Sides

Vegetable Soups

One of the easiest and most pleasant ways I know to bump up our servings of vegetables is by way of soup. I'm not talking about a meal-in-a-pot type soup like the *Crowded Chowder* on page 194, but the kind of simple-themed soups that feature one or two vegetables. If the ingredients and method are simple enough we are more likely to include an extra serving or two of vegetables in our meals.

My favorite soup making method begins with three or four cups of water in a 5-quart pot over medium-high heat. I always chop up a large onion and add it to the water with a teaspoon of salt. Then I add another four cups of chopped vegetables. After the vegetables have simmered for about half an hour (or until completely tender), I usually add evaporated whole milk and purée the soup with my immersion blender.

(Puréed soups have at least two advantages: the creaminess can cover a multitude of sins, and the texture makes them easier to eat than broth-and-vegetable-type soups. These soups alone are worth the purchase of an immersion blender, which you can stick directly into the hot soup to purée it without having to transfer the soup to a processor or blender.)

These are very basic recipes that I can generally put together without planning ahead; most of the ingredients are my pantry standards. With a handful of these easy recipes standing by, you can add a vegetable without much trouble.

(A creamy vegetable soup is a good way to use frozen vegetables, too. See the *Quick Green Pea Soup* on page 115, with the spinach and zucchini variations.)

Two Potato Soup

This is a simple and luscious soup. Not complex, but comforting and easy to make. Because I always have the ingredients on hand, and because the soup takes only an hour from start to finish, this is a favorite. (The name *Two Potato Soup* is not actually accurate, as yams are not potatoes.)

(Serves about 4)

3 cups water
1 large onion in ¼-inch dice
1 medium–large garnet yam, grated
1 medium baking potato, grated
2 teaspoons salt
2 teaspoons freshly crushed garlic
½ teaspoon freshly ground pepper
¼ teaspoon Tabasco sauce
1 can (14 ounces) coconut milk (not low-fat)

1. Bring water to the boil in a 5-quart soup pot over medium high heat. Add diced onion and grated vegetables as you prepare them. You will have roughly 3 – 4 cups of each. Add salt and bring back to the boil, then reduce heat and simmer for about 30 – 45 minutes, stirring and scraping the bottom every 10 minutes or so to keep it from sticking. (Don't worry if it seems too thick.)

2. Add garlic, pepper, Tabasco, and coconut milk, and simmer 10 minutes longer.

3. Whisk vigorously, both to blend ingredients and to smooth the texture of the soup. For a creamy version use an immersion blender or food processor. Bring back to a simmer and serve.

Cauliflower Butter Broth

The cauliflower is one of the most sensible vegetables a busy person could have in the refrigerator. They're quick to clean and easy to prepare, with almost no waste. (Before you buy one, though, make sure its snowy complexion is natural and not the result of cosmetic surgery. Few vegetables age gracefully.) The cauliflower is mild mannered enough to be generally liked but with enough of the crucifer family spunk to be interesting. This is a simple, satisfying, single-note soup that uses the whole cauliflower, and makes a good first course while giving you one or two servings of vegetables.

(Serves about 4)

1 cauliflower
½ stick (4 tablespoons) butter
1 medium-large onion, diced (about 3 cups)
1 tablespoon freshly crushed garlic
2 tablespoons all purpose flour
4 cups water
1½ teaspoons salt
1 teaspoon freshly-ground black pepper
(½ cup chopped fresh parsley)

1. Rinse and trim cauliflower of leaves and stem. Separate into clumps and split clumps into smaller florets with a paring knife. Dice the core and the remaining bits and pieces. You should have at least 6 cups total. Set aside.

2. Heat a heavy 5-quart pot over medium-high heat. Add butter. When bubbling, add onions. Sauté 12 minutes or until onion is tender.

3. Reduce heat to low, add garlic, and sauté another minute. Sprinkle the flour over the top and blend in thoroughly. Add 1 cup of water and blend until smooth. Add remaining water, salt, and pepper.

4. Scrape cauliflower into the soup. Some will probably poke above the surface but that's fine. Bring soup to a simmer and cook for about 35 minutes or until cauliflower is very tender. Stir in parsley, if you have it.

Note:

▸ Broccoli instead of (or combined with) the cauliflower is just as good but the broccoli does tend to fade.
▸ You can replace all or half the butter with extra-virgin olive oil – I may not even notice.

Cauliflower Cream Soup
Gently Curried

(Serves 4)

4 cups water
1 medium-large onion, diced (about 3 cups)
1 cauliflower, chopped (about 6 cups)
1 tablespoon freshly crushed garlic
1½ teaspoons salt
½ teaspoon freshly ground black pepper
½ teaspoon curry powder
1 cup evaporated whole milk
(¼ cup finely chopped fresh parsley or cilantro – optional)

1. Bring water to a boil and add diced onions.

2. Quarter cauliflower lengthwise and slice into ¼ - ½-inch slices, including core. Add to pot, bring back to a boil, and then reduce heat and simmer 35 minutes.

3. Add garlic, salt, and pepper, and curry powder, and simmer another 10 minutes.

4. Add evaporated milk and purée until smooth with an immersion blender. *(If you use a food processor, let soup cool a bit before puréeing it in 2 batches.)* Serve each bowl with a sprinkle of cilantro or parsley.

Creamy Thai Tomato Soup

The Thai reference is actually culinary license on my part but this is a great soup: rich and vivid, yet with the comforting quality of creamy tomato soups. This can be made from scratch quickly and uses ingredients I always have on hand.

(Serves 6)

¼ cup extra-virgin olive oil
½ teaspoon crushed chilies
1 medium – large onion, diced (about 3 cups)
1 tablespoon freshly crushed garlic

1 can (28 ounces) crushed tomatoes
1½ cups tomato juice (or a 12-ounce can)
1 teaspoon salt
1 teaspoon minced fresh ginger
2 teaspoons fish sauce (see *Note*)
1½ tablespoons honey
1 can (14 ounces) coconut milk (regular, not low-fat)
2 tablespoons fresh basil leaves, thinly sliced

1. Heat the oil over medium-high heat in a heavy 5-quart soup pot. Add chilies and onion. Sauté 15 minutes, or until onions are very soft. Add garlic and sauté another minute.

2. Add crushed tomatoes, tomato juice, salt, ginger, fish sauce, and honey. Bring to a simmer, then reduce heat and simmer for about 20 – 30 minutes, stirring now and then. Remove from heat, add coconut milk, and blend thoroughly with whisk or purée. (See note below.) Add fresh basil just before serving.

Note:

▶ I like the smooth-textured version of this soup. If you have an immersion blender, purée soup directly in pot. If you use a food processor, purée cooled soup in 2 batches. Return soup to pot and bring to a simmer again. The fresh basil is a grand addition, but the soup is bright enough in color and flavor to stand alone.

▶ Thai fish sauce is potently fishy, so don't let the smell put you off. I use it also in the *Tom Kah Gai* on page 196. It is available in most supermarkets and probably has a shelf life of a hundred years or so. You can substitute a teaspoon of mashed anchovies, or about 1 good-sized anchovy. I dice the anchovy finely first, then mash it with the side of the blade until it's a smooth paste. (See the box on page 176 for more anchovy talk.)

Smoooth Butternut Bisque

This can be made from scratch very quickly, and takes kindly to experiments in the field of flavors, especially the spices. The heat of this soup is important, I think, and depending on the audience you could add more Tabasco sauce. You could use all kinds of squash for this soup, leftover or fresh-cooked, roasted or steamed. (The roasting method allows you to prepare the squash without having to peel and chop it.) Butternut squash happens to have the smoothest texture. The tomato juice counters the sweetness of the squash and onions nicely. This soup tends to be thick; you may prefer the smaller amount of squash.

(Makes about 8 – 10 cups)

> 2 – 3-pound butternut squash (about 3 – 4 cups cooked)
> ¼ cup extra-virgin olive oil
> 1 medium-large onion, chopped (3 – 4 cups)
> 1 teaspoon curry powder
> 1½ teaspoon salt
> 1 tablespoon freshly crushed garlic
> (1 tablespoon finely minced fresh ginger, if available)
> ¼ – ½ teaspoon Tabasco sauce
> 2 cups water
> 3 cups tomato juice
> 1 can (12 ounces) evaporated milk

1. ***To roast squash:*** *Preheat oven to 450 degrees and place the rack in top third of oven.* Halve squash lengthwise and scoop out seeds. Line a baking sheet or shallow pan with foil. Mist with non-stick spray or rub cut side of squash with olive oil. Place squash cut side down on foil. *(The foil's job is simply to make the clean up easy.)* Roast for about an hour, or until squash is very tender. When cool, scrape squash from skin and chop roughly.
   To steam squash: Peel squash with vegetable peeler and trim each end. Separate neck from bulb end. Cut both in half vertically, and scrape out seeds in bulb end. *(To roast seeds, see page 122.)* Chop squash into roughly evenly sized chunks. Steam in a steamer basket in a 4-quart saucepan for 30 minutes or until tender.

2. Meanwhile, heat the oil in a heavy 5-quart soup pot over medium-high heat and add onions, curry, and salt. Sauté 10 – 15 minutes or until onion is soft. *(I would always use the larger quantity of onion. You don't need to be fussy about chopping when you're going to purée the soup anyway, but make sure the onion is sautéed until soft.)* Add garlic and sauté another 2 minutes.

3. Stir in ginger (if you have it), Tabasco, water, and cooked squash pieces. Bring to a boil, and simmer 15 minutes. Remove from heat.

4. Add tomato juice and evaporated milk. Purée soup in 2 or 3 batches in food processor, or use immersion blender. *(At this point you could store soup in the refrigerator for a few days.)* Return soup to pot. Bring to a simmer and serve.

Gazpacho
(Cold Mediterranean Soup)

Salad in a blender! Summer in a glass! Cold and zesty, and a pleasant way to perk up wilted limbs and drooping taste buds. This traditional Spanish soup has countless versions, but this is mine and it may be one of the simplest. You can make and chill the vegetable base days ahead (except for the tomato juice, which makes more sense to chill in its can), and transport it to a picnic or potluck in a bottle surrounded with ice.

(Makes about 8 cups)

> 6 ripe tomatoes (about 1½ pounds)
> 1 medium cucumber
> 1 cup chopped sweet onion
> ¼ cup apple cider vinegar
> ¼ cup extra-virgin olive oil
> ½ teaspoon salt
> ½ teaspoon freshly crushed garlic
> ½ teaspoon Tabasco sauce
> 2 cups tomato juice
>
> **Suggested garnishes**
> ½ cup fresh chopped cilantro
> 1 red bell pepper, diced finely
> 1 avocado, diced, tossed with a tablespoon of lime juice
> ½ cup drained yogurt (page 97) mixed with a tablespoon of cream
> 2 boiled eggs, chopped

1. *To prepare tomatoes:* Place a couple at a time in a pot of boiling water for about 10 seconds, then peel. (I stick a fork in the core end and strip the skin off with a paring knife.) Slice into quarters, core, and scoop seeds into a sieve. *(You can strain at least ½ cup of juice from the seeds to add to the gazpacho ingredients.)*

2. Peel cucumber, quarter lengthwise, remove seeds, and chop roughly. You should have about 2 cups. Peel and chop onion.

3. Combine tomatoes, cucumber, onion, vinegar, oil, salt, garlic, and Tabasco in food processor in two batches and process for about 30 seconds, or until smooth. Add tomato juice. Transfer to a bottle and chill for a few hours or overnight. Serve cold with garnishes. (See *Note*.)

Note:

▸ Traditional garnishes are croutons and finely diced green peppers and cucumbers. Cooked, chilled shrimp and diced avocado would be spectacular additions.

Mirepoix
(Sautéed Vegetable Base)

Mirepoix (pronounced *meer-PWAH*) is a simple sauté of diced vegetables and aromatics, but is one of the most useful cooking basics you can know. The classic French version is about two parts onion to one part each celery and carrot, and can provide the critical underpinning for simple soups like the *minestrone* on this page, chowders (see page 194), pot pies (see page 201), stews (you could add it to the beef stew on page 206), and sauces. In Italy it is called *soffrito,* a more fitting name for my olive oil version, anyway. Whatever the name, it can be adjusted to suit your purpose or supplies. Mine sometimes has bell pepper instead of carrots and/or celery (see *Chili* on page 209 or *Tuna Tetrazzini* on page 191), but it is usually the one below. The time it takes to sauté the vegetables has much to do with the pot; the larger the surface area, the faster they'll cook.

(Makes about 2½ cups)

¼ cup extra-virgin olive oil
3 cups onion in ¼-inch dice
1½ cups carrot in ¼-inch dice
1½ cups celery in ¼-inch dice
1 tablespoon freshly crushed garlic
(¼ cup of minced fresh parsley)

1. Heat oil in a heavy wide-bottomed pot or large skillet over medium-high heat. When oil is hot, add vegetables (they should sizzle when they hit the oil) and sauté for about 12 – 15 minutes or until vegetables are tender. *(After about 10 minutes begin to stir vegetables more diligently. They brown quickly once they've begun to soften.)*

2. Add garlic (and parsley, if you have it) and sauté for another minute, stirring constantly. Remove from heat.

Minestrone

It might seem outrageous to give this simple little recipe the title of *minestrone* but – I do.

(Serves 4 – 6)

Mirepoix (this page)
 6 cups of chicken broth or water
4 cups of bite sized cauliflower florets
or 3 – 4 cups ½-inch diced cabbage
3 cups diced zucchini
1 can (28 ounces) diced tomatoes
1 can (15 ounces) chickpeas
1 teaspoon of salt
1 teaspoon of freshly ground pepper

Optional last minute addition: ½ cup fresh basil puréed in blender with 2 tablespoons extra-virgin olive oil and 2 teaspoons freshly crushed garlic.

1. Combine mirepoix and broth in a 5-quart pot over medium high heat and bring to a simmer.

2. Add cauliflower (or cabbage) and simmer for 10 minutes.

3. Add zucchini, tomatoes with their juice, drained chickpeas (no need to rinse them), salt, and pepper and bring back to a simmer. Reduce heat to low and cook gently for another 20 minutes, or until vegetables are tender.

4. *Stir in optional basil purée just before serving. Freshly grated parmesan is a good thing to offer on the side*

Note:
▸ Just about any greens are good additions to this soup. If you have a half bag of baby spinach languishing in the refrigerator, don't think twice – just chop roughly and add in the last 5 minutes.

Vegetable Sides

Very few of us eat enough vegetables, so it is a good idea to develop a repertoire of simple recipes and do them often enough so that they become very familiar. Roasted vegetables (page 123-28) get a whole section to themselves because most people like them. The simple salads (starting on page 129) can be easy do-ahead-or-serve-a-day-later vegetables, as can the soups (starting on page 138). Using frozen vegetables is perfectly legal (some suggestions start on page 114) and expands your options well beyond your fresh vegetable (pages 117-22) inventory.

Butternut Squash Purée

This is fun to serve to people who don't trust squash under any circumstances. I have seen some touching scenes of reconciliation. The preparation is simple and each ingredient important. Butternut squash is dependably smooth and creamy, and has easy-to-peel thin skin. Also, puréed squash is a more useful leftover than the roasted squash described on page 128, which is best eaten freshly roasted.

(Serves about 4 – 6)

Butternut squash (about 3 pounds raw whole or 4 cups cooked)
2 tablespoons butter
½ teaspoon salt
½ teaspoon freshly ground pepper

1. Peel squash with vegetable peeler and trim each end. Separate neck from bulb end. Cut both in half vertically, and scrape out seeds in bulb end. *(To roast seeds, see page 122.)* Chop squash into roughly evenly sized chunks. Steam in a steamer basket set in a 4-quart saucepan for about 30 minutes or until tender.

2. Purée in a food processor or in a bowl with an electric mixer, with butter, salt, and pepper. *(This re-heats well if you want to prepare it in advance.)*

Butternut Custard

Any leftover squash purée can be turned into the dessert custard or pie filling below. Makes a fine treat on a rainy afternoon.

(Serves about 6)

4 – 6 eggs
½ cup honey
½ teaspoon salt
1½ teaspoons cinnamon
1 teaspoon garam masala *(see page 149)*
¼ teaspoon ground cloves
1 can (12 ounces) evaporated whole milk
1½ cups butternut purée
1 tablespoon soft butter *(for spreading over the bottom and sides of casserole dish)*

Preheat oven to 325 degrees.

1. Beat eggs in an 8-cup Pyrex jug, then add remaining ingredients and beat it all together until well blended. (If purée is unsalted, add ½ teaspoon more salt.)

2. Pour into a buttered 1½ quart dish and bake for about 50 – 60 minutes, or until it is just barely set in the center. (Just jiggle the dish to test.)

Colcannon
(Mashed Potatoes with Cabbage)

Colcannon is a traditional Irish mashed potato and cabbage dish that lends itself to all kinds of variations. (One suspects that the garlic and olive oil would *not* be an Irish variation. Call it poetic license.) Here the green cabbage is cooked to a buttery tenderness and stirred through the mashed potatoes with or without the onion suggested below. *(See **Note** for other options.)* The name combines the German word for cabbage, *Kohl*, and 'cannon', as in *smash*. Wonderful.

(Serves about 4 – 6)

> 3 – 4 medium potatoes (russets or Yukon gold)
> (1 medium onion or about 2 cups in ¼-inch dice - optional)
> ¼ cup extra-virgin olive oil
> 1 teaspoon freshly crushed garlic
> ¼ - ½ green cabbage, or about 4 – 8 cups shredded
> 1 cup milk
> 1½ teaspoons salt
> 1 teaspoon freshly ground pepper

1. Peel and cut potatoes into quarters or eighths. Steam or boil until tender, about 30 – 40 minutes. *(I prefer steaming to boiling; boiled potatoes tend to break down and dissolve into the water if left too long.)*

2. ***Optional but strongly recommended:*** Meanwhile, peel and dice onion. Heat olive oil in skillet over medium heat, add onions, and sauté for about 10 minutes or until very tender. Stir in the garlic, turn off heat, and set aside.

3. Combine cabbage and milk in a skillet over medium heat. Bring to a simmer and cover; reduce heat to low, then cook gently for 20 minutes or until very soft. *(If you don't include the sautéed onion, stir the garlic and olive oil into the cabbage in the last few minutes of cooking.)* Add salt and pepper.

4. Mash cooked potatoes, and then combine with onion and cabbage mixtures. Blend well. Serve hot. Colcannon is especially good with meatloaf (page 208).

Note:
▶ The creamy blandness of the mashed potato is a natural vehicle for other vegetables to be slid into the meal almost undetected. Two or three small turnips cooked and mashed with the potatoes are generally safe for any audience. So are small rutabagas, although the yellow tint is not as subtle and can make some people nervous. But you can *always* get away with the sautéed diced onions (described in Step **2** of the instructions above) with the mashed potatoes. (Remember, two cups of raw diced onions cook down to just one cup.)

Cauliflower Custard

Using custard as a vehicle is a great way to serve cauliflower, and lots of other vegetables, for that matter. This dish is bliss for cauliflower lovers and pretty good for the rest of you. It is a bit pallid without the chopped parsley, and the fresh green bite provides a contrast in flavor that is even more important than the color.

(Serves 4 – 6)

> 1 cauliflower
> 4 eggs
> 1½ cups 2%, whole, or evaporated milk
> 4 – 6 ounces sharp cheddar cheese, grated (about 1½ cups)
> 1 teaspoon salt
> ½ teaspoon freshly ground pepper
> ¼ cup minced fresh parsley, if possible

Preheat oven to 325 degrees. Mist a 1½-quart casserole with non-stick spray.

1. Clean and trim cauliflower of leaves, and trim stem. *(I prefer to remove stem and most of the core up inside the cauliflower and save for Cauliflower Butter Broth on page 139. However, if it's a small cauliflower I use the whole thing.)* Place cauliflower in steamer basket, stem side down. Steam until tender, about 15 – 25 minutes, depending on the size of the cauliflower. Set aside until cool enough to handle.

2. Meanwhile whisk eggs in a mixing bowl (an 8-cup Pyrex jug works well) and add milk, cheese, and seasoning.

3. Chop steamed cauliflower into bite-sized pieces. You will probably have between 4 – 6 cups. Add to egg mixture and mix gently.

4. Don't worry if there are bits of cauliflower sticking up. Bake in the middle of the oven for about 50 minutes or until custard is golden on the edges and no longer wet in the center. *(I suggest reducing the heat to 300 degrees after 30 minutes.)*

Sweet onion custard

An all-onion version is real soul food for us onion lovers, especially during Walla Walla season – although I make this any time with any sweet onions available. Whether you use onions or any other substitute vegetable, you can keep the other ingredients the same. Roasted zucchini and onion (page 128) is a fine variation.

1. Chop 2 medium-large sweet onions into 1 x ½ -inch chunks (about 6 cups).
2. Roast onions until meltingly tender, according to the directions on page 126.
3. While onions are roasting, complete Step **2** of the instructions above.
4. Add roasted onions to the egg mixture. (You will have about 3 cups of onions.)
5. Bake custard according to the instructions in Step **4** above.

Scalloped Corn

This is a variation on a traditional American recipe, sometimes called corn pudding, and is solidly in the category of comfort food. Those who like vegetables to arrive at the table subdued and creamed especially appreciate it. You can use canned or fresh corn instead of frozen, of course. More importantly, you can hide at least one onion in this dish without anyone noticing!

(Serves 4 – 6)

> 10 ounce or 16 ounce frozen petite yellow corn (2 – 3 cups)
> 2 tablespoons extra-virgin olive oil
> 1 medium onion in ¼-inch dice (about 2 cups)
> 1 red or green bell pepper in ¼-inch dice (at least 1 cup)
> 4 eggs
> 1 cup 2%, whole, or evaporated milk
> 4 – 6 ounces sharp cheddar cheese, grated (about 1½ cups)
> 1 teaspoon salt
> ¼ - ½ teaspoon Tabasco sauce
> (**Optional:** 4 ounce can whole green mild chiles, diced – see **Note**)

Preheat oven to 300 degrees. Mist a 1½-quart casserole with non-stick spray.

1. Empty frozen corn into a strainer and run under very hot water for about 10 seconds, then set aside to drain. Drain very well.

2. Heat oil in 8 – 10-inch skillet over medium high heat and sauté onion 5 minutes. Add bell pepper and continue sautéing another 5 – 10 minutes or until barely tender. Add drained corn and sauté for another few minutes to cook off any water still hanging onto the kernels. (An optional step.)

3. Whisk eggs in a mixing bowl (an 8-cup Pyrex jug works well) and add milk, cheese, seasoning, sautéed vegetable mixture, corn, and chiles.

4. Scrape into oiled casserole dish and bake custard in the middle of the oven for about 1¼ hours or until custard is golden on the edges and no longer wet in the center.

Note:

▸ If you have no bell peppers, the canned green chiles are a fine stand-in. There are many who prefer the more distinctive green flavor which also is so compatible with the flavors of corn and cheese. I suggest buying canned *whole* chiles and dicing them yourself – diced canned chiles occasionally include bits of tough skin and stem, and whole chiles are easier to check for stray skin and whatnot.

▸ A more serious chile is an option if you like your corn pudding to pack heat.

Marinated Carrot Matchsticks

Cooked carrots are hard for some of us to enjoy but they are easy to prepare *plus* they provide a splash of bright color. A solution is to slice carrots into thin sticks, steam until barely tender, and toss in vinaigrette. Carrots are dominant enough to handle aggressive flavors like cumin, cilantro, and garlic, and a recipe like this allows one to sneak a few of the more assertive root vegetables onto the table. A turnip sliced into matchsticks can be steamed with the carrots; the peppery flavor and clean white color contrast nicely with the carrots. (See **Note** below.)

(Serves 4 – 6)

> 4 – 5 cups ¼-inch matchstick carrots and turnips
> 2 tablespoons lemon juice or apple cider vinegar
> 2 teaspoons honey
> 1 teaspoon freshly crushed garlic
> 1 teaspoon salt
> 1 teaspoon ground cumin
> 1 teaspoon freshly ground pepper
> 3 tablespoons extra-virgin olive oil

1. Trim and peel vegetables. Slice carrots diagonally into ¼-inch slices, and then into ¼-inch matchsticks. Slice turnips in half lengthwise, then into ¼-inch slices. Slice into matchsticks, as with carrots. Combine matchsticks to make about 5 cups, and steam for 7 – 10 minutes, or until tender-crisp. *(If you overcook them they will fall apart when you toss them in the vinaigrette.)*

2. Combine dressing ingredients in mixing bowl and whisk together. Add steamed matchsticks and toss gently but thoroughly to mix. Serve hot, warm or room temperature. Makes great leftovers.

Note:

▸ You can buy julienne carrots in some stores, if you need to. You can also make matchsticks with a food processor attachment or a tool like a mandolin. There is even a peeler look-alike that is actually a julienne slicer made by Oxo, which can create linguini-type matchsticks.

Reach out to a rutabaga

Two other vegetables I like to bring in under cover of vinaigrette are rutabagas and kohlrabi. Their names may make it difficult to take them seriously, but the point here is not to bring these vegetables to the table just for the sake of diversity or a concern for their self-esteem. (Although how can we like them if they don't like themselves? There are some deep issues here.) More importantly, the peppery brightness of these root vegetables is a welcome foil for the sweetness of the carrots. (Kohlrabi or rutabagas are best when quite small, about the size of plump lemons.)

Creamy Spinach
with fresh cheese
(*Palek Paneer*)

This is offered with apologies to northern India. Many Indian restaurants serve a version of this, and this is my interpretation. An Indian cook told me that as long as the ingredients included *whole* cumin seeds and *did not* include curry powder, anything else was fine. Sadly, whole cumin seeds are not an ingredient used in this book, and curry somehow found its way in. By the time I finally came across some authentic Indian recipes, mine was settled. So, here we are.

(Serves 4 – 6)

8 ounces (or thereabouts) *paneer* (see **Note**)
½ stick butter (4 tablespoons)
2 tablespoons extra-virgin olive oil

1 medium onion (about 2 cups, ¼-inch dice)
¼ teaspoon crushed chilies
½ teaspoon ground cumin
½ teaspoon curry powder
½ teaspoon turmeric
½ teaspoon freshly ground pepper
1 teaspoon garam masala (See **Note**)
1½ teaspoons salt
1 tablespoon freshly crushed garlic
1 tablespoon minced fresh ginger

1 bag (16 ounces) frozen chopped spinach
1 teaspoon honey
1 can (14 ounces) coconut milk

Brown basmati rice (recipe on page 171)

1. Slice *paneer* into ½ inch slices. (See **Note**.) Heat butter and oil in a medium skillet over medium heat. *(You'll want a skillet with a lid because you're going to use the same pan for the spinach later.)* Add cheese and sauté in one layer, turning them when they are golden-speckled, about 2 – 3 minutes on each side. *(If you sauté the cheese a bit too long, the pieces tend to dry out and are not the succulent chunks they should be.)* Remove the cheese with tongs, leaving the butter and oil mixture behind in the skillet. Cut each slice of cheese into six pieces and set aside.

2. Scrape butter and oil from the skillet into a 2½-quart pot and set pot over medium heat. Add spices, salt, garlic, and ginger, and blend. When mixture bubbles add diced onion. Cook for about 15 minutes, reduce heat to low, and then cook for another 20 minutes or until onions are meltingly soft and beginning to brown.

3. Meanwhile, set the skillet back over low heat and empty frozen chopped spinach into it. Place over a low heat, covered, and cook very gently for about 20 – 30 minutes, or *only* until spinach is fully thawed and hot through. Tilt the pan and press out about ½ cup of liquid, which you can save for your next pot of soup. You should have about 2 cups of spinach. (For more on frozen spinach see page 116. You could also use fresh spinach or a combination of fresh and frozen.)

4. Add spinach, honey, and coconut milk to the sautéed onion and spice mixture. Bring to a simmer and add *paneer* chunks. Cook gently for about 15 minutes. Serve over hot brown basmati rice.

Note:

▸ *Paneer* is a fresh Indian style cheese that I have no trouble finding in specialty stores. It is firm and mild like mozzarella, but it doesn't melt or even soften when fried. Recipes usually call for cubing the cheese before frying, but working with slices is easier than with little chunks.

▸ *Garam masala* is a powdered spice with warm, not hot overtones – a mixture of black pepper, cinnamon, cloves, cardamom, coriander, and cumin. It is easy to find, but I would buy it in small quantities from a good source.

Ratatouille
A (Roasted) Mediterranean Medley

Ratatouille (*Rah-tah-TOO-ee*) was born in the Provence region of France, and could define the term 'Mediterranean' both by its ingredients and simplicity. Ratatouille pops up commonly in cookbooks and menus in this country and it is probably safe to say that rarely is justice done to it. Ratatouille is juicy, flavorful, rich, and particularly good served over polenta (on pages 184), and also over whole grain pasta or brown rice (page 171). Leftover ratatouille can end up over a hot baked potato, or in an omelet or *frittata*, and makes a fine pizza topping (drained well first). It can be served at any temperature, from hot to room temperature, and is especially delicious the day after it's made. And the day after that. And so on.

(Serves 6 – 8)

> 2 small eggplants (about 1½ pounds total) firm and smooth
> 3 sweet red, orange, green, and/or gold bell peppers
> ⅔ cup extra-virgin olive oil, divided
> 1½ teaspoons salt, divided
> 1 teaspoon freshly ground black pepper, divided
>
> ¼ cup finely chopped fresh garlic
> 2 medium-large onions, preferably sweet
> 1 can (28 ounces) peeled diced tomatoes, drained
> ¼ cup fresh chopped basil or 1 teaspoon dried basil

Preheat oven to 450 degrees.

1. Line a large shallow roasting pan, about 11 x 16 inches or the largest that will fit into your oven, with heavy duty foil coated with non-stick spray. Trim eggplant (I prefer to leave the glossy purple skin intact) and cut into 1 x ½-inch chunks. Core and seed peppers, and chop into 1-inch chunks. Toss eggplant and peppers together in a large bowl with ⅓-cup olive oil. Spread in the pan, sprinkle with about half the salt and pepper, and roast in the top third of the oven for 20 minutes, or until just barely tender.

2. Peel onions and chop into 1 x ½-inch chunks. *(Onion plays the part of a vegetable here, not just a flavoring. Sweet onions tend to have thicker, juicier layers.)* Heat 1/3-cup of the oil in a sturdy pot (5-quart or preferably larger, so the onions can spread out and thus steam less) and sauté onions briskly for 12 minutes or until tender. Add garlic and sauté another 2 minutes. *(You could roast the onions like the eggplant and peppers if you prefer.)*

3. Empty diced tomatoes into small strainer to drain. You do not want 'petite diced' tomatoes here, by the way. Larger chunks are better. As for fresh tomatoes, they don't have enough flavor for this dish. (Save the juice, which should amount to about 1 cup or more, for something like *Creamy Thai Tomato Soup* or *Smoooth Butternut Bisque* on pages 140-41.)

4. Add eggplant and pepper mixture, drained tomatoes, basil, and remaining salt and pepper to the sautéed onions in the pot. Mix gently to avoid mushing soft vegetables. *(The name ratatouille translates literally as 'stirred dish', but this recipe tries to avoid any unnecessary stirring. This dish is so much prettier and more appetizing when it's not mushy.)*

5. Reduce oven temperature to 350 degrees and bake ratatouille, uncovered, for about ½ hour to meld the flavors. *(If you have chosen to roast and sauté more vigorously, as I tend to do, the ratatouille obviously needs no cooking, but the tomatoes need some time to get acquainted.)*

6. Serve at any temperature. Liquid will collect, so serve the ratatouille with plenty of good dipping bread.

7. Ratatouille will keep for several days in the refrigerator, but make sure it has completely cooled before covering and chilling.

Note:

▶ You should not have to bother with the salting-rinsing-drying business with eggplants if you choose them carefully. Always buy eggplants that are smooth, shiny, and tight in their skin, with green, fresh-looking caps, or don't bother buying them at all. Don't forget to check out the slim little Asian eggplants, too.

▶ The extra-virgin olive oil is an ingredient in its own right, not just a sautéing medium. If you have to substitute with another kind of oil for some unthinkable reason, there's nothing I can do about it – just don't call the dish ratatouille. Fresh garlic also has no substitute, but if you choose to use less than this recipe calls for, the dish will still be perfectly legal. I mince rather than crush the garlic for longer-cooking dishes like this and the beef stew on page 206.

▶ It's important not to roast the vegetables beyond the just-tender stage. The eggplant will melt into indistinguishable blobs and the skin will lift off the peppers. It's best if the vegetables maintain their shape while you combine everything, and they will cook a bit more during the brief baking.

▶ Many ratatouille recipes call for zucchini. I happen to like zucchini served just about anywhere but in a stew. Texture is not a quality for which zucchinis are admired. I love them diced and sautéed quickly in olive oil with salt and pepper, or roasted with onions as described on page 128.

▶ … but if you would like to include zucchini in your ratatouille, choose slim, smallish ones, if possible. Trim both ends, quarter lengthwise, and slice into 1-inch lengths. Toss with 2 tablespoons extra-virgin olive oil, spread in a foil-lined pan, sprinkle with salt and pepper, and roast in the top third of a 450-degree oven for about 15 – 20 minutes, or until zucchini is barely tender but not yet translucent or beginning to brown. It will continue to cook after you take it out of the oven, too. Add it with the eggplant in Step **4**.

Caponata
(A Sicilian Antipasto)

For every one of us who loves eggplant, there may be three who don't. There is a lot of passion on both sides. A good caponata is so lively and complex and rich, however, that it has a good chance of slipping under the most sensitive eggplant radar. Caponata is related to ratatouille, but is more a sweet-and-sour relish than a stew. It can be served as a sauce for pasta or rice, or fish (see suggestion on this page), or as a topping for pizza, or with hot or cold meat as a relish, or on *bruschetta*, and so on and so forth.

(Makes about 6 cups)

1 eggplant, about ¾ pound *(see **Note** about choosing eggplants on previous page)*
½ cup extra-virgin olive oil (divided)

2 – 3 stalks celery
1 medium onion
1 red bell pepper
¼ teaspoon crushed chilies
1 fat teaspoon freshly crushed garlic

1 can (15 ounces) *petite* diced tomatoes
½-cup pitted chopped green olives
2 tablespoons apple cider vinegar
2 tablespoons honey
1 teaspoon salt, or to taste
1 teaspoon freshly ground pepper
1 tablespoon capers
¼ cup currants
½ cup minced fresh parsley

1. Preheat oven to 450 degrees. Line a large baking pan with foil and mist with non-stick spray. Trim ends of eggplant and cut into ½-inch cubes. Toss with ¼ cup olive oil and spread evenly in one layer in pan. Roast eggplant in oven for 20 minutes or until beginning to soften.

2. Meanwhile prepare other vegetables. Slice celery lengthwise into halves or thirds, and slice crosswise into ¼ -inch dice. Peel onion, and core, quarter, and seed pepper. Cut each into ¼-½ inch dice. (You should have about 2 cups of onion and 1½ cups each of celery and peppers.)

3. Heat remaining ¼ cup olive oil in a heavy 5-quart pot over medium-high heat. Add dried crushed chilies and celery. Sauté 5 – 7 minutes, and then add onion and bell peppers. Sauté until just tender, about 10 minutes longer, depending on the level of heat and the sturdiness of the slices. Add garlic and cook for another minute.

4. Stir in half-roasted eggplant and sauté until eggplant is soft. Add petite diced tomatoes with their juice, olives, vinegar, honey, salt, and pepper. (Add capers, currants, and parsley, if you have them.) Bring to a simmer and cook gently for about 10 minutes, uncovered. If making in advance, cool thoroughly before covering and refrigerating.

Halibut with caponata
(Serves 4 – 6)

Caponata livens up a mild white fish like halibut. (You can slice through the middle of very thick slabs to make 2 fillets out of one.)

1. Spread half of the *caponata* recipe over the bottom of a shallow 1½-quart casserole dish.
2. Place 1½ pounds of fresh halibut fillets on the caponata.
3. Cover fish with the remaining caponata.
4. Bake uncovered in a 350-degree oven for 30 minutes or until fish can be flaked gently with a fork at its thickest point.

▸ This dish pairs nicely with roasted asparagus (page 125). Leftover fish and sauce can be integrated into a tasty version of *Crowded Chowder* on page 194.

10   Beans

About Beans

Why eat beans? Besides being rich in protein, iron, and B vitamins, beans are a superb source of soluble fiber, and one of this world's best defenses against diabetes, heart disease, cancer, obesity, and osteoporosis. Beans are perhaps the cheapest and safest lipid lowering drugs on the market, *and* they come in pretty colors. In fact, the richer the color, the higher the antioxidant level.

Beans also happen to be cheap, available everywhere, simple to cook, and easy to store. You don't even have to *cook* them yourself; you can find a bean for any occasion canned and ready to drain and use in soup, chili, salad, dip, or whatever.

Canned beans

■ Home-cooked beans are easy but for spontaneous bean eating there are canned beans. These should be absolute standards in any pantry. They easily stand in for home-cooked beans, and have all the health benefits *plus* a great shelf life, huge variety, and wide availability. As usual, read labels. Most of the regular brands have added sugar, among other things.

■ A standard 15 ounce can holds about 1½ cups of beans. There are generally several cans each of black beans and chickpeas in my pantry. (There is also a can or two of red kidney beans, partly because they're so pretty and partly because they feature in the bean marinade on page 165.)

■ I find that the most useful canned beans are black beans. Their color contrasts nicely with rice and polenta, and they are small. (Bean size can be important when you are feeding anti-bean folks.) Larger beans are sometimes not as easy for non-bean-lovers to eat.

■ Chickpeas (garbanzo beans) are among the richest sources of the anticancer compounds called *protease inhibitors*[1], as well as soluble and insoluble fiber, folate, and iron. They are best known for their role in the Middle Eastern dip called *hummus*. (See page 102.)

Frozen beans

■ You should also be able to find fresh frozen beans, like baby lima beans, speckled butter beans (delicious name!), black-eyed peas, and fresh soybeans (*edamame*) in the frozen vegetable section of your supermarket. These cook relatively quickly straight from the freezer, and are delightful hot and buttered with salt and pepper, or tossed with olive oil, freshly crushed garlic, salt, and pepper, or dressed with vinaigrette and served at any temperature.

Dried beans

Once you slide into a bean cooking routine, you may wonder why you used to think it was so much work.

1. For about 5 – 6 cups cooked beans, start with 2 cups of dried beans. (This is about 1 pound of beans.) Check beans for sick, shriveled or broken beans, or any non-bean material like rocks or little lumps of dried mud, both of which can look bean-like if you're not alert. (Sometimes other types of beans will turn up, like a glossy red kidney bean in a batch of chalk-white Great Northern beans, which is fun. You can always include visitors.)

2. Rinse in a strainer and place in a large heavy-bottomed pot or saucepan (at least 3-quart size) and add enough cold water to cover beans by about 3 inches. (Beans can swell to almost 3 times their original volume.) Remove any floaters.

3. Place cleaned and picked-over beans in a 5-quart pot and cover with about 8 cups

---

[1] *The Food Pharmacy Guide to Good Eating*, Jean Carper©1991

of cold water. (Beans should be covered by about 3 inches of water.)

4. If you opt to soak the beans, set them aside for 4 – 12 hours. For a pound of beans, which is about 2 cups, use about 10 cups of cold water. (See more about soaking on the other side of this page.)

5. Place pot over a medium-high heat and bring to a rolling boil. Reduce the heat to low and let the beans simmer very gently. Don't try to rush the cooking – slow and gentle is best for beans. Boiling beans damages their little coats and they tend to disintegrate.

6. After about 30 minutes, add a couple of teaspoons of salt. Some say that cooking beans with salt toughens them, but others say it improves their texture. However, *no-one* disagrees with the fact that beans taste much better cooked with salt, so adding salt in the second half of the cooking period is a good compromise.

7. Simmer beans until tender. Test several beans – one or two beans can fool you. I think it's better to err on the side of tenderness, for taste as well as maximum digestibility. (See more about digestion on this page.) This can take from about 1 – 3 hours, depending on their size and age. (Older beans are dryer and take longer.) Lentils take only about 30 minutes to cook, while chickpeas can take 3 hours.

8. Cool beans in their cooking broth (if the recipe allows) for better texture and flavor. It's also handy to store the beans in the refrigerator in the cooking liquid; they keep nicely, and the bean broth can be added to soup, with or without beans.

9. Never add acidic ingredients like tomatoes or vinegar to beans before they are completely cooked; the acid will inhibit the softening process. No-one seems to argue with that, thank goodness.

More about soaking

Bean-cooking experts still seem to disagree as to whether or not soaking beans is important. Soaking may improve the texture of the beans and help them cook more evenly, as well as reduce the cooking time a bit. Soaking also reduces the potential for certain digestive problems, if you discard the soaking water. I never discard the soaking water. *(More about the digestion issue further on.)*

If you're in a hurry or gripped by a sudden and impatient craving, skip the soak step or use the quick-soak method: cover beans with several inches of cold water and bring to a boil, then remove from heat, cover, and let sit for an hour. **However**, some experts say that if you can't soak the beans for at least 4 hours, just cook them longer, as the quick-soak method is ineffectual. One begins to suspect that soaking beans before cooking is simply not a life-or-death matter.

The digestion issue

It is suggested by other experts, or perhaps even the same experts, that gastrointestinal problems associated with beans are minimized by pouring away the soak water with most of the pesky water-soluble oligosaccharides. But you're also pouring out valuable nutrients and antioxidants leached out by soaking.

Some say that a better solution is to cook them longer, eventually making the offending carbohydrates more digestible. (Julia Child suggests that anyone concerned about the minimal loss of nutrients that get thrown out with the bean soaking water should just eat a minimal amount *more* of the beans.)

Also, cooking the beans with garlic is said to help – although I'm not sure it should be legal to cook beans *without* garlic. One sensible approach would be to eat a couple of tablespoons of beans every day until your digestive system learns to appreciate them.

Easy Beans

You could call this a sort of soup. Should you prefer something soupier, add more liquid and mash some of the beans. If you choose to double the recipe, turn leftovers into a type of minestrone by adding broth and the mirepoix recipe on page 143, or use the mini-minestrone recipe on the same page. My favorite beans are Anasazi, but a white bean like cannellini may be more traditional.

(Serves about 4)

1½ cups dried beans
6 cups water

1½ teaspoons salt
1 large onion in ½-inch dice
1 tablespoon chopped fresh garlic
¼ teaspoon dried thyme
¼ teaspoon dried oregano
¼ teaspoon crushed red chilies
¼ cup extra-virgin olive oil

1. (See *Beans* on the preceding pages for more preparation information.) Combine beans and cold water in a 3-quart pot and bring to the boil. Reduce heat to low and cook uncovered at a slow simmer for about 1 hour.

2. Add salt, diced onion, garlic, herbs, crushed chilies, and olive oil, and stir into the beans. Continue simmering gently until beans are very tender. (If the water level drops to the bean level, add another cup or so of water.) Cooked beans should mash easily with a fork.

3. Serve the beans in bowls with their broth, like soup. A heaping tablespoon (at least) of freshly grated Parmesan on each bowl is a good idea, and a fresh focaccia sliced into wedges (recipe on page 230) would make this into a feast.

Lazy Lentils
A lentil stew

I love lentils for their peppery nuttiness and simplicity of preparation. Whether or not *you* love them, they are useful beans to know because they cook so quickly. This is a favorite last-minute dinner. There are red, yellow, brown, black, and little French green lentils, but the brown are the biggest and most versatile.

(Serves about 4)

1½ cups brown lentils
6 cups of water, or water and chicken stock
1½ teaspoons of salt

¼ cup extra-virgin olive oil
1 large onion, diced (3 – 4 cups)
¼ teaspoon crushed chilies
1 teaspoon ground cumin
1 tablespoon freshly crushed garlic
½ teaspoon freshly ground pepper
(¼ cup chopped fresh cilantro)

1. Combine lentils and cold water in a 3-quart pot and bring to the boil. Reduce heat to low. Add salt and cook partly covered at a slow simmer for 40 minutes or until tender.

2. Meanwhile, dice onion. Heat oil in a sturdy 10-inch skillet and add the onion, chilies, and cumin. Sauté about 10 minutes or until onion is tender. Add garlic and sauté another 2 minutes.

3. Add onion mixture to pot of cooked lentils. Add pepper and simmer for another 5 minutes. Stir in fresh cilantro, if you have it, and serve in soup bowls with a side of *Tabbouleh* (page 178) or hot brown rice (page 171).

Note:
▶ Replacing the sautéed onions with the mirepoix on page 143 would turn this into more of a meal but still qualify as lazy.

Sprouting Lentils

Sprouting can be done easily anywhere, anytime, and can give you a tiny crop of vegetables to harvest from just a handful of dry beans or seeds. Sprouting often improves a seed's vitamin content and digestibility, according to Harold McGee in *On Food and Cooking* (page 460, 2004 edition). There are just a few steps to sprouting: pick over, rinse, soak, drain, and then rinse and drain about two times each day until sprouts are to your liking. Lentil sprouts are my personal favorites among sprouts; they're plump and crunchy and delicious tossed through a salad. Plus, they're easy to do.

1. First, find ½ cup of brown lentils. Check them as usual for rocks or other foreign bodies, then place into a wide-mouthed jar, and rinse by filling the jar with water, stirring vigorously to settle the floating lentils, and pouring off most of the water and any floating things. Repeat, then half-fill the jar with water and set aside for about 6 hours or overnight.

2. Tip soaked lentils into a wire meshed sieve, rinse well, and cover with a couple of layers of wet paper towel. Place in a bowl or something to drain. (I use a 6-inch sieve that fits perfectly inside a 1½-quart bowl.) *If you are using a jar with a screened sprouting lid, which you can generally find at natural food stores, simply drain the lentils, then fill jar with fresh water and drain again immediately.*

3. Set drained lentils aside in a cool spot out of direct light. Now, all you have to do is to remember to rinse and drain the lentils twice a day. **Drain thoroughly.** That's all there is to it. The lentils will have sprouted enough to be eaten in just a couple of days.

4. Keep well-sealed (so sprouts don't dry out) and refrigerated.

Note:

▶ You can apply these instructions to lots of other grains, seeds, or beans. Some require a longer soaking time than wheat, and most require a longer sprouting time, but one sprouting rule never varies: sprouts will spoil if allowed to stay too wet or too warm. (Bad bacteria flourish under these conditions.) The idea is to maintain a moist, cool environment.

Other Sprout Options

- **Wheat** sprouts are a fresh and slightly chewy addition to cold cereal like rolled oats or muesli. I think wheat sprouts taste best if the sprouts are only about ¼-inch. This takes just a couple of days.

- **Sunflower seeds** are *fast*; they sprout in about one day, and become delicately crunchy. Eat them when their sprouts are only barely showing. I only soak them for two hours or so before draining and setting aside to sprout. They don't store well after they've sprouted (they develop black speckles) so eat them or toss them into salads within a day or two. They taste so good that it is hard *not* to eat them quickly.

- **Mung bean** sprouts are good, but you need to shake the sprouted beans a handful at a time in a metal pie pan to check for the rock-like unsprouted beans. (You can find them by the distinctive rattle they make in the pan.) Home-sprouted mung beans are nothing like the long, juicy bean sprouts you find in Asian markets and some produce sections of supermarkets, but are tasty raw or stir-fried briefly in butter with lemon juice.

Fresh Frozen Beans

The most commonly available of the fresh frozen bean varieties are baby green lima beans, green soybeans, speckled butter beans (delicious name) and black-eye peas. Try to buy beans that break up fairly easily when you handle them. If the beans are in a solid icy clump it's a bad sign.

Check for freezer burn before you cook them: if the beans look shriveled when you open the bag or box, the situation is possibly hopeless. They will probably taste freezer-burnt and won't soften much as they cook. If you want to try anyway, cover with water and simmer until tender. I've been surprised by some startling recoveries. Fresh frozen beans, whether leftover or straight from the freezer, are a welcome addition to minestrone-type soups.

Green soybeans cook in about 5 minutes, baby limas in about 10 minutes, speckled butter beans in about 15 minutes and black-eye peas in about 30 minutes.

Fresh Soybeans

The Japanese call them *edamame (ed-uh-MAH-may)*. They have a nutty, sweet quality and firm texture that some may prefer to the more beany texture of the similar looking baby green lima beans.

The availability of fresh soybeans in supermarket freezer departments is amazingly widespread, probably because they are arguably the most delicious soy product on the market. You can even find them fresh in the pod (Asian markets are your best bet) as well as cooked and ready-to-eat.

Fresh green soybeans are a particularly sensible source of unprocessed soy. (See page 53.) I usually serve them on their own, because they are such a pretty shade of green and taste so nutty and good.

Seductive Soybeans
Edamame

This is a very simple treatment and a lovely side dish all by itself. These soybeans also make a fine replacement for lima beans in my *Succotash Salad* (page 162) or anywhere else.

(Makes about 3 cups)

1 cup water
1 teaspoon salt
16-ounce bag frozen green soybeans (*edamame*)

2 tablespoons extra-virgin olive oil
1 tablespoons apple cider vinegar
1 teaspoon freshly crushed garlic
½ teaspoon salt
¼ teaspoon freshly ground pepper

1. Bring water to a boil in a 2-quart saucepan and add salt and soybeans. Bring back to a boil, gently shaking the pan to break up any clumps of beans. Reduce heat to low, cover, and simmer for about 5 minutes.

2. Meanwhile combine olive oil, vinegar, garlic, salt and pepper in a mixing bowl.

3. When soybeans are cooked, drain and add to the oil and vinegar mixture. Toss to thoroughly coat beans. Let sit for 10 minutes, tossing a few times. Serve at any temperature. (Freshly cooked or room temperature is best, I think.)

Note:
▸ A cooked soybean has a naturally firm texture, not soft like the limas on page 161.

Soybeans in the Pod

These look like slightly furry and flattened versions of sugar snap peas and are generally in the freezer next to the regular green soybeans (edamame). In fact, they're easier to find than shelled edamame! You can even find them fresh in some Asian grocery stores in season. They make great finger food; some Japanese restaurants serve a little bowl of them on the table as a sort of pre-appetizer.

(Serves a small group as appetizer)

1 bag (16 ounces) frozen soy bean pods
1 heaping tablespoon of salt (see *Note*)

1. Bring 2 – 3 quarts of water to a boil. Add salt. Empty frozen pods into the boiling water. Bring back to the boil, and cook for about 3 – 5 minutes.

2. Drain well and serve anywhere, anytime.

Note:

▶ The salted water does a lot for the flavor. Obviously it will be subtle, but it makes a difference.

▶ These are good hot, cold, or anywhere between. Just squeeze the soybeans from their pods straight into your mouth. (Lay out a bowl to hold the empty pods.)

▶ Store cooked pods in a bag or covered dish in the refrigerator. You can snack on them for days, whenever you feel like nibbling. These are also great company on car trips.

▶ If you would prefer to steam the pods instead of boiling them, that works fine, too.

Tofu

There are those who consider tofu to be a sort of practical joke played on the gullible Americans (the same ones who eat shark cartilage) by a fun-loving Japan. That certainly might be true, but it's nice when something as practical as tofu can be fixed up to taste so good.

The two tofu recipes in this book use extra firm tofu — *Tofu (in Soy Ginger Marinade)* on the following page, and *Tofu Pâté* on page 101. The marinated tofu doesn't last long in our house: if I marinate tofu for the purposes of a stir-fry, I have to make extra for snacking. *Tofu Pâté* is a wonderful egg salad substitute.

What is it?

Tofu is pressed soy milk curds made from soybeans. Tofu's very blandness and ability to absorb flavors makes it a perfect candidate for marinating, and then either being served as an appetizer or tossed through a stir-fry. It comes in a wide range of textures, from "silken", which is soft enough to disappear into dips and smoothies, to "extra firm", which you can buy in a ready-to-prepare form that requires no draining or pressing to remove excess liquid. If you find it in your refrigerator with an expired use-by date, don't automatically toss it out. I've found tofu months beyond the date that tastes fresh!

Draining Tofu

If you buy tofu packed in water in a plastic tub, you should press out the excess water. Wrap tofu in a clean kitchen towel and place on a plate. Place another plate over the wrapped tofu, and put something heavy on top, like a telephone book. Set aside for about ½ hour or so. (If you're hungry, 15 minutes works fine, too.) Tofu absorbs flavors more effectively after this step.

Tofu in Soy Ginger Marinade

These tasty tofu sticks have been gobbled happily by people who have assured me they *hate* tofu. And it's so easy with extra-firm tofu packed in minimal water; all you have to do is pat it dry with a paper towel.

(Serves about 4 as a hearty snack, and more as an appetizer)

10 ounces extra-firm tofu

Soy Ginger Marinade
⅓ cup soy sauce
2 tablespoons toasted sesame oil
1 tablespoon apple cider vinegar
1 tablespoon honey
1 tablespoon freshly crushed garlic
1 tablespoon finely minced fresh ginger
½ teaspoon crushed red pepper, or to taste

1. Drain tofu, pat dry, and slice into sticks about ½-inch x ¼-inch. For that matter, make any sized sticks you want: if you want tofu to marinate quickly, make the sticks thinner, but if you plan to store the marinated tofu in the refrigerator to snack from during the week, chunkier slices are easier to handle.

2. Combine marinade ingredients in a shallow storage dish and whisk to blend. (A container wide enough to hold the tofu sticks in one or two layers is ideal.)

3. Add tofu, making sure all surfaces are covered with marinade. Set aside for at least 10 minutes, and then tilt dish back and forth to allow marinade to flow around tofu before setting aside for another 10 minutes or so. Taste. It should be ready to eat. It will keep happily in your refrigerator for several days although the tofu will darken to the color of the soy sauce.

Note:
▸ Your personal tastes can dictate amounts of ginger, garlic, or crushed peppers. In any case, the marinade works equally well for marinating chicken or any other meat, or for saucing a stir-fry, or for dressing an oriental noodle salad, and so forth. You can also recycle the marinade in a stir-fry, with or without the tofu.

Fresh ginger is an easy item to keep on hand. Buy a firm, smooth-skinned knob of ginger and cut it into one-inch chunks. Store the chunks submerged in *mirin*, a sweet rice wine used in Japanese cooking, in a glass jar in the refrigerator. (You could use white wine, too.) The ginger will last indefinitely this way, although it will lose a certain amount of its fresh bite over time. Peeling the ginger is optional, but it's easy to peel or scrape off the thin skin. You can store it for months. By the way, some people find that ginger relieves nausea and motion sickness; you can make your own ginger tea by steeping sliced ginger in boiling water with a bit of honey for taste.

Luscious Limas

The lima bean is a victim of a cultural bean bias. There are otherwise open-minded grown-ups who won't touch lima beans on principle, and who think lima beans aren't even an acceptable subject of conversation. Unlike canned peas, which some consider irredeemable, lima beans don't deserve their reputation. At least green baby lima beans don't.

Innocent children, untainted by the cultural bias and with tastes uncorrupted by their parents' preconceptions, generally love these particular lima beans. I presented this recipe for the first time to my buddy Robbie when he was about 1½ years old, and he thought they were *very* good. (He was a man of few words but he had strong opinions about food, and his judgments were usually accurate.) At the time of this writing Robbie is now a teenager, but he *still* thinks these lima beans are good. Is there a higher recommendation?

(Enough for Robbie and me, and maybe a few close friends.)

> 1 bag (16 ounces) frozen baby lima beans
> 1 cup water
> ½ teaspoon salt
>
> ¼ cup extra-virgin olive oil
> 1 – 2 tablespoons apple cider vinegar
> 1 teaspoon freshly crushed garlic
> ½ teaspoon salt
> ¼ – ½ teaspoon freshly ground pepper

1. Bring water to boil in a 2-quart saucepan, and add salt. Add frozen lima beans and bring back to a boil, gently breaking up any big clumps of beans. Reduce heat to low, cover, and simmer for about 7 – 15 minutes. Beans should be tender but not mushy. *(Packet directions may say anything from 10 – 20 minutes, but the key words are 'until tender'. Don't judge doneness by testing beans with wrinkly skins; they take much longer to soften.)*

2. Meanwhile, combine the olive oil, vinegar, garlic, salt, and pepper in your mixing bowl. When lima beans are cooked, drain in a colander and add to the oil and vinegar mixture and toss. Let sit for 10 minutes, and then toss again. Yum. Serve hot, warm, or room temperature.

Note:

▸ If lima beans are unable to gain a toehold in your freezer for whatever tragic reasons, you can substitute any fresh frozen beans, like speckled butter beans, green soybeans (edamame), or black-eye peas. Robbie found them all acceptable. Check for freezer burn: if the frozen beans look shriveled they will probably taste freezer-burnt. Yuck. Not a good way to introduce *Luscious Limas* to anyone.

Succotash Salad

This is a good dish for a picnic, a potluck, or any kind of hungry gathering. It looks pretty and is sturdy enough for even hot weather. I think it tastes better if it isn't eaten straight from the refrigerator. You can substitute the lima beans in this succotash with green soybeans (*edamame*) or speckled butter beans. (See note following the recipe for *Luscious Limas* on the preceding page.)

(Serves 6 – 8)

1 box (10 ounces) or 1 bag (16 ounces) frozen baby lima beans (2 – 3 cups)
1 cup water
½ teaspoon salt

1 box (10 ounces) or 1 bag (16 ounces) frozen petite corn (2 – 3 cups)
1 – 2 cups finely diced sweet onion
1 large sweet red pepper in ¼-inch dice (or about 1½ cups)
¼ cup extra-virgin olive oil
¼ cup apple cider vinegar
1 teaspoon salt
½ teaspoon freshly ground pepper

1. Bring water to boil in a 2-quart saucepan, and add salt. Add frozen lima beans and bring back to a boil, gently breaking up any big clumps of beans. Reduce heat to low, cover, and simmer for about 7 – 10 minutes. Beans should be tender but not mushy.

2. To thaw frozen corn, empty into a colander and run under very hot water for a few seconds, then shake off excess water and toss gently in a colander lined with paper towels.

3. Combine diced onion and peppers with oil, vinegar, salt, and pepper in a mixing bowl. Add drained corn and lima beans and toss gently with a large rubber spatula. (Don't be stingy with the salt and pepper. Beans and corn can overwhelm your average flavoring efforts.)

Note:

▶ To thoroughly remove residual water from corn, heat a tablespoon of olive oil in a hot skillet, add the thawed corn and sauté it quickly, until the corn begins to brown. It's not necessary, but it makes the corn taste better.

▶ For warm winter succotash, add the onion and peppers to 2 tablespoons of olive oil in a hot 8-inch skillet, sauté briskly for about 5 minutes, and then add the corn and sauté for another 5 minutes. Then add to the hot lima beans and remaining olive oil, vinegar and seasoning.

Tuscan Bean Salad

This is an example of a classic Mediterranean treatment of beans, and a point of departure for your own tastes. You can turn this salad into a Tuscan meal by adding a finely sliced fennel bulb (see Step 3 on page 189) and some very good tuna packed in olive oil. Bean salad variations are endless, and their relaxed attitude toward time and temperature are legendary, but the mix of tang and richness make practical considerations seem irrelevant. It's nice to know a salad you can trust.

(Serves about 6)

> 1½ cups small white beans, uncooked (or about 3½ cups cooked)
> several cloves of garlic, peeled and sliced or smashed (see *Note*)
> 1 tablespoon salt
>
> ¼ cup lemon juice
> (zest from lemon – see page 68 for more on lemon zest)
> ¼ cup extra-virgin olive oil
> 2 teaspoons freshly crushed garlic
> 1 teaspoon salt
> 1 teaspoon freshly ground black pepper
> 1 cup finely diced red pepper
> 1 cup finely diced sweet onion
> ½ cup minced fresh parsley

1. Check and rinse beans, then place in a 3-quart pot or saucepan with the garlic and enough water to cover by 3 inches. Bring to a boil, then reduce heat to low and simmer quietly for about 1 — 1½ hours or until beans are tender. *Add salt after 45 minutes.*

2. Scoop out ¼ cup of the bean cooking water and set aside. Pour cooked beans into a strainer, and then tip drained beans into a large mixing bowl. Add the ¼ cup hot cooking water and the remaining ingredients. Toss thoroughly but gently with a big rubber spatula. It may seem wet just after it's made but the beans absorb liquid as time goes by, which is the reason for the dollop of bean water. Bean salads should be luscious.

3. Serve any time. This salad is especially good when eaten while still warm, but is also delicious after a night in the refrigerator.

Note:
▸ For the garlic cooked with the beans this is a good time to use those skinny slippery little cloves that tend to cluster at the center of the heads. One firm but restrained tap with the bottom of a glass should barely crush the cloves and conveniently loosen their skins for easy peeling.

Black Bean, Corn, and Jicama Salad
with Lemon and Cilantro Vinaigrette

This salad is crunchy, colorful, flavor-packed, easily made, and good for two or three days of snacking or supplementing a meal. Leftovers are intentional. Sometimes it can be difficult to track down a happy, healthy-looking jicama but it's actually a fine salad without it. The red bell pepper is important for color, however. (For more on jicama, see final **Note**.)

(Serves about 6 – 8)

> 1 can (15 ounces) black beans
> 1 box (10 ounces) frozen corn (about 2 cups)
> 1 medium-sized jicama (1 – 1½ lbs)
> 1 red bell pepper
> 1 cup ¼-inch diced sweet onion

1. Rinse black beans and set aside to drain very well. Place frozen corn in a strainer and thaw by running briefly under hot water while shaking the corn gently. *(Make sure corn is thoroughly drained by tossing in a colander lined with paper towels until the towels stop absorbing water. Use the same method for beans, if necessary.)*

2. If jicama (see **Note**) has tough brown skin, strip off with paring knife, and then peel once more with regular peeler. Slice into ¼-inch dice. *(You will have 2 – 3 cups.)* Dice onion and red bell pepper.

3. Combine beans, corn, jicama, onion, and bell pepper in a mixing bowl. Add vinaigrette (see below) and mix thoroughly with a rubber spatula. Cover and chill until ready to serve, mixing again just before serving.

Lemon and Cilantro Vinaigrette

You can use this anywhere a Southwestern flourish is needed.

(Makes about ½ cup)

> ¼ cup lemon or lime juice
> 2 teaspoons freshly crushed garlic
> 1 teaspoon chili powder
> 1 teaspoon ground cumin
> 1 teaspoon salt
> ½ teaspoon Tabasco sauce
> ½ teaspoon freshly ground black pepper
> ¼ cup extra-virgin olive oil
> ½ cup chopped fresh cilantro

Combine all ingredients in a 2-cup measuring jug and whisk thoroughly.

Note:

▶ This salad should be lively: the beans and corn tend to absorb a lot of flavor, so don't skimp on the salt and heat.

▶ Green bell pepper substitutes nicely for red, but the salad could use a bit of red color. I like to peel the peppers with a regular vegetable peeler. The skins can be a bit tough and they are certainly easier to slice without their skins.

▶ Jicama (*HEE-kuh-muh*) is a vegetable that looks like a tan oversized turnip, has the crisp texture of a water chestnut, and a flavor that is both slightly sweet and starchy. Choose a jicama with smooth, hard skin.

Three Bean Thing

Variations of this appear on salad bars everywhere. Something only becomes a cliché when it is used often, and it usually means that it works. You can use any beans you like but these are sturdy and still look fresh a week later. If the onion is mild I would definitely use 2 cups. Diced bell pepper of any color is a good addition (and traditional, too) if you have some. See *Note* for leftover ideas.

(Makes about 5 cups)

> 1 – 2 cups sweet onion, sliced in strips no more than ¼ -inch x 1 inch
> 2 tablespoons extra-virgin olive oil
> 2 tablespoons apple cider vinegar
> 1 teaspoon freshly-crushed garlic
> 1 teaspoon salt
> ½ teaspoon freshly ground pepper
>
> 1 can (15 ounces) red kidney beans
> 1 can (15 ounces) garbanzo beans (chickpeas)
> 1 can (15 ounces) cut green beans

1. Combine onion with oil, vinegar, garlic, salt, and pepper, and set aside. (This marinates the onions slightly, and makes them taste milder if they are hot. If onions are mild, I always use at least 2 cups to balance the beans.)

2. Drain and rinse kidney beans and chickpeas and set aside in colander to drain thoroughly. (Tossing beans in the colander with a dry paper towel helps.)

3. Drain green beans. (S&W cut green and wax beans are pretty if you can find them.) Combine all drained beans with onions in dressing and mix well.

Note:

▶ This makes quite a bit (it's hard to find these beans in smaller tins) but you can combine leftovers with cooked whole grain pasta spirals as a quick main dish salad. Leftovers are also a surprisingly good addition to *Tuna and Broccoli Pasta* on page 190.

Warm Lentil Salad

People who recoil at bean salads can relax. Lentils have a peppery nuttiness and a disarming daintiness that allow them to slip under the radar. Furthermore, this is possibly impossible to dislike. As well as being simple and relatively last minute (lentils cook in about 30 minutes), this recipe is very forgiving. You can use ½ cup of any dressing you happen to like or have already made. You can substitute your own choice of vegetables, like green onions and sweet red bell peppers, or just minced onion. It's an especially good dish to have ready when you're expecting to feed a group that may include vegetarians. Personally, I like to make enough for me to snack on for a week.

(Serves 6)

> 1½ cups brown lentils
> 6 cups water
> 1 tablespoon salt
>
> ¼ cup apple cider vinegar (or lemon juice)
> ¼ cup extra-virgin olive oil
> 1 teaspoon freshly crushed garlic
> 1 teaspoon salt
> ½ teaspoon freshly ground pepper
> ½ teaspoon ground cumin
> 1 cup minced sweet onion
> 1 cup ¼ -inch diced cucumber
> 1 cup ¼ -inch diced tomato
> (½ cup chopped fresh cilantro, if you have it)

1. Rinse lentils, and then combine with the water and the tablespoon of salt. Bring to a simmer and simmer until lentils are tender, 30 – 40 minutes. (Check after 30 minutes.) You should have about 4 cups of cooked lentils.

2. While lentils are cooking, combine vinegar, olive oil, garlic, seasoning, and onion in a mixing bowl. Set aside until lentils have finished cooking. Drain lentils in a colander. Add hot, drained lentils to dressing and onion mixture and toss thoroughly but gently. Set salad aside for about 15 minutes to marry flavors, tossing once or twice.

3. Add cucumber, tomato, and fresh cilantro, if you have it. Toss again. Serve hot, warm, or room temperature.

Note:

▸ Like any type of bean salad, this begs to be part of a buffet. It pairs nicely with something like *Marinated Carrot Matchsticks* on page 148.

Quick Little Black Bean Chili

Serious chili cooks would probably object to the use of the name *chili*, given that there is neither meat nor an honest chile in the ingredient list. It doesn't even use pinto beans! Its attraction is that it is quick, satisfying, and assembled from ingredients I always have on hand. We love it, whatever it is. Sometimes I include thinly sliced leftover meat or a bit of good ground fresh sausage that I add with the spices.

(Makes about 4 cups of chili, to serve 2 – 3)

> 2 – 4 tablespoons extra-virgin olive oil
> 1 medium – large onion in ¼ inch dice (2 – 3 cups)
> 1 tablespoon chili powder
> 1 teaspoon ground cumin
> 1 teaspoon salt
> 1 tablespoon freshly crushed garlic
> 1 tablespoon honey
> ¼ teaspoon Tabasco sauce, or more to taste
> 1 can (14 ounces) black beans, rinsed and drained (about 1½ cups)
> 1 can (14 ounces) crushed tomatoes in purée
> 1 can (7 ounces) mild whole green chilies, diced

1. Heat olive oil in a heavy 3-quart pot over medium-high heat. Sauté diced onion for 10 minutes or until onions are tender.

2. Add chili powder, cumin, salt, and garlic. Sauté for another two minutes.

3. Add honey, Tabasco sauce, black beans, tomatoes, and diced chilies. Bring to a simmer, and then cook gently for about 10 minutes. Mighty tasty served over *Easy Cheesy Polenta* (page 184). Or melt some grated cheddar cheese over a pile of hot brown rice in each dish, then top with chili.

Note:

▸ This is easily expanded to serve more people or to make enough for leftovers. Just double the beans and tomatoes and increase the seasoning by about half. Any bell peppers or celery tops that look like they might be feeling neglected should be diced finely and sautéed with the onions.

▸ Of course, minced fresh hot chiles are an authentic alternative to Tabasco, but fresh chile users don't need me to tell them. For more on chili see the recipe on page 209.

11

Whole Grains

Brown Rice
Basic Baked Brown Rice
Nutty Brown Rice
Quick Brown Rice Pilaf
Green Eggs and Rice
Brown Rice Power Patties
Mexican Brown Rice (with Black Beans)
Brown Rice Salad
Brown Rice Pudding
Tabbouleh
Barley Salad (with Red Peppers and Corn)
Quinoa Salad (with Corn and Radish)
Buckwheat (Kasha)
Millet
Basic Polenta
Easy Polenta
Easy Cheesy Polenta
Polenta with Vegetables

Brown Rice

> **B**rown rice has twice as much fiber as white rice because it has not been stripped of its bran. It may be the least likely of all grains and cereals to provoke intestinal gas and is anti-diarrheal as well as a natural laxative. It will not irritate sensitive colons and discourages peptic ulcers. Brown rice contains anti-cancer protease inhibitors, lowers cholesterol, and tends to block the development of kidney stones. However you happen to feel about brown rice, it certainly seems to like you, anyway.

Brown rice is nutrition-dense, fiber-rich, and fluent in just about any language or culture you choose. It can be a side dish, main dish, salad, bread, or dessert. Also, brown rice is equally agreeable with beans, cheese, meat, eggs, nuts, fish, and cooked or raw vegetables. Some of us even enjoy brown rice as a hot or cold breakfast cereal with milk and honey.

This is the most useful of all the grains, in my opinion, which is why most of my whole grain recipes call for brown rice. I suggest making a batch at least once a week and storing it in the refrigerator for snacks or meals any time of day.

Which Variety?
In large stores with bulk grain sections you can find a mind boggling selection of long, short, and medium-grain rice, both domestic and imported, organic and otherwise, and including brown, white, red, black, sticky, sweet, jasmine, and basmati. (Wild rice, by the way, is the seed of a wild grass and not technically part of the rice family.)

The delicate and aromatic brown basmati rice is my preference for most purposes, so I tend to buy it and cook it without giving any thought to other varieties. Short grain brown rice, however, is better for recipes where plumper, moister rice is appropriate, like

Brown Rice Power Patties (page 174). Also, if you are serving rice as a simple side dish, the stickier short grain rice is easier to pick up with a fork.

Sticky rice
For *Brown Rice Pudding* (page 177) you could experiment with sweet (also called sticky) brown rice. It is very glutinous and clumpy when cooked, and has an intriguing texture that suits rice pudding. If you cook sticky rice as you do regular brown rice, it will turn into wet, glutinous sludge. Sticky rice should be soaked for 8 – 24 hours, and then steamed for an hour. (I use a sieve that fits snugly in a 3-quart saucepan. The lid happens to fit the rim of the sieve perfectly, but you can use foil to make your own lid.) Make sure the water underneath doesn't touch the rice.

Freezing rice
Brown rice freezes well. I pack it in 2-cup portions in 1-pint plastic bags, removing as much air as I can before sealing the bags. I then place the bag of rice (dated, if I happen to remember) into a similarly-sized plastic container and freeze it. When I need the rice I remove the frozen lump from the bag and steam it over a half-inch of water in a 1-quart saucepan. (More below.)

Reheating rice
The best way to reheat brown rice is by steaming. It will taste freshly made, as well as wait patiently over the steam until you are ready to serve. Let the steam escape so the rice doesn't get soggy, and don't let the pot boil dry! One method is to set a basket steamer in a saucepan (the size of the basket and saucepan depend on the amount of rice being heated) with water added to just below the basket. Place the cold (or frozen, as mentioned above) cooked rice in the basket, bring the water to a boil, and cover. Three cups of cold cooked rice takes about 15 minutes to heat through.

Basic Baked Brown Rice

A lot of people think they don't like brown rice because they have only eaten badly cooked or undercooked brown rice. There is no good reason for this. If you are not familiar with cooking brown rice, try my directions below.

The most common cooking directions for brown rice involve simmering the rice and water on the stovetop for about 45 minutes. My directions call for starting it on the stove top, then sticking it in the oven and forgetting about it until the timer rings an hour later. With the baking method I can forget the rice while it is cooking and am never at the mercy of capricious burners.

There are other cooking options you may prefer but the important thing is that the final texture of the rice should be tender and moist. In any case, it is one of the most intelligent leftovers you could hope to find in your refrigerator. (The re-heating method mentioned on the previous page is an invaluable tip, not only to give you hot, tender rice in 10 minutes, but also to rescue imperfectly-cooked rice.)

(Makes about 6 cups cooked brown rice)

4 cups water (see **Note**)
1 teaspoon salt
2 cups brown *basmati* rice (see **Note**)

Preheat oven to 300 degrees.

1. Bring the water to a brisk boil in an ovenproof 2½-quart pot with a lid. Stir in salt and rice and bring back to the boil. Check for any husks that may have floated to the surface. (Some of us are phobic about getting a husk in a mouthful of rice.) Cover and place in the oven for 60 minutes.

2. Remove from the oven and leave pot covered for 10 minutes. Take off lid and fluff cooked rice with a fork, loosening it from the sides of the pot at the same time. Cover with a towel (a paper towel works fine) until cool. (This allows steam to escape without drying the surface of the cooked rice.)

3. Whatever you don't use the same day, store in the refrigerator, covered tightly. (Make sure rice is completely cool before you cover it.) Keeps well for up to a week, but if you don't think you will use it within a few days, it would be a good idea to freeze it. (Freezing and reheating suggestions are on the previous page.)

Note:

▸ I find I have to use less water – about 3¾ cups – if I cook regular short or long grain rice. Whichever rice you decide you like, it is probably wise to stick to one source, to avoid being surprised with wet rice one time and too-dry rice another time.

> ▸ Brown basmati rice has a nutty fragrance and a more delicate texture than regular brown rice and I use it pretty much exclusively. However, I have found that even different brands of brown basmati rice absorb water differently. For that reason, as I suggest above, I buy the same kind every time. My current favorite is from *Trader Joe's*.

▸ If you choose to rinse the rice before cooking it, rinse it *after* you measure, and drain in a strainer to remove excess water.

▸ I never cook less than 2 cups of rice, which makes about 5 – 6 cups of cooked rice. I sleep a lot better if I know there is leftover rice in the refrigerator.

Nutty Brown Rice

This is a great rice dish: simply made, interesting-looking, and decadent tasting. It is a particularly good last-minute dish if you keep pecans and sesame seeds on hand in the refrigerator, as I do. My instant version leaves out the green onions and nuts.

(Serves 4 – 6)

¼ cup extra-virgin olive oil
¼ teaspoon crushed red chili flakes
1 bunch green onions, thinly sliced
4 cups *cooked* brown rice (see previous page)
1 scant teaspoon salt
½ cup raw or toasted chopped nuts (walnuts, almonds, or pecans)
¼ cup sesame seeds, toasted

1. Heat oil over medium heat in large skillet (preferably a heavy stovetop-to-table sort of pan) and add chili flakes. Cook gently in the oil for a couple of minutes, and then add green onions. Sauté for about 30 seconds; onions should be barely softened and still bright green.

2. Add rice, salt, nuts, and seeds. Toss until heated through.

Toasting Raw Sesame Seeds:
Tip about ½-cup or so (you might as well toast enough for a couple of batches) into a shallow baking pan and toast in a 325-degree oven for 5 – 10 minutes. Keep an anxious eye on the seeds and shake the pan after a few minutes. They cook quickly and it takes very little time for golden and sweet to become brown and bitter. Remember also that they will continue to cook in the hot pan even after you take them out of the oven.

Quick Brown Rice Pilaf

This is another easy way to present brown rice to an unsympathetic audience. In pilafs the grain is cooked with the liquid (often broth) and vegetables. Here the pilaf concept is an afterthought, but it works well with leftover rice and last minute dinners.

(Serves 4 – 6)

¼ cup extra-virgin olive oil
1 medium onion in ¼-inch dice, or 1½ cups
1 red bell pepper in ¼-inch dice
8 ounces fresh mushrooms, chopped
1 teaspoon freshly crushed garlic

3 cups *cooked* brown rice (see previous page)
1 teaspoon salt
½ teaspoon freshly ground pepper
½ cup of minced parsley

1. Heat oil in 10 – 12-inch skillet or a sturdy 3 – 5-quart pot over medium high heat. Sauté onion 5 minutes, then add peppers and mushrooms. Sauté another 10 minutes or until vegetables are tender. Add garlic and sauté another minute.

2. Add rice, salt, and pepper (and minced parsley, if you have it) to onion and garlic mixture. Toss to blend thoroughly and reduce heat to low. When mixture is hot, it's ready to serve.

Note:

▸ You could also add a cup or so of frozen peas, especially if you haven't any other green accent available.

▸ Instead of rice you could use cooked barley, bulgur, or *kasha* (see page 181.)

Green Eggs and Rice

This is an easy one-dish whole food meal rich in protein, fiber, healthy fat, and vegetables. It also allows lots of flexibility. A diabetic-friendly alternative to rice would be quinoa. (See page 180.) You can use fresh spinach instead of frozen (just steam it a bit first), or replace the spinach with other fresh or frozen greens, or something like chopped cooked broccoli or asparagus. You can use sliced green onions instead of regular onions, and a different type of cheese or milk. You can use any leftover brown rice – or cooked quinoa or millet, or whole grain pasta – but white rice does *not* have the nutritional caliber to qualify. For people getting used to brown rice you can reduce the amount of rice. Leftovers are delicious heated for lunch the next day. Using this recipe as a basic model, and given that you probably have eggs, milk, and cheese on hand, you may want to put this on the *Ten Most Useful Recipes* list.

(Serves 4 as a main dish, more as a side dish)

> 1 bag (16 ounces) or 2 boxes (10 ounces each) frozen chopped spinach
> 2 tablespoons extra-virgin olive oil
> 1 medium-large onion in ¼-inch dice (about 3 cups)
>
> 4 eggs
> 1 teaspoon salt
> 1 teaspoon freshly ground black pepper
> 1½ cups fresh or evaporated whole milk
> 4 ounces sharp cheddar cheese, grated (about 1½ cups)
> 2 cups *cooked* brown rice (see page 171)

Preheat oven to 300 degrees. Oil a shallow 1½-quart casserole dish.

1. Place frozen spinach into a pot or skillet with a lid. Place over a low heat, covered, for 20 – 30 minutes or until completely thawed and hot through. There is no need to drain the spinach at all.

2. Heat oil in a sturdy 10-inch skillet over medium-high heat and sauté onion for 10 – 15 minutes or until very tender. It's fine if the onions are just beginning to turn brown at the edges. (If you use a non-stick skillet you shouldn't use more than medium heat, so it will take longer.) Remove from heat and set aside.

3. Whisk eggs in a mixing bowl or an 8-cup Pyrex jug. Add seasoning, milk, cheese, and rice, and mix well. Blend in spinach and onions. *(You can combine the whole mixture hours or even a day ahead, but bring to room temperature and stir again before you transfer it to the cooking dish.)*

4. Scrape into oiled casserole and bake uncovered at 300 degrees for about 60 minutes or until it is no longer wet in the center. *You can cook it at 325 degrees if you want it to finish cooking a little sooner, but a custard-based dish like this will have a better texture cooked at a lower temperature. If you notice mixture bubbling around the edges, reduce heat by 50 degrees.*

Brown Rice Power Patties

These nutty little patties are convenient for lunch at your desk, snacks when you're peckish, meals on the road, or after-school snacks. They're good straight from the refrigerator or at room temperature, which makes them ideal for hiking or camping.

(Makes 12 patties)

> 2 cups *cooked* brown rice (see page 171)
> 4 ounces sharp cheddar cheese, grated (about 1½ cups)
> 1½ cups finely-grated carrot (about 1 large)
> ½ cup raw sunflower seeds
> ***and/or*** ½ cup sesame seeds, raw or toasted
>
> 3 eggs
> 1 teaspoon dried basil
> 1 teaspoon salt
> ½ teaspoon freshly ground pepper
> 1½ cups toasted slivered almonds or dry roasted peanuts

Preheat oven to 350 degrees. Mist a baking sheet with non-stick spray.

1. In a mixing bowl, combine *cooked* rice, grated cheese, carrots, and seeds.

2. Combine the eggs and seasonings in the food processor and blend for about 5 seconds. Add nuts and process another 5 seconds. If using dry roasted peanuts you may need to process them an extra 5 seconds. *Don't over-process the nuts; their texture is important.* Add to rice mixture and mix thoroughly.

3. Use a ¼-cup measuring cup to scoop mixture onto baking sheet, and form into plump patties about ¾-inch thick. *I pack the measuring cup firmly and rinse it between scoops so that the mixture drops out more or less cleanly formed, ready to be patted out a bit more and shaped the rest of the way.* Bake at 350 degrees for 15 minutes, then turn patties over and bake 10 minutes more. Transfer patties to rack, flipping them so their toastier side shows.

4. If you're not eating them the same day, keep in the refrigerator. They will easily last at least a week if kept cold and stored in an airtight container.

Toasting slivered almonds

Spread them in a shallow baking pan and toast for about 10 minutes in a 325-degree oven. You want them barely golden, not browned. Cool before using. It's a good idea to toast a lot more than you need for this recipe — extra is always useful to have on hand for other recipes like *Nutty Brown Rice* or *Brown Rice Salad* or instead of walnuts in *Oatmeal Cookies*, and so on. (For toasting sesame seeds, see page 172.)

Mexican Brown Rice
with Black Beans

This is a last-minute one-skillet dinner that also offers complete protein in the bean-and-rice partnership. If *Mexican Brown Rice* didn't taste so good, you might suspect some other reason for its existence, like nutritive value or ease of preparation. It is at its best freshly made, but it still makes lovely leftovers.   It should be mentioned that if you don't have fresh cilantro on hand when the occasion for this dish presents itself, nobody would probably miss it. Parsley is a fine substitute.

(Serves 3 – 4 as main dish)

¼ cup extra-virgin olive oil
3 cups diced onion (a medium-large onion)
1 tablespoon chili powder (mild)
1 teaspoon ground cumin
1 teaspoon salt
1 green bell pepper, diced
1 fat teaspoon freshly crushed garlic

2½ cups *cooked* brown rice (see page 171)
¼ cup lemon juice
½ teaspoon freshly ground pepper
1 can (14 ounces) black beans, rinsed and drained
1 can (14 ounces) diced tomatoes, drained
(½ cup chopped fresh cilantro, if available)

1. Heat oil in 10-inch skillet over medium high heat and sauté onion, chili powder, cumin, and salt for about 5 minutes.

2. Add diced green pepper and sauté for another 5 minutes. Reduce heat to medium. Add garlic and sauté for another 2 minutes. *(This dish seems to call for a fresh crunchiness, so sauté with an easy hand and a reckless Latin spirit. The green pepper should be tender but still bright green.)*

3. Add rice, lemon, pepper, black beans, tomatoes, and cilantro. Toss gently, breaking up any lumps of rice, until the mixture is hot throughout. *(Check to make sure there's enough salt – you may need to add another ¼ teaspoon.)* Serve and eat while steaming hot.

Note:
▸ If you use chopped fresh tomatoes, use plenty – they have a milder flavor than the canned, and their fresh juiciness is a lovely addition. Make sure you add them just before serving, if possible — cooking tends to turn them to mush.

Brown Rice Salad

This salad can be a meal in itself if you toss it with cooked chicken or shrimp. Like any grain salad it's a sensible choice for buffets or picnics – it can be served warm, at room temperature or chilled, and can be made a day before or an hour before it's served. Leftovers can be transformed with additions like chopped olives or fresh tomatoes or marinated beans, or enjoyed for lunch or snacks until the last spoonful is gone.

(Serves about 6, hopefully with leftovers)

Lemon Vinaigrette
¼ cup lemon juice
1 teaspoon freshly crushed garlic
1 tablespoon honey
1 teaspoon salt
1 teaspoon freshly ground black pepper
¼ cup extra-virgin olive oil
(*Optional*: 1 tablespoon anchovies in olive oil – see box below)

3½ cups *cooked* brown basmati rice, still hot or warm, preferably (page 171)
1 bunch (or at least 1 cup) thinly sliced green onions
1 – 2 cups celery in ¼-inch dice
1 red bell pepper (the color is important) in ¼-inch dice
½ cup raw almonds with skins, chopped in thirds

1. Combine lemon juice, garlic, honey, salt, pepper, and oil in a 2-cup measuring jug and whisk thoroughly. Drain anchovies, mince and smash into a smooth paste, and add to dressing. (See **Note**.)

2. Pour lemon vinaigrette over rice (freshly cooked, if possible) and toss. Add green onions, celery, bell pepper, and almonds. Set aside for about 30 minutes, tossing a couple of times. *(The salad may seem wet but the rice will absorb vinaigrette as it sits.)* If you don't plan to serve the salad the same day, cover and refrigerate.

Anchovies

Anchovies give a richness and depth of flavor to this salad. Great source of omega-3 oils, too. The best I've had is an 8.4-ounce bottle of *Scalia* anchovies packed in extra-virgin olive oil and imported from Italy. The *King Oscar* brand has been dependable, but anchovies can vary pretty wildly in quality. Even if the thought of anchovies makes you squirm, please at least try adding two of the little fellows, mashed to a creamy anonymity with a fork, to the dressing of this salad. You can store anchovies in the refrigerator for an indefinite amount of time.

Brown Rice Pudding

This is actually rice custard, but Mother always called it rice pudding. It is best warm from the oven, but straight from the refrigerator at midnight works just fine, too. You can use any kind of leftover rice, and I especially like using cooked millet instead. Any kind of milk works but I think the milk needs to be rich to balance the assertive rice and maple syrup. Some like raisins in rice pudding but Mother and I prefer a diced ripe banana. This recipe has neither.

(Serves 4 – 6)

> 1½ - 2 cups *cooked* brown rice, hot or cold (see page 171)
>
> 4 – 6 eggs, beaten
> ½ cup pure maple syrup (or honey)
> ½ teaspoon salt
> 1 tablespoon lemon juice
> 1 teaspoon lemon zest (see page 68)
> 1 can (12 ounces) evaporated whole milk (1½ cups)
>
> 1 tablespoon butter

Preheat oven to 300 degrees, and set rack in middle of oven.

1. Break up any clumps of rice thoroughly. (I keep a sharp eye out for rice hulls, about which I have a phobia.) If I have the time or energy, I like to heat the rice before using it in this recipe to give it as tender a texture as possible. See heating tips on page 170.)

2. Whisk eggs in an 8-cup measuring jug, and then add maple syrup (or honey), salt and lemon juice with the zest, if you have it. (Lime juice is fine, too.) Add milk and rice and whisk thoroughly.

3. If butter is soft, spread over bottom and sides of shallow 1½-2 quart casserole. Otherwise, melt butter in casserole (easily done by popping it into the preheating oven for about 5 minutes). Or, if you must, use non-stick spray.

4. Scrape rice mixture into casserole and place in the oven. Check pudding after 30 minutes. At this stage I suggest stirring the rice pudding gently to help keep the rice from settling into a firm layer on the bottom. The sides will have already started to set, but don't worry. If it is bubbling around the edges, reduce heat to 250 degrees. (Custards should be cooked very gently or they tend to separate.) Bake for about 50 minutes, or until just barely set in the middle.

Note:

▶ One or two finely diced ripe bananas or ½ cup raisins or whatever are additions enjoyed by some. If you use honey, it should be a mild clover honey or it will affect the flavor of the custard. If you have neither mild honey nor maple syrup, use ½ cup brown sugar.

Bulgur

Bulgur is whole wheat that has been steamed or parboiled before being dried and chopped. It is not interchangeable with raw cracked wheat — bulgur absorbs water much more quickly. Except for the *Bulgur and Oat Bread* on page 227 there are no other recipes using bulgur in this book. Most of us have a disproportionate amount of wheat in our diets, and it makes sense to emphasize other whole grains.

Bulgur is available in fine, medium, or coarse grind. Fine or medium bulgur can be prepared with just a soak in boiling water (directions below) but coarse bulgur needs to be simmered for about 20 minutes.

The recipe for *tabbouleh* that follows the preparation instructions uses fine or medium bulgur, which is tender and recipe-ready after a soak in boiling water for half an hour. By using no more water than absolutely necessary you avoid the extra step of squeezing excess water from the bulgur.

To prepare bulgur

(Makes about 2 cups)

1 cup uncooked bulgur, fine or medium
1 cup boiling water

1. Place bulgur in a small bowl (clear 4-cup Pyrex measuring jug works well) and add boiling water. (Just hot water isn't good enough.) Cover with plastic wrap and set aside for 30 minutes. Fluff up with a fork. The water should be completely absorbed.

2. Use for *tabbouleh* while still warm, or substitute for rice in *Nutty Brown Rice* or *Quick Brown Rice Pilaf,* both on page 172.

Tabbouleh
Lebanese wheat salad

Authentic Lebanese *tabbouleh* (*tah-BOO-lee*) can call for more or less *equal amounts* of bulgur and minced parsley as well as fresh mint. This recipe is a pleasant perversion of the real thing but feel free to follow your conscience.

(Serves 4 – 6)

2 cups *cooked* bulgur *(see preceding directions)*
¼ cup lemon juice
¼ cup extra-virgin olive oil
¾ teaspoon salt
½ teaspoon freshly ground pepper
½ - 1 cup thinly-sliced green onions (3 – 6)
2 – 4 tomatoes in ¼-inch dice (at least 2 cups)
½ - 1 cup minced fresh parsley

1. Combine lemon juice, oil, and salt and pepper in a mixing bowl and add softened bulgur, onions, tomato, and parsley. Toss to blend thoroughly. Serve at room temperature or chilled. Keeps well in the refrigerator for a few days, and goes very nicely with the *Lazy Lentils* on page 156.

Note:

▸ For a more substantial *tabbouleh* I like to add 2 cups of cucumber in ¼-inch dice and a 14-ounce can of thoroughly drained chickpeas.

▸ If you choose to include chickpeas, try this treatment: heat a tablespoon of olive oil in a skillet over medium heat and add the chickpeas, shaking the pan to settle them into a single layer. Sprinkle with ¼ teaspoon of salt and a grinding of pepper and cook them until they start to turn a toasty brown, giving the pan a shake now and then. Chickpeas fixed this way are tasty on their own *or* in *tabbouleh.*

Barley (Whole)

Barley is a great source of soluble fiber, lowering blood sugar, insulin, and cholesterol. It may also have a significant cancer-fighting effect through its beta-glucan content. Because of its assertive personality it is not used as much as the easygoing and all-purpose brown rice, but it is worth getting to know.

Whole barley (also called 'whole hulled' barley) is the form we recommend using. It generally takes a good hour to cook, and even then one would never accuse it of being tender. (Pearled barley is by far the most common form of barley — its hull and bran have been polished off so it takes about half the time to cook.)

It is often suggested that one soak the barley overnight, and also to dry roast the grains to improve the favor. As usual, I choose the simplest route and just boil barley in plenty of water for at least an hour.

To cook barley

(Makes about 3 cups)

6 cups water
1 teaspoon salt
1 cup *whole* barley (not pearled — see above)

1. Bring water to the boil in a 4-quart saucepan. Add salt and barley. Turn heat down to allow a slow boil and cook for 1 – 1½ hours, at least.

2. Check a few grains for doneness. If they are the least bit rubbery, simmer for another 10 minutes before testing again.

3. Drain barley, saving liquid for soup stock. Use as a brown rice substitute (try with recipes on page 172), or in place of quinoa in the *Quinoa Salad* on the next page.

Thermos option

If you have a Thermos with at least a 3-cup capacity, try this: place 1 cup of barley in the thermos and add ½ teaspoon salt and 2 cups of boiling water. Seal Thermos and leave for 10 hours or overnight.

Barley Salad
with Red Peppers and Corn

This is one of those popular but unusual salads that go anywhere and wait patiently and taste best at room temperature.

(Serves about 4 – 6)

3 tablespoons lemon or lime juice
or apple cider vinegar
2 tablespoons extra-virgin olive oil
1 teaspoon freshly crushed garlic
½ teaspoon salt
½ teaspoon freshly ground pepper

2 cups *cooked* whole barley
½ - 1 cup ¼-inch diced sweet onion
1 cup frozen petite corn
1 cup ¼-inch dice red bell pepper (about 1)
1 cup ¼-inch diced celery
½ cup walnut pieces (toasted, if possible)
¼ cup minced fresh parsley

1. Combine lemon juice, oil, garlic, and salt and pepper in a mixing bowl and add barley and diced onion. Mix thoroughly.

2. Add corn, peppers, celery, walnuts, and parsley, and toss to blend. Serve at any temperature.

Quinoa

Quinoa (*KEEN-wah*) is a South American grain that looks like ivory-colored millet. (Actually, it isn't strictly a grain; it's the fruit of an herb.) It is particularly high in protein and a good alternative to brown rice, especially since it cooks in about half the time. Quinoa is also our preferred substitute for couscous. It has a natural coating that supposedly can give the quinoa a bitter taste, so most recipes will tell you to rinse the grain before cooking — even though most quinoa is apparently pre-washed.

To cook quinoa

(Makes about 4½ cups)

1½ cup quinoa
2¼ cups water
½ teaspoon salt

1. I don't rinse my quinoa. If you do, make sure the sieve is fine enough — quinoa can sneak through some pretty small holes. Set aside to drain. (Measure the quinoa *before* you rinse it – it swells.)

2. Bring water and salt to a boil in a 2-quart pot (one that has a lid) and add rinsed quinoa. Bring back to a boil, then reduce to a simmer, cover, and cook for about 20 minutes. The water should be absorbed and quinoa should be tender.

3. Remove quinoa from the heat. Fluff grains by tossing with a fork, reaching down to the bottom of the pot. Cover and set aside for 5 – 10 minutes.

Note:
▸ Leftover quinoa is a great substitute for brown rice – for example, in *Green Eggs and Rice* on page 173 – as well as for the couscous in *Southwest Chicken Salad* on page 202.

Quinoa Salad
with Corn and Radish

Quinoa pairs nicely with corn, and the chopped fresh radishes give crunch, color, and pep in one fell swoop. This salad is also suited to the assertive texture of barley (see previous page).

(Serves about 6)

1 cup frozen petite corn *(See note)*

3 tablespoons lime juice or apple cider vinegar
3 tablespoons extra-virgin olive oil
1 teaspoon freshly crushed garlic
1 teaspoon ground cumin
½ teaspoon salt
½ teaspoon freshly ground pepper

3½ cups *cooked* quinoa
1 – 1½ cups ¼-inch diced radishes (see **Note**)
1 cup finely sliced green onion
½ cup chopped fresh cilantro
½ cup walnut pieces, toasted if possible

1. Place frozen corn in a strainer or colander and thaw by running briefly under hot water while shaking the corn gently. Make sure corn is thoroughly drained by tossing in a colander lined with paper towels.

2. Combine lime juice, oil, garlic, cumin, and salt and pepper in a mixing bowl and add corn, radishes, green onions, walnuts, cooked quinoa, and cilantro. Toss to blend thoroughly. Serve at any temperature. Keeps nicely in the refrigerator for several days.

Note:
▸ Mother prefers this salad without corn. (Surprisingly, it's barely missed.) Also, two finely diced *small* turnips can substitute for the radishes.

Buckwheat (Kasha)

Buckwheat is neither related to wheat nor is it even a cereal — the buckwheat groat is technically a fruit that belongs to the same family as rhubarb. My favorite form of buckwheat is called *kasha*, whole toasted buckwheat groats. I love the deliciously aggressive flavor and aroma of hot cooked kasha, but it is certainly not your Grandma's *Cream of Wheat*.

(Makes about 2 cups)

1 cup water
¼ teaspoon salt
1 teaspoon butter
½ cup toasted buckwheat

1. Bring water to a boil in a small saucepan. Stir in salt, butter, and buckwheat. Turn heat down very low, cover pan, and simmer 15 minutes.

2. Remove from heat and fluff with a fork. Cover again and set aside for 5 – 10 minutes.

3. (I recommend eating half of it right away with a teaspoon of honey and a bit of milk, and storing the rest in the refrigerator to eat cold or hot some other time. See *Note*.)

Note:

▸ Leftover cooked buckwheat is a hot commodity in our refrigerator, either for a between-meal snack or in a loaf of bread. (I use it instead of the millet in the recipe for *Millet Bread* on page 224.)

▸ Cooked kasha can also be substituted for rice in *Quick Brown Rice Pilaf* on page 172.

▸ Uncooked buckwheat has a benign crunch and can be added directly to muesli or granola. (See *Muesli* on page 77.)

Millet

Millet is a protein-rich grain with a mild but curious flavor. The round yellow grains are tiny but swell amazingly when cooked. (Be sure to buy hull-less millet.) Actually, raw millet looks much like quinoa and couscous at first glance.

Properly cooked millet should be almost fluffy and can expand to almost four times the original quantity. I will admit I have found millet to be a bit tricky to cook, and the texture can be unpredictable. (Lots of the millet grains are still encased in their shiny little hulls so they can be a bit crunchy even after being cooked.) Should you find yourself with a soggy pot of millet, use it in the *Millet Bread* on page 224, or instead of rice in *Brown Rice Pudding* on page 177. I also love it as a hot cereal with honey and milk.

(Makes about 1½ cups)

½ cup millet
1¼ cups water
¼ teaspoon salt
(1 teaspoon butter)

1. **Toasting millet (optional):** Place millet in a 1½-quart pot or sturdy skillet (one that has a lid) over medium-high heat. In a few minutes, or as soon as the grains begin to pop and smoke, begin to shake the pan every few seconds. In about 1 – 2 more minutes the grains begin to look and smell toasty. *(Toasting is optional but it improves the flavor of the millet.)*

2. **Cooking millet:** So, with the skillet still on the heat, add the water, salt, and butter, and bring to a boil. Turn the heat to low, cover, and cook millet for about 20 minutes. Remove from heat and fluff deeply and thoroughly with a fork. Cover again and set aside for 10 more minutes.

Cornmeal (Polenta)

Cornmeal is a term that covers a wide range of possibilities: it can be almost flour-like or impossibly gritty, and the stone-ground versions are often a mixture of the two. It can be bland or dominating, organic or degerminated, stone-ground or not. So, know your cornmeal. For our purposes we usually mean stone-ground whole grain cornmeal.

Polenta is the coarse golden stuff used for the Italian dish by the same name. It is made from degerminated corn, so is not strictly a whole grain but it has a longer and more stable shelf life as a result. You can find polenta as well as cornmeal in the bulk food sections of natural food stores and others, and here in Oregon packaged by Bob's Red Mill.

Polenta can generally be used as you would pasta or rice, or even mashed potatoes, and it has the perfect personality to partner with rich and garlicky meat or bean stews like chili, or vegetable stews like *ratatouille*.

Cooking polenta

You can cook polenta in water, milk, stock, or a combination of any of those. I recommend using water as the cooking liquid, and adding ingredients for flavor and richness later, if you choose

Even the proportion of polenta to liquid is flexible – but the most common proportions are one part of polenta to four parts of water. The higher the ratio of water, the softer the polenta will be. Recipes for grilled or fried polenta would usually call for a lower ratio of water, like one-to-three.

There are two cooking methods I use: cooked on the stovetop or baked in the oven. (Both methods are on the following pages.) You can also use the microwave to cook polenta in 15 minutes, but we avoid using the microwave where possible.

Oven baked polenta is the easiest method. *And* there is no polenta cooked onto the bottom of the pot, which generally happens when I cook polenta on the stovetop. (… but if you have a pot with a layer of polenta cooked onto the bottom, let it soak in cold water overnight. It should be easy to scrape off in the morning. Our chickens think it is delicious.)

Flavoring polenta

Polenta loves strong flavors, and can be austere (with just the necessary salt) or decadent (with some injudicious additions of butter and cheese). You can stir in any cheese, fresh herbs, sliced green onions, diced green chilies, frozen or canned corn, or just plain butter, salt, and pepper. (Consult your refrigerator for ideas.)

Serving polenta

Cooked polenta firms so quickly that it can be frustrating to work with for the busy cook who has a tight meal-prep schedule. When polenta is hot, it's soft and easy to serve in a luscious heap on the plate. But — wait ten minutes and you will be serving odd-shaped chunks. One solution is to keep it hot in a double boiler.

My usual strategy is to scrape the still-hot polenta mixture into a clear Pyrex loaf pan, from which it can be served in neat slices once it firms slightly. If you have made it in advance you can just refrigerate it, and then decide how you want to serve it another day.

Polenta can be turned out of its serving dish after it cools for 15 minutes or so, especially if you rinse the bowl beforehand.

Polenta leftovers

Cooked polenta may be stored in the refrigerator, covered, for several days. Reheat in a 350-degree oven, covered with foil, for about 30 minutes. Or gently heat thick slices in a nonstick skillet, covered. A really delicious treat is slices of polenta fried in olive oil until beginning to turn brown, or brushed with olive oil and broiled in the oven.

Basic Polenta
(Stovetop method, plain)

Contrary to rumor, polenta does not need constant stirring. It is perfectly happy to be stirred at your convenience while you are working on other things. *(However, I would not recommend cooking polenta on the stovetop if you can cook it in the oven as described on the next page. There is no substitute for the bake-and-busy-yourself-elsewhere method.)* Using a heavy pot is helpful, but a layer of polenta stuck to the bottom will be easier to scrape off after an overnight soaking in cold water. (For more about polenta see previous page.) This is one of my favorite and most versatile dishes to have as leftovers, especially with the additions mentioned in the recipe for oven baked polenta on the next page.

(Serves 4 – 6)

> 6 cups water
> 2 teaspoons salt
> 1½ cups polenta
> 1 – 2 tablespoons butter

Have available the dish in which you want to store or serve the cooked polenta before it cools.

1. Bring water to a boil in a 4-quart pot, add salt, and then slowly and steadily pour in the polenta, at the same time stirring with a wooden spoon or a whisk to prevent lumping. Turn the heat down to low and simmer polenta for 30 – 45 minutes, sprinting over to the stove every few minutes or so to stir it. If you find it beginning to stick because you forgot to stir, just patiently scrape the bottom of the pan with your wooden spoon or whisk until all or most of the roughness is gone. If you catch it too late it doesn't really matter — it will soak off later. The longer you cook it, the thicker it will become.

2. When polenta is cooked (grains should be soft, with no core) which should take at least 30 minutes and preferably longer for the best results, stir in butter.

3. Scrape into a serving dish while hot and freshly cooked and serve right away, *or* if you're making the polenta in advance, transfer to a loaf pan and smooth the top. It will become firm quickly. If you would like to keep the polenta soft and scoop-able for a couple of hours, transfer to a double boiler over simmering water or cover and place in a 200-degree oven.

Easy Polenta
(Oven baked)

This is the method I use the most for cooking polenta. Done in the oven, it's a low maintenance dish, and — best of all — the polenta never sticks to the bottom.

(Serves about 4)

5 cups hot-to-boiling water
2 teaspoons salt
1½ cups polenta
1 – 2 tablespoons butter

Preheat oven to 325 degrees.

1. Place hot water in a 2-quart oven-safe dish (like Pyrex). Whisk in salt, polenta, and butter, and place uncovered in oven. Ignore polenta for 30 minutes.

2. Remove from oven and whisk to blend fast-cooking edges with liquid center. *Be very careful* – being splashed with molten polenta can ruin your night. Scrape sides of dish and return to the oven for another 15 – 30 minutes; the longer time may increase succulence.

3. (If you are making the *Easy, Cheesy Polenta* on this page, now is the time to stir in the sliced green onion or fresh herbs, and the grated cheese.)

4. Scrape polenta while hot into a serving dish or Pyrex loaf pan. Serve hot, warm, or reheated.

Note:

▶ The polenta will take on the form of the dish you use, and a loaf shape is convenient for slicing and heating (or frying or broiling) leftovers. For more polenta talk, go back to page 182.

Easy, Cheesy Polenta
(Mexican translation)

Polenta is especially suited to bright Mexican flavors. With the addition of cheese and sliced green onions or diced chiles, this makes a terrific partner to *Quick Little Black Bean Chili* on page 167 or *Chili (con carne)* on page 209.

Follow the recipe for the *Easy Polenta* on this page, adding these ingredients:

1½ – 2 cups grated sharp cheddar
 or Monterey jack cheese
1 cup thinly sliced green onion
 or 1 can (3½ ounces) whole mild chiles, diced
(I suggest buying canned whole chiles and dicing them yourself – the ready-diced chilies sometimes have too much skin and stem in them.)

1. Just before the final 15 minutes of cooking, add cheese and onions or chiles. Blend thoroughly with polenta. Continue with step 4 of *Easy Polenta* on this page.

Easy, Cheesy Polenta
(Mediterranean)

For a Mediterranean accent which transforms *Easy Cheesy Polenta* into a natural partner for any kind of rich meat or vegetable stew like the *Beef Stew* on page 206 or the *Ratatouille* on page 150, stir in these ingredients:

¼ cup finely chopped fresh basil
or 1 tablespoon minced fresh rosemary
½ cup of freshly grated Parmesan

1. Just before the final 15 minutes of cooking, add fresh herbs and Parmesan. Blend thoroughly with polenta. Continue with step 4 of *Easy Polenta* on this page.

Polenta with Vegetables
(Oven baked)

This is a way to turn polenta into a one-dish meal, with diced vegetables and cheese cooked directly into the polenta in a succulently textured casserole. The directions seem almost too simple, but it really works.

(Serves 4)

1 cup polenta
3½ cups hot water
2 tablespoons butter
2 teaspoons salt
1 medium onion, ½-inch dice (about 2 cups)
2 slim zucchini, ½-inch dice (about 2 cups)
2 medium tomatoes, ½-inch dice (2 cups)
½ cup freshly grated Parmesan
or 4 ounces sharp cheddar cheese, grated (about 1½ cups)

Preheat oven to 350 degrees.

1. Whisk polenta with the hot water, butter, and salt in a 1½- or 2-quart ovenproof casserole. Add diced vegetables and stir to distribute as evenly as possible. Place uncovered in the oven and ignore it for 40 minutes.

2. Remove polenta from the oven. Fold grated cheese into polenta and vegetables to gently but thoroughly blend. Smooth the top and clean up the sides before returning to the oven. Bake for another 20 minutes or until vegetables are soft and the polenta has absorbed the liquid. Let polenta firm up for 5 – 10 minutes before serving.

Note:

▸ As simple as this recipe is, it can't be rushed. Try it when you have the time to allow it at least the full hour of cooking.

12　Main Dishes

Fish

Canned Tuna

There are good reasons to eat more tuna, or any high-fat fish, for that matter — wild salmon, sardines, anchovies, and so on. Deep-sea fish like these are rich in omega-3 fatty acids and are also a valuable source of fat-soluble vitamins A and D. Canned tuna can be incorporated into all kinds of cooked and uncooked dishes, and its availability makes it practical to keep a good supply in your cupboard. It's a particularly easy way to lift your fish consumption and answer last-minute dinner questions at the same time. (See recipe for *Tuna Salad* on page 104, as well as several tuna based main dishes on the following pages.)

Plain or fancy?

When it comes to canned tuna, I favor fancy. Good tuna, whether imported from Italy or from somewhere in the Pacific Northwest of the U.S., is worthy of being the centerpiece of a meal you would serve to anybody. The variety of canned tuna on the supermarket shelves has increased considerably since the Mediterranean approach to eating has become newsworthy. The price for a six ounce can of tuna ranges from under one dollar to around ten dollars and there is a tremendous variation in quality, but you should be able to find a moderately priced one that you like.

Solid or chunk?

Solid tuna is always my choice. I always prefer to deal with as intact a fillet as possible, to serve whole or to flake myself, depending on my purposes. Chunk tuna costs less than solid, and tends to be stronger tasting and softer textured. It can even be a bit mushy, and it is harder to squeeze the liquid out when one is making something like tuna salad.

Light or white?

'Light' tuna (from yellowfin tuna, for example) probably contains less mercury than 'white' tuna (from albacore) and has been found to have higher levels of omega-3 fatty acids. Albacore is the mildest tasting of the tunas. If color or subtlety of flavor is an issue, or if you are serving tuna to a wary eater, solid white is probably the best bet.

In oil or water? Or its own juice?

Our first choice is tuna packed in its own juice. Our second choice is tuna packed in extra-virgin olive oil. If neither is available, we would choose tuna packed in water. If you are planning to drain tuna before using, as in the tuna salad on page 104, for instance, it may be best to buy tuna packed in water. Tuna packed in olive oil may leach a high proportion of the important omega-3 fatty acids into the oil, so you don't want to discard the oil. (There are recipes that can incorporate the tuna and the olive oil it is packed in, like *Tuna and Broccoli Pasta* and *Tuna and White Bean Salad*.)

Mercury contamination

The issue of mercury contamination in fish could be summarized this way: smaller, younger fish have the lowest mercury levels. Highest mercury levels are found in large fish like swordfish and shark, which eat other fish and live long enough to build up significant mercury. Moderate levels are found in the large albacore tuna most commonly used in canned white tuna. The general recommendation is two servings (12 ounces total) of canned tuna per week, with only one of the servings to be albacore. 'Light' tuna may not need to be limited. For more on this issue try the following website: www.epa.gov/waterscience/fish

Tuna and White Bean Salad
with Fresh Fennel

Fennel can usually be found in the produce section near the celery. It is deliciously crispy and with a delicate licorice flavor. If I can't find nice young fennel I don't make this salad; the tops should be fluffy and delicate, the bulb smallish and rounded for the best crunch. Instead of fennel you could use celery, preferably cut in long, slim diagonal slices.

(Serves 3 – 4)

> 1 can (6 ounces) solid light tuna packed in olive oil
>
> 1 can (15 ounces) great northern or cannellini beans
> 1 fennel bulb
> ½ cup onion in ¼-inch dice
>
> ¼ cup lemon juice and/or apple cider vinegar
> (2 tablespoons extra-virgin olive oil, drained from tuna)
> 1 teaspoon freshly crushed garlic
> ½ teaspoon salt
> ½ teaspoon freshly ground pepper

1. Open can of tuna and drain 2 tablespoons of the oil and reserve. Tip tuna and remaining oily juices into a small bowl and break up into nice pieces – not too small – with a fork. Set aside.

2. Drain and rinse beans and set aside to drain thoroughly. (A quick method is to toss the beans in a colander lined with paper towels.)

3. Trim root end of fennel bulb, and slice off everything just above the bulb. Trim feathery parts of the stalks; mince and set aside. Sample the stalks; if they are tender and tasty, slice thinly on the diagonal and include them in the salad. Quarter bulb lengthwise and remove any tough layers and core. Cut in ¼-inch (or thinner) slices; you will probably have about 2 cups. Set aside.

4. Dice onion and combine with lemon juice (or vinegar), reserved olive oil (drained from tuna), garlic, salt, and pepper in a medium to large bowl. Add sliced fennel and beans and toss thoroughly. Scatter tuna over the top of the salad and toss gently, just enough to mix but not enough to break up the tuna into indistinguishable bits. Serve room temperature or cold.

Note:

▸ Local or imported solid light tuna packed in its own juice is the best tuna for this dish but it can be comparatively expensive. I save the juice (about ¼ cup) for the next time I make chowder (page 194) or *Tuna Tetrazzini* (page 191). (If you use this kind of tuna, just add 2 tablespoons of extra-virgin olive oil to the dressing.)

Tuna and Broccoli Pasta

This is delightfully simple in ingredients and construction, with no cooking beyond boiling a pot of pasta water. This is a great way to cook broccoli, by the way. Critical to the looks and taste of this meal, though, is not allowing the broccoli to overcook. Undercooking is safer.

(Serves 4 – 6 as main course)

>12 ounces *whole-grain* pasta spirals (brown rice, whole wheat, etc.)
>(large pot of water with 1 tablespoon salt)
>
>8 cups of broccoli florets (about 3 heads)
>2 – 3 cans (6 ounces each) solid light tuna in olive oil
>
>2 tablespoons lemon juice or apple cider vinegar
>1 – 2 teaspoons freshly crushed garlic
>1 teaspoon salt
>1 teaspoon freshly ground pepper
>1 cup freshly grated Parmesan

1. Set a big pot (8-quart is a nice size) of water on the stove to boil with 1 tablespoon salt.

2. Prepare broccoli florets: rinse about 3 heads of broccoli and slice off just the actual florets from each. *(I find it easiest to hold the stalk in one hand with the broccoli head against the cutting board.)* Divide larger florets into bite-sized mouthfuls. You can save the stems for another meal, or peel and slice in ¼-inch slices and add to florets.

3. Drain about 2 tablespoons of oil from each can of tuna and reserve oil. Tip tuna into a small bowl and break up tuna into bite-sized chunks with a fork. *(Please do not use chunk tuna! If you choose a solid tuna packed in water, drain thoroughly, discarding the liquid, and then add ½ cup extra-virgin olive oil.)*

4. In a large bowl, combine reserved olive oil, lemon juice (or vinegar), garlic, salt, pepper, and Parmesan. Mix vigorously.

5. Add pasta to the pot of boiling water and cook according to instructions, or until pasta is just *barely* done. Crank the heat up to high and add the broccoli to the boiling water and pasta. Watch for water to come back to a boil, and then remove in about 30 seconds, while broccoli is still vibrant green and tender-crisp. The delicate florets mush quickly.

6. Empty broccoli and pasta into a strainer and drain for about 5 seconds, tossing gently in strainer a couple of times. Tip drained pasta and broccoli into the large bowl with the dressing, add tuna, and mix thoroughly. Serve hot or warm.

Tuna Tetrazzini

This is a good way to introduce pasta alternatives to your family (or yourself) and to increase your consumption of tuna fish and omega-3 fatty acids. You may raise your eyebrows at all the dicing but try it first. Remember that this is a one-dish meal so it's a good idea to add *more* vegetables, not less. Chopped cooked broccoli is another good addition. The diced red bell pepper is helpful for color, but any bell pepper is good. *Tuna Tetrazzini* can be made a day or so in advance, or eaten a day or so later as leftovers. Cooked brown rice can replace the pasta.

(Serves 4 as main course)

> 2 cans (6 ounces each) solid light tuna in olive oil
> 8 ounces *whole grain* pasta spirals (brown rice, whole wheat, etc.)
>
> 1 medium-large onion in ¼ inch dice (2 – 3 cups)
> 2 – 3 stalks celery in ¼-inch dice
> 1 sweet red bell pepper in ¼-inch dice
> ¼ cup all-purpose flour
> 3 cups milk or chicken stock (or combination)
> 1 teaspoon salt
> ½ teaspoon freshly ground pepper
> ¼ teaspoon dried thyme, rubbed fine
> ½ teaspoon Tabasco sauce
> 2 tablespoons fresh lemon juice and chopped zest from 1 lemon
> 6 ounces sharp cheddar cheese, grated (a generous 2 cups)

Preheat oven to 400 degrees. Oil a 2-quart casserole dish.

1. Drain about 2 tablespoons of olive oil from each can of tuna and reserve oil. Tip remaining tuna with oil into large mixing bowl and break up tuna into even-sized flakes with a fork.

2. Cook pasta according to instructions and drain. Add pasta to tuna in bowl.

3. In pasta cooking pot, heat the 4 tablespoons of reserved olive oil. Sauté onion and celery for about 15 minutes or until tender. Stir in diced red bell pepper.

4. Sprinkle flour over sautéed vegetables and stir over a medium-low heat for about 2 minutes. Blend half of the milk/stock into the mixture. When it's smoothly blended add remaining liquid. Bring to a simmer, and cook about 10 minutes, stirring often. (Sauce will thicken slightly.)

5. Add remaining ingredients to sauce and blend. Combine with pasta and tuna mixture and mix thoroughly but gently. Scrape into an oiled 2-quart casserole dish. Bake uncovered at 400 degrees for 30 minutes or until hot through.

Salmon (or Tuna) Cakes

This is a good way to bring canned salmon or tuna – or any leftover cooked fish – to the dinner table while shamelessly exploiting the weakness most of us have for hot fried things. These are golden brown and crispy, speckled with green onion, and lively tasting. You could serve them as appetizers if you made them nice and small.

(Serves 3 – 4)

> 1 can (14 – 15 ounces) salmon
>> *or* 2 cans (6 ounces) solid light tuna packed in olive oil –
>> *or* – about 2 cups flaked leftover cooked salmon or other fish
>
> 2 eggs
> 1 tablespoon lemon juice
> 1 bunch thinly sliced green onion
> ¼ teaspoon salt (more if using fresh fish)
> ¼ teaspoon freshly ground pepper
> ½ teaspoon Tabasco sauce
> ½ cup old-fashioned rolled oats
>
> (About 4 tablespoons extra-virgin olive oil for frying cakes)

Preheat oven to 200 degrees (for keeping fish cakes warm).

1. Drain canned fish and break up with a fork. (See *Notes* below.)

2. In a mixing bowl, beat eggs briefly with a fork and add lemon juice, green onion, seasoning, and oats. Add to fish and mix gently but thoroughly.

3. Using a ¼-cup measure, scoop mixture into about 6 – 8 portions and form into patties. A spoon and a fork make good tools for this job. *(You can form the patties in advance and lay them between plastic wrap misted with non-stick spray until ready to cook.)*

4. Heat 2 – 3 tablespoon of olive oil in a non-stick skillet over medium heat. Fry patties in 1 – 2 batches, about 3 – 5 minutes on the first side and 3 minutes on the second, or until browned and crisp. Transfer to a plate in the oven to keep warm. Serve with a side of *Rich Yogurt Aioli* (found on page 98) mixed with some minced green tops of green onions, if possible.

Note:

▸ If using canned salmon, include the nutrient-rich skin and bones attached to the salmon. I just break them up with a fork so they are completely undetectable. If you tend to look sideways at canned salmon, try canned red Alaskan sockeye. It's beautiful stuff, and worth the extra expense if it means you eat more salmon. Save drained salmon juice for *Crowded Chowder* on page 194.

▸ If using tuna packed in olive oil, save oil for another fish-friendly recipe; for example, in place of the olive oil in *Crowded Chowder* (page 194). At this writing, Trader Joe's sells a good solid light tuna in olive oil.

Kedgeree
Tuna and Rice: Variation on an Anglo-Indian Classic

Kedgeree (pronounced *kedger–EE)* is a simple but rich and complex tasting meal you can stir up quickly on the stovetop, calling for ingredients you probably have on hand anyway. The traditional kedgeree calls for smoked haddock and chopped hard-boiled egg and *certainly* doesn't mention canned tuna, but this rendition is practical and delectable. Don't be intimidated by the generous (and untraditional) amounts of celery and onion – they provide balance and freshness and help turn kedgeree into a complete meal. If you have all the ingredients measured and waiting, this can be started within 15 minutes of serving.

(Serves 4 as main dish)

> 2 cans (6 ounces each) solid light tuna in olive oil
> 1 box (10 ounces) frozen petite peas, or about 2 cups
> (¼ cup extra-virgin olive oil)
> 2 cups diced onion (a medium-big onion)
> 2 cups thinly sliced celery, including leaves
>
> 1 teaspoon crushed fresh garlic
> 1 teaspoon curry powder
> 1 teaspoon salt
> 1 teaspoon freshly ground pepper
> 4 cups *cooked* brown rice (see page 171)
> ¼ cup lemon juice
> (½ cup minced fresh parsley, if you have it)

1. Drain about 2 tablespoons of olive oil from each can of tuna and reserve oil. Tip tuna and remaining oily juices into a small bowl and flake gently with a fork.

2. Thaw frozen petite peas in a sieve under hot running water and drain well.

3. Heat reserved oil in a deep 10-inch skillet and sauté celery and onion for 10 minutes or until barely tender. Add garlic, curry powder, salt, and pepper, and sauté for another minute.

4. Add rice, tuna, lemon juice, peas, and parsley (if available), and toss gently, breaking up any lumps of rice, until mixed thoroughly and heated through.

Note:

▸ Flaked smoked salmon can substitutes nicely for the tuna.

▸ Make sure the peas taste good before you add them. Or just serve them (or petite green beans) on the side, which certainly helps make for a pretty plate of food, especially if you don't have any parsley to add to the kedgeree.

Crowded Chowder

This creamy chowder, or a variation thereof, is in the top five of the world's ten most useful recipes. The recipe can just as easily be transformed into clam chowder or vegetable chowder (see *Note*). Leftover cooked salmon added at the end makes a delicious variation, and barbecued salmon gives a nice smoky taste. The large amount of diced vegetables makes it inefficient to sauté all together, so I prefer to simmer them separately to make sure everything is tender in a reasonable time. Not conventional, but it works.

(Serves 4 as a main dish)

¼ cup extra-virgin olive oil
¼ teaspoon crushed red chilies
1 – 2 large onions (4 – 6 cups diced)
1 teaspoon curry powder
1 tablespoon freshly crushed garlic
¼ cup all purpose flour (½ cup if you prefer thicker chowder)

6 cups water or chicken stock or mixture
2 teaspoons salt
2 – 3 cups celery in ¼-inch dice, including tender leaves
2 – 3 cups carrots in ¼-inch dice
4 cups potatoes in ¼ inch dice

½ teaspoon dried thyme
1 teaspoon dried oregano
1 teaspoon freshly ground pepper
1 pint half-and-half or 1 can (12 ounce) evaporated whole milk (see *Note*)
2 pounds fresh fish in ½ x 1 inch chunks (see box on next page)
(1 cup minced fresh parsley or finely sliced green ends of green onions)

1. Heat a heavy pot (about 8 quarts) over medium heat and add oil. When oil is hot, add crushed chilies, onions, and curry powder, and 1 teaspoon of the salt. Sauté until onions are tender, 10 – 15 minutes, depending on the size of the pot. Stir in garlic and sauté for another minute. Sprinkle flour over onions and cook for a minute or two, stirring to make sure flour is thoroughly blended. Remove from heat.

2. Meanwhile, bring water/stock to a boil in another pot (about 6 quarts) and add remaining teaspoon of salt, celery, carrot, and potatoes. Bring back to a boil and then reduce heat and simmer uncovered until vegetables are tender, about 20 minutes.

3. Return pot with the sautéed onion mixture to medium heat. Add 2 cups of the vegetable cooking water and stir until smooth. Carefully tip in the remaining water and cooked celery, carrot, and potatoes and blend thoroughly. Add herbs and pepper. (The soup should taste pretty lively at this point; the milk/cream will mute the flavor somewhat.)

4. Stir half-and-half (or milk) and fish pieces into soup, and bring soup just to a simmer. The fish cooks in a flash, and the chowder is done. Add the minced parsley (or thinly sliced green onion tops, as an alternative) and serve it forth.

Note:

▶ I generally have a supply of olive oil from previously drained tuna, which I use instead of regular olive oil, including any tuna liquid that comes with it.

▶ You can adjust the richness to your taste. The richer the milk, the less you need. Cream or half-and-half are good and traditional, but evaporated whole milk is always in my pantry, and a 12-ounce can is 1½ cups. Speaking of liquids, any combination of water and/or fish or chicken stock for the liquid will work, and adding a cup of white wine to the water is a fine idea.

▶ For vegetable chowder increase the vegetables and include more variety like broccoli florets, diced zucchini and red bell peppers, and a bag of baby spinach. Some people like to add corn. For clam chowder, add perhaps a 10-ounce can of whole baby clams and a can or two of 6½-ounce minced clams. For liquid you can use clam juice, stock, and/or water.

About the fish

Halibut is always my first choice, especially if I am making the chowder for people I don't know. It is often expensive but it's dependable in texture (not too firm and not too soft) and has a mild flavor. Also, with halibut fillets I don't have to deal with bones or scales. Individually packed frozen fillets of fish like tilapia can be thawed quickly in a bowl of cool water for a last-minute addition of fish.

If for any reason I find myself with fish that hasn't been skinned, or fish steaks instead of fillets, I prefer to poach the fish separately. The skin and bones are easy to remove from the cooked fish and I can strain the poaching water to make sure no scales or bits of fin sneak into the chowder. The trimmings add flavor to the stock, and I can remove any dark-colored flesh (which can have a strong taste) before I add the fish to the chowder. Naturally flaked fish also integrates nicely with the chowder. (You can still cook the vegetables in the water, before or after you poach the fish.)

Poaching fish for chowder

Bring 6 cups water/stock to a boil in a 4 – 6 quart pot and add salt. Rinse fish quickly under tap and place in water. *(Don't bother to remove skin and bones from the fish; the skin adds flavor to the stock, and the bones are much easier to see or feel and remove from the cooked fish.)* Reduce heat and simmer for about 7 minutes or until fish turns opaque at its thickest point. **It needs only to be barely cooked.** Lift fish from water with a slotted spoon and set aside. When cool enough to handle, remove any skin and bones. I also remove any dark-colored flesh which I find too strong-tasting. Break the cooled cooked fish into large flakes and add to chowder ½ hour before serving.

Chicken

Tom Kah Gai
a Thai Chicken Soup, loosely translated

This is a liberal interpretation of a classic Thai soup, some version of which is on every menu of every Thai restaurant I've visited. Composition and presentation vary wildly from restaurant to restaurant as well as among recipes in magazines and cookbooks, but Tom Kah Gai is usually a thin but potent soup exploding with flavors of chilies, ginger, lime, and fresh cilantro, mellowed with coconut milk, chicken, and mushrooms.

At least three authentic elements are missing from this recipe: kaffir lime leaves, lemongrass, and galangal, all of which are available in the produce sections of some specialty stores. Straw mushrooms (available in cans) are optional, but their texture is a bit odd for some tastes. Fresh sliced supermarket mushrooms are my preference.

The intention here is to offer a recipe that anyone can make after a brief stop at the supermarket on the way home from work. (Some authorities find it acceptable to replace galangal with fresh ginger, but consider the lime leaves and lemongrass to be non-negotiable. You decide.)

For maximum impact, this soup should be served shortly after adding the mushrooms, green onions, chicken, and cilantro. The mushrooms should be creamy and fresh looking (barely cooked, to my taste) and the green onions and cilantro need to be still bright green and fresh tasting. It is not only possible, but actually preferable, to serve this soup within an hour of actually starting to make it. The ingredients all need to be prepared and standing by, of course.

(Serves about 4 as a main dish)

1 quart chicken stock (4 cups)
½ - ¾ teaspoon crushed red chili flakes
2 tablespoons curry powder
2 tablespoons finely minced fresh ginger
2 tablespoons freshly crushed garlic
2 tablespoons honey
½ cup fresh lime juice
¼ cup Thai fish sauce
1 teaspoon salt
2 cans (14 ounces each) coconut milk

2 packets sliced mushrooms (8 ounces each)
2 bunches green onions (about 12)
1½ pounds skinless boneless chicken breast
lime zest from juiced limes (see page 68)
½ – 1 cup chopped fresh cilantro

Brown basmati rice (page 171)

1. Heat chicken stock in a 5-quart pot over medium heat. While stock is heating, add chili flakes, curry, ginger, garlic, honey, lime juice, fish sauce, and salt. (Don't add the lime zest, yet. It gets tired and khaki-colored when cooked the whole time.) Simmer for about 15 minutes. Add coconut milk.

2. Meanwhile, slice green onions on the sharp diagonal. You want them to be fairly substantial but with a bit of elegance created by the long tapering edges. I like plenty in this soup.

3. Thinly slice chicken. Try to slice against the grain, which you can see if you squint at the meat in a good light. The slices can be long but they should be less than ¼-inch thick.

4. When you are close to being ready to eat, bring soup to a simmer again. Add sliced mushrooms and sliced chicken. Stir to separate chicken slices. Add green onions and lime zest. *If you use already cooked chicken, stir it in now.* The thin slices of chicken will cook very quickly, so only allow the soup to come back to a gentle simmer.

5. Finally, stir fresh cilantro through soup. Serve with a steaming pot of brown basmati rice (see page 171). To use a common Thai expression, *yum*.

Note:

▸ This recipe is mild by Thai standards, but you can fix that easily enough by adjusting the chili factor. If you are chili savvy you could use fresh Thai chilies. I have also often used Thai red chili paste for flavor and heat. Sample paste for firepower by mixing a smidgen with a bit of soup liquid.

▸ A few whole fresh red chilies floating around have a certain dramatic appeal, and anyone who likes it hot can catch one and release it in their own bowl.

▸ I prefer chicken thigh meat even though it is certainly fussy to trim and slice. Chicken breasts are definitely easier. Another option is simply to use the meat liberated from a chicken you have cooked yourself – about 4 cups of cooked chicken in delicate bite-sized shreds. I have even made this soup with fresh halibut. All liked it and some loved it, but the chicken always gets the most votes.

▸ Thai fish sauce is available in most supermarkets, and is an important ingredient here. (However, I have successfully substituted a tablespoon of mashed anchovies, or about 3.) In fact, every ingredient is critical in this soup. It needs every element present to do it justice.

Coconut Milk

Canned
Canned coconut milk is available under many labels almost anywhere for a wide range of prices. Before you decide on any brand, always read the ingredient label; the brand I like has only xanthan gum and soy lecithin added as natural emulsifiers. As usual, it's a good idea to buy this sort of product from a busy store.

If you open the can and the contents have separated into a solid white layer on top and the liquid below, don't worry. Just scrape out the firm creamy part (which will melt quickly into the soup) and use both it and the liquid.

Homemade
Making your own coconut milk is pretty straightforward. For an absolutely decadent version, try this:

1. Combine **3 cups dried unsweetened shredded coconut** with **3 cups of 2 percent milk** in a saucepan and bring slowly to a simmer, watching that it doesn't scorch while your back is turned.

2. Remove from the heat and cool for about 30 minutes. Blend in 3 batches in a blender at high speed for about 30 seconds, pouring each batch then through a strainer.

3. Pour **1 cup of boiling water** over the coconut in the strainer and press it with the back of a big spoon to extract all the milk you can. (You can also squeeze the drained coconut in 2 layers of cheesecloth or a tea towel to get every bit of milk.)

4. Store in the refrigerator until ready to use.

Chicken and Rice Soup, Mexican-style
Caldos de Arroz con Pollo

This recipe combines the comfort of a simple and unassuming chicken soup with the explosive contrast of cold, hot, crunchy, smooth, and spicy. It is an especially useful soup to serve to strangers in that it can be customized to suit any tastes – soothing and well-behaved in the pot, but as exciting as you choose to make it with the toppings.

(Serves 4)

2 tablespoons extra-virgin olive oil
2 cups onion in ¼-inch dice
2 cups celery in ¼-inch dice
1 red bell pepper in ¼-inch dice (1 – 2 cups)
1 tablespoon freshly crushed garlic

6 cups chicken stock (see page 199)
1½ teaspoons salt
½ teaspoon freshly ground pepper
¼ – ½ teaspoon Tabasco sauce
4 cups shredded cooked chicken (see page 203 for cooking ideas)
2 cups *cooked* brown basmati rice (page 171)

Toppings
1 cup sweet onion in ¼-inch dice
1 – 2 avocados in ¼-inch dice
2 – 3 tomatoes in ¼-inch dice
½ - 1 cup chopped fresh cilantro (I like *lots*.)
½ cup minced seeded jalapenos

1. Heat oil in a heavy 5-quart pot over medium-high heat. Add onions and celery and sauté 10 minutes. Add diced peppers and garlic and sauté for another 5 minutes. Vegetables should be tender.

2. Add chicken stock, salt, pepper, and Tabasco. Bring to a simmer and cook gently for 10 minutes, then add shredded chicken and cooked rice and bring back to a simmer. The soup is ready, but make sure you have enough Tabasco sauce to be interesting.

To serve: Set separate bowls of diced onion, avocado, tomatoes, cilantro, and jalapenos on the table to be added to each bowl of soup.

Note:
▸ This recipe can also double as a basic chicken soup, suitable for the care and feeding of people who are looking for comfort, not excitement. Just follow the directions through step 2, using the smaller amount of Tabasco. Mind you, if the chicken soup is treating the sniffles, chilies act as effective decongestants for some.

Roasted Chicken Thighs

Buy them with their skin on to protect the meat during cooking, and remember that leftover chicken is very useful. This might be the simplest treatment of chicken I know.

(Serves about 4 – 6, depending on thigh size)

8 chicken thighs, with skin
salt
freshly ground pepper

Preheat oven to 400 degrees.

1. Trim excess fat and skin overhang from chicken thighs and save for stock.

2. Lay thighs skin side down in an 8 x 10-inch casserole dish and sprinkle undersides with salt and pepper. Then turn the thighs over so the skin side is up and sprinkle with more salt and pepper.

3. Roast in the upper third of the oven for about 45 – 60 minutes at 400 degrees. (Large thighs take the longer time. The meat should pull easily from the bone.)

Note:

▸ Another flavor option is to combine a teaspoon of salt with a tablespoon *each* of whole grain mustard, olive oil, and honey in the casserole dish, and roll the chicken thighs to thoroughly coat before roasting.

▸ …or squeeze lemon or lime juice over the undersides of the thighs before continuing with the directions in step 2.

▸ For an easy and comforting meal, place the seasoned chicken thighs in a large roasting tray and surround them with a selection of vegetables (see pages 123-28 for ideas), cut into ½-inch chunks, tossed in extra-virgin olive oil, and sprinkled with salt and pepper. Everything should be ready together. Yum.

Simple chicken stock

1. Collect the bones and skin (including the raw skin and fat trimmings mentioned earlier) in a container and store it in the refrigerator until you can boil it all up for stock. Tip all the chicken juices from the pan of cooked thighs into the container, too, scraping every bit out with a spatula.

2. When you're ready to make the stock, just transfer the contents of the container to a pot (I generally use a 4-quart saucepan) and add enough water to just cover. I usually peel an onion and add the skin (I can always make use of a peeled onion in the refrigerator) and any celery leaves and trimmings you find. Bring to a boil. Reduce heat and simmer uncovered for a couple of hours.

3. Strain the whole mess into a bowl and set aside to cool. Empty contents of strainer onto several sheets of newspaper, then wrap up like a package and seal in a plastic bag and throw in the garbage can.

4. Store cooled stock in the refrigerator or freezer. The fat will solidify on top and seal off the stock from the air. The fat is easiest to remove when very cold. You can store the stock in the refrigerator for a few days or in the freezer for up to several months. Boil for at least 5 minutes before using.

Chicken stock, ad hoc

For easy homemade chicken stock any time use about 3 pounds of chicken wings with a quart of packaged chicken stock and enough water to cover. Follow the directions above. Chicken wings produce a particularly gelatin-rich stock with so little fat that it can be used immediately – ideal for a rustic sort of recipe like the soup on the preceding page.

Just Plain Old Roast Chicken

This is one of those recipes that aren't really recipes, but could be classified under *Things Mother Taught Me*. When it comes to roasting chickens, one is faced with all kinds of questions. Low and slow? Hot and fast? A combination? Truss? Baste? (… and if so, with what?) Covered or uncovered or both? With or without a thermometer? Who cares? Just do what Mother did.

> chicken, 4 – 5 pounds, a drug-free, free-range, clean-living bird
> extra-virgin olive oil
> salt and freshly ground pepper
>
> (Optional: onion, celery tops, lemon, garlic)

Preheat oven to 425 degrees. Find a pot with lid that will fit your chicken: I use a 3-quart enameled cast iron pot or a 5-quart Dutch oven.

1. Check the cavity of the chicken. If there is a neck, toss it back into the cavity. If there is a bag of giblets, rip it open. There are usually a couple of funny little things that I believe are the heart and gizzard and which I throw in with the neck. If the liver looks inviting it gets sautéed briskly in butter, salted and peppered, and eaten while it's hot. Mm-mm.

2. If you choose to rinse the chicken, pat it dry with paper towels. Rub a teaspoon of olive oil around inside the pot before putting the chicken in. Stuff chicken with a squeezed lemon, if you have one (save the juice for something else), a quartered onion (no need to peel it, but strip off any loose brown papery skin), a couple of leafy celery tops, and some garlic cloves, not necessarily peeled but lightly smashed. Coat visible surfaces of chicken with olive oil – although Mother says nothing browns chicken skin more nicely than butter. (Paprika helps, too, she says.) Dust generously with freshly ground pepper and salt.

3. Cover pot, place in oven, ***reduce heat to 400 degrees***, and roast for about 1½ hours. Check for doneness by wiggling a drumstick; if it moves with any reluctance, or tends to bounce firmly back to its original position, cook it for another ½ hour or so. If the drumstick moves easily in the joint, the chicken is cooked. (If the drumstick comes away in your hand — well, it's probably overcooked, and therefore more meltingly delicious, according to Mother.)

4. Give the cooked chicken 15 minutes to brood before serving.

Chicken options

Save carcass for *Simple Chicken Stock* on previous page. If you are looking for uses for your leftover cooked chicken, some ideas would be *Chicken Salad* (page 105), *Chicken Pot Pie* (page 201), *Southwest Chicken Salad* (page 202), *Chicken and Rice Soup, Mexican-style* (page 198), *Tom Kah Gai* (page 196), and a substitute for the lamb in *Lamb Curry* (page 204).

Chicken Pot Pie

Most of us love a good chicken pot pie. There are all kinds of options for the crust, including phyllo (traditional Greek pastry sold in rolls of paper-thin sheets) and puff pastry. I usually make buttery whole wheat scone topping using my recipe on page 239.

(Serves 6)

2 carrots, ¼-inch dice (about 2 cups)
2 celery stalks, ¼-inch dice (about 2 cups)
3 cups chicken broth (*see directions*)

½ stick (4 tablespoons) butter
3 cups ¼-inch diced onion (1 medium-large)
1 teaspoon freshly crushed garlic
¼ cup plus 2 tablespoons white flour
1 cup whole milk or half-and-half
1½ cups reserved broth
2 tablespoons lemon juice
(zest from lemon – see page 68)
½ teaspoon dried thyme
1 teaspoon salt
1 teaspoon freshly ground pepper
½ cup freshly grated Parmesan (see page 67)
(½ cup fresh minced parsley, if you have it)
1 cup frozen petite peas

4 cups cooked chicken *(I prefer chicken torn into succulent shreds rather than cubed for this recipe)*

Whole wheat scone recipe (page 239)

1. Dice carrot and celery. Bring chicken broth to boil in a 2-quart saucepan and add diced carrot and celery. Bring broth back to a boil and then reduce heat and simmer uncovered until vegetables are tender, about 10 minutes. Drain vegetables and set aside. Reserve 1½ cups of broth. *(Save remainder for another use.)*

2. Melt butter in a sturdy 5-quart pot over medium-high heat and sauté onions for about 10 minutes or until tender. Reduce heat to medium, add garlic, and sauté for another minute.

3. Sprinkle flour over the onion mixture and blend thoroughly. Add milk and stir briskly with a wire whisk until smooth, making sure all of the floury onion mixture is scraped from the corners. Add broth, lemon juice (and zest, if you have it), and seasoning, and whisk until blended. Bring to a simmer, whisking now and then to keep it smooth as it thickens.

Preheat oven to 400 degrees.

4. Add Parmesan, frozen peas, chicken, cooked carrot and celery, and parsley. Bring to a simmer again, and then remove from heat and scrape into a 2-quart baking dish.

5. Roll out whole wheat scone dough to ¼ - ½ inch. *(Don't try to use the whole recipe. Too much biscuit topping overwhelms the filling.)* Because I cook the pie in a round casserole dish, I cut a circle of dough into wedges, and then lay each wedge individually on the pie. For a rectangular baking dish, squares work well. If the topping pieces are serving sized, dishing up the pot pie is much easier.

6. Bake in a 400-degree oven for 30 minutes, or until crust is golden and filling is bubbling around the edges.

Note:

▶ If cooking chicken from scratch for this recipe, see simple directions for poaching chicken on page 203. The directions will give you the 4 cups of cooked chicken you need for the pot pie, and you can use the stock for this recipe, too

▶ One could fill another page with the options this recipe invites. You could add other vegetables, like broccoli florets or mushrooms, or use any combination of vegetables at all. You could make an all-vegetable pot pie, for that matter.

Southwest Chicken Salad
with Couscous and Jicama

This salad is wonderfully easy to make, lively and rich tasting, good warm or cold, and makes for popular leftovers. Couscous is not a grain, so this is essentially a pasta salad. Whole wheat couscous is not as easy to find as the regular couscous, but it is available in both bulk and packaged forms. (For a whole grain version of this salad, replace the couscous with cooked quinoa, using the quinoa recipe on page 180.)

Jicama (*HEE-kuh-muh*) is a vegetable that looks like a tan oversized turnip, has the crisp texture of a water chestnut, and a flavor that is both slightly sweet and starchy. Choose a jicama weighing about 1½-lb (they tend to range between 1 – 3-lbs) with smooth, hard skin.

(Serves 4 – 6 as main course)

> 1 box (10 ounces) or 1½ cups *whole wheat* couscous (about 4 cups cooked)
> 2½ cups water and/or chicken broth (see directions)
> ¾ teaspoon salt
>
> *Or* about 4½ cups cooked quinoa (1½ cups raw quinoa cooked according to
>   directions on page 180)
>
> 2 lbs skinless boneless chicken breasts or thighs
> 1 bunch green onions, sliced (or about 1½ cups)
> 1 medium jicama, peeled and sliced into matchsticks (or about 3 cups)
> ½ - 1 cup chopped fresh cilantro
>
> 1 cup *Southwest Dressing* (recipe below)

Southwest Dressing:
⅓ cup lemon juice
2 teaspoons freshly crushed garlic
2 teaspoons mild chili powder
2 teaspoons ground cumin
1½ teaspoon salt
¾ teaspoon Tabasco sauce
⅔ cup extra-virgin olive oil

To prepare couscous
Note: For the proportion of water to couscous, follow directions on the box. Some brands of couscous are 12 ounces or 2 cups couscous, so be aware.

1. In a saucepan with a lid bring 2½ cups chicken broth/water and salt to a boil. If you use the chicken poaching liquid (details next page), don't add any more salt.)

2. Stir in whole wheat couscous and bring back to the boil. Allow to boil for 30 seconds, and then remove from heat. Cover pan and set aside for 10 minutes.

3. Remove lid and fluff couscous with a fork. Set aside.

To prepare dressing

1. For dressing, combine all ingredients except oil in a 2-cup Pyrex jug and whisk thoroughly.
2. Add oil in a thin stream, whisking as you pour. If possible, allow dressing to sit for an hour at room temperature.

To prepare jicama

1. For jicama with tough brown skin, strip off with paring knife and then peel once more with regular peeler.
2. To slice into matchsticks, halve or quarter jicama so you have a flat side to place on cutting board, and slice into ⅛-inch slices. Lay slices flat and cut into ⅛-inch sticks. (They will vary in length because of the shape of the jicama.) You should have about 3 cups of matchsticks.

To assemble salad

1. Place sliced green onion, jicama matchsticks, chopped cilantro, and chicken pieces in a large mixing bowl and add hot or warm couscous.
2. Pour dressing over the top and toss to blend thoroughly. Serve at any temperature.

To Poach Chicken

When I start with raw chicken, I usually poach it this way. It's easy, and the chicken meat ends up tender and moist. I prefer the richer meat of thighs, but it takes long to extract the meat. The chicken breasts are easier to work with if your timing is tight. You can use the poaching liquid to cook the couscous.

1. Pour 3 cups of chicken broth (or broth and water mixed) and a teaspoon of salt into a 1½-quart pot with a tight-fitting lid. Bring liquid to a boil, then reduce heat and add 2 pounds chicken breasts and/or thighs (skinless and boneless), arranging it to submerge as much of the meat as possible.

2. Bring broth back to a simmer, and gently simmer chicken for 10 – 15 minutes, depending on the size of the chicken pieces. Avoid letting the broth boil – it will make the meat tougher. Remove from heat and cover pot, and let chicken finish cooking in the hot broth for another 10 – 15 minutes.

3. Transfer chicken to a bowl and set aside until meat cools enough to handle. *(If you're cooking chicken in advance, return cooled chicken to poaching liquid to keep it moist.)* Reserve 2½ cups of the poaching liquid for cooking the couscous. If necessary, add water to make correct amount.

4. Cut cooked chicken into thick slices (about 1 inch) and tear slices into bite-sized pieces. Set aside; you should have about 4 cups.

Lamb

Lamb Curry, Seven Boy
(or chicken, if you prefer)

This is a three-part meal: the curry itself, the accompaniments, and the rice. The 'seven boy' part refers to the traditional Indian curry meal where boys carried around the side dishes that accompanied the curry. These accompaniments are a critical element in the symphony of flavors and textures that make up this meal. Hot, sweet, spicy, rich, crunchy, smooth, soft, and crisp.

While both satisfying and exciting in its rich, hot, meaty complexity, this curry is perfectly sensible in that it supplies vegetables, meat, salad, fruit, nuts, and brown rice in one fell swoop. In fact, the meat is not really the main character here. As long as you know everyone at the table can enjoy curry, it's a superb company meal. This recipe is mildly hot and safe for anyone. For those of you who don't enjoy curry unless it requires an eighth boy to stand by with a wet towel to put out the flames, you probably know what to do. The way I usually raise the heat is with *Thai Red Curry Paste*, first mixing the stiff paste with a tablespoon of water before blending it into the curry. Remember that you can add it but you can't subtract it.

Curry is best made a day in advance. We do not recommend reducing the quantities of this recipe because we like it a *lot* and hope to be able to eat it for another meal or two. (It may need to be thinned out slightly with a bit of stock or coconut milk the next day.) The preparation involves a lot of chopping but is otherwise uncomplicated.

(Serves 6 – 8)

>   3 pounds lamb or chicken, ½-inch cubes (see **Note** for alternatives)
>   ¼ cup (4 tablespoons) curry powder (or more to taste)
>   1 tablespoon turmeric
>   1 tablespoon salt
>
>   ½ stick butter or ¼ cup extra-virgin olive oil
>   6 cups diced onions (about 3 medium – large)
>   2 tablespoons crushed fresh garlic
>
>   2 tablespoon minced fresh ginger
>   juice from a fresh lemon or lime (about ¼ cup)
>   4 cups finely diced butternut squash
>   6 cups finely diced Granny Smith apples (about 3 – 5 apples)
>   2 cans (14 ounces each) coconut milk
>   1 cup raisins

1. Combine meat pieces with curry and salt. Mix thoroughly and set aside.

2. Heat a heavy pot (about 8-quart) over medium high heat and add oil. When oil is hot, add onions and sauté 15 minutes. Stir in garlic and seasoned meat, and sauté for another 10 minutes or until meat is brown.

3. Add diced squash and apples, ginger, lemon juice, coconut milk, and raisins. Bring to a simmer, uncovered. ***Preheat oven to 300 degrees.***

4. Place in oven, uncovered. Cook for an hour, and then reduce heat to 250 degrees and cook for another hour. Remove from oven and taste for flavor. If you decide to add more curry powder (or chili paste for pure heat), first mix with a small amount of curry until smooth, then add to the pot. Cool completely before covering and chilling overnight.

5. To serve, bring to room temperature. Place in 300-degree oven, partially covered to allow steam to escape, and heat for 1 hour. Stir and check temperature. Return to oven until good and hot. Serve over brown basmati rice with accompaniments.

Accompaniments

These are our standard, non-negotiable favorites. I bring them to the table in mismatched earthenware bowls of various sizes. The diced avocado and banana need to be tossed with a bit of lemon or lime juice to keep their clean colors intact. The bowl of fresh grated coconut is a lovely touch, and I think is worth the trouble. (For anyone unfamiliar with fresh coconuts, some preparation tips are in box below. You can extract the coconut meat a couple of days before, grate it, and store it in a plastic bag in the refrigerator.

- 1 bunch green onions, thinly sliced
- 1 cucumber, peeled, seeded, and finely diced
- 2 tomatoes, seeded and finely diced
- 2 avocados, diced
- 2 bananas, diced
- 1 cup coarsely chopped unsalted dry-roasted peanuts
- Fresh coconut, grated on the medium holes of a box grater.

Note:

▶ If you would prefer to use already cooked meat, I suggest shredding it and mixing it with the curry just before you place it in the oven for the final cooking.

Not sure about fresh coconuts?

If you buy the coconut a day or two before you need it, you will be able to make sure it's fresh while you still have time to replace it. A taste of the milk inside will tell you if it is a good coconut. There are three eyes at one end of the coconut, and one of them is soft enough to drill through – I poke each with an oyster knife (see page 69) to find the soft one, then twist the blade through the shell and meat until I've made a hole big enough so the coconut milk (actually a cloudy, watery looking liquid) can come out. I set the coconut on a Pyrex measuring jug to drain. The liquid should be clean and sweet-tasting. I love to drink it, but if you don't, just add it to the curry. If the coconut liquid tastes the least bit sour, the coconut is past its prime. Bring it back to the store!

Beef

Beef Stew
Rich beef stew with red wine and onions

This stew is rich and simple, with an intense meat presence. The only vegetable in the stew is onion. I prefer to cut the meat up myself, and it's a pretty easy task when you start with chuck steaks. Not lean, either; nicely marbled meat is preferable. My stew calls for an equal volume of meat and chopped onion, but the onion pretty much melts into the stew by the time it's done. One of the nicest things about a stew like this is that one should make it a day ahead, which makes it very convenient to prepare a selection of side vegetables like roasted butternut squash, cauliflower, and asparagus (see *Roasted Vegetables* on page 124), and steamed baby red potatoes. (If you would prefer a one-dish meal, add vegetables to the stew before serving.)

(Serves about 6)

3 pounds beef chuck steaks sliced into ½-inch chunks
2 tablespoons paprika
2 teaspoons salt
1½ teaspoons freshly ground pepper

1 bottle (750 ml) full-bodied red wine, like merlot
6 tablespoons extra-virgin olive oil, divided
2 tablespoons butter (or extra-virgin olive oil)
2 medium-large onions, diced (about 6 cups)
¼ cup minced or crushed fresh garlic
½ teaspoon dried thyme
¼ cup all purpose flour

1. Place meat chunks in a large mixing bowl, spreading meat out to create as much surface area as possible. Use a half-cup measure to combine and blend paprika, salt, and pepper, and sprinkle over meat. Toss thoroughly to make sure the meat chunks are all seasoned. Open the bottle of wine.

2. Heat 2 tablespoons olive oil in a large heavy-bottomed pot over medium-high heat. When oil is good and hot – but not smoking, so don't walk away – add half of the meat mixture, spreading it out into one layer. Sauté briskly until mostly brown. This should only take a few minutes. (It is entirely acceptable to rescue smaller pieces of meat and eat them as you work.) Tip the sautéed meat into a waiting 3-quart casserole.

3. Place the pot back on the heat and immediately add half of the wine. It should start to bubble quickly, and any stuff stuck to the pan will gradually loosen. Scrape with a heat-proof silicone spatula (gently, to avoid being splashed) as wine boils and reduces to close to half its original volume. Scrape the reduced wine mixture over the sautéed meat.

4. Place the pot back on the heat and add another 2 tablespoons of oil, and then the last half of the meat mixture. (The pot will still be good and hot so you don't want to get distracted at this point.) Sauté remaining meat as before and add it to the previous batch. Place pot back on the stove and add remaining wine. Repeat the deglazing procedure, and when the wine is reduced roughly by half, add to meat.

5. Have chopped onions standing by. Combine butter and remaining 2 tablespoons of olive oil in same pot over medium-high heat, and add onions when butter and oil are bubbling and hot enough to sizzle a bit of onion you toss in. Sauté onions for about 10 minutes, and then reduce the heat to medium and sauté for another 5 minutes or until onions are soft and golden. Add thyme and garlic, and cook a couple of minutes more while you blend in the garlic. Add flour and stir to blend thoroughly. Cook for another minute and remove from heat.

6. Add the meat and juices to the onion mixture and mix well. Set aside until completely cool and chill overnight or for a day or two. *(If you don't think it's cool enough to store, cover stew with a couple of sheets of paper towel held down with a spatula to keep it from sagging into the stew as it absorbs the steam. Otherwise the steam condenses and drips back into the stew.)*

7. **To finish cooking the stew**, place in 250-degree oven, partly covered to allow steam to escape, and cook for about 4 hours. The long, gentle cooking will allow the meat to become tender and the sauce to richen deliciously.

Beef Stew, Easy Method

1. Place meat chunks in a large mixing bowl.

2. Combine wine with paprika, salt, pepper, thyme, flour, and garlic. Pour the wine mixture over the meat and blend thoroughly. (You can do this a few hours before Step **2**.)

3. Heat 4 tablespoons olive oil and the 2 tablespoons butter in a large heavy-bottomed pot over medium-high heat. Have chopped onions standing by and add when oil is bubbling and hot enough to sizzle a bit of onion you toss in. Sauté onions for about 15 minutes or until onions are tender.

4. Add meat and wine mixture and blend thoroughly. Allow stew to come to a simmer.

5. Pick up with Step **7** of *Beef Stew* (main recipe)

Note:

▸ *For crock pot or slow cooker:* Transfer stew to slow cooker after step **3**. Cook on low, partially covered to allow steam to escape, for 8 hours or until meat is very tender. (Crock pots vary so much in size and performance that you'll probably need to adjust the timing to suit your situation.)

Meat Loaf

A rich and redolent meat loaf is a truly great dish. It is also a sensible way to serve meat when you don't know exactly how many you are serving, or when. Meat loaf can be last minute or mixed ahead of time and stored in the refrigerator, and preferably brought to room temperature before cooking. It even waits cheerfully *after* it's cooked without losing its appeal. As for leftovers, there is the legendary meat loaf sandwich, or you can chop it up and use it in chili (page 209), or with tomato sauce (page 109) over pasta or with polenta (page 184), and so on.

(Serves 4 – 6)

1 Tbl crushed dried tarragon (or is it rosemary??)

2 eggs

~~¼ cup yogurt~~

1 cup minced onion

3 2 tablespoons Dijon-style or whole grain mustard

1 teaspoon freshly crushed garlic

1 teaspoon salt

1 teaspoon freshly ground pepper

~~¾ cup old-fashioned rolled oats~~

~~1½~~ - 2 pounds finest quality ground meat of your choice
(we like our ground beef to be about 15 percent fat)

Preheat oven to 350 degrees.

1. In a small bowl combine everything but the meat and whisk until well blended.

2. Spread ground meat out into a thick layer in a mixing bowl and pour egg mixture over it. Blend thoroughly. (This is the only part of making meatloaf that could be considered work. I use a big fork.)

3. Use a spatula to pat meat mixture into a vaguely loaf-shaped lump while it is still in the mixing bowl, and then tip it into a shallow 1½-quart oven-to-table casserole. Finish shaping the meat into a free-form loaf, trying not to compact it too much in the process. Bake in a 350-degree oven for about 1¼ hours.

Note:

▸ Meat loaf is not an inherently glamorous thing, so I like to serve it under or over the *Tomato Sauce* on page 109. Tastes good and is also an extra serving of vegetables.

Meatballs are a useful variation but they do take a bit more time to form. Shape the meat into shaggy nuggets no larger than 1½ inches in diameter. Crowd them in a shallow pan and bake them for about 20 minutes. (Test one for doneness.) Serve them on a bed of hot *Tomato Sauce* (page 109). You can also place the raw meatballs on a couple of plates and freeze them for an hour, then transfer to a bag and store in the freezer for another day.)

Chili

(*con* beans and *con carne*)

This can be simple or complex, fancy or plain, vegetarian or not. You can use whatever beans you like. I cook my own anasazi beans (see page 156) or use canned pinto beans. You can make it hot, or tame like this version. You also may prefer a soupier chili than this one. We generally serve chili over brown rice, but a decadent alternative is to serve it over *Easy Cheesy Polenta* (page 184).

(Serves 4 – 6)

> ¼ cup extra-virgin olive oil
> 2 medium-large onions, diced (about 6 cups)
> 1 – 2 bell peppers, diced (1½ – 3 cups)
> 1 – 2 jalapenos, seeded and finely diced (optional)
> 1 – 2 tablespoons freshly crushed garlic
> 2 tablespoon chili powder
> 1 tablespoon ground cumin
> 1 teaspoon oregano
> 1 fat tablespoon honey
> 2 teaspoons salt
> 1 teaspoon freshly ground pepper
>
> 1 pound raw chopped or ground meat
> 1 can (28 ounces) crushed tomatoes
> 3 cups cooked beans (15-ounce can is about 1½-cups drained beans)
> (1 cup chopped cilantro, if available)

1. Heat oil in 6-quart heavy pot over medium high heat and sauté onions briskly for about 8 minutes, then add peppers (and jalapenos, if you have them) and cook for 5 more minutes, or until onions and peppers are tender. Stir in garlic and seasonings and cook for another few minutes.

2. Add meat and sauté briskly until browned.

3. Add tomatoes and drained beans. Bring to a simmer and cook very gently, uncovered, for about 30 minutes, stirring from time to time. Avoid letting the chili boil. Keep in mind that the longer you cook it, the drier it gets. Taste for flavor – the chili may need a dose of bottled fire of your choice, depending on the amount of beans and/or meat you ended up using. Add cilantro within an hour of serving, to maintain color and flavor. *(If made in advance, let cool completely, uncovered, before storing in refrigerator.)*

Note:

▶ I like to either serve chili with sides of *Pico de Gallo* and *Avocado Salsa* (both on page 131) or with side dishes of topping options like grated sharp cheddar cheese, sliced green onions or diced mild white onions, diced avocado, extra chopped cilantro, and minced fresh jalapenos.

Meat-Free Main Dishes

Zucchini Frittata

The *frittata* is basically an omelet with the filling and eggs combined, so there is obviously lots of room for experimentation here. The possibilities range from complex to simple and this recipe is *very* simple. The seasoning is understated, so this dish goes down nicely anytime from breakfast to midnight snack.

(Serves about 2 – 4)

> 4 eggs
> 3 slim zucchini grated on medium grater (about 4 cups)
> ¼ cup freshly grated Parmesan or crumbled feta cheese
> ½ teaspoon salt
> ½ teaspoon freshly ground pepper
> 1 tablespoon extra-virgin olive oil

1. Crack eggs into a mixing bowl and beat with a fork, just enough to blend. Add grated zucchini, cheese, and seasoning, and mix well. *(If you grate the zucchini ahead of time, toss with a teaspoon of salt and set aside in a sieve for 30 minutes. Press out excess liquid before adding to egg mixture, and reduce recipe salt to ¼ teaspoon.)*

2. Heat oil in a 10 – 12-inch non-stick skillet over medium high heat until a drop of the frittata mixture sizzles wildly. Give mixture a final stir and pour it into the skillet, spreading it evenly. Reduce heat to medium-low and cook until mixture is almost set, about 10 – 15 minutes, shaking pan from time to time in the first few minutes to prevent sticking. (The smaller sized pan will make a thicker frittata, which will take longer to set.) The frittata will be wet on top.

3. To finish cooking, place pan under broiler for about 3 minutes **or** cut frittata in quarters and flip carefully. Or if you're feeling deft, place a plate over the skillet and, holding plate and skillet tightly together with hot pads, invert so frittata falls onto plate, and then slide frittata back into hot skillet to finish cooking the top. I don't recommend doing this the first time with an audience.

Note:

▸ A favorite variation of mine is made with spinach. Prepare a 10-ounce packet of frozen chopped spinach using the directions on page 116, draining it of about ¼ cup of liquid. Use it instead of the zucchini in the recipe above. It's a great emergency meal because I always have eggs and frozen spinach on hand. A frittata made with leftover cooked vegetables can be wonderful. Chopped cooked potato and broccoli make a satisfying combination, for example, and thinly sliced green onions are always a welcome addition (and can be added raw, of course).

▸ You can also cook the frittata in an oven. Scrape mixture into a shallow 2-quart casserole and bake in a 400-degree over for about 20 minutes or until just set.

Black Bean Polenta

This one-dish meal delivers beans, grains, and vegetables in one fell swoop. It can be made easily in less than an hour, keeps for days in the refrigerator, re-heats by the slice as needed, and, except for the green onions, requires only ingredients you could easily keep on hand in your cupboard. You can adjust the level of heat in *Black Bean Polenta* by way of the salsa or chilies, and you can certainly adjust the amount of cheese, beans, or any other ingredient.

(Serves about 6)

> 6 cups water
> 2 teaspoons salt
> 1½ cups polenta, or preferably stone-ground coarse cornmeal
>
> 8 ounces sharp cheddar cheese, grated (about 3 cups), divided
> 1 bunch green onions, thinly sliced (about 1 – 1½ cups)
> 1½ cups salsa, bottled or fresh, mild or hot, drained of excess liquid
> 1 can (7 ounces) mild whole green chiles, diced (see *Note*, page 147)
> 2 cans (14 ounces each) black beans, drained and half-mashed

Preheat oven to 400 degrees. Oil a shallow casserole dish, about 9 x 11 inches.

1. Bring water to a boil in a 4-quart heavy-bottomed pot, add salt, then slowly and steadily pour in the polenta while stirring constantly with a whisk to prevent lumping. Reduce heat to low and simmer polenta for 30 minutes, stirring frequently and scraping the bottom of the pan regularly to prevent sticking. The cooked polenta grains should be soft, with no noticeable core.

2. Meanwhile, prepare the grated cheese (in two piles), green onions, salsa, chiles, and beans. Line them up in the order you'll need them. Oil casserole dish.

3. When polenta is cooked, stir in the sliced green onions and half of the grated cheese. Mix well, making sure to reach the polenta at the very bottom, and then remove pot from heat.

4. Scrape half of the polenta mixture into the casserole and spread evenly. (The remaining polenta will begin to firm as it cools, so work briskly at this point.) Spread with the salsa, the black beans, the diced chiles, and the remaining cheese. Cover with the rest of the polenta mixture, and smooth the top.

5. Heat uncovered at 400 degrees for about 30 minutes, or until hot in the middle. (Check by poking a paring knife into the middle and pulling it out immediately. If the blade is hot, the dish is ready.) Set aside for 10 minutes to firm slightly so it will be easier to slice.

Note:

▸ If you are not going to serve it the same day, set aside to cool completely, then cover and chill. To serve, bring to room temperature before cooking.

Spinach and Cheese Crêpes
with Tomato Sauce

This is a vegetarian dish in three parts, all of which may be made days ahead, if necessary, and demand no last minute shopping. Good for potlucks and those suppers for tired and hungry houseguests who arrive a couple of hours later than they're supposed to. One filled crêpe topped with the bright sauce makes a first course that doubles as a vegetable and can boost a simple meal. Two crêpes make a main course finished with an easy salad.

(Makes 12 filled crêpes)

Crêpes

(If you haven't made crêpes before, don't wait any longer. Crêpes are surprisingly easy and a great addition to any cook's repertoire. They even freeze well.)

(Makes about 16 x 6-inch crêpes.)

> 4 eggs
> 1 cup milk
> 2 tablespoons extra-virgin olive oil
> ½ teaspoon salt
> 1 tablespoon sugar
> 1 cup whole wheat pastry flour

For crêpe batter:

1. Combine ingredients in a food processor or blender and process until smooth,

   or beat eggs in a 4-cup measuring jug, add remaining ingredients, and blend until smooth with an immersion blender or whisk. (The whisk method is adequate, but will not give you a completely smooth batter.)

2. Set batter aside for 1 – 2 hours if you can; this technically relaxes the gluten and makes more tender crêpes. If you store the batter overnight in the refrigerator, it will separate; just whisk to a smooth consistency again. For the same reason, stir batter regularly while cooking crêpes.

To cook crêpes:

1. Heat crêpe pan, or a 6 - 7 inch skillet with sloping sides, over moderate-high heat. When drops of water sizzle in the pan, it is ready. Wipe with oil-soaked paper towel. Pour batter into pan from a spoon or scoop holding about 3 tablespoons, holding pan handle in your other hand and swirling pan quickly to cover the bottom evenly with batter. Keep swirling pan until batter no longer runs and set pan back on heat.

2. When the crêpe's surface is dry and the underside is a lacy golden-brown it is ready to flip – this will probably take about 20 – 30 seconds. (One clue that it is ready to flip is a slight darkening of the very edge.) After flipping, cook for

another 10 seconds and then flip again onto a plate covered with a paper towel. (The second side will be pale and freckled.)

3. Stack crêpes as you cook them. You will notice there are enough crêpes to allow for some disasters or hungry passers-by or whatever. The crêpes may be made up to a week in advance and stored in the refrigerator sealed in plastic.

Spinach and Cheese Filling
> 1 box (10 ounces) frozen chopped spinach, thawed and drained
> 2 eggs
> 1 teaspoon freshly crushed garlic
> 1 teaspoon salt
> ½ teaspoon freshly ground pepper
> 8 ounces mozzarella cheese, grated (about 2½ cups)
> 1 cup freshly grated Parmesan (about 3 ounces)

For spinach and cheese mixture:

1. Thaw and drain spinach. *(Either leave frozen spinach in a bowl in the refrigerator overnight, or at room temperature for a few hours, or place in a covered skillet over a low heat for about 10 – 15 minutes, breaking up spinach as it thaws. Drain off excess liquid in a sieve, pressing spinach with a spatula; you should be able to extract ½ cup.)*

2. Whisk eggs in a medium bowl and add spinach, garlic, seasoning, and cheeses, mixing very thoroughly.

To assemble crêpes:

1. Butter or oil shallow casserole dish, about 8 x 12-inch.

2. Lay 12 crêpes out on counter, pale freckled side up. Divide filling between crêpes, about ¼ cup on each. Spread filling across the lower three-quarters of each crêpe and roll up.

3. Place in baking dish and cook, covered loosely with foil, at 400 degrees for about 30 minutes. (If crêpes were made ahead and chilled, bring to room temperature before baking.) Serve with *Tomato Sauce* (page 109).

Note:

▸ If these filled crêpes are overcooked they can easily become dry. Don't put them in the oven unless you are confident you can serve them as soon as they are cooked.

▸ You can also spread the spinach and cheese filling on strips of cooked whole wheat lasagna, then roll them up, crowd them in the casserole, and cover with the tomato sauce. To cook, follow instructions in Step **3** above.

Macaroni and Cheese

It's easy to justify a meal of macaroni and cheese if you don't compromise on the ingredients. This recipe is a departure from the traditional in that it is based on custard, which offers added nutrition, protein, and good fat from the eggs that you won't get from a cheesy sauce. (…but if you would like a cheesy sauce, add the cheese in this recipe to the Béchamel sauce on page 108.)

This version also incorporates an onion and whole grain pasta. Remember that diced onion, when sautéed according to the directions below, will melt down to less than half its original volume and will virtually disappear into the macaroni and cheese. (I have successfully used more than 3 cups of onion before!) The 'don't ask, don't tell' policy works here.

(Serves 4 as main dish)

4 cups **cooked** whole grain macaroni
        (brown rice, whole wheat, etc.)

2 tablespoons extra-virgin olive oil
1 medium onion, in ¼-inch dice

6 eggs
1 can (12 ounces) evaporated whole milk
8 ounces sharp cheddar cheese, grated
1 tablespoon whole grain mustard
1 teaspoon salt
½ - 1 teaspoon Tabasco sauce

Preheat oven to 300 degrees.

1. Cook pasta according to directions. (About 2 cups of dried pasta should yield about 4 cups of cooked.)

2. Heat olive oil in 10-inch pot. (I like to use the heavy-bottomed pasta pot – I just tip the cooked, pasta into the colander to drain, and put the still-hot pot back on the stove and add the oil.) Sauté onion for 15 minutes or until very tender. (If the onion has any crunch it will be too obvious.)

3. Whisk eggs in a 2-quart mixing bowl. Add milk, cheese, and seasoning, and blend thoroughly. Combine with cooked macaroni and onion.

4. Scrape into an oiled 2-quart casserole dish. (You will have slightly less than 2 quarts of macaroni and cheese mixture.) Bake uncovered at 300 degrees for 45 minutes or until set in the middle. Check after 30 minutes and lower the heat if it is browning around the edges. Gentle cooking for just enough time to set the custard will give the best results.

Note:

▸ A dish like this begs to be customized, but keep it real. Use real cheese, not 'lite' or processed, and with real flavor, if possible. Eight ounces of grated cheese is about 3 cups. A cup of grated feta cheese is one of our favorite additions, if there is any left over from the last *Greek Salad* (page 134).

▸ If you don't use evaporated whole milk, use fresh milk with respectable butterfat content, like 2 – 4 percent.

▸ A variation that some prefer includes a 4- or 7-ounce can of diced green chiles, mild or medium. (See **Note** about chiles on page 147.)

▸ Brown rice macaroni is softer and milder than whole wheat pasta, so is probably the more acceptable substitute for regular white pasta. (See more about whole grain pastas at the top of page 85.) Be aware that pasta sold as quinoa pasta may have corn as the first ingredient.

13 Bread

Breadmaking:
Eight common questions

One problem is that it's *too* easy to make bread; that's why so many of us make bread without really understanding how bread is made. Then, when our plump and soaring loaf emerges from the oven pocked and sullen, it's just one more unsolved mystery that knocks another leg out from under our confidence. The point is, once you understand the few basic principles governing the action of yeast and gluten, you'll never again be bullied by breadmaking or all the silly misconceptions about it.

How bread works

Water, yeast, and flour: there you have the framework on which hang all yeast-risen breads. Mixed together in a bowl, the water moistens the wheat proteins to develop the gluten, which during the stirring and kneading is stretched and toughened to form an elastic network of little pockets (a sort of honeycomb effect) able to trap the gases produced by the fermenting yeast.

So the bread rises. The only way it won't rise is if the yeast is dead, or we kill it. Now, yeast is sensitive, but it's not fragile, and will usually survive in spite of us. Once you master a simple loaf and understand how and why it works, you'll know when to ignore unnecessary and sometimes crazy recipe instructions.

From there it takes only practice and an awareness of the effect of other ingredients – like salt, sweetening, and fat – on the teamwork of gluten and yeast. Following are the most-asked questions about making bread, with answers that I hope will simplify the process for you.

How important is water temperature?

Just don't scare the yeast! It doesn't like hot water or cold water. Yeast is inactive when cold, sluggish when cool, thriving when warm, hysterical when hot, and dead when the temperature hits 140 degrees. The ideal temperature for activating dry yeast is about 110 degrees. Anything within the range of warm is fine. Bread recipes often urge you to use a thermometer (I never have), but as long as yeast has such a casual approach to the warm water issue, you may as well.

What kind of yeast?

The active dry yeast granules are easier to find, use, and store than the fresh compressed yeast (which is usually sold in little cakes in the refrigeration department). Any brand of active dry yeast is fine. If you find yourself with past-dated yeast, test it before you toss it – it's probably fine.

The common supermarket brands come in 4-ounce jars or ¼-ounce packets; unless you plan to make only three loaves of bread a year, the jars are more economical. But by far the best deal is pre-packed bulk baking yeast from a good natural food store. As for something called 'rapid-rise' yeast, I've used it interchangeably with regular yeast. (This all may sound haphazard but that's one of the charming aspects of bread making. A bit of yeast either way will not raise the eyebrows of any dough.)

How much yeast?

Yeast is not like baking powder. Yeast cells are alive and grow by multiplying; given enough time, a half-teaspoon of yeast is able to aerate a batch of dough just as well as a tablespoon of yeast. This is an especially important point to make in view of the fact that you may come across recipes that call for *two packages* (almost 2 tablespoons) of yeast, even for a standard batch of white bread. Obviously more yeast works faster and makes both the recipe-writer and the baker feel safe, but once you get used to tipping in that amount of yeast, you're more likely to feel doubtful when a perfectly sane recipe calls for one third of that amount. Excess yeast rushes dough fermentation along, as well as causing the loaf to dry faster.

Whole grain dough can use more yeast and doesn't benefit from long or multiple risings. (Technically, dough that is allowed a leisurely rising period undergoes a ripening process which develops its natural acidity; this is one of the keys to those crusty, fragrant artisan breads with Italian names in paper bags we pay so much for.)

Does it matter what flour I use?

You bet it does. For yeast raised breads you should be using mostly flour made from what is called 'hard' (high protein) wheat. Look for something called **stone-ground whole wheat bread flour**. My choice is *Bob's Red Mill* stone-ground whole wheat bread flour, which is ground and packaged here in Oregon and easy to find in most supermarkets. Whether you buy flour packaged or from the bulk food department, choose a food store with high standards and a brisk turnover. (See *Some favorite Portland sources* on page 65.)

The critical factor is gluten, the protein in wheat which becomes elastic when moistened, and which is what makes yeast breads possible. Yeast works relatively slowly and depends on the strength of the gluten to trap and hold the gases it produces. (*Pastry flour* is made with 'soft' low-gluten wheat and is best for quick breads like scones and muffins which call for a fast acting rising agent like baking powder.)

If you're using high-gluten flour, you should never need to add gluten flour (which is pure, powdered gluten), even in 100 percent whole wheat bread. Once you have handled the springy, exuberant dough made from high-gluten flour, you won't give up until you find it.

Can I substitute other kinds of flour instead of wheat?

Unless you are confident of producing a successful loaf of bread using wheat flour, you probably should put off experimenting with recipes using non-wheat flours. Most non-wheat flours have no appreciable gluten, and gluten is a critical factor in yeast-risen breads. (For that reason, non-wheat flours are generally supplemented with white flour, and that would seem to defeat the purpose.)

Keep in mind, too, that it is hard to be sure of buying fresh flour of the less popular and slower selling varieties like oat, barley, rice, and even rye flour. However, if you do decide to experiment, start with about one part non-wheat flour to three parts whole wheat flour. (See page 224 about using cooked whole grains in bread.)

How do I know when I've added enough flour?

Never take the flour quantities in recipes too seriously. Flours absorb at different rates and people measure different ways. (For that matter, recipes make mistakes and sometimes include misprints.) Once dough is too stiff to stir, add no more than one or two tablespoons of flour at one time. Never mind how much flour the recipe calls for – let the dough have the last word. Dough should feel soft, but bouncy. (The bounce comes from well-developed gluten, which is the result of adequate kneading.) It may take a good bit of practice, though, to feel the bounce in sticky whole wheat dough.

'Wet' dough is inherently less stable than drier dough, and if left to rise too long before baking will tend to collapse more easily in the oven, coming out dimpled and flat or misshapen on top. However, it will certainly have a better flavor and moister texture than the loaf with more flour and a nice rounded crust. The trick is to find the right balance, and that comes with practice.

Can I over-knead dough?

Probably not, unless you're using a food processor or some other mechanical kneader. Kneading manually, your arms would drop off before the dough was even tired. (In fact, dough made from high-gluten flour begs to be kneaded much longer than most of us are willing.) The trick is to avoid adding too much flour to the dough during kneading because of the temptation to try to remove the stickiness from the dough. Too much flour makes dense, dry, bland bread.

Can I make good bread without salt/ fat/ sugar?

Certainly without fat or sugar (consider the traditional baguette, for example), but salt is critical for the overall taste. Salt is technically important in the development of dough (it tightens the gluten network) but more important to the home baker is its role as a flavor enhancer. Leave it out at your own risk.

Sweetening is not necessary for the dough at any stage, but it will make the dough rise faster by exciting the yeast. Directions to add a dab of sugar with the yeast are always safe to ignore; although it can make even shy yeast foam excitedly (yeast loves sugar), it serves more to reassure an anxious baker.

Honey is my preferred sweetener, and is an important ingredient in the versions of my *Whole Wheat and Honey Loaf* recipes on pages 220 and 222. Added sweetening also makes the crust brown quicker and darker, as does fat.

Fat makes bread more tender, and even a small amount, like a tablespoon per pound of dough, can increase the final loaf volume by 20 percent. More fat, like ¼ cup or more per pound of dough will require more yeast to get the work done. Remember that milk and eggs have the effect of fat in dough. (Eggs can create a fine, close crumb, which is useful if you use bread for sandwiches.)

Whole wheat bread making

It has always seemed curious that most recipes for what is called 'whole wheat bread' require only about *half* the flour to be whole wheat. On one hand it's not surprising, because half-white dough is simply easier to work with and produces a more predictable loaf than whole wheat dough.

However, it's confusing (and certainly inaccurate) to call bread made with any proportion of white flour *whole* wheat, regardless of how enriched, unbleached, organic, and untainted by genetic modification it is. There are times, though, when the addition of white flour is especially welcome for texture and handling, and examples of this are my recipes for pita pockets, focaccia, and pizza (pages 228-32).

100 percent whole wheat dough is trickier to handle because whole wheat flour absorbs more liquid than white flour, and takes longer to absorb the liquid. The dough is stickier, so we tend to either add too much flour or knead too briefly (thus under-working the gluten).

The easier option is to find a way to knead it apart from your hands. These days we have options like electric mixers, bread machines (see page 222), and food processors (see *Pita Bread by Processor* on page 228), which make that part of the job simpler. My preference is for the dough cycle of a bread machine — I find that this is the easiest way to deal with the needs of whole wheat dough.

Make the same loaf again and again until you feel comfortable enough to adjust the ingredients and methods to suit yourself. Starting on page 220 are my recipes. These include examples of three different methods to mix the dough by hand, bread machine, and food processor.

Tips and Rules of Thumb

▸ Becoming a confident bread-maker is easy if you make bread often in small batches. Familiarity builds confidence.

▸ When making bread by hand, always start with the liquids in the bowl, and then add the flour. The flour, not the liquid, should be the variable. (An exception is when mixing dough in a food processor. See page 228.)

▸ You never need to sift flour in bread making. However, before measuring flour from the bag it's a good idea to stir it first with a fork to fluff it up. You'll find that measuring will be more consistent once compacted flour is loosened.

▸ The best way to measure flour is always to spoon or pour flour from the bag into your measuring cup. Flour quantities vary quite a bit, depending on whether flour is packed firmly or loosely. If you reach in with a measuring cup and scoop out flour, it will be compacted, and this variable can throw off your proportions.

▸ As a rule of thumb, you will need *about* 2¼ cups of whole wheat flour or 2¾ cups of white flour for every cup of liquid, but always let your dough decide. Whole wheat flour absorbs more liquid, *and at a slower rate*, than white flour.

▸ Remember to handle dough briskly and authoritatively. When dough senses uncertainty, it sticks to the hands. It's also handy to know that dough will be slower to stick to wet hands.

▸ Oiled plastic wrap over rising dough is easy to remove later, and will keep the dough moist and skin-free. Spray the plastic briefly with non-stick cooking spray.

▸ Non-stick spray is also the most convenient and efficient way to oil your bread pans, too. Avoid washing your bread pans; buy the best quality (**not** non-stick) pans you can find, and just wipe them out with paper towels between loaves.

▸ To clean a doughy counter, scrape thoroughly with a dough scraper (see *Useful Cooking Tools* on page 69) first. And to clean a bowl or bread machine bucket, scrape out as much dough as you can. When you do use water, you'll find that cool water works better than hot water, which tends to set the dough.

▸ *Do not store bread in the refrigerator*, even if your mother always did. Bread turns stale faster in the refrigerator than at room temperature. (The exception is if the bread is moist or a bit undercooked, and the air is warm or humid.)

▸ … but it is critical to cool a loaf completely before storing in a plastic bag – any moisture from condensation will mold bread quickly, especially in warm temperatures. Double-wrap and freeze extra bread.

▸ If you're new to bread making, keep things simple at first. Start with a basic, useful recipe, (like the *Little Whole Wheat and Honey Loaf* on the next page) and then experiment within the recipe. Note what happens when you add more or less flour, more or less sweetening or fat, milk instead of water, less yeast with longer rising times, and so on. It's the best way to learn how to control the texture, moistness, crust, flavor, and shape of your bread, and with the least chance of failure.

▸ Always eat your failures while they're still warm.

Little Whole Wheat and Honey Loaf
using wooden spoon method

Making a small loaf like this is the best way to learn to make a good loaf of 100 percent whole wheat bread, in my opinion. It is pretty easy to mix by hand and makes a fairly manageable lump of dough; if you mess it up somehow, it's not a big deal. However, I wouldn't recommend making a loaf this small once you get comfortable with the breadmaking process. It makes more sense to put the effort into a larger loaf (See *Whole Wheat and Honey Family Loaf*) and freeze several slices for future need. I suggest you slice it thin for sandwiches and thicker for toast.

(8 x 4-inch loaf)

> 1¼ cups warm water
> 1 tablespoon active dry yeast
> 2½ - 3 cups stone-ground whole wheat bread flour, divided
>
> 1½ teaspoons salt
> 2 tablespoons extra-virgin olive oil
> ¼ cup honey

1. Sprinkle yeast over warm water in mixing bowl and set aside about 3 minutes to soften. Add 1½ cups of flour and stir until smooth. The mixture should feel like very thick batter. (If not, add flour 2 tablespoons at a time until it feels very thick but still beatable.) Beat vigorously by hand - a wooden spoon works best - for about 150 strokes. (Switching hands keeps your arm from having to stop to rest. Feels clumsy but it works.) Scrape sides of bowl, cover with plastic wrap, and let dough rise for about an hour, or until at least doubled. (This mixture of water, yeast, and flour is called a 'sponge', which is the perfect environment for the development of yeast and gluten.)

2. Add salt, oil, honey, and ½ cup of flour and stir until smooth. Beat for 50 strokes. Stir in another ½ cup of flour, blending until smooth. Stir spiritedly for 100 strokes, if possible. (The stirring develops the gluten and reduces your kneading time later.) If the dough is still slack enough to be stirred, work in more flour a tablespoon or two at a time until dough becomes too stiff to stir. Scrape sides of bowl clean, making sure all loose flour is blended into dough. Cover with plastic wrap, and set aside to rise for about an hour or until doubled.

3. Using a rubber spatula, deflate dough and gather into a sticky ball. Sprinkle with a tablespoon of flour and scrape out onto a floured patch of countertop. Knead the dough for a minute or two, dusting the counter with only as much flour as you absolutely need. The dough should be soft and tacky. (Until you get used to handling whole wheat dough, you may find your palms constantly gathering a layer of dough during kneading.)

4. Pat dough into a flattened oval cushion on the flour-dusted counter, roll it up into a fat sausage about 8 inches long, then tuck it into an oiled 8 x 4-inch loaf pan. Pat the dough down evenly and cover with oiled plastic wrap. Preheat oven to 400 degrees. Allow dough to double, which should take about 30 – 45 minutes, depending on the warmth of your kitchen.

5. Place in the lower third of your oven (or directly on preheated baking stone) and bake for 30 minutes. The bottom crust should be a toasty golden-brown, and have a hollow-sounding *thok* when you knock it, rather than a dull *thud*.

6. Don't try to slice off more than the crust in the first half-hour of cooling. Allow it to cool for at least a couple of hours before sealing in a clean plastic bag. And don't store it in the refrigerator!

Note:

▸ If you would rather ease more gradually into an all whole wheat loaf, replace the last cup of whole wheat flour with unbleached white bread flour.

▸ As for the honey, we like the level of sweetness in this loaf but it can naturally be adjusted to suit you. (It is important to remember that honey counts as a liquid, so if you reduce the honey, the recipe will take less flour.)

▸ The amount of flour you add will determine the height and roundness of the crust as well as the moistness of the bread, but don't forget that a dramatically soaring loaf probably is a symptom of too much flour. The secret to moist, well-textured *wholly* whole wheat bread is well-kneaded yet sticky dough, but it's hard to knead sticky dough for long without adding too much flour. One answer is to give the dough a good thrashing while it is still slack enough to be stirred, but there's no escaping the fact that hand-mixing whole wheat dough does require significant arm-work.

▸ The temperature of your kitchen and the time of year can make a significant difference in the time your dough takes to rise. (The final rise generally takes less than 30 minutes in my kitchen.) Keep an eye on it, and begin preheating your oven as soon as you have set the loaf aside to rise. If you let the dough over-rise, the shape of the top crust will not be as nice and the bread will tend to be very weak in the middle.

The Bread Machine

Bread machines are hard working helpers with impressive white uniforms but no brains. They are tireless, unquestioning, cheerful in the face of the wettest dough, and easy to clean.

However, because you need a brain to deal with the variables that affect the loaf's moistness and the timing of the final rising and baking, that part of the process is their weakness. I never use bread machines to actually bake the bread.

Brainlessness notwithstanding, bread machines do a splendid job of mixing and kneading, and are worth their expense as a dough-making machine. The gentle, thorough, supervision-free kneading of dough too sticky to knead by hand is one way to perfect 100 percent whole wheat bread.

Also, bread machines have managed to do what no amount of written reassurance could; they have proved that bread making is a very simple science. You combine the flour, water, and yeast, and the machine simply baby-sits, applying prescribed doses of a little paddling here, a little nap there, and gentle heat as needed.

Eventually, a loaf is hatched. Technology trampling art? No, it's just an uncluttered view of the essence of the bread-making process.

If you're shopping for a bread machine, avoid those that take themselves too seriously. Do you really want one that can make jam and boil water? Too many bells and whistles can invite temperament issues. All you need is a sturdy machine that starts when you push the button and can handle two pounds of dough.

The following recipe uses the machine only for kneading and rising purposes. I have tasted bread baked in bread machines and I simply don't think it's as good as bread baked in a conventional oven.

Whole Wheat and Honey Family Loaf
made with a bread machine

This is a family-sized version of the recipe for *Little Whole Wheat and Honey Loaf*, with the wooden spoon replaced with a bread machine.

(9 x 5-inch loaf)

2 cups warm water
1 tablespoon active dry yeast
3 cups stone-ground whole wheat bread flour

2 tablespoons extra-virgin olive oil
½ cup honey
2½ teaspoons salt
2 cups stone-ground whole wheat bread flour

1. Place warm water in bucket of bread machine and sprinkle yeast into water. Allow a few minutes for yeast to soften, and then add 3 cups of flour. (Measure the flour by pouring or spooning flour into the measuring cup.) **Set bread machine on dough cycle and push start button.** Check after 10 minutes, and scrape down sides with a spatula. You should have a mixture that looks like very thick batter but not yet beginning to gather into dough. (This mixture of water, yeast, and flour is called a 'sponge', which is the perfect environment for the development of yeast and gluten. If it doesn't look thick enough, add flour ¼ cup at a time.) **Allow machine to complete the kneading stage of the dough cycle,** after which the machine rests and the rising cycle begins.

2. When the sponge has had 30 minutes to raise, during which time it has probably tripled in volume, push stop button. **Start dough cycle again,** and with a rubber spatula scrape down the sponge from the sides of the bucket. Add oil, honey, salt, and remaining 2 cups of flour.

3. Check after 10 minutes, scraping clean the sides of the bucket again. When mixed, the dough should be able to form a soft ball that pulls away from the sides of the bucket, tending to climb slightly upward rather than slop around in a relaxed mass as it is kneaded. If dough forms a ball that looks patchy and dry, add 1-2 tablespoons of water. If you think dough might be too wet, be very cautious about adding flour. However, if dough really seems too sloppy and only forms a half-hearted sort of ball, add flour cautiously, a couple of tablespoons at a time. Avoid adding any more flour than necessary. It's safer to err on the moist side with 100 percent whole wheat dough. **Allow the dough to continue through kneading cycle, and then 20 minutes of rising cycle.**

4. **Start kneading cycle again.** Meanwhile, mist a 9 x 5-inch bread pan with non-stick spray and set aside. Position oven racks so that there is room for the loaf on the bottom shelf. If you have a baking stone, place it on the bottom rack.

5. Check back again in 10 minutes, when dough should be kneaded down into a soft ball again. (If it seems too wet or dry, refer back to instructions in Step 3.) **Push stop button.**

6. Shake and scrape dough out of bucket onto a floured patch of countertop. It will feel warm from the bread machine. With extra flour at hand, knead the dough briefly to form it into a ball of sorts; the point is not to knead more flour into the dough, but to keep adequate flour between the dough and your hands and the counter. The dough needs no more kneading, but only shaping. A dough scraper (see page 69) can be very useful. Pat dough into a rough oval cushion, fold or roll up into a fat sausage about the length of the pan, and lift it quickly into the pan. (If the dough is very soft it pays to handle it briskly. Quick movements and dustings of flour help keep dough from sticking)

7. Pat the dough down evenly and cover with oiled plastic wrap. Take a good look at it so you have an idea what it should look like when doubled.

Preheat oven to 400 degrees.

8. Check dough after 30 minutes. (It should only take that long because the dough's warmth from the machine's kneading process accelerates the rising.) If you think it has doubled, go ahead and put it in the oven. It's easy to let the dough rise too far, which means the top crust will collapse and the loaf will have an airy, weak center.

9. Place loaf on the lowest rack in the oven (or directly on a preheated baking stone). Bake for 40 minutes. The loaf should tip out of the pan with just a shake or two of encouragement on your part, and the bottom crust should be golden-brown. If you knock it with your knuckle you should hear *thok thok* rather than *thud thud*.

10. Allow loaf to cool completely (about 3 hours) before sealing in a clean plastic bag. Try to avoid slicing off more than the crust in the first half-hour of cooling. And don't store it in the refrigerator!

Note:

▸ The best place to store bread that you are not going to use in a few days is the freezer. I suggest placing four or five slices in a quart-sized zip lock bag, and then in another bag before storing in the freezer. You can just pull out packets as you need them, and the slices should separate easily even while frozen.

Cooked grains in bread

Conventional bread has a hard time getting my attention. I am not safe, however, in the same room — nay, the same *house* — as a buttered slice of my millet or buckwheat or brown rice bread. There is no snack more tempting, no breakfast more satisfying, no hyperbole more gloriously justified.

Personal preference aside, whole wheat bread made with cooked whole grains is not only more nutrient-dense and full of delicious character, but it also stays moist longer. Toasted and buttered? Oh boy.

The idea is to achieve bread with delightful character while avoiding anything reminiscent of baked porridge. If you decide to experiment, I suggest being conservative at first, especially if you're working with dense-textured mixtures.

Speaking of porridge, this is a fine way to use leftover cooked cereal. You can mix hot water with cooked grain straight out of the refrigerator, for instance, and then add the yeast as soon as the mixture cools to a yeast-friendly temperature.

The three following recipes use different methods, but they all try to incorporate generous doses of cooked whole grains. In the following recipe I call for cooked millet, a grain I don't tend to use often enough. (My personal favorite is cooked toasted buckwheat, called *kasha*. Cooking directions are on page 181.)

The *Millet Bread* here can be used as a master recipe, and you can substitute any **cooked** whole grain cereal like cracked wheat, bulgur, or cracked rye. If you're using a denser porridge like cooked cornmeal or oatmeal, start with one cup.

This recipe is not complicated; it is deliberately detailed in its directions so that even a beginning bread maker can handle it.

Millet Bread
Master Recipe for bread
with cooked whole grain

You can replace the millet in this recipe with buckwheat, brown rice, cornmeal, or oatmeal, or a cooked cereal or grain of your choice. If it is densely textured like cooked cornmeal or oatmeal, start with just one cup of porridge. Although the amount of cooked millet I call for here is two cups, it's fairly fluffy. Well, unless it's soggy or mushy or lumpy (millet can be tricky to cook for the novice), which is a very good reason to make this bread.

(Makes 9 x 5-inch loaf)

1 cup warm water
1 tablespoon active dry yeast
1½ – 2 cups **cooked** millet (See page 181.)
3 – 4 cups whole wheat bread flour, divided

1 tablespoon extra-virgin olive oil
¼ cup honey
1½ teaspoons salt

1. Place warm water in a mixing bowl. (See **Note**.) Sprinkle yeast over the top and let soften for about 5 minutes.

2. Add cooked millet and 1 cup of flour and stir until smooth. Firmly smash any lumps of millet you find. Add another ½ cup of whole wheat flour. The mixture should be like very thick batter, but stirable. Stir briskly for about 150 strokes. (You can do it if you keep switching arms. As your arms tire, you may find it works to switch every 10 strokes or so.) Scrape sides of bowl clean, then cover with plastic wrap and set aside for 45 minutes or until at least doubled. (This mixture is called a 'sponge', which is the perfect environment for the development of yeast and gluten. If it doesn't look thick enough, add flour ¼-cup at a time.)

3. Add oil, honey, salt, and ½ cup of flour. Stir until smooth, and then blend in another ¼ cup of flour and stir vigorously for at least 50 strokes. (By now you may have decided to buy a bread machine, in which case you can follow the directions starting on page 222. Much easier.)

4. Thoroughly mix in another ¼ cup of flour. (Keep bottom and sides of the bowl scraped to avoid ending up with dried shreds of dough hanging around the outskirts.) By now the dough will probably be too stiff to stir but too sticky to knead. If not, add another ¼ cup of flour.

5. Sprinkle a tablespoon of flour over the dough and scrape it free of the bowl so it is gathered into a floury lump, and then turn it out onto a heavily floured patch of countertop. The dough should be soft and sticky at this point, so just begin by folding part of the dough's floury bottom up and over onto its top. Do this until the sticky surface of the dough is more or less tucked inside the floury surface pulled up from the bottom.

6. Continue with this same up-from-the-bottom-and-over-the-top motion, but start giving the dough a quarter-turn between each fold-over motion. Dust the counter, not the dough, as you notice it sticking. As the dough becomes easier to handle, try to develop a rhythm to your kneading: fold over, push down, quarter turn, fold over, push down, quarter turn. Handle dough lightly and briskly; it will have less opportunity to stick to your hands.

7. Knead for at least 5 minutes, adding only as much extra flour as you need to keep the dough from clutching your palms or grabbing the counter. You should not be trying to remove the dough's stickiness. Your goal is soft but springy dough with no lumps or wet patches.

8. Put dough into a mixing bowl misted with nonstick spray and cover with plastic wrap. Set aside to rise for 30 – 60 minutes. The dough should double.

Preheat oven to 400 degrees. Mist a 9 x 5-inch loaf pan with nonstick spray.

9. Deflate risen dough with a spatula and scrape out onto a lightly floured patch of countertop. Knead for a few minutes in order to form the dough into a smooth ball. (The dough might feel sloppy at first but will quickly tighten as the gluten springs back into action, so resist the impulse to add any more flour than you have to.)

10. Pat dough into a plump oval cushion about 9 inches long, fold in half, and tuck into loaf pan. Cover with oiled plastic wrap and let rise for 30 – 45 minutes or until nearly doubled.

11. Place loaf on the lowest rack in the oven (or directly on a preheated baking stone) and bake for 40 minutes. You should hear a *thok* rather than a *thud* sound when you knock the bottom.

12. Allow loaf to cool completely (about 3 hours) before sealing in a clean plastic bag. Store at room temperature and slice as you need it. Don't store in the refrigerator!

Note:

▸ If you start with cold cooked cereal from the refrigerator, mix it with ½ cup of boiling water, mashing any lumps out of it at the same time. Meanwhile, soften the yeast in the remaining ½ cup of warm water.

▸ It is difficult to predict how much flour will be needed, even if you follow directions precisely each time. The variations in the cooked grain alone, both in quantity and water content, are enough to affect the flour needs of the dough.

Brown Rice Bread
Using hot cooked rice

Cooked brown rice makes moist and nubbly bread that is substantial yet mild
mannered. Its slightly chewy texture makes especially good toast. You can use any
well-cooked whole grain or any sort of rice with this method, but I like my version
below the best. If I haven't any freshly-cooked rice (see page 171), I steam leftover
rice in a steamer basket over boiling water for about 10 minutes.

(Makes 9 x 5-inch loaf)

1 cup warm water
1 tablespoon active dry yeast
⅓ cup honey

2 cups hot cooked brown rice
3 cups stone-ground whole wheat bread flour, divided
1½ teaspoons salt

1. Mix together warm water and yeast in a measuring jug and set aside for at least 5
   minutes.

2. In a separate mixing bowl combine 2 cups whole wheat flour and salt with hot
   cooked rice. Blend thoroughly. (It will feel like a bowl of floury rubbery pellets.)
   Scrape the sides of the bowl clean.

3. Stir honey into yeast mixture and add to the warm rice and flour. Mix well, and
   then stir vigorously with a wooden spoon for about 100 strokes. Add another ½
   cup of flour and stir for another 100 strokes. (This is an important step in
   developing the gluten. It's not as hard as it sounds if you switch arms after each
   50 strokes or so.) Work another ½ cup of flour into the dough. Don't bother
   counting at this stage. Just work it in.) When the flour is thoroughly blended in,
   scrape the sides of the bowl and cover with plastic. Let rise until doubled.

4. Scrape risen dough away from sides of bowl and into a lump. Sprinkle with ¼
   cup flour and tip out onto floured counter. Have handy more flour for dusting
   counter. The dough should be too soft and sticky to handle easily, but you only
   have to handle the dough enough to prepare dough for shaping. Form dough
   into loaf and place into an oiled 9 x 5-inch loaf pan. Cover with oiled plastic
   wrap.

Preheat oven to 450 degrees and place rack in lower third of oven.

5. Let dough rise for 30 – 60 minutes or until not quite doubled. Bake at 450
   degrees in the lower third of oven for 15 minutes, and then reduce the
   temperature to 350 degrees and bake for another 20 minutes. Remove from pan
   and put back into oven on its side for another 10 minutes.

Bulgur and Oat Bread
Using quick-cooking whole grain

This is a full-bodied and mildly chewy little loaf. If you don't like the taste of molasses, substitute honey. Even mild molasses has a dominating presence, but it's compatible with these grains. If you have blackstrap molasses, use just one tablespoon with two of honey.

(Makes one loaf)

⅓ cup medium or fine bulgur
1 cup boiling water
⅓ cup rolled oats

¼ cup warm water
1 tablespoon active dry yeast
1 tablespoon extra-virgin olive oil
2 tablespoons mild molasses
1 tablespoon honey
1 teaspoon salt
1¼ cups stone-ground whole wheat bread flour
egg white (optional)

1. Put the bulgur into a medium-sized mixing bowl (like 2-quart size) and add boiling water. Sprinkle the oats over the top, then cover and set aside for 30 minutes, or until the bulgur is completely soft and mixture is just warm. Meanwhile, stir yeast into warm water and set aside.

2. Add oil, molasses, honey, and salt to grain mixture and blend well. Add yeast mixture and 1 cup whole wheat flour and mix well. Stir vigorously with a wooden spoon for a minute or two, if you can. Scrape sides of bowl and gather dough into a lump, then cover with plastic wrap and leave for about 1 hour or until doubled.

3. Mist a regular pie pan or baking sheet with non-stick spray. Scrape dough into a lump again. Sprinkle it with 2 tablespoons of flour, then tip the floury lump onto the counter and knead for a few minutes. Dust counter with flour as needed but don't try to get rid of the dough's stickiness. You only have to knead dough just enough to shape it into a plump little loaf, either oval or round. Place in pan and cover with oiled plastic wrap.

Preheat oven to 450 degrees and place rack in lower third of oven.

4. Let loaf rise for about an hour or until it has almost doubled. If you want it to look fancy, brush with a bit of beaten egg white and sprinkle with rolled oats. Place loaf on the lowest rack in the oven (or directly on a preheated baking stone) and bake at 400 degrees for 35 minutes.

Pita Bread
By processor

Pita, or pocket, bread is the fastest bread to make that I know of, whether by food processor or by wooden spoon. With the processor you can make the dough at 5 p.m., and have the pockets out of the oven and ready to eat by 6 p.m. The best part is watching the pockets puffing up in the oven; they always look like they're in such a hurry. And if you are in a hurry, it's comforting to have the bread rushing right along with you.

These directions for making dough using the food processor method can be applied to any recipe of this general size. The standard 7-cup processor can easily handle this amount of dough, which is about 1½ pounds. Consider using a plastic blade, if you have one – the metal blade works better but it is too easy to cut yourself when extracting it from the dough.

You will find this recipe, through Step **5**, used as a Master Recipe for preparing the dough for the *Focaccia* and *Pizza Margherita* recipes further on.

(Makes 9 x 7-inch pita pockets)

> 1½ cups warm water
> 1 tablespoon (or 1 packet) active dry yeast
>
> 2 cups stone-ground whole wheat flour
> 2 cups unbleached white bread flour, plus extra if needed (see Step 3)
> 2 teaspoons salt
>
> 2 tablespoons extra-virgin olive oil
> 2 tablespoons honey

1. Pour warm water into a 2-cup measuring jug (with pouring spout) and stir in yeast. Set aside for about 5 minutes for yeast to soften.

2. Measure whole wheat and white flour and salt into the processor bowl, and process a few seconds to mix.

3. Add oil and honey to yeast and water mixture. With processor running, pour yeast mixture slowly (but within 5 seconds) through food chute. Within another 5 seconds the dough should lump together and begin to revolve under the cover. Let it revolve about 10 times, then stop the machine and let the dough rest 5 minutes or so.

> ### STEP 3 continued: dough troubleshooting
>
> *If the dough stubbornly remains a thick batter instead of forming a roughly cohesive lump, add white flour while the machine is running, a tablespoon or two at a time, until a rough ball forms. As usual, add flour cautiously; everything happens pretty fast, and dough that is choking up the blade one moment may be riding friskily around in a ball on the blade the next, with the addition of a scant tablespoon of flour. If the dough is too dry, add water while machine is running, 1 tablespoon every few seconds, until ball forms. Let ball rotate under cover about 5 times before stopping machine.*

4. After dough has rested, turn on machine and let ball of dough rotate under the cover again another 30 times. The kneading process should not last longer than 60 seconds altogether. Cover processor bowl with plastic wrap and set aside for about 30 – 45 minutes or until doubled.

5. Turn on machine and process dough for about 5 – 10 seconds, just enough to gather it back into a lump. Scrape dough out of processor and turn out onto lightly floured surface.

Preheat oven to 500 degrees and place rack in top third of oven.

6. Knead dough briefly to shape into a ball and divide ball in thirds, and then divide each third into 3 pieces. Beginning with 3 pieces, form each into a ball, as if you were making rolls. When you have finished with the third ball, return to the first. Flatten it with your hand, then use a rolling pin to roll it out into a circle about 7 inches across. When you have rolled out the first 3 this way, place them on the baking sheet and let rest 10 minutes. (No need to cover them for this length of time.)

7. Bake at 500 degrees for 4 - 5 minutes. (If your oven has a window, you will notice that in about 3 minutes the pita pockets will be swelling up and practically standing on their tiptoes.) Because of the high temperature, whip them out as soon as you think they're ready, which may be after 4 minutes in your oven. Cool them on a rack between the folds of a clean tea towel.

8. Needless to say, repeat the process with the remaining pieces of dough. When the pitas have cooled completely, seal in a clean plastic bag. If you don't plan to serve them within 2 days, seal them in a second bag and freeze.

Focaccia
Italian flatbread with olive oil and seasoning

Focaccia was originally just the homemade version of pizza. The name comes from the Latin word *focus* (the hearth), which is where women baked bread at home. Traditionally it was simple: pizza dough topped with olive oil and salt, and maybe garlic and fresh herbs like rosemary or sage.

Naturally, it's been worked over thoroughly in this country and often turns up looking like a sort of deep-dish pizza. And that's fine, I hasten to add, but I prefer my version. If I want pizza, I make pizza. If I want focaccia, I make this.

This is wonderfully versatile bread; you can serve it either as an appetizer or at the table as you would any bread — except it doesn't need butter, so you don't need butter or butter knives at the table, and you don't have people waiting for the butter to be passed. You can make it thick or thin. You can serve it in wedges or squares, or just tear off chunks, which has a certain reckless earthiness. You can also split it and use it for sandwiches.

I like a thinnish focaccia with a simple olive oil, salt, pepper, and herb topping. It's tempting to add minced garlic, but overcooked bits of garlic on the cooked focaccia are not nice. It's a hot oven, and any shred of garlic that pokes its head up is, literally, toast. However, there are *endless* variations with both dough and toppings.

(Makes enough focaccia to serve about 6 - 8 rational people)

Focaccia dough:
1½ cups warm water
1 tablespoon (or 1 packet) active dry yeast
2 teaspoons salt
2 tablespoons extra-virgin olive oil
2 tablespoons honey
1¾ cups stone-ground whole wheat flour
1¾ cups unbleached white bread flour, divided

To mix dough –
1. In food processor: follow directions on page 228-229 through step **5**, **-or-**
2. with bread machine: follow directions on next page, **-or-**
3. by hand: follow directions on page 220 through step **2**.

Focaccia topping:
½ cup extra-virgin olive oil
kosher or coarse salt
freshly ground pepper
Optional: 1 tablespoon fresh rosemary or thyme. Don't use dried rosemary.
-or- ½ teaspoon dried thyme

Bread machine method:

1. Place warm water in bucket of bread machine and sprinkle yeast into water. Allow a few minutes for yeast to soften, and then add whole wheat flour and 1 cup of white flour. (Remember to measure the flour by pouring or spooning flour into the measuring cup.) Set bread machine on dough cycle and start. In 10 minutes add salt, oil, honey, and remaining white flour. Scrape down sides with a spatula. You should have soft dough – softer than regular bread dough. (See *Note*.) Allow machine to complete the kneading stage of the dough cycle.

2. When dough has completed most of the raising stage, or when dough at least doubles in volume, push stop button and remove bucket from machine. Tip dough directly into prepared pan.

Preheat oven to 450 degrees and place rack on lowest position.

3. Place 2 tablespoons olive oil in 13-inch pizza pan or a 9 x 12-inch pan and spread to edges with fingers. Scrape dough out of bucket (or food processor) into pan and pat out to edges as evenly as possible. If the dough is wet enough it will spread easily, but you will need to oil your hand(s) to keep the dough from sticking to you. If the dough acts stubborn and difficult to spread, it is probably not wet enough: ignore it for 5 minutes and it will relax. Set aside to rise until about doubled. (It's harder to judge with bread as flat as focaccia, but it takes about ½ hour in my kitchen.)

4. Using the tips of your fingers, firmly poke the surface of the dough, pushing your fingers right through the dough until it is covered with deep dimples an inch or two apart. Use a pastry brush to spread the remaining oil over the dough. (This is not the time to be squeamish; the olive oil is a critical element of the focaccia, and the finished bread should taste rich enough to banish any heretical suggestions – or even thoughts – of butter.)

5. Sprinkle with the kosher salt, freshly ground pepper and herbs. Bake at 450 degrees on the lowest rack or baking stone for about 15 minutes.

Note:

▸ The secret to achieving a chewy, moist, airy focaccia is wet but well-worked dough, so don't add any unnecessary flour. However, that will mean the dough is going to be hard to handle without getting stuck to your hands. It will help if your hands are oily (which is easy to arrange).

▸ Focaccia really is a terrific last minute masterpiece, because even a technically failed focaccia is going to delight and amaze. (Take it from one with a past littered with technically failed focaccias. I don't apologize for them anymore.)

Pizza Margherita

Opening up the subject of pizza is scary. It's vast, cluttered, and altogether subjective, and trying to pin down definitive recipes and methods is impossible. In colloquial Italian, *pizza* just means a pie of any kind – and apparently was made in some form or other all over Europe long before tomatoes were even cultivated there. For that matter, the *Armenians* claim to have invented the pizza! What most of us know for certain is what we happen to like on a pizza, and that's as deep as some of us are interested in digging.

This version was apparently born in Naples in 1889, created and named for Queen Margherita. The crust is thin and crisp, the topping simple and fresh. (For the record, neither whole wheat flour nor garlic belongs in the original recipe; the poor queen was born well before the benefits of fiber and garlic were understood.)

(Makes 2 x 12-inch pizzas)

Pizza Dough:
Follow directions for the preceding *Pita by Processor* through step **5**,
-or- mix dough by hand using the directions on page 220 through step **3**.

Topping:
2 pounds tomatoes, approximately (preferably Roma – more flesh, less core)
¼ - ½ cup torn-up fresh basil leaves
¼ cup extra-virgin olive oil
2 tablespoons minced fresh garlic
½ - 1 pound whole milk mozzarella, sliced
kosher salt and freshly ground pepper

Preheat oven to 500 degrees and place rack in lowest position. *(If you have a baking stone that doesn't live full time in your oven, place it on the lowest rack before turning on the oven.)*

1. Quarter tomatoes and scoop out seed clusters with your thumb. (Don't discard! Eat or save for soup or something.) Remove bits of core, which in Roma tomatoes are usually pretty inoffensive. Dice in ¼ -inch chunks and combine with basil, olive oil, and garlic. Slice mozzarella.

2. Divide dough in half and form each half into a smooth ball. Roll out first half to a 12-inch circle on well-floured surface. Transfer to baking sheet sprinkled with cornmeal or misted with non-stick spray. Spread with half of tomato mixture and arrange half of sliced mozzarella over the top. (You don't need a whole pound of mozzarella, but ½ pound is a bit stingy.) Sprinkle with salt and freshly ground pepper.

3. Bake for about 10 - 12 minutes or until edges and bottom crust are at least golden. Prepare second pizza the same way.

14 Quick Breads *and* Treats

Serious Muffins
Extreme Muffins
Banana Bread
No Frills Muffins
Almond Teacakes
Scones
Cornbread
Scottish Oatcakes
Oatmeal Cookies
Coconut Macaroons
Hot Chocolate (Cocoa)

Quick breads
and other baked treats

Quick breads come into their own on Saturday morning when you want to serve a basket of fresh baked muffins, or an hour before dinner when you decide to bring a pan of hot fresh cornbread to the table. In the following collection of quick breads muffins get the most attention. Even the banana bread and cornbread recipe can be turned into muffins, for that matter. On the subject of versatility, the scone recipe can be tweaked to make pastry, or used for the topping for pot pie, like the *Chicken Pot Pie* on page 201.

Muffin stuff

People generally seem to like muffins, and they're relatively simple and quick to make. The only type of muffin worth making, though, is one that delivers a hefty dose of fiber and the minimum of refined sugar and flour. Fiber-rich muffins can serve a useful purpose when you're dealing with people who haven't made the transition to a better diet, philosophically or otherwise.

However, expectations are key. For example, anyone who is used to muffins that are like large, fluffy cupcakes is going to be horribly disappointed in the sort of muffins we're talking about here. Whole grain muffins can be pretty dense and tend to make a bit of a statement.

The following muffin recipes are 100 percent whole grain. You can adjust the level of whole wheat flour and bran to suit, but *at the least* you can start with 50 percent whole wheat without any problem from picky eaters who may be used to muffins made with white flour. You can gradually increase the proportion of whole wheat flour over time to an unsuspecting audience.

Muffin tips

▸ I have never noticed a difference in muffins whose wet and dry ingredients have been mixed "only until just blended" and muffins whose ingredients have been "thoroughly mixed". I thoroughly mix.

▸ Muffins are especially quick to make if you happen to have ingredients like nuts prepared in advance. (Some of us have a strong preference for nuts in muffins.)

▸ I've noticed that amounts of baking powder and baking soda seem to be fairly random out there in the world of muffin recipes, so I do what works for me.

▸ When you're using whole wheat flour the batter may seem too runny right after it's mixed. I find that if I let it sit while I clean up the kitchen, it not only thickens, but the muffins rise better in the oven. This is especially useful to know when you have forgotten to preheat the oven.

▸ I bake muffins at 400 degrees, and I don't wait for them to brown. I want a moist muffin, and whole grain muffins can be dry, if you're not careful. Naturally, though, your oven may behave differently than mine; you can test a muffin by breaking it in half immediately after pulling the tin out of the oven, and if it's still wet in the center bake the rest for another 2 – 4 minutes. Keep in mind, however, that a muffin hot from the oven can *seem* undercooked but will firm up as it cools.

▸ Using the general proportions in these recipes you can easily create your own variations. There are so many options, it's dizzying. **Don't forget, though, that muffins generally should still be classified as high-fiber cake and not your daily bread.**

Serious Muffins
with Flaxseed Meal and Carrot

It should be understood that this is not your average superficial, giddy sort of muffin. This is a muffin of substance and conviction. The recipe was adapted from the version printed on the flaxseed meal package from Bob's Red Mill of Milwaukie, Oregon. Natural food stores and some supermarkets carry flaxseed meal — and it should be refrigerated. In any case, you *can* buy whole flaxseeds and grind your own meal in a coffee grinder dedicated to that purpose.

(Makes 12 muffins, ½-cup size)

> ¾ cup flaxseed meal
> 1¼ cup whole wheat pastry flour
> 2 teaspoons baking powder
> 2 teaspoons baking soda
> 1 teaspoon salt
> 1 teaspoon cinnamon
> ¼ teaspoon ground cloves
>
> 1 cup chopped walnuts
> 1 cup golden raisins
>
> 2 eggs
> ½ cup plain yogurt or milk
> ½ cup honey
> 2 raw carrots, finely grated (about 2 cups)

Pre-heat oven to 400 degrees. Oil muffin tins and set aside.

1. Combine dry ingredients and mix thoroughly. (A dry wire whisk works well.) Stir in nuts and raisins and set aside.

2. In a mixing bowl or an 8-cup Pyrex jug, whisk eggs. Add yogurt/milk and honey, and whisk for about 30 seconds to dissolve honey.

3. Grate carrot on fine holes of grater (the ⅛ inch teardrop-shaped holes). Add to egg mixture and blend well.

4. Tip dry ingredients into wet and blend thoroughly. Set batter aside while you clean up your mess. Scoop into muffin tins – I like using a ⅓-cup measure. You can fill muffin cups ¾-full.

5. Bake in center of 400-degree oven for about 20 minutes. Using a butter knife, ease muffins from tins and cool on wire rack.

Extreme Muffins
Wheat-free

These are favorites of mine partly because they are so unconventional and partly because they are so sensible. A muffin this sensible has an uphill battle in the taste department but these are good. They are also short and stubby with a flat top and tender crumb. They are wheat-free and gluten-free, and call for oat bran instead of any kind of flour. They are sweetened with maple syrup instead of sugar, have yogurt instead of milk, and include fresh apple, dried prunes, and olive oil. These muffins rise very little in the oven.

(Makes 12 – 15 muffins, ½-cup size)

2 cups oat bran
2 teaspoons baking powder
1 teaspoon baking soda
1 teaspoon salt
2 teaspoons cinnamon

2 eggs
½ cup plain yogurt
½ cup pure maple syrup
¼ cup extra-virgin olive oil
zest from 1 orange (see page 68) minced (or 1 tablespoon)

1 apple, peeled and grated (about 1- 1½ cups)
1 cup dried pitted prunes, chopped (¼-inch pieces or smaller)

Pre-heat oven to 400 degrees. Oil muffin tins and set aside.

1. Combine dry ingredients and mix thoroughly. Set aside.

2. In a mixing bowl or an 8-cup Pyrex jug, whisk together egg, yogurt, maple syrup, oil, and orange zest. Stir in grated apple and prunes.

3. Tip dry ingredients into wet and blend thoroughly. The mixture will probably be quite wet; set it aside while you clean up your muffin mess and the mixture will thicken and make a slightly more rounded muffin.

4. Spoon into the oiled muffin tins. *Muffin cups should be no more than ⅔ full; if the muffins rise above the level of the cups, they will spread out, not up.*

5. Bake in center of 400-degree oven for about 20 minutes. Using a butter knife, ease muffins from tins and cool on wire rack.

Banana Bread
(or Muffins)

Most homes seem to have bananas, and most bananas are over-ripe at some time in their lives. This is where banana bread comes in. For those of us who feel vaguely guilty about our frank distaste for eating bananas straight, especially when the banana is such a practical and well-meaning fruit, there is a tremendous sense of satisfaction in being able to use *three bananas* in one recipe.

(Makes one 9 x 5-inch loaf or 12 muffins, ½-cup size)

> 1 cup wheat bran
> 1¼ cup whole wheat pastry flour
> 2 teaspoons baking powder
> 1 teaspoon baking soda
> 1 teaspoon salt
> 2 teaspoons cinnamon
> ½ teaspoon ground nutmeg
>
> 1 cup chopped pecans or walnuts
>
> 2 eggs
> ½ cup plain yogurt
> ½ cup honey
> ¼ cup melted butter
>
> 3 ripe bananas, or about 1¾ cups after being diced and roughly mashed

Pre-heat oven to 350 degrees. Oil loaf tin and set aside.

1. Combine dry ingredients and mix thoroughly. (A dry wire whisk works well.) Add nuts and set aside.

2. In a mixing bowl or 8-cup Pyrex jug, whisk eggs. Add yogurt, honey, and butter, and whisk until honey is blended. Add banana and mix well. *If you dice the bananas first and then only roughly mash them, you will end up with nice little bits of creamy banana in the cooked muffins.*

3. Tip dry ingredients into wet and blend thoroughly. The mixture may seem too wet but it will thicken up a bit if you let it rest for 10 minutes while you clean up your mess and wash the dishes.

4. Scrape mixture into oiled loaf tin. Bake in center of 350-degree oven for about 60 minutes. Let the loaf sit in the tin for 10 minutes, then run a butter knife around the edges and ease loaf out onto a wire rack to cool.

   For muffins, bake at 400 degrees for about 20 minutes, and then use a butter knife to gently ease muffins from tin. Cool on wire rack.)

No Frills Muffins
Plain and simple

The fact remains that there are times when one may want to make a muffin with no frills, no fruit, no flaxseeds, or anything at all starting with the letter f.

(Makes 12 muffins, ½-cup size)

2 eggs
1 cup milk
½ cup yogurt
½ cup honey (or pure maple syrup)
¼ cup melted butter

2¼ cups whole wheat pastry flour
2 teaspoons baking powder
1 teaspoon baking soda
1 teaspoon salt

Pre-heat oven to 425 degrees. Oil muffin tins and set aside.

1. In a mixing bowl or an 8-cup Pyrex jug, whisk eggs. In a 2-cup Pyrex jug, measure milk and then add yogurt to bring level to 1½ -cup mark. Add to eggs along with the honey and butter.

2. Combine dry ingredients and mix thoroughly. (A dry wire whisk works well.) Add to egg mixture and blend thoroughly. The mixture will seem too wet; just ignore it for 5 minutes while you clean up your mess. The batter should thicken considerably.

3. Scoop batter into muffin tins (a one-third cup measure works nicely) to fill them about three-quarters full.

4. Bake in center of 425-degree oven for about 18 – 20 minutes. Using a butter knife, ease muffins from tins and cool on wire rack.

Almond Tea Cakes
Wheat-free

In this recipe, ground almonds replace flour. These are rich, sweet, and nutty-textured – perfect for the times you want a bit more than a cookie, but something less than dessert.

(Makes 12 tea cakes, ½-cup size)

2½ cups ground almonds
1 teaspoon cinnamon
½ teaspoon baking soda
½ teaspoon salt

2 eggs
¼ cup melted butter
½ cup honey

Pre-heat oven to 375 degrees.
Line 12 ½-cup muffin tins with paper liners and set aside.

1. Combine ground almonds with cinnamon, soda, and salt, and mix very well.

2. Combine eggs, butter, and honey, and beat together with electric beaters or a whisk.

3. Add almond mixture to egg mixture and blend thoroughly. Line muffin cups with paper liners, and fill half full with mixture.

4. Bake in lower third of oven for 15-20 minutes, or until golden.

5. Transfer muffins to a wire rack to cool, and carefully remove muffin liners.

Scones
Whole wheat

For us, scones are mainly something one eats with jam and cream for afternoon tea. These are more like pastry than biscuits, flaky rather than cakey. For that reason this recipe works nicely for shortcakes (with two or three extra tablespoons of sugar) or as the top crust for *Chicken Pot Pie* (page 201). In fact, with a bit of tweaking this is also my recipe for pastry, so I've included it on this page.

(For about 12 scones)

2 cups whole wheat pastry flour
1 tablespoon baking powder
½ teaspoon salt
1 tablespoon sugar

1 stick butter (¼ pound or 8 tablespoons)
¾ – 1 cup whole milk

Preheat oven to 450 degrees and place the butter and milk in the freezer to chill quickly.

1. Combine flour, salt, baking powder, and sugar, and blend thoroughly. (A wire whisk works well.) Grate stick of butter using medium holes of grater into flour mixture and toss together until well mixed. (See **Note** for more on butter.)

2. Pour ¾-cup of very cold milk over the flour and butter mixture and blend briskly with a fork. Add only as much of the remaining milk as you need to incorporate any floury residue, and knead briefly in bowl to blend in the dry bits. Try not to handle dough any more than necessary and try to keep the bits of butter intact.

3. On a floured countertop, roll out dough to about ½-inch thick. Using a biscuit cutter or a knife, cut into circles or wedges and arrange on an ungreased baking sheet.

4. Push the remnants together, handling as little as possible, and roll out and cut remaining dough.

5. Bake for 15 minutes or until golden brown and puffy.

Note:

▸ I always keep a back-up supply of butter in the freezer. Frozen butter is hard to grate at first, but it softens quickly. It is easier to grate butter if it is at least half-frozen.

▸ To avoid the inevitable last messy inch of butter, grate two half sticks of butter instead. It also helps to stand the grater directly in the bowl of flour mixture.

Whole Wheat Pastry
(For an 8 – 9-inch single-crust pie)

1½ cups whole wheat pastry flour
½ teaspoon salt
1 tablespoon white sugar
1 stick (¼ pound or 8 tablespoons) butter
¼ – ½ cup ice water

1. Mix together the flour, salt, sugar, and butter according to the preceding directions for scones through Step 1.

2. Briskly blend in ¼ cup ice water, adding only as much extra water as you need to be able to gather the dough together into a barely moistened lump. Use lump of dough to gather up the remaining floury residue, and knead briefly in bowl to blend in the dry bits and even out the texture.

3. Pat dough into a fat disk about the diameter of a saucer. Wrap in plastic and chill while you clean up your mess. (Chill dough ideally for about 2 hours.) It is ready to roll out when you are.

Cornbread
Northern style

When I serve a one-pot meal like chili (pages 167 and 209) or chowder (page 194), a pan of cornbread rounds out the meal nicely. Warm, fresh cornbread is a treat, yet it can be so easy to make that you shouldn't have to give it a second thought. This particular recipe takes less than ten minutes, including clean-up. Plus, the smell of baking cornbread is a quiet but compelling call to dinner.

Lots of Southern-style variations are possible here, like buttermilk, bacon fat, and cast iron skillets, or chilies, cheese, and corn. For anyone new to cornbread, though, this is a safe starting point. You can make muffins instead of cornbread, of course. They are a bit more work but handier to serve.

(Makes an 8 x 8 inch pan)

½ stick (4 tablespoons) butter
1½ cups stone-ground cornmeal (see **Note**)
½ cup whole wheat pastry flour
2 teaspoons baking powder
¾ teaspoon salt
1¼ cups milk
1 egg
¼ cup honey

Pre-heat oven to 400 degrees and put an 8 x 8-inch pan in middle of oven.

1. Put the half stick of butter into the pan in the oven. I like to bake the cornbread in a pan I can bring to the table. An 8-inch Pyrex is fine, but I have a 13-inch Pyrex pie dish which allows me to serve the bread in wedges. Any ceramic dish would work, too, if the size is right. If you accidently add an extra little chunk of butter, that's just fine.

2. Meanwhile, combine dry ingredients in a mixing bowl and mix thoroughly. (A dry wire whisk works well.)

3. In another bowl combine milk, egg, and honey. Whisk until well mixed and honey is dissolved, about 30 seconds.

(Remember that there is butter in the oven! If you must answer the phone, take out the butter so it doesn't turn brown.)

4. By now the butter in the pan should be melted. Carefully (this is no time to move quickly) take out the pan and pour about three tablespoons of the butter into the milk mixture. Stick the pan back in the oven and whisk the butter and milk mixture vigorously for a few seconds to blend. Tip into the dry ingredients and blend thoroughly.

5. Pull the hot buttery pan out of the oven again and scrape cornbread batter into it. Bake for about 25 minutes, or until top is golden and bread has pulled away slightly from the sides.

Note:

‣ Whether or not you use fine or medium cornmeal, always buy whole grain meal. You do not want degerminated cornmeal. If you can find a cornmeal ground locally, that's wonderful. (Here in Oregon we have Bob's Red Mill.) Medium grind cornmeal makes a thin batter and a much coarser cornbread. We like it, but you may prefer the smoother texture of finely ground cornmeal.

‣ Don't worry if you use regular whole wheat bread flour instead of pastry flour. Technically, for baked goods raised with baking powder, low-gluten flour is preferable.

Scottish Oatcakes
Whole grain crispbread

These oatcakes are not for wimps. Neither cracker nor cookie, these are stalwart, simple, rich little repositories of cardio-friendly fiber. I love them. To me these are as good as cookies, yet a person can feel almost self-righteous eating them. They keep well for at least a week, in my opinion, but they're best freshly baked. I serve oatcakes as snacks anytime or with morning or afternoon tea with a chunk of extra sharp cheddar cheese on the side. (I always keep a few packets of Bob's Red Mill Scottish oatmeal on hand.)

(Makes about 18 x 1½-inch oatcakes)

1½ cups Scottish oatmeal
½ cup whole wheat pastry flour
½ teaspoon salt
½ teaspoon baking powder

½ stick butter, melted (¼ cup)
2 tablespoon honey
⅓ cup boiling water

(extra ¼ cup Scottish oats for sprinkling on counter)

Preheat oven to 325 degrees.

1. In a mixing bowl combine Scottish oatmeal, flour, salt, and baking powder.

2. Combine melted butter, honey, and boiling water and add to oatmeal mixture, blending thoroughly. The mixture will be moist and sticky. Set aside for 5 minutes while some of the liquid is absorbed.

3. Sprinkle countertop thickly with extra Scottish oats and pat out oat mixture. Using a rolling pin dusted with flour, roll out mixture to ⅛ inch thick. Cut out circles or wedges or whatever shapes you prefer, and place on an ungreased baking sheet. (You can crowd them.)

4. Bake in the middle of a 325-degree oven for 20 – 40 minutes, or until oatcakes are golden. (See ***Note***.)

Note:

▸ Whether or not you have rolled your oatcakes out as thinly as I do or your oven runs hotter than average can make a significant difference in the timing. Once you have made these in your own kitchen you can adjust my directions. I like them good and crispy, but you can experiment by removing a couple after 20 minutes and comparing them to the toastier ones that stay in the oven longer.

▸ Do *not* confuse Scottish oatmeal with steel cut oats. They look similar but are not interchangeable. Believe me – your teeth will know the difference. (For more on the two kinds of oats see page 75.)

▸ Using sugar instead of honey would make a slightly crispier oatcake. Nutritionally it is not a big issue; my choice of honey is more general principal than anything else.

▸ Adding ¼ cup of whole flaxseeds to the oatmeal and flour mixture is a good idea.

Oatmeal Cookies
with nuts and raisins

This recipe produces a sort of all-purpose oatmeal cookie, but with a higher proportion of rolled oats and a lower proportion of flour than most recipes. Even though these cookies still qualify as a treat, at least they also can be considered real food, especially with the nuts and raisins included.

(Makes about 18 x 3-inch cookies)

1 cup (½ pound or 2 sticks) butter
1 cup brown sugar, packed (see *Note* below)
2 eggs

1 cup whole wheat pastry flour
1½ teaspoons cinnamon
1 teaspoon baking powder
½ teaspoon salt

3 cups old-fashioned rolled oats
1 cup chopped walnuts or pecans
3/4 cup raisins

Preheat oven to 350 degrees and set rack in middle of oven.

1. Beat together butter and sugar until creamy, and then beat in eggs.

2. Mix together flour, cinnamon, baking powder, and salt. Stir into the butter mixture until well blended.

3. Combine rolled oats, nuts, and raisins in a mixing bowl. (I prefer a large bowl – the oats tend to be a bit frisky during the mixing.) Add butter/flour mixture and blend thoroughly.

4. Using 2 spoons, drop tablespoon-sized lumps of cookie dough 1½ inches apart on an ungreased baking sheet. (I press them out a bit – I don't like them too thick in the middle.) Bake in 350-degree oven for about 15 minutes or until golden brown.

Note:

▶ I have a friend who says these cookies are ready to pull out of the oven after only 8 minutes. Such a large variation in oven temperature is remarkable, but it's a good reminder to never take cooking times too seriously until you have made a recipe at least once.

▶ More sugar will produce a crispier version and less sugar will produce a more cakey texture that I don't like. You can customize your cookies to suit the occasion; if you need a more traditional oatmeal cookie, add ¼ - ½ cup of white sugar.

▶ Honey doesn't work well as a sugar substitute in most cookies, especially if you are looking for a crisp texture.

Coconut Macaroons

These particular coconut macaroons are disgracefully simple to make, they store well, and they even freeze beautifully. (In fact, I have served them directly from the freezer.) You can generally find dried unsweetened shredded coconut in the bulk food section of natural food stores or packaged by Bob's Red Mill.

(For reasons that are not clear, many patients with irritable bowel syndromes such as Crohn's disease or ulcerative colitis seem to get a noticeable degree of improvement in their symptoms by having a small amount of coconut each day. Not surprisingly, the most popular coconut delivery system is 1 – 2 of these macaroons.)

(Makes about 2 dozen)

2 egg whites (scant ⅓ cup)
½ cup white sugar
1 teaspoon pure almond extract
¼ teaspoon salt

2 cups dried unsweetened shredded coconut

Preheat oven to 350 degrees. Set rack in middle of oven. Mist baking sheet with non-stick spray.

1. Whisk egg whites, sugar, almond extract, and salt in a mixing bowl until well blended.

2. Add coconut and mix thoroughly with a large fork or a sturdy rubber spatula. The mixture should be thick and sticky.

3. Form walnut-sized mounds of mixture and place about an inch apart on the oiled baking sheet. The cookies won't spread unless the mixture is too wet. *(Stir mixture from time to time, as the egg white tends to settle.)*

4. Bake at 350 degrees in the middle of the oven for 20 minutes, or until macaroons are golden top and bottom. Transfer from baking sheet to cooling rack with a thin-edged metal spatula. Store in covered container for a week (I've kept them successfully for 2 weeks) or store for a few months in the freezer, well sealed.

Note:

▸ Macaroons are a favorite use for egg whites. (See mayonnaise recipe on page 96.)

▸ I use the tablespoon from my Oxo measuring spoon set to make evenly sized and shaped macaroons. I scoop it full of the coconut mixture, scrape off the excess on the edge of the mixing bowl, and unmold it with a firm tap on the cookie sheet. I rinse the spoon about every 3 cookies or so, which keeps the coconut mixture from sticking to the inside of the spoon.

▸ This recipe uses what I think is the minimum of sugar; another ¼-cup of sugar will make a crispier cookie.

▸ Macaroons made with a higher egg-white-to-coconut ratio will spread slightly as they cook, be chewier, and will stay moist longer.

Almond Macaroons

Replace all or part of the coconut with toasted ground almonds. *(See directions for toasting slivered almonds on page 174.)* Depending on the proportion of almonds to egg white, the cookies may spread a bit; place them at least 1½ inches apart on the baking sheet. Otherwise, the other ingredients and instructions are the same. I love these cookies but they can be too hard for some. It is safer to err on the side of too wet for this batter; if crunchiness is a problem, a thinner cookie is better.

Hot Chocolate (Cocoa)
Basic model

Here is a recipe for a simple mug of hot chocolate. Ordinary pure unsweetened cocoa from most suppliers is perfectly suitable and satisfying; there is no need to use one of the premium products, even if it is grown on a private plantation in a remote corner of South America. When choosing one, just be sure you are starting with pure cocoa — sweetened cocoa mixes are mostly sugar. Where we live, plain unsweetened Hershey's cocoa is a good choice, and available in most supermarkets. 'Dutch process' cocoa may not be as good a choice due to the damage the process does to the phenolic nutrients. (Phenols are an important class of antioxidants.) Remember to check the baking section if you can't find what you want on the beverage shelves.

(Makes 1 mug, or about 1¼ cups)

> 1 cup whole milk
> 2 tablespoons pure unsweetened
>   cocoa powder, like Hershey's
> ¼ cup boiling water
> 1 – 2 teaspoons honey, or to taste
> ⅛ teaspoon salt

1. Heat milk over medium heat in a little saucepan (1-quart size is perfect for this amount of milk) until it is steaming energetically *but not bubbling*. It's a good idea to set a timer for 5 minutes – by then the milk should be steaming. If you let the milk boil it will develop a skin and an overcooked flavor.

2. Meanwhile, combine cocoa, water, honey, and salt, and blend with a spoon or a little whisk until cocoa lumps are gone.

3. Add chocolate mixture to hot milk and whisk vigorously. Pour into a warmed mug. Drink immediately or thereabouts.

Note:

▸ Salt enhances most food, sweet or savory. It also has a way of reducing the need for as much sweetening.

▸ Vanilla essence is a traditional addition to cocoa, but a good-quality pure vanilla is more expensive than its effect is worth, in this opinion. Orange extract is delicious to some.

▸ Honey is the best choice for a sweetener but it has more flavor than sugar. Use a very mild-tasting variety like clover honey.

Dark chocolate
(From page 17)

One of the most surprising and heartwarming nutritional discoveries of the last 20 years is that dark chocolate appears to be associated with less heart disease[1], more flexible arteries, better cholesterol, and lower blood pressure. Much of the benefit probably is associated with a group of chemicals in dark chocolate called phenols, which are also present in tea, extra-virgin olive oil, and many other foods.

Definitive studies using dark chocolate to prevent heart disease have not been done, so don't go crazy with this idea; however, it is reasonable to use up to one or two ounces daily. Choose dark chocolate with a cocoa content of 70 percent or higher.

However, when you add something like chocolate to your diet, remember to remove calories somewhere else. Gaining weight on chocolate would tend to defeat the purpose.

---

[1] Buijsse et al. Arch Int Med 2006;166:411-7

Index

Recipe Index

Beans

Whole Grains

Brown Rice Recipes

Other Whole Grain Recipes

Main Dishes

Baking

Yeast Breads

Quick Breads and Treats

General Index

GOOD FOOD, GREAT MEDICINE

A HOMEMADE COOKBOOK, SECOND EDITION

Evidence-based diet and lifestyle guidelines for optimal health using the Mediterranean diet

by Mea Hassell and Miles Hassell, M.D.

WITH ADDITIONAL RECIPES
AND NEW CHAPTER:

TEN-STEP PLAN *for*

TREATING *and* PREVENTING HEART DISEASE

Date:	
Name:	
Street:	
City: State: Zip:	
Telephone:	
E-mail address:	

QUANTITY	DESCRIPTION	COST	TOTAL
	copies of *Good Food Great Medicine*	$ 30	
	case(s) of *Good Food Great Medicine* (14 books @ $18 each)	$ 252	

POSTAGE & HANDLING: *Books will be sent via media mail.*

$7.00 for one (1) book and $1.00 for each additional book to the same address *(up to 13 books)* For 14 or more books shipping is $19.00 per case.	

Please contact our office if you need quicker delivery or for shipping charges outside the United States.

TOTAL ENCLOSED [ ]

PAYMENT OPTIONS:

○ I want to pay by check or money order *(payment enclosed - payable to: Miles Hassell, M.D.)*
○ I want to pay by Visa or Mastercard
Card number:
Expiration date:

Miles Hassell, M.D.
Attn: Cookbook
9155 SW Barnes Road, Suite 302
Portland, OR 97225

Voice: (503) 291-1777   **Web:** www.goodfoodgreatmedicine.com   **Fax:** (503) 291-1079